Writing Doubt in Montaigne's *Essais*

Edinburgh Critical Studies in Renaissance Culture

Series Editors: Lorna Hutson, Katherine Ibbett, Joe Moshenska and Kathryn Murphy

Selected titles available in the series

Legal Reform in English Renaissance Literature
Virginia Lee Strain

The Origins of English Revenge Tragedy
George Oppitz-Trotman

Crime and Consequence in Early Modern Literature and Law
Judith Hudson

Shakespeare's Golden Ages: Resisting Nostalgia in Elizabethan Drama
Kristine Johanson

Refusing to Behave in Early Modern Literature
Laura Seymour

Shakespeare's Virtuous Theatre: Power, Capacity and the Good
Kent Lehnhof, Julia Reinhard Lupton and Carolyn Sale

Writing Europe in Renaissance France: Travels in Reality and Imagination
Niall Oddy

Epistolary Courtiership and Dramatic Letters: Thomas Overbury and the Jacobean Playhouse
Jackie Watson

Writing Doubt in Montaigne's Essais: *Thinking Relationally with Seneca and Plutarch*
Luke O'Sullivan

For a full list of titles in the series, visit the Edinburgh Critical Studies in Renaissance Culture website at www.edinburghuniversitypress.com/series/ECSRC

Writing Doubt in Montaigne's *Essais*

Thinking Relationally with Seneca and Plutarch

Luke O'Sullivan

EDINBURGH
University Press

Edinburgh University Press is one of the leading university presses in the UK. We publish academic books and journals in our selected subject areas across the humanities and social sciences, combining cutting-edge scholarship with high editorial and production values to produce academic works of lasting importance. For more information visit our website: edinburghuniversitypress.com

© Luke O'Sullivan 2024, 2026

Edinburgh University Press Ltd
13 Infirmary Street
Edinburgh EH1 1LT

First published in hardback by Edinburgh University Press 2024

Typeset in 10.5/13 Adobe Sabon by
Cheshire Typesetting Ltd, Cuddington, Cheshire, and
printed and bound by CPI Group (UK) Ltd,
Croydon, CR0 4YY

A CIP record for this book is available from the British Library

ISBN 978 1 3995 2296 0 (hardback)
ISBN 978 1 3995 2297 7 (paperback)
ISBN 978 1 3995 2298 4 (webready PDF)
ISBN 978 1 3995 2299 1 (epub)

The right of Luke O'Sullivan to be identified as the author of this work has been asserted in accordance with the Copyright, Designs and Patents Act 1988, and the Copyright and Related Rights Regulations 2003 (SI No. 2498).

Contents

Acknowledgements	vi
Note on Texts, Translations and Style	viii
Series Editor's Preface	x
Introduction: Leaky Business	1
1. A Doubtful Combination	17
2. Writing Between Authors	44
3. Forming Thoughts I: Thinking About Form	84
4. Forming Thoughts II: Writing Doubly	122
5. Simple Truths	147
6. Paradoxical Truth-Telling	180
Conclusion: Communicating Doubt	217
Bibliography	224
Index	238

Acknowledgements

Over the course of writing this book, I have been generously supported by a good number of individuals and institutions, and it is a pleasure to record those debts here. *Writing Doubt* began as a PhD thesis at Durham University, funded by a Durham Doctoral Scholarship. A Leverhulme Early Career Fellowship, held at King's College London, followed by a Career Development Fellowship at St Hilda's College, Oxford, allowed me to substantially rework the thesis in the most supportive and enriching of academic environments. As this book neared completion, I was delighted to be elected Gerard Davis Fellow in Early Modern French by the Governing Body of St Hilda's College. I would like to express my sincere gratitude to the Senior Tutor, Sarah Norman, to the Principal, Dame Sarah Springman, to the members of the Governing Body, and especially to Helen Swift. I am immensely thankful for the continued support provided by St Hilda's as this book goes out into the world.

I am enormously grateful to my doctoral supervisors, John O'Brien and Kathryn Banks, and to my generous and incisive examiners, Neil Kenny and Marc Schachter. I was incredibly fortunate to have such supportive postdoctoral mentors, Emily Butterworth and especially Helen Swift, whose advocacy and collegiality are unparalleled. I could not have asked for a better run of supervisors, readers and colleagues. John in particular has been a constant source of encouragement and insight over the years and this book would not have been possible without him.

I have benefited tremendously from the excellent community of researchers in early modern French studies. Many people have generously provided advice on various aspects of this project, and I have profited significantly from conversations, questions and feedback. In addition to the names above, I would like to thank Warren Boutcher, Colin Burrow, Terence Cave, Tim Chesters, Emma Claussen, Vittoria Fallanca, Raphaële Garrod, Olivier Guerrier, Tom Hamilton, Emma Herdman, Rachel Hindmarsh, Katherine Ibbett, Ian Maclean, Lisa

Nicholson, Jenny Oliver, Jonathan Patterson, Marina Perkins, Alice Roullière, Richard Scholar, Andrew Sillett, Gemma Tidman and Wes Williams. The Montaigne Reading Group at Oxford is an exceptional community of experts and I have learned so much by sharing their company. I am grateful also to the group of early career *seiziémistes* based around Oxford and thankful for our online meetings that preserved a sense of *sodalitas* in the depths of the pandemic. I am especially grateful to Vittoria Fallanca: for the conversations about Montaigne, academia and everything else, but also for her ability to pull people together when we have had an idea for a reading group or workshop.

Parts of this book first appeared in several articles. Parts of Chapter 2 appeared as 'In-Between Authorship in Montaigne's *Essais*', *Early Modern French Studies*, 41.2 (2019), 106–25. An early version of Chapter 3 and part of Chapter 4 was published as '"Double et divers": Writing Doubly in Montaigne's *Essais*', *Modern Language Review*, 112.2 (2017), 320–40. Parts of Chapter 6 are based on aspects of an article first published in French: '"Feuilletant ces petits brevets descousus": consolations fausses et l'écriture de la vérité', *Bulletin de la société internationale des amies et amis de Montaigne*, 74 (2022), 187–205. All are substantially revised and reused with permission. Many thanks to the editors and publishers for their support. I am grateful also to the anonymous reviewers of those articles, whose feedback continued to influence revision as I prepared this book manuscript for publication.

Thanks are due also to the editorial team at EUP, especially Emily Sharp and Elizabeth Fraser, and to the editors of this series, Lorna Hutson, Katherine Ibbett, Joe Moshenska and Kathryn Murphy. I am especially grateful to Katherine and Kathryn, as well as the two anonymous readers, for their immensely constructive and insightful comments. The book would have been very different and much poorer would their input.

I would like also to thank my family for their support during the long process of writing this book. My greatest thanks are owed to Lucy, whom I can't thank enough. Her support, patience, love and belief mean everything, and, without her, the doubt would have been too much.

Note on Texts, Translations and Style

Unless stated otherwise, all references to Montaigne are to *Les Essais*, edited by Pierre Villey and V.-L. Saulnier (Paris: Presses Universitaires de France, 2004 [1965]). References give book, chapter and page number parenthetically followed, after a slash, by page numbers for Donald Frame's English translation, *The Complete Essays of Montaigne* (Stanford, CA: Stanford University Press, 1958). With rare exceptions signalled in the footnotes, the translations provided in brackets are Frame's.

References to the first edition of the *Essais* are to *Essais de Messire Michel Seigneur de Montaigne* (Bordeaux: Millanges, 1580). Page numbers are given in the footnotes with the abbreviated reference: *Essais* 1580, I.1.1.

Where relevant to my argument, I have included Villey's 'couche' markers: [A] indicates that the text is from the first 1580 edition, [B] text from 1588, and [C] text from after 1588, which is to say text from the Bordeaux Copy and/or the posthumous 1595 edition prepared by Marie de Gournay. In most cases, I have preferred to refer directly to the Bordeaux Copy, available online via the Montaigne Project ('Les Essais de Montaigne d'après l'Exemplaire de Bordeaux', https://www.lib.uchicago.edu/efts/ARTFL/projects/montaigne/index.html). References to the Bordeaux Copy are given parenthetically: (Bordeaux Copy, fol. 1).

References to Plutarch's *Moralia* are to Jacques Amyot's *Les Œuvres morales et meslées de Plutarque* (Paris: Michel de Vascosan, 1572). When quoting from the *Lives*, I refer to the second, revised edition of Amyot's *Les Vies des hommes illustres, Grecs & Romains* (Paris: Vascosan, 1565), a copy of which has recently been discovered bearing Montaigne's signature. Translations are my own. In producing these translations, and in examining Amyot's French version, I have consulted the Greek text and English translation found in the respective Loeb editions: Plutarch, *Lives*, trans. Bernadotte Perrin,

11 vols (Cambridge, MA: Harvard University Press, 1914–26); Plutarch, *Moralia*, trans. Frank Cole Babbitt et al., 15 vols (Cambridge MA: Harvard University Press, 1927–69).

Quotations and, unless otherwise noted, English translations of Seneca's *Epistles* and *Moral Essays* are from the respective Loeb editions: Seneca, *Epistles*, trans. Richard M. Gummere, 3 vols (Cambridge, MA: Harvard University Press, 1917–25); Seneca, *Moral Essays*, trans. John W. Basore, 3 vols (Cambridge, MA: Harvard University Press, 1928–35). References to the *Epistles* are included parenthetically following the abbreviation *Ep*.

Quotations from Sextus Empiricus are from Henri Estienne's Latin text, the translation known to Montaigne: *Sexti philosophi Pyrrhoniarum hypotyposeon libri III* ([Paris]: Henri Estienne, 1562). References in the footnotes give book, chapter and page number: I.1.1. Translations into English are based on those of the Loeb edition, *Outlines of Pyrrhonism*, ed. and trans. R. G. Bury (Cambridge, MA: Harvard University Press, 1933), with occasional modification to reflect Estienne's Latin. I refer to the Loeb edition when discussing points of Greek language in the *Outlines of Pyrrhonism*.

Unless stated otherwise, all quotations and translations from other ancient texts are based on those of the Loeb library, with occasional modification. Full details are included in the bibliography, with short references included in footnotes. All other translations are my own.

In transcribing early modern printed material, I have distinguished 'i' from 'j', 'u' from 'v'. Contractions have been resolved though I have otherwise reproduced original spelling and punctuation.

Series Editor's Preface

Edinburgh Critical Studies in Renaissance Culture may, as a series title, provoke some surprise. On the one hand, the choice of the word 'culture' (rather than, say, 'literature') suggests that writers in this series subscribe to the now widespread assumption that the 'literary' is not isolable, as a mode of signifying, from other signifying practices that make up what we call 'culture'. On the other hand, most of the critical work in English literary studies of the period 1500–1700 which endorses this idea has rejected the older identification of the period as 'the Renaissance', with its implicit homage to the myth of essential and universal Man coming to stand (in all his sovereign individuality) at the centre of a new world picture. In other words, the term 'culture' in the place of 'literature' leads us to expect the words 'early modern' in the place of 'Renaissance'. Why, then, 'Edinburgh Critical Studies in *Renaissance Culture*'?

The answer to that question lies at the heart of what distinguishes this critical series and defines its parameters. As Terence Cave has argued, the term 'early modern', though admirably egalitarian in conception, has had the unfortunate effect of essentialising the modern, that is, of positing 'the advent of a once-and-for-all modernity' which is the deictic 'here and now' from which we look back.[1] The phrase 'early modern', that is to say, forecloses the possibility of other modernities, other futures that might have arisen, narrowing the scope of what we may learn from the past by construing it as a narrative leading inevitably to Western modernity, to 'us'. *Edinburgh Critical Studies in Renaissance Culture* aims rather to shift the emphasis from a story of progress – early modern to modern – to a series of critical encounters and conversations with the past, which may reveal to us some surprising alternatives buried within texts familiarly construed as episodes on the way to certain identifying features of our endlessly fascinating modernity. In keeping

---

[1] Terence Cave, 'Locating the Early Modern', *Paragraph*, 29.1 (2006), 12–26 (p. 14).

with one aspect of the etymology of 'Renaissance' or 'Rinascimento' as 'rebirth', moreover, this series features books that explore and interpret anew elements of the critical encounter between writers of the period 1500–1700 and texts of Greco-Roman literature, rhetoric, politics, law, oeconomics, *eros* and friendship.

The term 'culture', then, indicates a license to study and scrutinise objects other than literary ones, and to be more inclusive about both the forms and the material and political stakes of making meaning both in the past and in the present. 'Culture' permits a realisation of the benefits to be reaped after two decades of interdisciplinary enrichment in the arts. No longer are historians naïve about textual criticism, about rhetoric, literary theory or about readerships; likewise, literary critics trained in close reading now also turn easily to court archives, to legal texts, and to the historians' debates about the languages of political and religious thought. Social historians look at printed pamphlets with an eye for narrative structure; literary critics look at court records with awareness of the problems of authority, mediation and institutional procedure. Within these developments, modes of research that became unfashionable and discredited in the 1980s – for example, studies in classical or vernacular 'source texts', or studies of literary 'influence' across linguistic, confessional and geographical boundaries – have acquired a new critical edge and relevance as the convergence of the disciplines enables the unfolding of new cultural histories (that is to say, what was once studied merely as 'literary influence' may now be studied as a fraught cultural encounter). The term 'Renaissance' thus retains the relevance of the idea of consciousness and critique within these textual engagements of past and present, and, while it foregrounds the Western European experience, is intended to provoke comparativist study of wider global perspectives rather than to promote the 'universality' of a local, if far-reaching, historical phenomenon. Finally, as traditional pedagogic boundaries between 'Medieval' and 'Renaissance' are being called into question by cross disciplinary work emphasising the 'reformation' of social and cultural forms, so this series, while foregrounding the encounter with the classical past, is self-conscious about the ways in which that past is assimilated to the projects of Reformation and Counter-Reformation, spiritual, political and domestic, that finally transformed Christendom into Europe.

Individual books in this series vary in methodology and approach, sometimes blending the sensitivity of close literary analysis with incisive, informed and urgent theoretical argument, at other times offering critiques of grand narratives of the period by their work in manuscript transmission, or in the archives of legal, social and architectural history, or by social histories of gender and childhood. What all these books have in common, however, is the capacity to offer compelling, well-documented and lucidly written critical accounts of how writers and thinkers in the period 1500–1700 reshaped, transformed and critiqued the texts and practices of their world, prompting new perspectives on what we think we have learned from them.

Lorna Hutson, Katherine Ibbett,
Joe Moshenska and Kathryn Murphy

Introduction: Leaky Business

If we take him at his word, Montaigne's relationship with books was distinctly casual and inexpert. He could see better than anyone, he claims, that his *Essais* are nothing but the 'resveries' of a man who has tasted only the outer crust of learning ('la crouste premiere') and retained none of it but 'un general et informe visage' [a vague general picture] (I.26.146/106). He likes history and poetry, and has something to say about them, but he can barely sketch the outlines ('les premiers lineamens') of the more serious stuff.[1] As for gnawing his nails studying Plato or Aristotle ('de m'estre rongé les ongles en l'estude de Platon, ou d'Aristote'), 'ce n'est pas mon occupation'.[2]

In what is now known as the Bordeaux Copy, a copy of the 1588 edition of the *Essais* covered in manuscript notes, additions and corrections, he crossed out the reference to Plato to crown Aristotle alone as 'monarque de la doctrine moderne' (I.26.146/107). But he made another change too. In a passage written in the left-hand margin, he set out his relationship with a rather different pair of classical authors:

> Je n'ay dressé commerce avec aucun livre solide, sinon Plutarque et Seneque, où je puyse comme les Danaïdes, remplissant et versant sans cesse. J'en attache quelque chose à ce papier; à moi, si peu que rien.

> I have not had regular dealings with any solid book, except Plutarch and Seneca, from whom I draw like the Danaïdes, incessantly filling up and pouring out. I stick some of it to this paper; to myself, next to nothing.[3]

---

[1] 'L'Histoire, c'est plus mon gibier, ou la poësie', I.26.146/106. On the 'casual', 'cool' delivery of this sentence in which the 'ou' describes not a choice but an almost gestural movement, see Terence Cave, 'The Transit of Venus: Feeling Your Way Forward', in *Montaigne in Transit*, ed. Neil Kenny, Richard Scholar and Wes Williams (Oxford: Legenda, 2016), pp. 9–18.
[2] *Essais* 1580, I.26.186.
[3] Translation modified. Frame gives 'Some of this sticks to this paper; to myself, little or nothing.'

Writing Doubt is a book about Montaigne's dealings with Seneca and Plutarch, about how this 'commerce' shaped the *Essais* and their peculiar mode of doubtful writing. Neither Seneca nor Plutarch was associated with the ancient Sceptical traditions that Montaigne played a key part in disseminating, and yet it was among precisely these authors that he identified 'une forme d'escrire douteuse' [a doubtful way of writing] (II.12.509/377). Their role as analogues for 'ce Seneque françois', this second Plutarch, was clear already to his earliest readers.[4] But Montaigne has a habit of 'thinking in twos' – a reflection of 'le plus universel membre de ma Logique' [the most universal member of my logic], 'distingo' (II.1.335/242) – and this study follows the essayist by insisting that Seneca and Plutarch are taken as a pair. Together, these authors provided Montaigne with the conceptual tools and formal, stylistic practices that underpin the writing of doubt in the *Essais*. Tracing their counterintuitive reception as doubtful writers, I argue that Montaigne's endless, leaky exchange with Seneca and Plutarch produced a form that reveals doubtful thinking. This is not a literary expression of ancient Scepticism but a distinct mode of thinking doubtfully in and with writing. Looking at Seneca and Plutarch askance, guided by Montaigne's curious association of doubt with two dogmatists, I show that doubtful writing is not only an illustration of an unresolved philosophy, and not simply a rhetorical provocation entangling the reader in thorny and obscure passages of prose, but a form of thinking, of forming thoughts. It is a 'forme d'escrire' that reveals the soul – to the author as much as to the reader – and a means of making oneself recognisable in writing. Filling up and pouring out, coming and going: Montaigne felt his 'esprit' to be endlessly, mercurially liquid. Drawing from these two 'livres solides', he found a way of giving it form.

Seneca and Plutarch are stitched together throughout the *Essais* and at every stage of composition. They are given a privileged place in Montaigne's writing and in his thoughts about writing. But why Seneca and Plutarch? What did they offer Montaigne? What did he do with them and what did they allow him to do? Answering these questions, *Writing Doubt* argues that it was with these authors that Montaigne found a way of doing what the Sceptics could not.

To suggest that Montaigne got his Scepticism from Seneca and Plutarch rather than from the ancient Sceptics would certainly cut against the grain of received wisdom. But one of the aims of this book

---

[4] For Montaigne as 'ce Seneque françois', see François Garasse, *Les Recherches des recherches* (Paris: Chappelet, 1622), p. 950. On Montaigne as an imitator of Plutarch, see La Croix du Maine's *Bibliothèque* (Paris: Angelier, 1584), p. 319.

is to step away from a model of sources and intellectual inheritance. Montaigne's habit of thinking relationally with Seneca and Plutarch produced a distinct form of doubtful thinking, a mode of thinking related to Scepticism without being subsumed by it; related to Senecan and Plutarchan ways of writing without simply reproducing them. Centring Seneca and Plutarch as doubtful dogmatists reorients our perspective on doubt in the *Essais*, not by introducing a competing line of inheritance but by aligning doubtful thinking positively with writing and communication, establishing doubt not as a method or mental habit in want of a language but as a style, a 'façon' or 'forme'. It is a shift in perspective that has implications beyond doubt too, destabilising authorship in this famously consubstantial book and entangling Montaigne's ethical and discursive simplicity – his 'façon simple' ('Au lecteur', p. 3/2) – with a doubleness that skirts dangerously close to dissemblance and duplicity.

When I say that Montaigne wrote 'doubtfully', I mean that he developed a form that is provisional and open-ended, tentative rather than resolved, enquiring rather than instructing ('enquerant plustost qu'instruisant', II.12.509/377). I mean also that it is hermeneutically doubtful: his prose is ambiguous, contradictory and 'double'; it employs rhetorical figures – prosopopoeia, for instance – and makes use of borrowed words in a manner that holds interpretation in check.

But, in addition to its open-endedness and its stylistic ambiguities, doubtful writing entails a specific conception of the relationship between thinking and writing. In the *Essais*, we see Montaigne thinking in and with doubtful writing, with writing as a material resource (thinking with bits of writing, whether his own or not; with writing on the page) and with the practice, activity or technology of writing. His 'forme' both reveals the doubtfulness of his thinking and sustains it, since it is in writing that he thinks as he does, which is to say doubtfully. In this regard, my approach draws influence from the recent 'cognitive turn' in literary studies and particularly the notion of extended cognition, whereby thought is understood to extend beyond the hardware of the brain.[5] Doubtful writing is not only provisional or ambiguous writing, and it is not simply a representation, record or illustration of doubtful

---

[5] The term 'extended cognition' was coined by Andy Clark and David Chalmers in 'The Extended Mind', *Analysis*, 58 (1998), 7–19. Cognitive approaches to literature and the humanities have proliferated in recent years. See, in the first instance, studies by Terence Cave: *Thinking with Literature: Towards a Cognitive Criticism* (Oxford: Oxford University Press, 2016), and *Live Artefacts: Literature in a Cognitive Environment* (Oxford: Oxford University Press, 2022). On parallels with early modern conceptions and the application of modern cognitive theories to Renaissance texts, see Miranda Anderson, *The Renaissance Extended Mind* (Basingstoke: Palgrave, 2015). On Montesquieu's claim that, in reading Montaigne, he sees not the man who is writing but the man who

thinking: it is a mode of doubtful thought. 'J'escoute à mes resveries par ce que j'ay à les enroller' [I listen to my reveries because I have to record them]: he hears his thinking pen in hand, giving his 'fantasie' body and form ('donner corps') not to describe his thinking but to conduct it (II.18.665/504).

Montaigne's relationship with doubt has long been read through his engagement with the arguments of the ancient philosophers and their schools. A century ago, Pierre Villey saw in Montaigne's textual and philosophical sources the outline of an evolution from Stoic to Sceptic to Epicurean.[6] Half a century later, a number of major studies established the sixteenth century as a moment wrapped up in a 'Pyrrhonian crisis', a moment that was seen to shape Montaigne and one on which the essayist was seen to have had significant influence, disseminating a humanist revival of Academic and Pyrrhonian Scepticism.[7] Critical frameworks have changed a good deal in the intervening decades to privilege new ways of looking at the *Essais* as well as the core ideas and concepts they deal in. But doubt has a tendency to cling to a history of philosophical schools and traditions.[8]

What don't we know about Montaigne and doubt? This relationship – encapsulated by those two mottos, 'epecho', 'Que sçay-je?' – is one of the most familiar aspects of the *Essais*. Studies of Montaigne invariably note his philosophical Scepticism, at least in passing, and histories of Scepticism likewise invoke Montaigne as a central player in its reception and dissemination. His role in the history of doubt is a critical commonplace. What else is there left to say? And how might we justify going back to this question? It is not as though we are in short supply of problems in the world. One recent volume dedicated to Montaigne

---

is thinking, see Olivier Guerrier, 'Dans la plupart des auteurs, je vois l'homme qui écrit; dans Montaigne, l'homme qui pense', *Montaigne Studies*, 27 (2015), 89–98.

[6] Pierre Villey, *Les Sources et l'évolution des Essais de Montaigne*, 2 vols (Paris: Hachette, 1908).

[7] Richard Popkin, *The History of Scepticism from Savonarola to Bayle*, first published as *The History of Scepticism from Erasmus to Descartes* (Assen: Van Gorcum, 1960). See also Charles B. Schmitt, *Cicero Scepticus: A Study of the Influence of the Academica in the Renaissance* (The Hague: Springer, 1972); Marcel Conche's 1974 article, 'Le Pyrrhonisme dans la méthode', reprinted in *Montaigne et la philosophie* (Paris: Presses Universitaires de France, 1996), pp. 27–42; and Elaine Limbrick, 'Was Montaigne Really a Pyrrhonian?', *Bibliothèque d'Humanisme et Renaissance*, 39 (1977), 67–80.

[8] See, for instance, Sylvia Giocanti's *Penser l'irrésolution: Montaigne, Pascal, La Mothe Le Vayer. Trois itinéraires sceptiques* (Paris: Champion, 2001) and Frédéric Brahami's *Le Scepticisme de Montaigne* (Paris: Presses Universitaires de France, 1997). More recently, see Celso M. Azar Filho, 'Sur les rapports entre l'ignorance, la science, la philosophie et le scepticisme chez Montaigne', in *Global Montaigne: Mélanges en l'honneur de Philippe Desan*, ed. Jean Balsamo and Amy Graves (Paris: Garnier, 2021), pp. 303–13.

addresses these questions of ethics and interest directly: it includes two essays sharing the same title – 'Montaigne, Scepticism, and Finitude' – in which the authors note the current popularity of this sixteenth-century 'guide to modern life', along with the comfortable familiarity of his 'moderate scepticism'.[9] 'What to do when your world is ending?', asks Jan Miernowski.[10] It is a question for us just as much as it was for Montaigne, surrounded by war and plague. His 'inexhaustible text', endlessly engaged in ongoing enquiry, made sense in an 'ever-expanding world', one that had only recently begun exploring new continents and might yet discover more.[11] But we do not share Montaigne's environment: living in a world 'whose resources are limited', we are obliged, argues Ullrich Langer, to question not only the utility of 'moderate' Scepticism, but also our own academic, intellectual and ideological investment in it.[12] Surely, Langer argues (though Miernowski confirms that he is only joking), the situation calls for nothing other than a 'moratorium on Montaigne studies'.[13]

If we are to disregard their prohibition, we ought to make sure our limited resources are put to good use and tell something other than the well-known story of Montaigne and the Sceptics. But even approaches that try to reorient our perspective – whether by foregrounding the 'art' of free-thinking, the 'nouveau langage' of the *Essais*, or the trace of emergent, inchoate forms of thinking in 'perturbations textuelles' – tend to associate doubt with its ancient philosophical practitioners and their early modern champions.[14] This should not be surprising. Montaigne and philosophical Scepticism is an immensely familiar pairing. But what happens when we follow Montaigne's lead and check our assumptions?

Reading doubt in the *Essais* through another of those immensely familiar Montaignian relations – his relationship with Seneca and Plutarch – is not an exercise in digging deeper into the history and sources of Scepticism, but an opportunity to look again, differently

---

[9] Ullrich Langer, 'Montaigne, Scepticism, and Finitude. Montaigne, Horkheimer: Unhelpful Scepticism in a Limited World', in Balsamo and Graves (eds), *Global Montaigne*, pp. 316–26 (p. 326).
[10] Jan Miernowski, 'Montaigne, Scepticism, and Finitude. Montaigne, Meillassoux: Helpful Scepticism and the Multiplicity of Worlds', in Balsamo and Graves (eds), *Global Montaigne*, pp. 327–44 (p. 327).
[11] Langer, 'Montaigne, Scepticism, and Finitude', p. 322.
[12] Ibid.
[13] Miernowski, 'Montaigne, Scepticism, and Finitude', p. 344.
[14] See Richard Scholar, *Montaigne and the Art of Free-Thinking* (Oxford: Peter Lang, 2010); André Tournon, *Route par ailleurs: le 'nouveau langage' des Essais* (Paris: Champion, 2006); and Terence Cave, *Pré-histoires: textes troublés au seuil de la modernité* (Geneva: Droz, 1999).

and with fresh eyes, at this most significant of Renaissance doubters. Doing so reveals a relationship with doubt distinct from those traced in histories of a resurgent philosophical Scepticism. Rather than adopting a philosophical programme of suspending judgement, Montaigne established a literary form with which to address the problem that ran through the crises surrounding him. Communicating himself truthfully and authentically, communicating what he called the 'double' nature of thought, he developed not a philosophy of doubt, nor a doubtful philosophy, but a mode of doubtful writing.

Material Books

The comparison with the Danaïdes, the daughters of Danaus who murdered their husbands and were condemned to spend the afterlife filling a leaky vessel (or carrying water in a sieve, or a mixture of the two), does not – on first impression, at least – paint a positive picture of this 'commerce'.[15] But in constructing this image, Montaigne approached it from a number of different perspectives, illuminating this key relationship in different ways. Studying its composition in the Bordeaux Copy, we can trace his revisions as he tried to express his understanding of the relation between himself, Seneca and Plutarch, and his book.

In its first iteration, his account lacked several of what seem now to be its most significant features:

> Je n'ay commerce aveq aucun livre materiel que par secousses, tantost a Plutarque tantost a Seneque parvenues, reiterees: ~~car ce que je lis qu'une fois je le lis pour neant~~ en faveur de ma maudite mémoire. Et y puise come les Danaïdes remplissant et versant sans cesse. J'en attache quelquechose a ce mien livre. A moi, si peu que rien. (Bordeaux Copy, fol. 53v).

---

[15] The image of the Danaïdes was commonplace; see Erasmus, *Adagia*, I.iv.60, in *Opera omnia Desiderii Erasmi Roterodami* (Amsterdam: Elsevier, 1969–), II-1 (1993), p. 452; *Adages: I i 1 to I v 100*, trans. Margaret Mann Phillips, in *Collected Works of Erasmus*, ed. R. A. B. Mynors (Toronto: Toronto University Press, 1974–), vol. 31 (1982), p. 361. Without wishing to suggest a direct line of influence or imitation, we might note a similar image in Seneca's contrast between true tranquillity and the 'iners negotium' [idle business] of the *otiosi*, who exemplify an idleness not unlike that described by Montaigne in 'De l'oysiveté': 'Abit igitur vita eorum in profundum; et ut nihil prodest, licet quantumlibet ingeras, si non subest quod excipiat ac servet, sic, nihil refert quantum temporis detur, si non est ubi subsidat, per quassos foratosque animos transmittitur' [And so life vanishes away into an abyss; and as it does no good, no matter how much water you pour into a vessel, if there is no bottom to receive and hold it, so with time – it makes no difference how much is given; if there is nothing for it to settle upon, it passes out through the chinks and holes of the mind], *De brevitate vitae*, 10.5.

> I have no dealings with any weighty book but by repeated short bursts, sometimes with Plutarch, sometimes with Seneca, ~~because whatever I read only once, I may as well not read at all~~ on account of my damned memory. And I draw from them like the Danaïdes, incessantly filling up and pouring out. I stick some of it to my book. To myself, next to nothing.

The Bordeaux Copy, a partial record of what would eventually be sent to the printer to become the 1595 edition, reveals Montaigne's textual practices, his equivocations and hesitations, and his modes of thinking on the page. He never intended for these notes to be read by anyone other than himself and those involved in the printing of his book, but they illuminate his relationship with writing in ways that support (rather than override) our understanding of the *Essais* as they were printed and as Montaigne expected them to be printed. The effects of these editorial practices, and the relationship with composition that underpins them, can be read in the printed editions of the *Essais* as much as in the Bordeaux Copy: both reveal a relationship with writing as an affordance, a means of conducting and exploring thought rather than simply expressing what had already been composed mentally. The Bordeaux Copy, with its dead ends and second thoughts, is valuable because it brings this relationship to the surface.

Montaigne's graphic hesitations reveal his ongoing thinking: we can see a stylistic concern in his efforts to avoid repetition while also recognising that those seemingly superficial choices reveal and direct understanding. What, for instance, is the difference between a 'livre materiel' and a 'livre solide'? That latter term had, in the printed text of the 1580 and 1588 editions, described the 'science solide' associated with Plato and Aristotle, but this was crossed out when it came to be associated with the books of Seneca and Plutarch. What are we to make of this migration? And how does this hard physicality correlate with the watery image with which the handwritten passage concludes?[16] It would seem that these books only become 'solides' once Montaigne's endless 'filling up and pouring out' has liquefied them. The image of grasping water keeps recurring in the *Essais* (as it does in Plutarch) to describe the vanity of trying to pin down a mobile world.[17] Here, the movement

---

[16] In addition to the movement from robust hardness to softness, Montaigne's leaky commerce is implicitly aligned with the 'womanly' incontinence of the Danaïdes more than with masculine metaphors of copious abundance. On Montaigne's tendency to 'place himself among the women', see Mary McKinley, 'Montaigne on Women', in *The Oxford Handbook of Montaigne*, ed. Philippe Desan (Oxford: Oxford University Press, 2016), pp. 581–99.

[17] See, for instance, II.12.601/455: here, he compares grasping the 'essence' of something in thought with someone trying to 'empoigner l'eau: car tant plus il serrera et pressera ce qui de sa nature coule par tout, tant plus il perdra ce qu'il vouloit tenir et empoigner'

from 'materiel' to 'solide', from 'solide' to liquid – a movement effected by the 'commerce' of reading and writing – seems telling: in Montaigne's hands, these solid books quickly become something else.

There is a further key shift in his choice of conjunction: Montaigne first addressed Seneca and Plutarch as examples of his sporadic and irregular reading of weighty 'livres materiels'. They might be particularly important examples, but 'tantost [...] tantost' [sometimes], unlike 'sinon' [except], admits additional authors and unnamed books. What determined this change? What is the significance of viewing Seneca and Plutarch not as examples but as exceptions? Montaigne's repeated reading of these authors was, in those earlier versions, attributed more to his own 'maudite memoire' than to anything specific to the authors themselves, but how might we interpret the erasure of this framing (or rather its double erasure, since it is rewritten before being crossed out again)? What does it mean for Montaigne's endless engagement with Seneca and Plutarch to *not* be governed by his poor memory or to *no longer* be governed by it? And, finally, what is the difference between attaching some of what he draws from Seneca and Plutarch to, on the one hand, 'ce mien livre' and, on the other, 'ce papier'?

The Bordeaux Copy is a witness to the material practices that played a central role in shaping Montaigne's pattern of thought: his doubtful and unresolved exploration of himself and the world was mediated though literary and compositional processes, by habits of thinking with 'livres materiels', thinking in writing, and using language – juggling terms and concepts and manipulating them on the page – to explore what it is that he thinks. The book of the *Essais* was not the only book belonging to his library that served such a habit. We might think, for instance, of the extensive annotations in his copies of Lucretius and Julius Caesar.[18] What, then, of his copies of Seneca and Plutarch? These would surely reveal the trace of engaged, active thinking.

Montaigne's copy, or perhaps copies, of Seneca remains undiscovered.[19] His copy of the *Moralia* is similarly unknown to us, though here we can be confident that he read Amyot's translation, first printed

---

[grasp water: for the more he squeezes and presses what by its nature flows all over, the more he will lose what he was trying to hold and grasp]. I will return to this passage and its debts to Plutarch in Chapter 2.

[18] For Montaigne's marginal annotations, see Alain Legros, *Montaigne manuscript* (Paris: Garnier, 2010); and, for Lucretius, see M. A. Screech, *Montaigne's Annotated Copy of Lucretius* (Geneva: Droz, 1998).

[19] Montaigne would no doubt have been quite familiar with the French translation of Seneca's *Epistles* published by his brother-in-law, Geoffroy de La Chassaigne, Seigneur de Pressac: *Epistres de L. Annæe Seneque, philosophe tres-excellent* (Paris: Chaudière, 1582).

in 1572.[20] Without access to these copies, we can only imagine how they might have been used. But it is not impossible that they will one day be uncovered in a private collection somewhere. Indeed, a copy of Plutarch's *Lives* belonging to Montaigne was found recently in just such a collection.[21] This discovery is undoubtedly significant, though perhaps as much for what it doesn't tell us as what it does. It bears Montaigne's signature on the title page but little else: only four marginal comments plus one vertical penstroke highlighting three lines in the life of Paulus Aemilius. As Alain Legros notes, the four comments show Montaigne to be a precise, careful reader, identifying inconsistencies between different accounts of the same event across different 'lives' or between Plutarch and another source.[22] The discovery of this edition is tantalising. It encourages us to reflect again on Montaigne's reading practices, on his interest in Plutarch and in life writing more broadly. But it also encourages us to assume that Montaigne must have had multiple editions: perhaps, as Legros suggests, a copy of the first edition published in 1559 – a copy full of marginal comments that would bear witness to the sustained engagement between these two authors and to the special place of Plutarch, along with Seneca, as one of the guiding stars of the *Essais*. But in the absence of such a copy, it is in Montaigne's own writing that this relationship can be discerned most clearly.

Reading Relations

To say that Montaigne was particularly fond of Seneca and Plutarch is to repeat what Montaigne himself says often enough. Identifying him as a Sceptic (of one sort or another) or as a doubtful thinker and writer similarly goes without saying. Both of these aspects of the *Essais* have been the subject of detailed and extensive scholarship, though few studies

---

[20] Montaigne notes in 'Des livres' that Plutarch is one of the authors he most frequents 'depuis qu'il est françois' (II.10.413/300), and he praises Amyot at length for the beauty and sensitivity of his translation, supposing that by 'longue conversation' Amyot had implanted in his own soul 'une generale Idée de celle de Plutarque' (II.4.363/262).
[21] The volume is a copy of the second edition of Amyot's translation, *Les Vies des hommes illustres, grecs & romains*, printed in Paris by Michel de Vascosan in 1565. See Alain Legros, 'Plutarque annoté par Montaigne', *MONLOE: Montaigne à l'œuvre* (published 15 September 2020), https://montaigne.univ-tours.fr/notes-de-lecture-de-montaigne/plutarque-annote-par-montaigne/ [accessed 6 November 2023].
[22] 'Ce jugement de Hannibal est autrement récité 267' [This judgement of Hannibal is recounted differently on folio 267]; 'Cicero dict lui mesme qu'il a eu trois jandres' [Cicero himself says that he had three sons-in-law]; Plutarch attributes only two. My quotations follow Legros' regularised edition published on the *MONLOE* website given above.

have considered them together.²³ This is presumably due to the fact that neither Seneca nor Plutarch seems, on the surface at least, to have much to do with doubt or Scepticism. They are dogmatists, as Montaigne made clear in 'Des livres': 'Plutarque a les opinions Platoniques, douces et accommodables à la société civile; l'autre [Seneca] les a Stoïques et Epicuriennes, plus esloignées de l'usage commun, mais, selon moy, plus commodes en particulier et plus fermes' [Plutarch's opinions are Platonic, mild, and accommodated to civil society; the other's are Stoic and Epicurean, more remote from common use, but in my opinion more suitable for private life and more sturdy] (II.10.413/300).

It is not my aim to show that Seneca or Plutarch were in fact the source for Montaigne's Sceptical philosophy, nor that Montaigne, having encountered the Pyrrhonian Sceptics and finding them in need of a 'nouveau langage' [new language] (II.12.527/392), found in the two dogmatists a literary form fit for expressing the philosophy outlined by Sextus Empiricus. I am not concerned with establishing a line of intellectual inheritance or a genealogy of ideas.

As Terence Cave has noted, sixteenth-century encounters with Pyrrhonism took this anti-dogmatic philosophy of contradiction and negation not only – indeed, not principally – as an apologetic tool to be adopted or imitated but instead as something rather odd, even comic: 'Imaginer le scepticisme, c'est imaginer une sorte de folie' [To imagine Scepticism is to imagine a sort of madness].²⁴ Renaissance authors grappled with this strange way of thinking not to establish a philosophical method but to open up a gap and tap into a new mental space.²⁵

Montaigne's relationship with Seneca and Plutarch might similarly be characterised as a connection that opens up a new way of thinking or, more precisely, a new relationship with thinking. The form of doubtful thinking practised in the *Essais* is not to be found in Seneca and Plutarch (just as it is not to be found among the Pyrrhonians). Rather than proposing a different genealogy for early modern Scepticism, this book argues that Montaigne's thinking is fundamentally relational: that he thinks with pairs, with his own doubleness ('Nous sommes, je ne sçay

---

²³ A notable exception is Nicola Panichi's 'Montaigne and Plutarch: A Scepticism that Conquers the Mind', in *Renaissance Scepticisms*, ed. Gianni Paganini and José Maia Neto (Dordrecht: Springer, 2009), pp. 183–212. Similarly, studies of Montaigne's debt to Seneca and Plutarch have tended either to treat these interlocutors separately, as in Isabelle Konstantinovic, *Montaigne et Plutarque* (Geneva: Droz, 1989), or as part of a broader examination of Montaigne's classical reading. Felicity Green's *Montaigne and the Life of Freedom* (Cambridge: Cambridge University Press, 2012), esp. pp. 45–88, demonstrates the value of reading Seneca and Plutarch in parallel.
²⁴ Cave, *Pré-histoires*, p. 25.
²⁵ 'Ils ouvrent un créneau sur un espace mental inédit', ibid., p. 25.

comment, doubles en nous mesmes' [We are, I know not how, double in ourselves], II.16.619/469). He also thinks not just with authors but with the space between authors, between different perspectives and scraps of writing ('pieces décousues' [detached pieces], as he describes the writing of Seneca and Plutarch, II.10.413/300). His doubtful dogmatists were central to both the conception and practice of this relational thinking: a practice of thinking with Seneca and Plutarch, with Scepticism, with the notion and status of authorship (including his own). It is a practice of thinking with writing. What emerged from Montaigne's mutually transformative, leaky dealings with Seneca and Plutarch is a cluster of stylistic and compositional habits, along with understandings of authorial ownership, identity and authenticity, that allowed him to explore thinking in new ways and to make that mode of thinking communicable in print.

Con-verser: Montaigne's relationship with Seneca and Plutarch is one of constantly filling up and pouring out, 'remplissant et versant'. But 'verser' is imbued with a very social sense of letting it all spill out, as Randle Cotgrave's 1611 dictionary makes clear: it is 'to shed, or spill; also, to converse with'.[26] Montaigne's 'commerce' with these authors is understood fundamentally as a conversation: provisional, open-ended, situated in time and vulnerable to loss. Crucially it is a conversation that structures another: the one between Montaigne and his readers. Writing doubtfully, spilling on to the page as he draws from and thinks with his favourite authors, Montaigne gushes forth, communicating himself – his character, his opinions, the patterns of his thinking – as he truly is. Doubtful writing, seen in this light, emerges not as the familiar habit of the enquiring, conservative, moderate Sceptic but as a radical, even desperate effort to salvage communication in a period of extreme social crisis. Responding to a social and ethical imperative, the *Essais* are a bizarre, paradoxical attempt to initiate a pouring forth *together*, in which doubtful writing serves as a means of holding on to one another precisely when that seems least possible.

This book takes as its starting point the association of doubtful writing with Seneca and Plutarch because it is an association that remoulds doubt into a type of thinking distinct from the strange and otherworldly madness of the Pyrrhonians.[27] 'Une forme d'escrire douteuse' is not, I will argue, merely an outlandish mental posture, a curiosity to be marvelled at, a fencer's last-ditch trick (II.12.558/418), or a (potentially

---

[26] Randle Cotgrave, *A Dictionarie of the French and English Tongues* (London: Adam Islip, 1611).
[27] It is for this reason that I differentiate 'doubt' and 'Scepticism', with 'Scepticism', capitalised following the manner of Stoicism, Epicureanism, Platonism, etc., understood as a category or, very loosely, a school of philosophy somewhat broader than Pyrrhonism.

dangerous) provocation: it is a mode of expressing what and, more importantly, how one actually thinks. Where early modern commentators, including Montaigne, took Pyrrhonism to be an essentially alien way of thinking, a disruption of ordinary, habitual patterns of thought, doubtful writing uncovers the doubleness that Montaigne understood to be natural and innate to him. He recognises that his thinking and his writing are foolish – indeed, it is in writing that he recognises himself as 'le badin de la farce' [the fool of the farce] (III.9.1001/766) – but his is a folly born within him. The Sceptics marshalled their arguments and 'refreins' (II.12.505/374) as a *facultas* to be deployed in argument, and their early modern commentators wondered at their feverish temper (one that would inevitably pass).[28] Montaigne's doubtful writing, by contrast, works to reveal him as he is. Doubtful writing is a mode of thinking, then, but crucially it is also a mode of communication: it is a mode of thinking in and with writing that facilitates Montaigne's ambition to reveal himself – an ambition entirely absent from Pyrrhonian or Sceptical practices and their rhetorical presentation.

Doubtful writing works through a cluster of relations. Some of these relations – a relational, dialectical thinking that opposes appearances or perspectives – are shared with the Pyrrhonians. Others are not. Thinking with Seneca and Plutarch, Montaigne established a form of thinking with writing, thinking with the 'papier' that sits at the centre of this 'commerce'. And by thinking with his book, he does something other than describe a doubtful disposition or present contradictions and ambiguities that prompt a reader to suspend judgement: he puts the movement and pattern of his character – doubtful, double, inconsistent and contradictory – into writing such that his reader can see him as he saw Seneca and Plutarch, 'jusques dans l'ame' [even into the soul] (II.31.716/541).

Outlines

The pattern of Montaigne's thought and writing is structured by doubles. This book focuses on the relationship with Seneca and Plutarch because, for Montaigne at least, they go together: his counterintuitive reading of these authors depends on their parallel relation. The first chapter considers their curious association with doubt. This link is

---

[28] On the relationship between Pyrrhonism and fever, see Estienne's prefatory letter to Henri de Mesme in his edition of the *Outlines of Pyrrhonism*, pp. 2–8, and, on this letter, Cave, *Pré-histoires*, pp. 31–5.

made explicit in Montaigne's reshuffling of the three philosophical sects – dogmatic, Academic, Pyrrhonian – given by Sextus Empiricus at the beginning of his *Outlines of Pyrrhonism*. Where the Pyrrhonians 'ne peuvent exprimer leur generale conception en aucune maniere de parler' [cannot express their general conception in any manner of speaking] (II.12.527/392) – the problem being that they speak affirmatively even in saying 'I doubt' – Seneca and Plutarch are presented not merely as Sceptics in disguise, and thus stuck in the same rut of thinking one way but speaking another, but as having landed on precisely the sort of self-expression that eluded the doubters. Their 'forme d'escrire douteuse' is one directed at and by the movements of the soul: they write in a way that reveals their character while moving the reader; their 'façons' harmonise with their souls while interlocking with each other, pushing and pulling the soul of the reader in parallel, reciprocal gestures. Far from illustrating a Sceptical suspension – 'je ne bouge' [I do not budge] (II.12.505/374) – Montaigne found in this pair of authors a set of relationships (between soul and style; between Seneca and Plutarch; between author and reader) suffused with movement.

Montaigne's book, consubstantial with its author, is nonetheless 'massonné purement' [built purely] from Senecan and Plutarchan 'despouilles' [spoils] (II.32.721/545). Chapter 2 argues that Montaigne thinks with a radically destabilised notion of authorial association: authorship in the *Essais* is, I argue, remoulded as insecure and impermanent, with scraps of text seeming to stick to different author figures weakly and temporarily. He expected at least some of his readers to be misled by his authorial practices: he describes himself setting traps and goading a reader into criticising a bit of Seneca or Plutarch, thinking it is him (II.10.408/296–7). But he also describes his own difficulties in working out what belongs to whom, who should be credited for a choice line in a modern author. Most significantly, he describes the experience of hearing his own words quoted back at him and not recognising the author. Montaigne capitalises on the ambiguities of authorship, on its perceived impermanence, to establish a way of thinking and writing with weak, temporary judgements on authorial association: a way of thinking that relies not on Sceptical *isostheneia* or 'equipollence' but on what Frédéric Brahami has called *astheneia*, the absence of strength that leads to a series of shifting, back-and-forth judgements.[29] It is a way of thinking seen most clearly in Montaigne's hesitations between Latin and French when borrowing a quotation from an ancient source – to what degree, he seems to be asking himself in his crossings-out and revisions,

---

[29] Brahami, *Le Scepticisme de Montaigne*, pp. 68–9.

is this phrase 'mine'? But the doubleness of authorial connections is seen elsewhere too, not least in a long patchwork of concealed Senecan quotations that stress again and again the importance of judging people on what is truly theirs and not on what is simply borrowed. Reading the *Essais*, we see now one 'visage', now another, such that ambiguous authorship becomes both the subject of doubtful enquiry and one of its principal strategies: it becomes a means by which Montaigne asks himself 'ce qui est sien et ce qui ne l'est point' [what is his and what is not], not just textually but ethically (III.8.940/718).

Chapters 3 and 4 examine the relationship between the form of the *Essais* and the 'subject informe' of Montaigne's 'cogitations' (II.6.379/274). He repeatedly describes himself and his way of thinking as not only inconstant or full of diversity but 'double'. Similarly, the movement of the 'esprit genereux' [spirited mind] is 'sans terme', without end, but it is also 'sans forme' (III.13.1068/818). The mode of writing developed in the *Essais* works to find a shape fit for such shapelessness. Here again, the foregrounding of Seneca and Plutarch reorients the *Essais* in ways that draw focus away from features that are privileged when read in a Pyrrhonian light: giving form to thought, Montaigne's doubtful writing is characterised not by the suspension of judgement (a posture he found difficult and painful), but by its proliferation; by the layering of judgements set down in temporally and temporarily fixed moments of writing. In Chapter 3, I read Montaigne's 'double and diverse' way of writing as related to two distinct modes of unresolved writing found in Seneca and Plutarch: Plutarch offers 'divers[es] et contrair[es]' interpretations of the subjects he examines, surveying possible opinions without offering definitive conclusion, while Seneca, in his serial epistolography, ties philosophy to the moment, with each letter subject to revision by those that follow. These forms are unresolved only in that they are 'sans terme': in drawing from them, Montaigne disrupts their linear irresolution to produce a form that responds to and communicates the shape of shapeless, double thinking. Having traced in Chapter 3 Montaigne's thought about form – the form of thinking; the form of writing – Chapter 4 develops three case studies that follow this practice of doubtful writing as it both reveals and sustains his thinking.

The *Essais*, like Montaigne, are characterised by doubleness. But to have 'une langue double' [a double tongue] is to be a liar, a flatterer or a hypocrite. Montaigne presents himself as something of an expert in matters of straight talking – a dangerous business in the context of the religious 'troubles'. And yet his own project of talking about himself is repeatedly held in suspicion and pre-emptively defended from imagined criticism. 'Mais, à qui croyrons nous parlant de soy, en une saison si gastée? veu qu'il en est peu, ou point, à qui nous puissions croire, parlant d'autruy, où il y a moins d'interest à mentir' [But whom shall we believe when he talks about himself, in so corrupt an age, seeing that there are few or none whom we can believe when they speak of others, where there is less incentive for lying?] (II.18.666/505).

Chapter 5 argues that the *Essais* stage a paradoxical reconciliation of simplicity and doubleness. Montaigne's *franchise* – his open, simple, 'naïve' truth-telling – draws readily from a commonplace association of *simplicitas* and *veritas* but, as the *Essais* reveal, Montaigne's 'façon simple' ('Au lecteur', p. 3/2) is one of doubleness. Writing doubly, Montaigne redefines the essential characteristics of *parrhesia*, that ancient model of frank, free speech exemplified and outlined in key works by Seneca and Plutarch, among others. Montaigne describes his book as 'un registre des essais de ma vie' [a record of the essays of my life] (III.13.1078/826). In this chapter, I argue that the *Essais* sit between the genre of the private *registre* and the Plutarchan 'life', drawing on these two models of writing that reveal the author's soul. Montaigne does not write a Plutarchan 'life' about himself, and nor does he write a diary recording his thoughts: he writes in a way akin to Plutarch, revealing his judgement to himself as much as to his reader. It is in this context that Montaigne complicates the equation of simplicity and truthfulness, again drawing from Plutarch and specifically his widely read treatise on 'How to tell a flatterer from a friend'. In the *Essais*, Montaigne employs his doubtful, double writing as a parrhesiastic tool with a difference: where Plutarch imagines the truth-teller using *parrhesia* as a corrective so that we might know ourselves, Montaigne, knowing himself to be double, asks how to tell the truth.

Chapter 6 traces the paradoxes that emerge from this contradictory and contrarian mode of truth-telling. It pays particular attention to Seneca's role as interlocutor and to the effect of this *conférence* in shaping Montaigne's inconstant, partial, contradictory veridiction. Seneca, Montaigne suggests, has a habit of repeating himself, and yet Montaigne draws attention to contradiction and inconsistency in his lessons. Curiously, it is in this teacher of *constantia* that one finds an advocate for inconstant raving, for letting loose the reins that might otherwise govern the spirit. We are inconstant, Montaigne and Seneca affirm, and we struggle to see ourselves in the round, 'en gros' (II.1.337/243). But where Seneca points to a unifying lesson and to a therapy that might bring about resolve and resolution, Montaigne stops short: his partial reading of Seneca takes him only as far as the diagnosis of inconstancy. Thinking with Senecan extracts, Montaigne abandons 'la forme du total' (II.1.337/243), revealing himself fully but – paradoxically – only by writing out his contradictory and shapeshifting parts. It is with this tension between part and whole that he developed a form of inconstant truth-telling, wherein he believes what he believes entirely in the moment, even in the knowledge that these beliefs will no doubt change just as they have in the past. Knowing his opinions will change does not temper his conviction: he contradicts himself but not the truth. Montaigne's writing of cognitive dissonance or doubleness and its relation to truth-telling is seen in a passage made up almost entirely of Senecan material and overloaded with techniques adapted from his letters and moral essays. The prosopopoeia of the 'esprit' flattering Montaigne, consoling him on the subject of his kidney stones, is an 'exemple' (III.13.1090/836) offered to the reader such that we might see the essayist fully and authentically, doing what everyone does in private but never in public. It works not by presenting the big picture, but by intercalating voices and perspectives, half-serious, half-joking, the better part lifted from Seneca, and yet entirely revealing Montaigne. It is a 'discours paradoxe' (III.5.875/667), a paradoxical, ridiculous discourse, but one that responds to the 'commandement paradoxe': know thyself (III.9.1001/766).

This is a book about how Montaigne thought about himself, his own book, and its relationship with those he read. It asks how he understood himself as doubtful, double, inconstant and self-contradictory, and argues that this relationship with himself was developed in a particular mode of writing. His doubtful 'forme d'escrire' emerged from a habit of thinking and writing with Seneca and Plutarch, two authors who superficially have little to do with doubt. But reading the *Essais* in light of this endless exchange uncovers a pattern of thinking with writing that lay at the heart of his project of self-recognition and self-communication. 'Remplissant et versant sans cesse' [incessantly filling up and pouring out], Montaigne developed a relationship with writing that structured a relationship with his reader: a means of communicating, authentically and in good faith, the doubtful, double movements of the soul.

Chapter 1

A Doubtful Combination

Playing the Fool

What does it mean to do philosophy? We might say that to do philosophy is to do what the philosophers do, whatever that might be. But where does that leave Montaigne, the self-declared 'accidental philosopher', and what of the practices of thinking and writing that make up his *Essais*?[1] In what sense does Montaigne do philosophy and what sort of philosophy might this be?

Montaigne addressed these questions directly at the beginning of 'Coustume de l'isle de Cea', a chapter arguing, in contrarian fashion, in defence of suicide: 'Si philosopher c'est douter, comme ils disent, à plus forte raison niaiser et fantastiquer, comme je fais, doit estre doubter' [If to philosophise is to doubt, as they say, then to play the fool and fantasticate, as I do, is all the more to doubt] (II.3.350/251).[2] It is for apprentices to enquire and debate ('à enquerir et debatre') and for the 'cathedrant', the authority who speaks *ex cathedra*, to resolve a dispute, but here as elsewhere Montaigne finds himself somewhere in the middle.[3] Between ignorance and authority, he seems to align himself with the philosophers, doubting – or, rather, playing the fool – though

---

[1] 'Nouvelle figure: un philosophe impremedité et fortuite!' [A new figure: an unpremeditated and accidental philosopher!] (II.12.546/409).
[2] Translation modified. Frame translates 'et fantastiquer' as 'and follow my fancies'. For 'fantastiquer', Cotgrave gives 'To conceive, imagine, devise, cast about, represent in the imagination; also, to affect fantastically; to fill with, or seed on, idle fancies' and, for 'fantastique', 'Fantasticall, humorous, new-fangled, giddie, skittish; inventive, conceited'.
[3] This is typical of Montaigne's preference for combinations, the middle ground and the hybrid: 'Les mestis qui ont dedaigné le premier siege d'ignorance, et n'ont peu joindre l'autre (le cul entre deux selles, desquels je suis, et tant d'autres)' [The half-breeds who have disdained the first seat, ignorance of letters, and have not been able to reach the other – their rear end between two saddles, like me and so many others] (I.54.313/227).

without quite placing himself among their number. The conclusion to his syllogism remains implied but unspoken and the link back to philosophy is left uncertain. What is philosophy? Doubting. Does Montaigne do philosophy? Perhaps – but he certainly doubts.

Montaigne was certainly well acquainted with the revived Sextus Empiricus: he borrows his arguments and at times paraphrases or translates his text very closely.[4] Uncovering the association of doubtful writing with Seneca and Plutarch is not to erase the influence of Sceptical philosophers, works or arguments on the *Essais*. Nor is it to argue that Seneca and Plutarch, or their Montaignian presences, are closet Sceptics. Montaigne thinks with and through his reading of Seneca and Plutarch in ways that are at times consonant with his thinking about Scepticism and sometimes concurrent with his reading of the Sceptics. To echo the opening of 'Coustume de l'isle de Cea', we might say that the Sceptics practised a form of doubt and that Montaigne, thinking and writing in innovative ways, thinks and writes doubtfully – though that is not to say that he thinks and writes like the Sceptics.

Throughout the *Essais*, Montaigne stresses the importance of Seneca and Plutarch, how theirs are the only books he could not be without. But what is it that he recognises and appreciates in them? What do they allow him to do that makes them so indispensable? Why are they so frequently considered together, in spite of the clear differences between them? And what might doubt have to do with a couple of dogmatists?

Three-Card Monte: Dogmatists and Doubtful Writing

In the 'Apologie', Montaigne outlined three types of philosophers. Anyone who goes looking for something, he says, will find themselves in one of three positions: they will have found what they were looking for; not found what they were looking for; or they will still be looking. 'Toute la philosophie', he says, 'est departie en ces trois genres' [All philosophy is divided into these three types] (II.12.502/371). The Aristotelians, Epicureans and Stoics say they have found truth, knowledge and certainty ('la verité, la science et la certitude'), the Academic Sceptics such as Clitomachus and Carneades have given up looking, while 'Pyrrho et autres Skeptiques ou Epechistes [...] disent qu'ils sont

---

[4] Most clearly in his account of the *phonai skeptikai* (II.12.505/374) and his own list of favourite words and phrases that 'amollissent et moderent la temerité de nos propositions' [soften and moderate the rashness of our propositions] (III.11.1030/788).

encore en cherche de la verité' [Pyrrho and other Sceptics and Epechists say that they are still in search of the truth].

The schema is not original to Montaigne but borrowed, silently, from the beginning of Sextus Empiricus' *Outlines of Pyrrhonism*.[5] This overview forms the basis of an extended reflection roughly halfway through the 'Apologie' on Scepticism, its relationship to other sorts of philosophy, and its relationship to different philosophical discourses. But it is not just a digest: Montaigne revises and twists Sextus' outlines, redrawing the links between doubt and expression in surprising ways, all the while pushing us to uncover doubtful writing where we would least expect to find it.

The Pyrrhonians have their own way of speaking and Montaigne lists their 'façons de parler', their 'refreins' such as 'I establish nothing' and their 'sacramental word', 'ἐπέχω, c'est a dire: je soutiens, je ne bouge' [*epecho*, that is to say, I hold back, I do not budge] (II.12.505/374). He notes that people often struggle to comprehend their philosophy and that even the Pyrrhonians themselves tend to describe their way of thinking obscurely. But having given as clear a picture as he can, he returns to his tripartite overview. Already though something has changed:

> Voylà comment, des trois generales sectes de Philosophie, les deux premiers font expresse profession de dubitation et d'ignorance; et, en celle des dogmatistes, qui est troisième, il est aysé à descouvrir que la plus part n'ont pris le visage de l'assurance que par contenance. (II.12.506)

> That is how, of the three general sects of philosophy, the first two make express profession of doubt and ignorance; and in that of the dogmatists, which is the third, it is easy to discover that most of them have put on the mask of assurance only to look better. (375)

We seem to be caught in a game of three-card monte: Montaigne has shuffled his three 'sectes' – the first two are now the Academic and Pyrrhonian Sceptics, not the dogmatists and the Academics – and, in any case, the three groups have collapsed into two. The initial criterion for categorisation (what the philosophers say about truth) has been replaced by their relationship with doubt.

But almost immediately, the new binary collapses again: dogmatists are, under their masks of certainty, Sceptics after all. This is not to say that Montaigne adopts Sextus' schema, scrubs out its distinctions, and then abandons it: he continues to refer to the 'tiers genre', though the principle governing the structure has changed yet again. It is not their epistemologies that separate them but rather the 'visages' with which

---

[5] *Outlines of Pyrrhonism*, I.1.9.

they practise their doubt. It seems that the three groups all think the same thing; what differentiates them is how they express their thought.

By the end of his survey, the dogmatists seem to be anything but dogmatic: Aristotle, Montaigne tells us, is constantly amassing piles of contradictory opinions to the point of covering himself in thick obscurity; Plato's Socrates does nothing but ask questions and stir things up; and, as for Plato himself, ten different sects, all disagreeing with one another, were born from his apparently dogmatic and certain teachings (II.12.507–9/375–6).

> [A]Il est ainsi de la plus part des autheurs de ce tiers genre [...] Ils ont une forme d'escrire douteuse [C]en substance [A]et un [C]dessein [A]enquerant plustost qu'instruisant, encore qu'ils entresement [C]leur stile de cadances dogmatistes. Cela se voit il pas aussi bien et en Seneque et [A]en Plutarque? [C]Combien disent ils, tantost d'un visage, tantost d'un autre, pour ceux qui y regardent de prez. (II.12.509)

> [A]It is the same with most of the authors of this third type [...] Their way of writing is doubtful [C]in substance [A]and their [C]plan [A]is to enquire rather than instruct, even though they sprinkle [C]their style with dogmatic cadences. Do we not see this as well in both Seneca and [A]Plutarch? [C]How much they say now one way, now another, for those who look closely. (377)[6]

Just look at Seneca and Plutarch, he writes, and you will find 'une forme d'escrire' that is doubtful not only in its 'substance' but also in its plan or method, in its 'dessein'.[7] The emphasis on writing is significant: these are 'autheurs' and Montaigne's attention is focused on hermeneutics and style. Theirs is a way of writing that expresses the doubtful, shifting perspectives of the author and demands that the reader apply their own enquiring scrutiny, looking closely to see the contradictions and to discern the irresolution interwoven with dogmatic cadences. For author and reader, it is a style that reflects a way of seeing things – including the text itself – 'now one way, now another'.

How are we to interpret this mode of writing, which has all the hallmarks of Scepticism, in relation to the categorisation of philosophers that governs this section of the 'Apologie'? Montaigne returns to the Pyrrhonians a few pages later. The difference is stark: 'les philosophes Pyrrhoniens [...] ne peuvent exprimer leur generale conception en aucune maniere de parler: car il leur faudroit un nouveau langage.

---

[6] Translation modified. Frame gives 'study them closely' for 'y regardant de prez'.

[7] On 'dessein' in the *Essais*, a term that refers to both a plan or intention and a sketch, see Olivier Guerrier, *Rencontre et reconnaissance: les Essais ou le jeu du hazard et de la vérité* (Paris: Garnier, 2016), pp. 151–60, and Vittoria Fallanca, 'The Design of Montaigne's *Essais*', unpublished DPhil dissertation, University of Oxford, 2020.

Le nostre est tout formé de propositions affirmatives, qui leur sont du tout ennemies' [the Pyrrhonian philosophers cannot express their general conception in any manner of speaking: for they would need a new language. Ours is wholly formed of affirmative propositions, which to them are utterly repugnant] (II.12.527/392). For the Pyrrhonians, language is too resolved, too affirmative, too dogmatic. They are caught in a bind, asserting, impossibly, 'Je doubte' and, the moment they speak, 'on les tient incontinent à la gorge' [you have them by the throat] (II.12.527/392). Drawing from Diogenes Laertius' 'Life of Pyrrho' (9.11.103–8), Montaigne takes Pyrrhonian 'aphasia', the technique of non-assertion whereby one avoids both affirmation and negation, presenting ideas and arguments without committing to them, and reads it as the sign of a philosophy in want of a language – a philosophical system without a means of expression.[8] And while the tongue-tied Pyrrhonians grapple with their impossible challenge, the dogmatists, paradoxically, appear to have landed almost by accident on a way of writing that is doubtful in both form and substance. Montaigne seems to have found the 'new language' that had eluded the Pyrrhonians precisely where one would least expect to find it: all one has to do is look closely ('regard[er] de prez').

If dogmatists are only Sceptics in disguise, what is it that draws Montaigne's attention? And if their dogmatism is only a pretence and they are really Sceptics after all, why does he follow Sextus' categorisation? It might be suggested that the point Montaigne is trying to make is that we are all Sceptics really, whether or not we admit it. But then why separate the philosophers into different groups in the first place? The distinctions are maintained, I want to suggest, because of the meaningful difference not in the content of their philosophical systems, in the beliefs they hold or the certainty of those beliefs, but in the way they express themselves. It is not simply that Scepticism leaches into everything and can be found everywhere, nor that everyone is really a Sceptic or ought to recognise that they are: the dogmatists have something positive to contribute, something the doubtful enquirer wants.

Montaigne's account of a 'dogmatic' way of writing characterised by doubt and irresolution seizes the reader's attention: it presents a strange,

---

[8] Emmanuel Naya has argued that this is in fact a promotion of Pyrrhonian aphasia, a paradoxical celebration of silence at the heart of a 'texte prolixe'; 'Les Mots ou les choses: le "nouveau langage" à l'essai', in *La Langue de Rabelais – La Langue de Montaigne*, ed. Franco Giacone (Geneva: Droz, 2009), pp. 325–49 (p. 326). As Naya has shown, Latin translations of *aphasia* and *epoché* tended to conflate *retentio assentionis*, the withholding of assent, and *retentio assertionis*, the withholding of speech, leading to a view of Scepticism as a voluntary silence (p. 348).

surprising paradox, one that overturns the relationship between dogmatism and doubt and points to a form of philosophical uncertainty that might be capable of expression – a way of thinking doubtfully that escapes both the aphasia of the Pyrrhonians and the dead end of affirming 'Je doubte'. This significant reimagination of the relationship between philosophical doubt and literary-philosophical writing emerged through an editorial process of revision, addition and redaction across the printed editions of the *Essais* and in the margins of the Bordeaux Copy. Tracing these revisions illuminates the shifting positions occupied the three 'genres' of philosophers, along with their relationships with writing and with each other. But it also uncovers Montaigne himself thinking with and through practices of rewriting – rewriting Sextus; revising his own, earlier work – to write in a way that is doubtful and unresolved, enquiring rather than instructing.

In its earliest version, Montaigne's account of the 'tiers genre' is much more concise and notably different at certain key points. It bears following Montaigne's lead, then, and asking what emerges when we look a little more closely ('regard[er] de prez'). He begins with Plato: for some he is a dogmatist, while others see him as a 'dubitateur', and others still see him as certain in some matters, doubtful in others. 'Il est ainsi de la plus part des autheurs de ce tiers genre' [It is the same with most of the authors of this third type]:

> Ils ont une forme d'escrire douteuse et irresolue, et un stile enquerant plus tost qu'instruisant: encore qu'ils entresement souvent des traitz de la forme dogmatiste. Chez qui se peut voir cela plus clairement que chez nostre Plutarque? combien diversement discourt il de mesme chose? combien de fois nous presente il deus ou trois causes contraires de mesme sujet, et diverses raisons, sans choisir celle que nous auons a suyvre? que signifie ce sien refrein: En un lieu glissant et coulant, suspendons nostre creance?[9]

> They have a form of writing that is doubtful and unresolved, and a style that is enquiring rather than instructing, even though they often sprinkle in a dash of the dogmatic style. Where can this be seen more clearly than in our Plutarch? How diversely he considers the same thing! How often he presents us with two or three contrary causes for the same subject, and diverse reasons, without choosing the one that we should follow! What else could be the meaning of his refrain, 'In a slippery and treacherous place, let us suspend our belief'?

In this earliest version, Plutarch alone exemplifies doubtful, unresolved writing, a style that combines perspectives but also combines a

---

[9] The passage remained unchanged in the 1588 edition. For the first edition, quoted here, see *Essais* 1580, II.12.268–9. For Montaigne's edits, see the Bordeaux Copy, fol. 213r.

'forme [...] irresolue' with the 'forme dogmatiste'. His 'refrein' – a rare word in the *Essais*, occurring only ten times – is, of course, one of the 'refreins' of the Pyrrhonians: *epoché*, 'suspendons nostre creance'.[10]

With the later additions, Montaigne hammers a series of textual wedges into this passage. After the various views on the extent of Plato's dogmatism, he fills the right-hand margin of the Bordeaux Copy with an anecdote about Socrates and his parallel between the work of the philosopher and the midwife.[11] The result is that the subsequent 'Il est ainsi de la plus part des autheurs de ce tiers genre' [It is the same with most authors of this third type] becomes significantly less intelligible. The section celebrating Plutarch is rewritten to include Seneca, though this is followed by the counterexample of legal discourses, 'le point extreme du parler dogmatiste' [the ultimate point of dogmatic speaking] (II.12.509–10/377–8).[12] Plutarch is separated from his 'refrein' to such an extent that 'sien' [his] is dropped altogether. Uncoupled from its author, this motto morphs into 'un lieu glissant et coulant', and Montaigne's question, 'Que signifie ce refrein', seems now a little less rhetorical.

In the 1580 version, Montaigne described the features he found attractive in Plutarch's way of writing, features that he would later ascribe also to Seneca. After 1588, he went much further. His discussion of the three types of philosophers has the appearance of being assertive and affirmative, made up of definitive categories put forth in resolute 'cadences dogmatistes', but, looking closely ('regard[ant] de prez'), it becomes apparent that the model borrowed from Sextus is not as simple as it seems. It is treacherous, 'glissant et coulant': the groups are simultaneously distinct and indistinct, depending on our perspective, and Montaigne juggles them in a way that leaves us unsteady, forced to check our assumptions. And it is not just Sextus' schema that is reworked: Montaigne disrupts and redirects the rhetorical and argumentative flow of his own writing, leaving us with a 'forme d'escrire' that is

---

[10] On this 'refrein', see André Tournon, 'Le Doute investigateur: métamorphoses d'un "refrein" de Plutarque dans les *Essais*', *Nouveau bulletin de la société internationale des amis de Montaigne*, 50 (2009), 5–22. Tournon notes how Plutarch, 'en dépit de ses attaches platoniciennes et aristotéliciennes, est pris pour exemple du *pseudo*-dogmatisme' [in spite of his Platonic and Aristotelian ties, is taken as the example of *pseudo*-dogmatism] (p. 7, my emphasis).
[11] Bordeaux Copy, fol. 213r.
[12] Montaigne regularly contrasts doubtful, unresolved discourse with the dogmatism of the *parlements*. See, for instance, III.11.1030/788. On Seneca's late inclusion and its relation to the conclusion of the 'Apologie', which will be discussed in Chapter 2, see Jan Miernowski, *L'Ontologie de la contradiction sceptique: pour l'étude de la metaphysique des Essais* (Paris: Garnier, 1998), pp. 65–8.

doubtful not only in its subject matter but also in its 'dessein', 'stile' and form. As André Tournon recognised, Montaigne does not limit himself to surveying disagreements between the philosophers – an inexhaustible source ('source inépuisable') of arguments against dogmatism.[13] He is more interested in how a single philosophical school, how individual philosophers contradict themselves. In showing how other authors, even seemingly dogmatic authors, constantly show things now one way, now another, Montaigne embraces similar tensions within his own prose. He shuffles his three 'sectes', changing the rules of the game and slipping in a digression that seems to come out of nowhere, before showing us a combination that catches us off-guard. Despite first appearances, this outline of philosophical schools is itself 'more enquiring than instructing' – not so much a dogmatic typology as an unfolding exposition that asks us to think things through from a new perspective.

In reworking this survey of philosophy, Montaigne outlined an unusual relationship between doubt and writing. The Pyrrhonians remain unable to say anything despite their 'refreins' and self-purging affirmations.[14] Doubtful dogmatists such as Seneca and Plutarch, on the other hand, allowing themselves a few 'dogmatic cadences', find a way of writing that is doubtful and unresolved, full of diversity and able to engage a reader while leaving them free to judge things for themselves. It is a strange reversal and one that relies on Montaigne's sleight of hand, the *legerdemain* of the juggler, the *bateleur*.[15] But that is not to say that this is just a trick: after all, 'niaiser et fantastiquer', to fool around, is to doubt, and to doubt is to philosophise. This paradoxical reversal is more than the adoption of a contrarian opinion, more than a provocative pose: in identifying the 'tiers genre' as one of doubtful

---

[13] Tournon, 'Le Doute investigateur', p. 12.

[14] 'Ils disent que cette proposition [Je doubte] s'emporte elle mesme [...], ny plus ny moins que la rubarbe qui pousse hors les mauvaises humeurs et s'emporte hors quant et quant elle mesme' [they say that this proposition carries itself away with the rest, no more nor less than rhubarb, which expels evil humours and carries itself off with them] (II.12.527/392–3). On the self-purging rhetoric of Scepticism, see John O'Brien, 'Si avons-nous une tres-douce medecine que la philosophie', in *L'Ecriture du scepticisme chez Montaigne*, ed. Marie-Luce Demonet and Alain Legros (Geneva: Droz, 2004), pp. 13–24.

[15] We might draw a connection here with what Alain Legros has seen as the 'culture du corps', the embodied movement latent in 'epecho'. See '"*Epékhô*, c'est-à-dire je soutiens, je ne bouge": jeu de paume, histoire et philosophie', in Balsamo and Graves (eds), *Global Montaigne*, pp. 411–23 (p. 412). Legros identifies in this 'refrein' 'la silhouette d'un funambule ou d'un equilibriste', a tightrope walker, or a tennis player ('joueur de paume'), characterised not by passive immobility but by a highly mobile balancing act. The skills of the funambulist and the trickster, analogous to those of the fool who is able to 'niaiser et fantastiquer', are apparent also in Montaigne's handling of Sextus' three categories.

writers, Montaigne drew a new relationship between literary 'forme' and philosophical 'substance' in which doubt finds expression, rather than impediments, in writing. In looking for that 'nouveau langage', we have, Montaigne seems to suggest, been looking in the wrong place, among the wrong group of philosophers, and looking not nearly close enough.

Parallel Lives

In 1580, Plutarch alone, 'nostre Plutarque', was picked out as the clearest example of doubt among the dogmatists. When Montaigne came to revise this passage, the author of the *Parallel Lives* had acquired his own Roman counterpart. What are we to make of Seneca's late inclusion in this roster of doubtful writers? And what exactly is his relationship, here and throughout the *Essais*, with Plutarch, a figure who seems to be his constant partner in Montaigne's reflections?

Seneca's introduction at this late stage certainly pushes against the traditional notion that Montaigne's admiration for the Stoic was on the wane.[16] But it points also to his deep association with Plutarch. The pairing is not unique to the *Essais*. In 1595, Simon Goulart printed *Les Œuvres morales et meslées de Sénèque*. The title of his translation, printed in the same year as his censored edition of Montaigne's *Essais*, was clearly intended to echo Amyot's translation of Plutarch's *Œuvres morales et meslées*, which he had also been printing in pirated editions since the early 1580s.[17] From Goulart's perspective at least, the two ancient texts had a good deal in common. In his preface to the Seneca volume, he notes that his pairing with Plutarch goes back at least as far as Petrarch, who records Plutarch 'en quelque endroit' [in some place or other] admitting that 'nul des Grecs n'est comparable à Seneque' [none of the Greeks is comparable to Seneca].[18]

But this conventional parallel rests on biographical and textual bases that are curiously flimsy. Goulart's 'quelque endroit' is Petrarch's letter to Seneca: 'Tu vero, venerande vir et morum, si Plutarcho credimus, incomparabilis preceptor' [You are, if we believe Plutarch, a venerable

---

[16] The argument that Montaigne's early chapters were marked by an appreciation for Seneca less apparent in his later writing goes back at least as far as Pierre Villey. See *Les Sources et l'évolution des Essais*, vol. 1, pp. 212–13.
[17] For Goulart's version of the *Essais*, see Michel de Montaigne, *Les Essais* (Lyon [Geneva]: François le Febvre, 1595).
[18] *Œuvres morales et meslées de Seneque* (Geneva: J. Arnaud, 1606), fol. 2r.

man and an incomparable teacher of morals].[19] No such passage is found in either the *Moralia* or the *Lives*.[20] This spurious compliment, from one 'preceptor' to another, nonetheless helped to establish the parallel by drawing on biography: Seneca tutored Nero, while Plutarch was thought, mistakenly, to have tutored Trajan. It was to this reputed role that Amyot referred, mixing self-promotion with flattery, in the dedicatory epistle to Charles IX prefacing his translation of Plutarch's Œuvres morales.[21]

Montaigne would have therefore encountered these authors as, in some way, a pair, a parallel 'set', with lives and books that reflect one another and interlock harmoniously. And it was a pair of authors to whom he had a particular, and particularly strong, attachment. His affection for them can be seen clearly enough in his 'Defence de Seneque et de Plutarque', the title of which prompts a comparison with the most famous of philosophical double acts (and the subject of the only other chapter in the *Essais* dedicated to two ancients), Democritus and Heraclitus. 'La familiarité que j'ay avec ces personnages icy [Sénèque et Plutarque]', writes Montaigne, 'et l'assistance qu'ils font à ma vieillesse, et à mon livre massoné purement de leurs despouilles, m'oblige à espouser leur honneur' [My familiarity with these personages [Seneca and Plutarch] and the help they give to my old age, and to my book, built up purely from their spoils, oblige me to espouse their honour] (II.32.721/545). As Warren Boutcher suggests, it is at least in part on account of this chapter, itself tied up with Montaigne's growing reputation as a new French Seneca or a French Plutarch, that, during his visit to the Vatican Library in 1580, he was presented with one or maybe two manuscripts brought out especially: 'un Seneque et les *Opuscules* de Plutarche'.[22] François Rigolot, surveying the items in

---

[19] Book 24, letter 5 in *Le familiari*, ed. Vittorio Rossi and Umberto Bosco, 4 vols (Florence: G. C. Sansoni, 1968), vol. 4, p. 232.

[20] Petrarch's error is not surprising, given that he had access only to intermediary sources and the pseudo-Plutarchan *Institutio traiani*. On Plutarch's medieval afterlife and particularly Petrarch's references to Plutarch, see Marianne Pade, *The Reception of Plutarch's Lives in Fifteenth-Century Italy*, 2 vols (Copenhagen: Museum Tusculanum Press, 2007), vol. 1, pp. 68–72. Petrarch may have encountered Plutarch's first Latin translator, Simon Atumanus, during his time at the papal court at Avignon. See Marianne Pade, 'Leonardo Bruni and Plutarch', in *Brill's Companion to the Reception of Plutarch*, ed. Sophia Xenophontos and Katerina Oikonomopoulou (Leiden: Brill, 2019), pp. 389–403 (p. 390).

[21] 'Epistre au roy', fols. A2r–A4v.

[22] Montaigne gives account of this visit in the *Journal de Voyage*, ed. Fausta Garavini (Paris: Gallimard, 1983), pp. 212–14. See Warren Boutcher, *The School of Montaigne in Early Modern Europe*, 2 vols (Oxford: Oxford University Press, 2017), vol. 1, pp. 269–84.

the Vatican Library, has suggested that this might have been the single-bound 1477 volume dedicated to Sixtus IV and containing Plutarch's *De cohibenda ira* and Seneca's *De ira* – a coupling of texts that further points to the reputation of this pair of authors as moral philosophers outlining compatible teachings on common themes.[23]

Montaigne's praise for Seneca and Plutarch is typically read in light of his comments on their works as 'pieces décousues' [detached pieces] (II.10.413/300). They serve as a model of informal writing that takes up a subject only to put it down again, a way of writing that accommodates 'le travail de détissage et de recomposition' [the work of unweaving and recomposition].[24] I will return to this key phrase – 'à pieces décousues' – in Chapter 3, but for the moment I would like to reconsider Montaigne's praise of Senecan and Plutarchan style in light of their association with doubt in the 'Apologie'. In what follows, I ask how Montaigne constructed his particular image of this couple, tracing the bonds by which he unites them. The fact that Seneca and Plutarch write in 'pieces décousues' certainly makes 'the job of disassembly and reassembly easier', as Nicola Panichi puts it.[25] But it is not just their words, stories and sayings that Montaigne pieced together. Thinking with these authors, with their ways of thinking, living and writing, he combined them, forging a model that is neither Senecan nor Plutarchan but the product of their combination. Seneca and Plutarch sit together in the *Essais* not only as moral instructors and not simply as figures who echo each other, expressing similar lessons in a similar fashion. They are parallel authors, shaping one another through relationships of similarity and difference.[26]

---

[23] François Rigolot, 'Curiosity, Contingency, and Cultural Diversity: Montaigne's Readings at the Vatican Library', *Renaissance Quarterly*, 64.3 (2011), 847–74 (pp. 851–4).
[24] The quotation is from Olivier Guerrier's entry on 'Plutarque', in *Dictionnaire de Michel de Montaigne*, ed. Philippe Desan (Paris: Garnier, 2018), pp. 1490–5 (p. 1491). Alexandre Tarrête makes much the same point in his entry for 'Sénèque', pp. 1705–12 (p. 1705). See also Floyd Gray, *Montaigne et les livres* (Paris: Garnier, 2013), p. 46. In the context of Renaissance miscellany more broadly, Marie-Claire Couzinet has shown how the 'mêlée' nature of Senecan and Plutarchan writing provided a model establishing a 'correspondance entre une philosophie et un style'; 'Les *Essais* de Montaigne et les miscellanées', in *Ouvrages miscellanées et théories de la connaissance à la Renaissance*, ed. Dominique de Courcelles (Paris: Ecole de chartes, 2003), pp. 153–69 (p. 169).
[25] Panichi, 'Montaigne and Plutarch: A Scepticism that Conquers the Mind', p. 209.
[26] On Montaigne's habit of thinking through pairs of authors, see Luke O'Sullivan, '"Un traict à la comparaison de ces couples": Seneca's Poets and Epicurean Senecanisms in Montaigne's *Essais*', in *Imitative Series and Clusters from Classical to Early Modern Literature*, ed. Colin Burrow, Stephen Harrison, Martin McLaughlin and Elisabetta Tarantino (Berlin: De Gruyter, 2020), pp. 223–42. Montaigne's parallel way of thinking bears the influence of Plutarch's use of *synkrisis* in the *Lives*, as shown by Alison Calhoun, *Montaigne and the Lives of the Philosophers: Life Writing and Transversality*

These authors of patchworks, 'bigarrures' not unlike Montaigne's own, are stitched together and, in the context of leaky business, it is the gaps, the seams, that make all the difference.

Listen up! Seneca, Plutarch and *Hoc age*

Speaking frankly and getting to the point – the horse has, it seems, already bolted; no need now to mince his words – Montaigne tells us in his chapter on books what he really thinks of Cicero: 'sa façon d'escrire me semble ennuyeuse' [his way of writing seems to me boring] (II.10.413/301).[27] He criticises the endless 'prefaces, definitions, partitions, etymologies' which 'consument la plus part de son ouvrage' [consume the greater part of his work], suffocating all that might once have been 'de vif et de mouelle' [of life and marrow]: 'je veux qu'on commence par le dernier point [...] qu'on ne s'amuse pas à les anatomizer [...] je veux des discours qui donnent la premiere charge dans le plus fort du doubte: les siens languissent autour du pot' [I want a man to begin with the conclusion [...] not waste his time anatomizing [his subjects] [...] I want reasonings that drive their first attack into the stronghold of the doubt; his languish around the pot] (II.10.414/301).

Montaigne's critique of Ciceronian fastidiousness is bookended by comments in praise of Seneca and Plutarch. I will return to the passage immediately preceding this review of Cicero later in this chapter, but I want to begin with Montaigne's 'dernier point'. Read in the light of doubtful dogmatism, this critique of Cicero and the comparison with Seneca and Plutarch that follows illuminate his understanding of how different styles make particular demands of their readers. What might be taken as a rather conventional opposition between, on the one hand, an overwrought 'ingenieuse contexture de parolles' (II.10.413/301) and, on the other, natural, inartificial eloquence is shown here to be concerned as much with ethics as aesthetics, with practical eloquence that not only cuts to the chase but compels its readers to think and act. Once again, Montaigne stresses the need to pay attention and look closely: where

---

in the Essais (Newark: University of Delaware Press, 2015), and Cara Welch, 'Beyond Stoicism: Plutarch's *Parallel Lives* and Montaigne's Search for a New Noble Ethos', in *Revelations of Character: Ethos, Rhetoric, and Moral Philosophy in Montaigne*, ed. Corinne Noirot-Maguire and Valérie M. Dionne (Newcastle: Cambridge Scholars Publishing, 2007), pp. 99–118.

[27] For the bolted horse, see II.10.413/301: 'puis qu'on a franchi les barrières de l'impudence, il n'y a plus de bride' [for once you have crossed over the barriers of impudence there is no more to curb].

Cicero and his imitators leave their readers struggling to keep their eyes open, he finds in Seneca and Plutarch a way of writing that both reflects and requires a state of alert, a readiness for action.

Ciceronian long-windedness is perfect for the schoolmaster's lesson, the barrister's defence or the preacher's sermon, moments 'où nous avons loisir de sommeiller, et sommes encore, un quart d'heure apres, assez à temps pour rencontrer le fil du propos' [where we have leisure to nap and are still in time a quarter of an hour later to pick up the thread of the discourse] (II.10.414/301). Their endless signposting is exhausting and Montaigne complains about authors who exert themselves 'à me rendre attentif' [to make me attentive], who 'me crie cinquante fois: Or oyez! à la mode de nos Heraux' [shout at me fifty times 'Listen!' in the manner of our heralds]. 'Les Romains', he continues, 'disoyent en leur Religion: *Hoc age*, que nous disons en la nostre: Sursum corda; ce sont autant de parolles perdues pour moy' [The Romans used to say in their religion *Hoc age*, as we say in ours: *Lift up your hearts*: these are so many words lost on me].

Montaigne would have encountered this phrase, *hoc age* (literally 'do this' but used to mean 'mind this' or 'pay attention'), in Plutarch, in the lives of Numa Pompilius and Coriolanus.[28] Whenever a magistrate is taking auspices or making a sacrifice, Plutarch writes, 'lon crie tout hault, Hoc age: qui vault autant à dire comme, fais cecy: & est un advertisement aux assistans, de soy recueillir pour penser à ce qui se fait' [people cry out 'Hoc age', which means 'do this' and is a warning to bystanders to gather themselves and pay attention to what is being done].[29]

Cicero and the barristers, teachers and preachers who imitate him have more in common with the heralds than the magistrates: they drive their readers to distraction with their constant calls to pay attention; they waste their time dawdling with prefatory matters without getting to the substance that ought to occupy us. Montaigne can spend

---

[28] On this phrase in antiquity, see John C. Rolfe, 'On *Hoc Age*, Plautus Capt. 444', *Classical Philology*, 28 (1933), 47–50. Rolfe notes that the religious context is absent outside of Plutarch, allowing us to identify Plutarch specifically as Montaigne's source. Emily Butterworth has noted the objection of the Roman Censors to Montaigne's comparison of the Roman 'hoc age' to 'sursum corda'. This comparison was suppressed in the 1582 edition but reinstated in the Bordeaux Copy and in the subsequent 1595 edition. See Emily Butterworth, 'Censors and Censure: Robert Estienne and Michel de Montaigne', in *Reading and Censorship in Early Modern Europe*, ed. María José Vega, Julian Weiss and Cesc Esteve (Barcelona: Studia Aurea Monográfica, 2010), pp. 161–79 (p. 174).

[29] 'Numa Pompilius', *Vies des hommes illustres* (Paris: Vascosan, 1565), fol. 48r. Plutarch repeats this point in similar terms in 'Coriolanus', fol. 155v. Montaigne alludes to Plutarch's comparison of the lives of Numa and Lycurgus in 'De la colere' (II.31.714/539).

an hour reading Cicero ('qui est beaucoup pour moy' [which is a lot for me]) but when it comes to accounting 'ce que j'en ay tiré de suc et de substance' [what juice and substance I have derived], he finds most often that he has come away with nothing at all ('la plus part du temps je n'y treuve que du vent') (II.10.413–14/301).

From thinking with Plutarch about Cicero, Montaigne turns to Plutarch himself, accompanied by Seneca: 'Les deux premiers [Sénèque et Plutarque], et Pline, et leurs semblables, ils n'ont point de *Hoc age*; ils veulent avoir à faire à gens qui s'en soyent advertis eux mesmes' [The first two, and Pliny, and their like, have no *Hoc age*; they want to deal with people who are already on the alert].[30] These authors get straight to the matter at hand and write in a way that expects a certain kind of reader: one already alert and attentive both to the practice of philosophy and the writing itself, a reader who can engage with the subject and with their interlocutor without the need for constant signposting, glossing and calls to attention.

But in writing in such a way that the reader must look for themselves, they teach a real, substantial philosophical lesson. Montaigne immediately qualifies his point that Seneca and Plutarch do without the *hoc age*: 'ou, s'ils en ont, c'est un *Hoc age* substantiel, et qui a son corps à part' [or if they have one, it is a substantial *Hoc age* that has a body of its own] (II.10.414/302). Their *hoc age*, their instruction to pay attention, is not a prelude to the main event but rather the lesson itself – something like the Delphic imperative to 'know thyself', to pay attention to oneself and to the world – and it is a lesson reflected in and taught through their way of writing. Seneca and Plutarch do not rouse the reader from their slumber, letting them nod off for a while but making sure they wake in time to hear a lesson ready to be extracted and copied into a commonplace book. They expect their readers to be alert to the movement of the argument, to its choice phrases, and to respond appropriately without a prompt. This reading experience mirrors the experience of living in the world. Reading Seneca and Plutarch teaches us to pay attention, to be alert, to think independently, not only in reading but in life.

Learning to read is a way of learning to live. The consonance between reading and philosophy illuminates Montaigne's own prose style in this passage. In both his critique of Ciceronianism and his praise of Seneca and Plutarch, he imitates the styles he is discussing, encouraging shifting

---

[30] Translation modified. Frame has 'they want to have to do with people who themselves have told themselves this'. Here I follow *The Complete Essays*, trans. M. A. Screech (London: Penguin, 2003), p. 465.

postures of attention and inattention in a reflection of the ways writing teaches us to be 'advertis'.

The discussion of Cicero's boring ('ennuyeuse') '[A]prefaces, definitions, partitions, etymologies, [qui] consument la plus part de son ouvrage' (II.10.413/301) is itself overloaded with possibilities, alternatives and negations, stretching out almost indefinitely. Montaigne begins by saying that an author should start with their last point, but his prose works to the opposite end, delaying his conclusion with caveats, with 'preparatoires et avant-jeux'. A long manuscript addition, included immediately before the discussion of Seneca and Plutarch and their 'substantial' *hoc age*, is especially florid:

> [C]La licence du temps m'excusera elle de cette sacrilege audace, d'estimer aussi trainans les dialogismes de Platon mesmes et estouffans par trop sa matiere, et de pleindre le temps que met à ces longues interlocutions, vaines et preparatoires, un homme qui avoit tant de meilleures choses à dire? Mon ignorance m'excusera mieux, sur ce que je ne voy rien en la beauté de son langage.

> [C]Will the license of the times excuse my sacrilegious audacity in considering that even Plato's dialogues drag and stifle his substance too much, and in lamenting the time put into these long vain preliminary interlocutions by a man who had so many better things to say? My ignorance will excuse me better in that I have no perception of the beauty of his language.

With his rhetorical question, his profession of ignorance (even as he nods to his familiarity with Plato), and the hyperbole of his 'sacrilegious audacity', Montaigne parodies the schoolmaster, the barrister, the preacher, all those who write tedious discourses that rely on the punctuating abilities of the *hoc age*. The Bordeaux Copy (fol. 172v) shows that he extended a prior, more concise version of this mock confession: the suggestion that Plato's dialogues drag was originally followed by the sentence about not knowing Greek, which was crossed out and moved to squeeze in the lament that this great thinker wasted his time with 'longues interlocutions, vaines et preparatoires'.

In what seems to be a different ink, Montaigne added a final sentence to this post-1588 addition: 'Je demande en general les livres qui usent des sciences, non ceux qui les dressent' [In general, I ask for books that use learning, not those that build it up]. This conclusion cuts through the verbiage to introduce Seneca and Plutarch. It is one of Montaigne's 'cadances dogmatistes' that ring out, not as a conclusion, summarising his argument so far, but as an abrupt tonal shift that seizes the reader's attention.[31] Rather than telling us to 'listen up!' ('Or oyez!'), he

---

[31] See Nicolas Le Cadet on Montaigne's use of maxims and assertive language as a figure of doubt: maxims, he suggests, work as 'lueurs de vérité qui jonchent le parcours de la

structures his prose so that we cannot help but recognise its movements ourselves. It is in the reading that we become 'advertis', alert both to the rhetorical movement of his argument and to the argument itself, both to his local point that learning should be practical and his broader point that style might teach us to see things and think for ourselves.

'J'entends que la matiere se distingue soy-mesmes', wrote Montaigne. 'Elle montre assez où elle se change [...] sans l'entrelasser de paroles, de liaison et de cousture introduictes pour le service des oreilles foibles ou nonchallantes, et sans me gloser moymesme' [I want the matter to make its own divisions. It shows well enough where it changes [...] without my interlacing it with words, with links and seams introduced for the benefit of weak or heedless ears, and without writing glosses on myself] (III.9.995/761). Montaigne's own style aspires to the substantial *hoc age* of Seneca and Plutarch, using form to ensure that his readers are 'advertis'. Those authors were able to grasp not only their subject but their reader's attention. Theirs is not the dogmatism of the pedant (they are still part of the 'tiers genre', more enquiring than instructing). Instead they offer a practical education in reading, interpreting and thinking for oneself. *Hoc age*, pay attention; 'regard[e] de prez', look closely: to read Seneca and Plutarch is a lesson in critical enquiry, a lesson Montaigne repeats for his own reader alert to the movement of his 'matiere'.

Parallel Movements: Writ(h)ing Bodies and Moving Souls

In Seneca and Plutarch, Montaigne identified a form capable of writing doubt, able to grasp a reader's attention, able both to reflect and promote independent thought. Theirs is a style that not only expresses but teaches what Richard Scholar calls the 'art of free-thinking', where free-thinking is 'nothing like a school of philosophy' but rather 'a set of attitudes'; a way of thinking and writing that calls on us to look again and to look closely, both in reading and in life.[32]

In the accounts considered so far in this chapter, Montaigne holds up Seneca and Plutarch as important examples of a broader community of authors, as members of the 'tiers genre' or as 'les deux premiers' [the first two] in a longer roll call including Pliny 'et leurs semblables' [and their like]. But these two authors are also repeatedly and consistently

---

pensée et rythment la quête jamais terminée du savoir' [glints of truth that litter the route of thought's trajectory and give rhythm to an endless quest for knowledge]; Nicolas Le Cadet, 'La Maxime et le "nouveau langage" des *Essais*', *Nouveau bulletin de la société internationale des amis de Montaigne*, 46 (2007), 85–109 (p. 103).

[32] Scholar, *Montaigne and the Art of Free-Thinking*, p. 45.

presented in parallel. As Alison Calhoun has noted, the parallel, that feature Montaigne describes as the 'most admirable part' ('la piece plus admirable', II.32.726/549) of Plutarch's *Lives*, 'complicates the idea that one person alone holds the key to perfection or knowledge about truth'.[33] It is a way of thinking with lives and interlocutors that brings about 'the necessity of judgement', a way of thinking that relies on those essayistic traits of 'weighing, comparing and contrasting, digesting'.[34] In pairing him with Seneca, Montaigne treats 'nostre Plutarque' as Plutarch treated others. But in addition to seeing Seneca as his biographical and generic double, he identified a contrasting but complementary relationship in their style and its effects. It is in relation to their parallel 'façons', I suggest, that Montaigne navigates his own path, not by following his models but by plotting out the space and the movement between them. What distinguishes these authors from those like them – what explains the shift in the Danaïdes passage from seeing them as examples ('tantost') to exceptions ('sinon') – is their interlocking affinity, their parallel movements that work in harmony and move their reader to see (and feel) things differently.[35]

Books can only help you so much. Montaigne makes this plain in his penultimate chapter, 'De la phisionomie'. You need hardly any learning ('guiere de doctrine') to live comfortably, he notes, and, if you would only look, 'vous trouverez en vous les arguments de la nature contre la mort, vrais, et les plus propre à vous servir à la necessité' [you will find in yourself Nature's arguments against death, true ones, and the fittest to serve you in case of necessity] (III.12.1039/794). And as for whether one needs to read Cicero's *Tusculan Disputations* to know how to die, 'J'estime que non' [I think not]. 'Les livres', Montaigne asserts, echoing a sentiment expressed earlier in his discussion of *hoc age*, 'm'ont servi non tant d'instruction que d'exercitation' [Books have served me not so much for instruction as for exercise] (III.12.1039/795). Pointing once again to readers capable of looking closely ('qui y regarde de pres'), he complains that even the best authors have a tendency to smother a 'bon argument' with others that are light ('legers') and insubstantial ('incorporels').

This critique of immaterial learning, separated from exercise, application and the real business of living, sets up a parallel with (and between) Seneca and Plutarch. It is a contrast that hinges on a complex harmony, in which words and bodies testify to, reveal and direct the movement of

---

[33] Calhoun, *Montaigne and the Lives of the Philosophers*, pp. 26–7.
[34] Ibid., p. 27. On Montaigne's preference not just for pairs of 'illustrious' men (the 'hommes illustres' of Plutarch's title) but for philosophers, see pp. 27–32.
[35] For the Danaïdes passage, discussed in the introduction, see I.26.146/107.

the soul.[36] It begins with Seneca, whose philosophical work was put to the test in his famous final hour:

> A voir les efforts que Seneque se donne pour se préparer contre la mort, à le voir suer d'ahan pour se roidir et pour s'asseurer et se desbatre si long temps en cette perche, j'eusse esbranlé sa reputation, s'il ne l'eut en mourant tresvaillamment maintenuë. (III.12.1040)

> To see the trouble to which Seneca puts himself to be prepared for death, to see him sweat from the exertion of steeling and reassuring himself, and writhe about interminably on his perch, would have shaken his reputation with me if he had not very valiantly maintained it in dying. (795)

Seneca's writing is entangled with his death. Indeed, he 'dies writing', as James Ker puts it in his analysis of this death scene in Tacitus, Suetonius and Cassius Dio: his final moments are occupied in dictating to his students, with the flow of blood from his veins mirroring the flow of ink.[37] The words Seneca dictated while dying have been lost: Tacitus, Montaigne's likely source, chose not to record them, noting that they had been published elsewhere.[38]

In the *Essais* too, Seneca's life and death are bound up with his words. Montaigne supports his judgement that Seneca died 'tres-vaillamment' with Latin quotations, but these are not, as one might expect, quotations from biographical accounts.[39] Instead, he quotes Seneca himself, albeit the Seneca of the *Epistles* – which is to say Seneca preparing for, rather than experiencing, that all-important final test. The quotations are taken from Letters 114 and 115: 'Magnus animus remissius loquitur et securius. Non est alius ingenio, alius animo color' [A great soul speaks more relaxedly and assuredly. There is not one colour for the mind, another for the soul.][40]

---

[36] This harmony of speech, life and character/soul defines *parrhesia*, a notion that will be discussed fully in Chapters 5 and 6.

[37] James Ker, *The Deaths of Seneca* (Oxford: Oxford University Press, 2009), p. 66.

[38] *Annals*, 15.60–5. On the Tacitus account and its afterlife, see Ker, *The Deaths of Seneca*, particularly pp. 20–34. Justus Lipsius, Montaigne's correspondent and editor of Seneca, would both laud this dying dictation and lament its loss: 'In ipsa etiam morte dictare, quod posteros iuvaret' [to dictate, even as he was dying, that which would help posterity!]; 'De vita et scriptis L. Annaei Senecae', in *L. Annaei Senecae philosophi opera*, ed. Justus Lipsius (Antwerp: Plantin, 1605), p. xxiii. On Lipsius' reading of Seneca's death scene, see Ker, *The Deaths of Seneca*, pp. 210–12.

[39] Montaigne borrows heavily from Tacitus' account in another retelling of Seneca's death, 'De trois bonnes femmes', II.35.747–9/566–7. There, Montaigne draws a parallel between Tacitus' version of Seneca's (and Paulina's) virtuous dying moments and a long account in Seneca's own words of his 'magnanimous' resolution to continue living – not for himself but for Paulina. On Montaigne's translation of Seneca's letter describing this resolution, see Chapter 3.

[40] Montaigne also quotes from letter 75, discussed below.

Strangely, these quotations are used to illustrate that Seneca did not quite live up to the standard he set himself. Stranger still, Montaigne's complaint has nothing to do with any final moment of weakness. Instead, his focus is on Seneca's character as revealed in his writing: where he advocated calm, constancy and assurance, his style – his 'agitation si ardante, si frequente' [agitation, so burning, so frequent], his tendency to break into a sweat in philosophising, in convincing himself and preparing himself for death – 'montre qu'il estoit chaud et impetueux luy mesmes' [shows that he was hot and impetuous himself]. Seneca's final moments are a test of character, a test not 'of the wit but of the soul' ('non ingenii sed animi negotium agitur'), as Seneca himself put it in a line quoted by Montaigne in this passage. His teachings, if they are to be more than weightless, 'incorporels' lessons, need to be judged against the character revealed in his life. And this is a test that Seneca passes. But it is in Seneca's writing that Montaigne sees not only his bodily toil but also his character, his disposition, his humour (literally – he is 'chaud', hot and impetuous).

To judge Seneca's arguments and determine whether they are 'bons' requires us to judge his life, his death, his body. Alison Calhoun has shown how Montaigne's discussion of philosophical lives makes routine reference to the body and to biological function, interrogating 'the Platonic and Stoic conceptions of the body's relationship to the soul'.[41] To say that the proof of the pudding is in the eating – that Seneca's lessons need to be seen in person, in practice, in the flesh – is conventional enough, but Montaigne's version of this argument seems back to front: he finds Seneca sweating, labouring, writhing around and steeling himself not in the hour of his death but in his epistles – not in the real, material ('corporel') world of life and death but in the writing up of philosophical arguments.

The relationship between words and deeds, between language, character and body, is not as straightforward as it might appear. It is not simply a case of establishing whether Seneca walks the walk: his life (and, more pointedly, his death) guarantee the worth of his philosophy because they reveal his character, his valiant resolve until the last. But that character, along with the toil and labour that went into preparing himself for death, discussed in overwhelmingly physical, embodied terms, are to be found not in his biography but in his own writing. There is something of a harmony – though not a straight equivalence – between Seneca's teachings and his life: indeed, Montaigne notes that the quotations he picks out show that Seneca still has something to learn from his own philosophy ('Il le faut convaincre à ses despens' [we have

---

[41] Calhoun, *Montaigne and the Lives of the Philosophers*, esp. p. 28.

to convince him at his own expense]). What emerges, then, is an understanding that, to judge a philosophy, one has to be a judge of character, a judge not of the *ingenium*, the intellect, but of the *animus*, the soul. What is surprising is that Montaigne discerns that character as much in Seneca's writing as in his death.

Seemingly out of nowhere, Montaigne introduces Plutarch. 'La façon de Plutarque, d'autant qu'elle est plus desdaigneuse et plus destendue, elle est, selon moy, d'autant plus virile et persuasive' [Plutarch's manner, inasmuch as it is more disdainful and less tense, is, to my mind, all the more virile and persuasive] (III.12.1040/795). Plutarch's introduction here is jarring: unlike Seneca, and unlike the Cicero of the *Tusculan Disputations* whom Montaigne had been discussing before, Plutarch has no clear association with the tradition of philosophy as *praeparatio mortis*. While it is true that he wrote a letter of consolation to his wife after their daughter's death, a text translated by Etienne de la Boétie and published by Montaigne, Plutarch himself had no exemplary death against which his philosophy could be judged, no 'life' of his own in which his character could be tested.[42]

Why, then, this sudden turn to Plutarch and his 'façon'? The link is immediately clarified by Montaigne. He thinks of Plutarch because here too he can read the movements of the author's soul: 'je croyrois ayséement que son ame avoit les mouvements plus asseurez et plus reiglés' [I would easily believe that the movements of his soul were more assured and more regulated]. In 'De la colère', written long before and on a theme that gestures to these two ancients as authors of 'De ira' and 'De cohibenda ira' respectively, Montaigne noted a similar capacity to read Plutarch's soul in his 'façon': 'les escrits de Plutarque, à bien savourer, nous le descouvrent assez, et je pense le connoistre jusques dans l'ame' [Plutarch's writings, if we savour them aright, reveal him to us well enough, and I think I know him even into his soul] (II.31.716/541).[43]

---

[42] For La Boétie's translation, see *La Mesnagerie de Xenophon. Les Regles de mariage de Plutarque. Lettre de consolation, de Plutarque à sa femme... Item, un Discours sur la mort dudit Seigneur De la Boëtie, par M. de Montaigne* (Paris: Fédéric Morel, 1571). On moral exemplarity and exemplary lives in the *Essais*, see Michel Jeanneret, 'The Vagaries of Exemplarity: Distortion or Dismissal?', *Journal of the History of Ideas*, 59.4 (1998), 565–79. Jeanneret suggests that Montaigne thinks with his examples, good and bad, rather than simply taking exemplars as virtuous models to be followed: 'Whether I agree or not [...] they work as an indispensable reference that helps me establish my thought' (p. 576). Alison Calhoun takes this further in *Montaigne and the Lives of the Philosophers*, tracing the essayist's 'subversion of exemplarity as an effective form of moral teaching' (p. 82).

[43] On Seneca's 'De ira' as a source for both Plutarch and Montaigne, see Peter Mack, *Reading and Rhetoric in Montaigne and Shakespeare* (London: Bloomsbury, 2010), pp. 9–10.

As Felicity Green has argued, Montaigne found in Seneca and Plutarch what she calls a 'language of the self' – a 'mode of self-figuration' concerned not with introspection and the uncovering of a 'hidden, psychological interiority', but with providing a rigorous account of one's 'moral preoccupations and sensibility'.[44] With both Seneca and Plutarch, Montaigne found authors who made themselves – their character – legible in their manner of writing.

Montaigne's reading of Plutarch recasts the account of Seneca and his toils. He began by suggesting that a philosophy had to be judged against biography, that one has to have seen Seneca maintaining his resolve to approve of his laborious philosophical programme. But the coupling with Plutarch suggests that it is not Seneca's life but his 'façon' that counts – his way of doing things, his 'style', both on and off the page.[45] The biographical details, which initially secured Seneca's 'reputation', are shown with increasing clarity to be supplementary, merely confirming the character that is revealed in reading.[46] Montaigne makes this point even more explicitly in 'Defence de Seneque et de Plutarque': he notes that Seneca's 'vertu paroist si vive et vigoureuse en ses escrits [...] que je n'en croiroy aucun tesmoignage au contraire' [virtue shows forth so live and vigorous in his writings [...] that I would not believe any testimony to the contrary] (II.32.722/545–6). Seneca and Plutarch are aligned in 'De la phisionomie', then, not because of their philosophy, nor because of their exemplary status as moral actors, but because Montaigne can read in their 'façons', their styles, the movement of their souls. It is a style that guarantees the harmony of speech and inward feeling as set out by Seneca in one of the letters Montaigne quotes in this passage: 'quod sentimus loquamur, quod loquimur sentiamus: concordet sermo cum vita' [let us say what we feel and feel what we say; let speech harmonise with life] (*Ep.* 75.4).

---

[44] Green, *Montaigne and the Life of Freedom*, pp. 46–77 (p. 53). Green's analysis shares a number of parallels with Warren Boutcher's study of the *Essais* as an 'index' of noble *liberté*, *The School of Montaigne*, esp. vol. 1, pp. 99–106.

[45] On 'façon' and fashion in the *Essais*, see John O'Brien, 'Fashion', in *Montaigne after Theory/Theory after Montaigne*, ed. Zahi Zalloua (Seattle: University of Washington Press, 2009), pp. 55–74. In his *Dictionarie of the French and English Tongues*, Randle Cotgrave gives the meaning of 'façon' as 'The fashion; forme; outward frame, or shape, a making, proportion, workemanship; manner, behaviour, order; custome, guise, wont', and points towards its use in the context of literary style: 'Le livre est de sa façon. *Is right of his phrase, or stile.*'

[46] The supplementary nature of biographical details for this knowledge of the soul is developed also in 'De la colère'. Montaigne declares that he knows Plutarch 'jusques dans l'ame', but notes that a biography would be welcome nonetheless: 'si voudrois-je que nous eussions quelques memoires de sa vie' [yet I wish we had some memoirs of his life] (II.31.716/541).

Seen another way though, the 'façons' of Seneca and Plutarch are diametrically opposed: 'L'un, plus vif, nous pique et eslance en sursaut, touche plus l'esprit. L'autre, plus rassis, nous informe, establit et conforte constamment, touche plus l'entendement. Celuy là ravit nostre jugement, cestuy-cy le gaigne' [The one, sharper, pricks us and startles us, touches our mind more. The other, more sedate, forms us, settles and fortifies us constantly, touches our understanding more. The former ravishes our judgement, the latter wins it] (III.12.1040/795). This parallel analysis of style and its effects shows Montaigne to be moving beyond what Felicity Green has described as an 'association of *stilum* [style] and *èthos* [character]'. He is complicating a commonplace sense that texts constitute 'vivid reflections of their authors'.[47] It is not simply that style reflects the movement of the soul – it also communicates and produces it, with the movement of the reader's soul drawn to the fore in Montaigne's analysis.

What's more, the movements seen in and produced by Seneca's and Plutarch's writing go together, establishing these authors as a pair and not simply as two preferred examples to be counted among a larger cohort. Seneca's writing sends us spiralling into a somersault, while Plutarch stills us, tethers us down, stops us in our tracks. Each of these movements only makes sense when it has its opposite, as Montaigne's insistent 'l'un [...] l'autre' makes clear. This alternating figure, which jumps from violent agitation in one clause to comforting assurance in the other, allows Montaigne to mirror in his own text the stop–start effect he experiences in reading theirs. Looking closely, he sees the relationship between them more as symbiosis than similarity: Seneca needs Plutarch to steady ('establi[r]') the reader before he can send them spinning, and vice versa.

The physicality of their effect is one that became more pronounced as Montaigne revised his comments on these dovetailed authors: 'd'autant plus forte', strong, became 'd'autant plus virile'; '[l]'un plus aigu', pointed, became 'vif', alive; and '[l]'autre plus solide' became 'rassis', sedate and settled.[48] As Richard Scholar has noted, Montaigne, in 'De Democritus et Heraclitus', describes his own process of essaying with

---

[47] Green, *Montaigne and the Life of Freedom*, pp. 42–3.
[48] Bordeaux Copy, fol. 460v. Montaigne's revisions here might also be designed to distinguish this 'façon' from the superficial qualities that he warned his reader not to mistake for deeper ones, discussed in another post-1588 addition made immediately before the account of Seneca's death scene: we must be careful, he says, not to call 'force ce qui n'est que gentillesse; et ce qui n'est qu'aigu, solide, ou bon ce qui n'est que beau' [strength what is only nicety, or solid what is only acute, or good what is only beautiful] (III.12.1040/795).

remarkable physicality, 'restoring, to the metaphors [he] uses, their literal senses'.[49] This same process is at work here. The movement of each author's soul is read in the push and pull between their 'façons', their styles. These are authors capable of moving their readers, and we feel those movements viscerally, in our bodies. The relationship between books and bodies, between philosophical lessons and real, lived experience, is by this point in Montaigne's discussion thoroughly entangled. So too, for that matter, is the relationship between Seneca and Plutarch. These parallel, contrary authors each have a style that tells us more about their character even than biography, a style that opens up their hearts, at once tracing and directing complementary, antithetical movements.

Keeping Things Simple

I have been suggesting that Montaigne's parallel account of Seneca and Plutarch, of their lives and their lessons, their ways of writing and its resonance with their own souls and those of their readers, is more complicated than it first seems. But from Montaigne's perspective at least, the experience of reading Seneca and Plutarch is characterised, like their 'façons', by a certain simplicity.

In 'Des livres', in the passage immediately before the discussion of *hoc age*, Montaigne once again sets up these authors as mirrors of one another in a long synchresis, not so much a competitive *paragone* as an articulation of harmony and consonance. They both ('tous deux') treat their material in a way that suits Montaigne's 'humeur', cutting it up into detached snippets ('pieces décousues'); they share most of the same opinions, at least those that are 'true and useful' ('utiles et vrayes'); and – once again linking their ways of doing and writing philosophy to their biographies – 'fortune' placed them both in the same century, more or less, and made both of them 'precepteurs' to Roman emperors. Both were strangers in a foreign country, both rich, both powerful (II.10.413/300).

This congruency culminates again in that key term, 'façon', which seems to encompass not only prose style but also their custom, their disposition and their approach to philosophy and philosophical writing: their teaching ('leur instruction') is 'présentée d'une simple façon et pertinente' [presented in a simple and pertinent fashion]. It is a phrase that recalls Montaigne's desire, in the 'Au lecteur', that his book might let people see him 'en ma façon simple, naturelle et ordinaire' [in my

---

[49] Scholar, *Montaigne and the Art of Free-Thinking*, p. 73.

simple, natural, ordinary fashion] ('Au lecteur', p. 3/2). 'Façon' marks a turning point in Montaigne's comparison of his two ancient analogues. Burrowing into this simple 'façon', he makes it clear once again that these authors go together on account of their tendency to pull apart. Where Seneca is 'ondoyant et divers' [undulating and diverse], Plutarch is 'uniforme et constant' (which is surprising – one would expect constancy of the Stoic).[50] Seneca is once again seen as labouring, straining and tensing himself ('se peine, se roidit et se tend'), while Plutarch is carefree, unwilling to quicken his pace or even raise a defence against vice ('semble [...] desdaigner d'en haster son pas et se mettre sur sa targue'). Seneca accommodated his speech to the 'tyrannie des Empereurs de son temps', while Plutarch 'est libre par tout' [is free throughout]. Plutarch is a Platonist, whose opinions are 'douces', soft and pliable, fit for 'l'usage commun', while Seneca's Stoic (and Epicurean) views are hard, 'fermes'. Seneca is full of sharp 'pointes', Plutarch full of matter, 'choses' (II.10.413/300–1).[51]

This parallel account concludes in a summary that reinforces not only the sense of embodied physicality that Montaigne associated with these authors but also his sense that the movement of their souls, reflected in the movement of their prose, impresses itself on the soul of the reader (this is no Pyrrhonian 'je ne bouge', 'I do not budge'): 'Celuy-là [Sénèque] vous eschauffe plus, et vous esmeut; cettuy-cy vous contente davantage et vous paye mieux. Il nous guide, l'autre nous pousse' [The former [Seneca] heats you and moves you more; the latter contents you more and pays you better. He guides us, the other pushes us] (II.10.413/301). Seneca warms you up and moves you, while Plutarch contents you; Plutarch gently guides while Seneca gives us a prod, and perhaps something a little stronger.

In this interlocking pair of authors, Montaigne recognised two ways of writing that move the reader in complementary ways. Together, their styles constitute a 'simple façon et pertinente' [simple and pertinent fashion], and it is with this pair that Montaigne developed his own 'façon simple, naturel et ordinaire'. Simplicity, here at least, is made

---

[50] The association of *constantia* and Stoicism was made explicit in Lipsius' *De constantia* (1583). On this notion in the *Essais*, see Sébastien Prat, *Constance et inconstance chez Montaigne* (Paris: Garnier, 2011).

[51] In 'Sur des vers de Virgile', Montaigne draws a further link between Plutarch, 'choses' and a material, physical relationship with language: 'Plutarque dit qu'il veid le langage latin par les choses; icy de mesme: le sens esclaire et produict les parolles; non plus de vent, ains de chair et d'os' [Plutarch says that he saw the Latin language through things. It is the same here: the sense illuminates and brings out the words, which are no longer wind, but flesh and bone] (III.5.873/665). He is referring to Plutarch's introduction to the life of Demosthenes, *Vies des hommes illustres*, fol. 583r.

up of antithesis, out of harmonious but opposed parts, out of parallel movements that need to be read between Seneca and Plutarch, between each author's soul and the trace it leaves in their way of writing, between the movements of their souls and those of their readers.[52] It is a 'façon', ultimately, that affords an extraordinary degree of communication, such that one might know an author by their *animus* and see them 'jusques dans l'ame' (II.31.716/541).

The simplicity of this 'façon' is what separates these authors from the Pyrrhonians. At the beginning of this chapter, I noted Montaigne's effort to set out their stall as clearly as he could, accepting that most people struggled to comprehend their philosophy and that they themselves tended to represent matters obscurely: 'Quiconque imaginera une perpetuelle confession d'ignorance, un jugement sans pente et sans inclination, à quelque occasion que ce puisse estre, il conçoit le Pyrronisme' [Whoever will imagine a perpetual confession of ignorance, a judgement without leaning or inclination, on any occasion whatever, he has a conception of Pyrrhonism] (II.12.505/374).

What would such a confession look and sound like? When it comes to talking about one's thoughts – when it comes to communicating – the doubtful enquirer seems caught in a bind, forced either to say nothing at all lest someone seize you by the throat (II.12.527/392), to stick to the small corpus of self-purging 'refreins', or to follow the lead of Pyrrho himself, at least as he is recounted by Diogenes Laertius.[53] Pyrrho, Diogenes records, would carry on talking even if the person to whom he was speaking had slipped away ('s'il avoit commencé un propos, il ne lassoit pas d'achever, quand celuy à qui il parloit s'en fut allé', II.29.705/533).[54] But Pyrrho was supposed also to have done a whole host of bizarre, unusual things, 'si esloignées de l'usage commun' [so remote from common usage] that his life was 'quasi incroyable' [almost unbelievable]: suspending judgement, he refused to move out of the way of oncoming traffic; others would have to pull him back to prevent him falling into a ditch; he would undergo surgery without batting an eyelid, and so on.

---

[52] I will return to the tension between simplicity and doubtful doubleness in later chapters, especially Chapter 5.
[53] A Latin translation of this 'Life' was printed as an appendix to Estienne's translation of Sextus' *Outlines*.
[54] On the reception of these 'incredible' tales in the *Essais* and in the early modern period more broadly, see Calhoun, *Montaigne and the Lives of the Philosophers*, pp. 79–89, and Emmanuel Naya, 'La Science-fiction pyrrhonienne: des perles aux cochons', *Littératures*, 47 (2002), 67–86.

Montaigne did not believe these stories. They were simply too ridiculous, and instead did no more than demonstrate the historian's desire to portray Pyrrho as 'stupide et immobile': 'Il n'a pas voulu se faire pierre ou souche; il a voulu se faire homme vivant, discourant et raisonnant, jouïssant de tous plaisirs et commoditez naturelles' [He did not want to make himself a stump or a stone; he wanted to make himself a living, thinking, reasoning man, enjoying all natural pleasures and comforts] (II.12.505/374). As Alison Calhoun has noted, Montaigne engaged with Pyrrho not as an outlandish marvel but as 'an ordinary person who can indeed live as a sceptic'; not someone who wanted to 'despouiller entierement l'homme' [entirely strip off the man] (II.29.706/533, translating a saying attributed to Pyrrho by Diogenes), but someone who lived according to 'observances communes' (II.12.506/375).[55] In his day-to-day life, Pyrrho lived according to convention, suspending judgement all while acting on common sense.

What, then, of the 'perpetual confession of ignorance' Montaigne asks us to imagine? It seems unimaginable, especially given that it lacks a case study, an example to serve as a guide. 'Discourant et raisonnant' – reasoning but also 'discoursing', speaking and discussing – Pyrrho seems to suspend not his judgement but his doubt when it comes to putting his thought into words. No matter which way they turn, the Pyrrhonians seem remarkably far from the straightforward symmetry of thought and writing, or feeling and speech, described by Seneca: 'quod sentimus loquamur, quod loquimur sentiamus; concordet sermo cum vita' [let us say what we feel, and feel what we say; let speech harmonise with life]. Seneca and Plutarch, at the heart of the 'tiers genre', illustrate not only a doubtful way of writing, 'une forme d'escrire douteuse', but one that is remarkably 'simple', capable of communicating thoughts and feelings, as well as pushing the reader to pay attention and to see things differently.

This chapter began with Montaigne the fool, keen to 'fantasticate' and offer up strange, doubtful suggestions, juggling his philosophical genres in a way that threatens to dazzle (and possibly lose) the reader. But the lesson to take from this performance is not that its conclusions should be dismissed. Montaigne took pains to stress the importance of paying close attention and, in the case of Seneca and Plutarch, it is clear that carefully following his moves reveals a way of thinking about doubt that places primacy on communication, on the power of certain ways of writing, certain 'façons', to express the movements of a shifting soul and to call on the reader to respond appropriately.

[55] Calhoun, *Montaigne and the Lives of the Philosophers*, p. 89.

Seneca and Plutarch can write doubtfully because they can variously push, prompt and goad the reader into looking carefully, seeing things differently and judging for themselves. And they can do this without falling into either the tedium of the schoolmaster's lecture or the aphasia, punctured only by stock sayings and 'refreins', of the Pyrrhonians. The relationship between these two authors, in which one counterbalances the other, is essential: in reading them together, Montaigne flits between them and finds a harmonious, sustaining interval. With this pair, he identified a 'façon' fit for practical, engaged enquiry, for open-ended, unresolved, doubtful free-thinking that speaks to and from the heart. To see it, one has to see doubt differently, bound up not with its philosophers but with the parallel movements within and between this fantastical pair: Seneca and Plutarch, doubtful dogmatists.

Chapter 2

Writing Between Authors

Negotiating Authors

In his chapter on philosophy as preparation for death, Montaigne went back to the beginning. He was born, he writes, at eleven thirty in the morning on the last day of February 1533. Thirty-nine years and two weeks separated the moment of his birth from the moment in which he was writing ('Il n'y a justement quinze jours que j'ay franchi 39 ans'), and he hopes that he will have at least as long until the moment of his death. It would be foolish, he asserts, to worry about death when it is surely still so far off, 'si esloignée', and yet 'les jeunes et les vieux laissent la vie de mesme condition' [young and old leave life on the same terms] (1.20.84/58).

More than fifteen years later, he returned to this passage. In the margins of the Bordeaux Copy, he coupled his personal reflection with a Latin tag taken from his reading: 'Nemo non ita exit e vita tamquam modo intraverit' [everyone goes out of life in the same way as if he had just entered it]. The quotation, which mocks old men for crying like babies in the face of death, restates what Montaigne himself had said in the line before. It is a line taken from Seneca (*Ep.* 22.14), one of the principal sources for this chapter, and it would seem that, in citing his source directly, Montaigne is acknowledging a debt that had hitherto run beneath the surface.

But then he changed his mind. It is not clear how long had passed – a moment or a couple of years – but at some point, and in a slightly lighter ink, he crossed out Seneca's Latin and rewrote it in French: 'Nul n'en sort autrement que comme si tout presentement il y entroit' [None goes out of it otherwise than as if he had just entered it].[1] It seems now that Seneca has been accommodated, silently incorporated into Montaigne's

[1] Bordeaux Copy, fol. 29r.

own prose, and any debt the essayist might owe his source is, if not concealed, less openly declared.

Except that these words are not Seneca's, or at least not originally. In his early letters to Lucilius, the Stoic practised the custom of closing each epistle with a choice phrase from Epicurus. At the end of letter 22, he explains that he had nearly forgotten to include 'aliquam magnificam vocem', 'some noble saying', and had to break the letter's seal in order to attach his customary gift ('munusculum'). 'Cuius inquis?', he imagines Lucilius asking him. 'Epicuri. Adhuc enim alienas sarcinas adorno' ['Spoken by whom?', you ask. By Epicurus; for I am still embellishing other men's belongings.][2] The line that ends up in the *Essais* started its journey not among the Stoics but in the 'enemy camp' of the Epicureans ('aliena castra', *Ep.* 2.5).

Seneca recognises, or rather pretends, that Lucilius will want to know where this quotation comes from – its provenance and its author are important – and he is clear that he is pilfering someone else's belongings.[3] But as he says in the previous letter, Epicurus' words, like everything else that is true and well said, are common property: 'Has voces non est quod Epicuri esse iudices; publicae sunt' [There is no reason why you should hold that these words belong to Epicurus: they are public property] (*Ep.* 21.9).

It is tempting to consider Montaigne's twice-borrowed words through the lens of intellectual communalism, reading this chain of quotations – *munuscula* – as evidence that literary property is 'communis'.[4] It is an

---

[2] Here I follow the Latin text of the 1557 edition used by Montaigne, *L. Annaei Senecae Philosophi Stoicorum omnium acutissimi opera quae extant omnia*, ed. Celio Secondo Curione (Basel: [Hervagius], 1557), p. 107. Modern editions give 'adsero' [I appropriate] for 'adorno' [I embellish]. On Montaigne's edition of Seneca, see Villey, *Les Sources et l'évolution des Essais*, vol. 1, pp. 240–2. It is overwhelmingly likely that Montaigne also made use of other editions, including French translations. Catherine Magnien-Simonin has convincingly argued that one of Montaigne's shortest chapters, 'Le profit de l'un est dommage de l'autre', uses the Latin text of Seneca's *De Beneficiis* alongside a 1560 French translation by Sauveur Accaurat. See Catherine Magnien-Simonin, '*Essais* I, 22: Montaigne lecteur d'un Sénèque français?', *French Forum*, 13.3 (1988), 277–85. Montaigne also knew the translation by his brother-in-law, Geoffroi de la Chassaigne, seigneur du Pressac, *Epistres de L. Annæe Seneque, philosophe tres-excellent*, reprinted in 1598 as an *Entière traduction des Epistres de Sénèque* (Lyon: Ancelin, 1598). Despite the claims made by its title, this is not a complete translation, and epistle 22, along with a number of others, is not included.
[3] On Seneca's quotations from Epicurus, see Ute Tischer, '"Nostra faciamus": Quoting in Horace and Seneca', in *Horace and Seneca: Interactions, Intertexts, Interpretations*, ed. Martin Stöckinger, Kathrin Winter and Andreas T. Zanker (Berlin: De Gruyter, 2017), pp. 292–313 (pp. 309–10). Seneca breaks the habit of closing his letters with Epicurean quotations after letter 29.
[4] On common ownership of intellectual property, see Kathy Eden, *Friends Hold All Things in Common: Tradition, Intellectual Property, and the Adages of Erasmus* (New

example, perhaps, of Montaigne making others say what he cannot express, finding in Seneca's Latin not so much an idea as a way of putting into words something shared, something universal.[5] Such a way of thinking, essential to early modern commonplacing practices, imagines true and elegant sayings as a sort of popular wisdom, a resource from which any given author might draw freely. Not all literary property is communal, of course: authors, including Seneca, routinely claimed individual ownership of their literary production, even when making use of common stock.[6] Authors of centos, for instance, 'new' works made up entirely of quotations, argued that their use of old material worked to digest and transform it. As Justus Lipsius put it in his *Politica*, a work made up almost entirely of quotations from classical authors, words and phrases might be borrowed, but their selection, their order and, consequently, their meaning belong entirely to him ('inventio tota & ordo a nobis sint').[7]

But what of Montaigne's hesitation between Latin and French? Similar examples are found throughout the *Essais* and the direction of traffic is not always the same. Consider another quotation from Seneca, again in the margins of the Bordeaux Copy.[8] In 'De l'art de conférer', Montaigne criticised those who cannot do anything without turning to some book or other, and did so by invoking Seneca, who said much the same: 'sub aliena umbra latentes, numquam auctores, semper interpretes' [lurking in the shadow of others, never authors, always

---

Haven, CT: Yale University Press, 2001), pp. 142–63; and, by the same author, 'Literary Property and the Question of Style: A Prehistory', in *Borrowed Feathers: Plagiarism and the Limits of Imitation in Early Modern Europe*, ed. Hall Bjørnstad (Oslo: Unipub, 2008), pp. 21–38.

[5] 'Je fay dire aux autres ce que je ne puis si bien dire, tantost par foiblesse de mon langage, tantost par foiblesse de mon sens' [I make others say what I cannot say so well, now through the weakness of my language, now through the weakness of my understanding] (II.10.408/296).

[6] *Ep.* 84.6. Scholarship on Seneca's metaphors describing digestive and apian imitation is expansive, but see, most recently, Colin Burrow, *Imitating Authors: Plato to Futurity* (Oxford: Oxford University Press, 2019), pp. 84–8. On the view common to Seneca and Plutarch of good imitation as a means of 'claiming a literary identity', see Benoît Castelnérac, 'The Method of "Eclecticism" in Plutarch and Seneca', *Hermathena*, 182 (2007), 135–63 (p. 139).

[7] Justus Lipsius, *Politicorum sive civilis doctrinae libri sex* (Antwerp: Plantin, 1604), p. 9.

[8] Bordeaux Copy, fol. 408r. There are many similar examples of graphic, linguistic hesitation, and these are not limited to borrowings from Seneca. See, for instance, a quotation from Livy crossed out and rewritten in French, Bordeaux Copy, fol. 289r. In 'Des loix somptuaires', Montaigne quotes Quintilian before rewriting the line in translation, only to change his mind again and return to the Latin, fol. 112v. Notably, when Quintilian's words were translated and accommodated into Montaigne's prose, he highlights the foreignness of this saying by ascribing it to 'un antien'.

interpreters] (III.8.927/707). The source is a letter in which Seneca encourages Lucilius to stop repeating others and to instead speak for himself (*Ep.* 33.8). The irony of Montaigne's quotation is clear. What is less clear is the degree to which the reader is encouraged to see this saying as, in some way, Montaigne's. Having first copied out the Latin quotation, he drew a line through it and wrote it again in French – an effort, perhaps, to partially conceal its provenance and thus the joke, refining his audience. But the translation is crossed out in turn and replaced with a partial, truncated Latin quotation, highlighting its foreignness and inviting us to see Montaigne not as *auctor* but as *interpres*, as precisely the sort of writer he is criticising. But those key terms, *auctor* and *interpres*, are silently dropped, leaving only 'sub aliena umbra latentes' [lurking in the shadow of others].[9]

These moments of linguistic fluidity are not limited only to the drafts and revisions of the Bordeaux Copy. The printed text of the *Essais* shows that, in borrowing from one passage, Montaigne might begin with a quotation in Latin, only to then swap into French translation, or vice versa, giving the impression that borrowed words are entirely and originally his or, alternatively, showing us that what we have just been reading as belonging to Montaigne was in fact taken from elsewhere.

In this chapter, I return from a different perspective to a question asked some thirty years ago by Floyd Gray: where is Montaigne among his borrowings?[10] In asking this question again, my intention is not to rehearse arguments about Montaigne's bilingualism or a late sixteenth-century 'rhétorique des citations', nor to extend the work of identifying his sources, nor still to contribute to a prehistory of plagiarism – though a complex understanding of authorial ownership and property rights will indeed be shown to emerge from Montaigne's handling of his materials.[11]

In the *Essais*, material passes between different authorial proprietors, figures with different claims to ownership, and some of that material gets stuck to Montaigne's 'papier'. This chapter, which focuses on

---

[9] Thus we end up with the following: 'Mais en ceux là (et il en est un nombre infiny de ce genre) qui en establissent leur fondamentale suffisance et valeur, qui se raportent de leur entendement à leur memoire, *sub aliena umbra latentes*, et ne peuvent rien que par livre, je le hay, si je l'ose dire, un peu plus que la bestise' [But in those (and their number is infinite) who base their fundamental capacity and worth on it, who appeal from their understanding to their memory, *lurking in the shadow of others*, and can do nothing except by the book, I hate it, if I dare say so, a little more than stupidity].

[10] Floyd Gray, 'Où se situe-t-il parmi tant d'emprunts?', in *Montaigne bilingue: le latin des Essais* (Paris: Champion, 1991), p. 76.

[11] On the 'rhétorique des citations' popular in *parlementaire* speech of the late sixteenth century, see Marc Fumaroli, *L'Age de l'éloquence* (Geneva: Droz, 1980), pp. 464–6, 471–4.

Montaigne's 'commerce', his leaky business with authors and books, will approach Renaissance theories of imitation only tangentially. Negotiating this 'commerce', recognising its stock in trade and asking what is at stake, requires a reassessment of authorship as it is developed in the *Essais*. The relationship between authors and texts is a perennial question in Montaigne studies, though it is one that has been revitalised in recent years.[12] In what follows, I suggest that Montaigne thinks with the ambiguities of authorial ownership, with the space between authors, to make authorship itself subject to volatile and inconstant judgements. Montaigne encourages his reader, invited into this unstable economy, to judge authorial association now one way, now another, and to find in the *Essais* a tool with which to see things differently.

Floyd Gray's question – where is Montaigne? – might lead us to imagine the essayist under threat of being crowded out by his sources, though a long history of scholarship has made this mode of acquiring common stock very familiar. The book that made Montaigne is itself 'massonné purement' [built purely] from Senecan and Plutarchan spoils (II.32.721/545): looting, repurposing and inheriting are the principal motifs of early modern imitation.

Less attention has been paid to the anxieties that run through the *Essais* concerning authorship's loss. In contrast to those dominant early modern ways of thinking about imitation as, in some way, digestive, transformative, acquisitive, cornucopian and so on, the *Essais* imagine authorship to be insecure, unstable, prone to being doubled up and contested. At certain points in the *Essais* there seem to be too many authors, and the result is not so much copious communalism as a vigilant, disquieting tension, a dispute that must be adjudicated.

We know that Montaigne made others speak for him: he constantly borrowed and stole from the authors he read, some more than others. He can barely pull himself away from Plutarch's banquet, compelled to take something to nibble on, be it a wing or a thigh ('je ne le puis si peu racointer que je n'en tire cuisse ou aile'). Plutarch offered him 'une main liberale et inespuisable de richesses' [a liberal hand, inexhaustible in riches] (III.5.875/666). But the cornucopia is at the same time

---

[12] In addition to Boutcher's *The School of Montaigne*, see Neil Kenny's *Born to Write: Literary Families and Social Hierarchy in Early Modern France* (Oxford: Oxford University Press, 2020), which makes the case for a 'family function' analogous to Foucault's 'author function'. See also Philippe Desan, *Montaigne: Penser le social* (Paris: Odile Jacob, 2018), which considers the social functions of the *Essais*, esp. 'Qu'est-ce qu'être sceptique dans les années 1560–1580?', pp. 52–74, focusing on Montaigne's 'scepticisme politique et social' (p. 74); and Jean Balsamo, *La Parole de Montaigne: littérature et humanisme civil dans les Essais* (Turin: Rosenberg & Sellier, 2019), esp. pp. 25–46 ('Le livre d'un gentilhomme').

a finite resource that demands careful stewardship. In thinking about readers encountering his own book, Montaigne worried that the riches he gained from Plutarch would be stolen from him in turn: 'Il m'en faict despit d'estre si fort exposé au pillage de ceux qui le hantent' [It vexes me that I am so greatly exposed to pillage by those who frequent him] (III.5.875/666). But he was not looking simply to hoard the common stock that had come under his purview: as we will see, he notes at several key points how rereading his own words leaves him feeling as though he is reading someone else, his words seeming no longer to be his. Montaigne is not a jealous keeper – he will open his gate to anyone (III.12.1060/812). What concerns him is rather the experience of glimpsing the exchange of textual property, catching the moment when one author is suddenly replaced with another.

What does it mean to be an author in the *Essais*? What is the relationship between an author and a given piece of literary property? In approaching these questions, I am guided by three related lines of enquiry. First, the questions that opened this chapter: why does Montaigne hesitate between translation and transcription and how do these choices reveal shifting degrees of authorial association? Second, if, as Montaigne claims, he shares a substance with his book, why does that book record so insistently an experience of dispossession? And third, if an author can not only acquire but also lose literary property, what practices of reading and interpretation would a text such as the *Essais*, alert to this impermanence and uncertainty, require of its reader?

The *Essais* stress with peculiar intensity the ways authorship can be lost. Uncovering this insecurity cuts against the grain of critical responses to Montaigne's relationship with his book, unsettling his role as 'patron' of his work along with the idea that the *Essais* operate under his signature.[13] This is not a postmodern anxiety about authorship or influence. Authors in the *Essais* are more than a function framing a text for a reader. They are felt to be vital, thinking and desiring interlocutors who make claims to the words and ideas attached to their names. Equally, Montaigne's sensitivity to authorial loss is not a complaint

---

[13] On Montaigne as 'patron-author', see Boutcher, *The School of Montaigne*, vol. 1. In referring to Montaigne's signature, I am alluding to André Tournon's argument that the revisions made on the Bordeaux Copy serve as an 'act de profération' – a legal declaration by a witness declaring their testimony in their own name. See 'Les Marques de profération dans les *Essais*', in *La Ponctuation à la Renaissance*, ed. Nathalie Dauvois and Jacques Dürrenmatt (Paris: Garnier, 2011), pp. 163–73. See also Terence Cave, *The Cornucopian Text: Problems of Writing in the French Renaissance* (Oxford: Oxford University Press, 1979), p. 272: Cave describes 'the activity of transmission or exchange ("commerce"), by which the textual substance of Plutarch and Seneca is displaced into a discourse bearing the signature "Montaigne"'.

about plagiarism.¹⁴ Reflecting on the relationship between authors and their works, he draws attention to acquisition and dispossession to ask how writing might extend and communicate a shapeshifting soul. In the *Essais*, authorship is a relation, an association, that must be interpreted and judged; it is a matter to be negotiated.

Plus ça change…

The *Essais* are full of borrowings from Plutarch, but the closing pages of the 'Apologie' are by far Montaigne's largest single serving. At the end of this unusually long chapter, he finally produces a conclusion. 'Finalement', he declares, 'il n'y a aucune constante existence, ny de nostre estre, ny de celuy des objects' [Finally, there is no existence that is constant, either of our being or of that of objects] (II.12.601/455). Everything is in flux, ourselves included: 'Et nous, et nostre jugement, et toutes choses mortelles vont coulant et roulant sans cesse' [And we, and our judgement, and all mortal things go on flowing and rolling unceasingly]. We are, it would seem, back in the world of Plutarch's 'refrein' from earlier in the 'Apologie', in 'un lieu glissant et coulant' [a slippery and flowing place] (II.12.510/378).¹⁵ And, as Plutarch taught in that refrain, in such a 'lieu', we must suspend judgement. 'Ainsin', Montaigne concludes, 'il ne se peut establir rien de certain de l'un à l'autre, et le jugeant et le jugé estans en continuelle mutation et branle' [Thus nothing certain can be established about one thing by another, both the judging and the judged being in continual change and motion] (II.12.601/455).

This statement of unrelenting, inescapable vicissitude is followed by four folio pages (in the 1588 edition) copied directly out of the closing section of Plutarch's 'Que signifioit ce mot E'i'.¹⁶ This extreme example of silent transcription is not entirely without acknowledgement, though the nod to Plutarch (who goes unnamed) comes only at the end: 'A cette

---

¹⁴ In addition to the volume edited by Hall Bjørnstad (*Borrowed Feathers: Plagiarism and the Limits of Imitation in Early Modern Europe*), see *Emprunt, plagiat, réécriture aux XVe, XVIe, XVIIe siècles*, ed. M. Couton et al. (Clermont-Ferrand: Presses Universitaires Blaise Pascal, 2006).

¹⁵ Translation modified. Frame translates 'coulant' as 'treacherous'.

¹⁶ There are some changes – additions (particularly in subsequent editions), suppressions, word substitutions, changes to punctuation – but this is no loose imitation or allusion: it is a faithful reproduction of nearly one thousand words, transcribed almost without acknowledgement. On changes to Amyot's punctuation, see André Tournon, 'Les Palimpsestes du "langage coupé"', in Giacone (ed.), *La Langue de Rabelais – La Langue de Montaigne*, pp. 351–69 (pp. 355–6). On Montaigne's additions and suppressions, see Luke O'Sullivan, 'In-Between Authorship in Montaigne's *Essais*', *Early Modern French Studies*, 41.2 (2019), 106–25 (pp. 107–8).

conclusion si religieuse d'un homme payen je veux joindre seulement ce mot d'un tesmoing de mesme condition' [To this most religious conclusion of a pagan I want to add only this remark of a witness of the same condition] (II.12.603/457). The *mot* that is added is a translated quotation from Seneca, and while this is also anonymous, the fact that it is borrowed is at least clear from the outset.

The passage taken out of Plutarch is much less clearly demarcated and it is by no means apparent that an early modern reader, even one familiar with Amyot's best-selling translation, would recognise it as a quotation.[17] Montaigne's reference to 'cette conclusion' seems, if anything, to muddy the waters. Prompted to look back over what we have read, we find that the preceding sentence – the last of the borrowed material – begins, 'Parquoy *il faut conclurre* que Dieu seul est, non poinct selon aucune mesure du temps, mais selon une eternité immuable et immobile, non mesurée par temps, ny subjecte à aucune declinaison' [Wherefore *we must conclude* that God alone is, not at all according to any measure of time, but according to an eternity immutable and immobile, not measured by time or subject to any decline] (my emphasis). The lexical echo highlights this sentence, differentiating it from what came before. Montaigne seems to be leading his reader to think that this, and only this, is the 'conclusion si religieuse'.

This unusual moment of extended transcription has prompted a range of critical responses. It has, on occasion, been seen as evidence of Montaigne's proclivity towards plagiarism.[18] At the other end of the spectrum, a very small number of readers have seen it as an example of Montaigne's 'emprunts' [borrowings] which are 'si fameux et anciens' that they virtually name themselves (II.10.408/296).[19] Most frequently, though, it is taken as evidence that Montaigne assimilated, digested and asserted ownership of his reading. But as Jean-Yves Pouilloux noted, these pages, often evoked but rarely analysed, demand that we keep in mind Montaigne's key insight: 'les paroles redictes ont, comme autre

---

[17] The passage is included, for instance, in *L'Esprit des Essais de Michel, Seigneur de Montaigne* (Paris: Charles de Sercy, 1679), p. 127, an abridged and reworked version of the *Essais* first published in 1677. *L'Esprit* and similar editions claimed to excise the essayist's quotations (though they were produced largely to circumvent the issue of the *Essais* having been placed on the *Index librorum prohibitorum* in 1676). Notably, these abridged versions avoid Montaigne's discussion of the 'homme payen' to whom some or all of this 'conclusion' is attributed.

[18] See, for example, Gisèle Mathieu-Castellani, *Montaigne: l'écriture de l'essai* (Paris: Presses Universitaires de France, 1988), p. 75; Bernard Sève, *Montaigne: des règles pour l'esprit* (Paris: Presses Universitaires de France, 2007), p. 269.

[19] See Joseph de Zangroniz, *Montaigne, Amyot, Saliat: étude sur les sources des Essais de Montaigne* (Paris: Champion, 1906), p. viii. Zangroniz's effort to uncover and compile such borrowings works somewhat against his claim.

son, autre sens' [words when repeated have a different sound and so a different meaning] (III.12.1063/814).[20] How, then, do these old words sound the second time around?

The borrowed material begins with the assertion that 'Nous n'avons aucune communication à l'estre' [We have no communication with being] (II.12.601/455).[21] One would have as much luck getting a good grip on water, it says, as grasping the essence ('son estre') of being ('l'estre'): the tighter you squeeze, the more it escapes you.[22] This watery image flows into a discussion of Heraclitus and his river before noting again, insistently, that it is not only the world but ourselves that are inconstant and forever changing. If we were 'tousjours mesmes et uns' [always one and the same], how would we account for our changing emotions, our changing opinions? We are defined by our inconstancy, an inconstancy that divorces us from real being: 'ce qui souffre mutation ne demeure pas un mesme, et s'il n'est pas un mesme, il n'est donc pas aussi' [what suffers change does not remain one and the same, and if it is not one and the same, it also is not]. With deft equivocation, the passage declares that we *are* inconstant and consequently we *are* not.

But the slipperiness of language is not just a rhetorical strategy. Opposed to our inconstancy is God, who 'n'a jamais eu de naissance, ny n'aura jamais fin; à qui le temps n'apporte jamais aucune mutation' [never had birth, nor will have end; to whom time never brings any change] (II.12.603/456). Only God truly is ('est veritablement'). In its original context, this statement of divine constancy solves the problem that prompted Plutarch's dialogue: what is the meaning of *ei*, that obscure word inscribed at the temple of Apollo in Delphi? 'E'i, c'est à dire, Tu es, comme pour tesmoigner de Dieu, que jamais il n'y a en luy changement ny mutation quelconque' [*Ei*, that is to say, Thou art, so as to show that, in God, there is no change nor any mutation whatsoever].[23]

---

[20] J.-Y. Pouilloux, 'Autour du *Ei* de Delphes', in *Moralia et œuvres morales à la Renaissance*, ed. Olivier Guerrier (Paris: Garnier, 2008), pp. 293–308 (p. 295). Translation modified. Frame translates 'redictes' as 'reported'.

[21] Amyot has 'participation', *Les Œuvres morales et meslées*, fol. 356v. Where minor, one-word differences occur, I follow Montaigne's text.

[22] 'Si, de fortune, vous fichez vostre pensée à vouloir prendre son estre, ce sera ne plus ne moins que qui voudroit empoigner l'eau: car tant plus il serrera et pressera ce qui de sa nature coule par tout, tant plus il perdra ce qu'il vouloit tenir et empoigner' [if by chance you fix your thought on trying to grasp its essence, it will be neither more nor less than if someone tried to grasp water: for the more he squeezes and presses what by its nature flows all over, the more he will lose what he was trying to hold and grasp] (II.12.601/455).

[23] 'Que signifioit ce mot Ei', fol. 357v.

The meaning of this one word has at last been pinned down. But in securing the present indicative – which is accessible only to God and with which we have no 'communication' – we seem to have lost our grip on everything else: time is a 'chose mobile, et qui apparoit comme en ombre' [a mobile thing, which appears as in a shadow], while matter is 'coulante et fluante tousjours' [ever running and flowing]. Even the ordinary, everyday habits of language, down to its basic building blocks, are suddenly without foundation: the present tense has no place in our world, 'à qui appartiennent ces mots: devant et apres, et a esté ou sera [...] car ce seroit grande sottise et faucété toute apparente de dire que cela soit qui n'est pas encore en estre, ou qui desja à cessé d'estre' [to which belong the words *before* and *after*, and *has been* or *will be* [...] for it would be a great stupidity and a perfectly apparent falsehood to say that that *is* which is not yet in being, or which has already ceased to be]. We presume to speak as though we and our world do in fact exist in the divine present, but it all comes crumbling down the moment we scrutinise it: 'la raison le descouvrant le destruit tout sur le champ' [reason discovering this immediately destroys it].

Nothing *is* in a world where things *were* or *will be* and our language of *now* is undone by reason and reflection. The opening line of this passage – 'Nous n'avons aucune communication à l'estre, par ce que toute humaine nature est tousjours au milieu entre le naistre et le mourir' [We have no communication with being, because every human nature is always midway between birth and death] – points to the fundamental tension between 'estre' and 'naistre', being and being born.[24] As Wes Williams puts it, 'estre' and 'naistre' 'sound the same in French, but for the "n"; but it's the extra "n" that makes the negative, but never quite conclusive, difference in our nature'.[25]

Our language misleads us in this unstable world. It leads us into the sin of saying that God 'was' or 'will be'; it lets us think that we can grasp things in the present, but we are mistaken and we have misunderstood. Taking 'ce qui apparoit pour ce qui est' [what appears for what is] (II.12.603/456), we are guilty of that 'grande sottise et faucété' of saying that things are when they are not.

This is Plutarch's 'conclusion si religieuse'. But in what sense is it Plutarch's? And how are we to read this passage as we find it in the

---

[24] This couple returns a few lines later: 'ce qui commence à naistre ne parvient jamais à perfection d'estre, pourautant que ce naistre n'acheve jamais' [what is beginning to be born never arrives at the perfection of being, forasmuch as this birth is never completed] (II.12.602/455-6).
[25] Wes Williams, 'Being in the Middle: Translation, Transition, and the Early Modern', *Paragraph*, 29 (2006), 27–39 (p. 36).

Essais? It seems that we read this conclusion assuming it to have been written by Montaigne and, at the end, are surprised to see that it was not (or, at least, that some of it was not). As Ann Hartle has noted, the sudden, unexpected citation 'creates a jarring break in the conversational flow' of Montaigne's writing, prompting us to check who we have been talking to.[26] But finding out is not straightforward.

Rather than reading this as a transformative digestion, an invocation of a proto-Christian authority, an appropriation of common stock, or as simple plagiarism, we can instead ask how this passage reshapes our understanding of authorship. These words cannot *be* Plutarch's; this passage *is* not his literary property. It certainly may have been, and it may be again – readers have identified and will identify these as Plutarch's words when they encounter them (whether that is in the *Œuvres morales et meslées* or in the closing pages of the 'Apologie'). But to speak of this literary or authorial ownership as being either 'stable' or 'permanente' is to forget the 'coulante et fluante' nature of all things. By the same token, we cannot speak of appropriation or imagine Montaigne to have stamped his mark of ownership on these words in having repurposed them, at least not definitively.

What does this mean for authorship? It means that authorship, which we might instead call authorial association, comes and goes: 'il ne se pouvoit trouver une substance mortelle deux fois en mesme estat [...] tantost elle dissipe, tantost elle rassemble; elle vient et puis s'en va' [no mortal substance can be found twice in the same state [...] it is now dissipated, now reassembled; it comes, and then goes] (II.12.602/455).

Flicking Noses

Montaigne expected at least some of his readers to be tripped up by his relationship with borrowed words. He even describes himself setting traps to 'tenir en bride la temerité de ces sentences hastives' [hold in check the temerity of those hasty condemnations] that are cast about at all sorts of writing, ancient and modern (II.10.408/296):

> [C]Ez raisons et inventions que je transplante en mon solage et confons aux miennes, j'ay à escient ommis parfois d'en marquer l'autheur [...] Je veux qu'ils donnent une nazarde à Plutarque sur mon nez et qu'ils s'eschaudent à injurier Seneque en moy. (II.10.408)

---

[26] Ann Hartle, *Michel de Montaigne: Accidental Philosopher* (Cambridge: Cambridge University Press, 2003), p. 75.

[C]In the reasonings and inventions that I transplant into my own soil and confound with my own, I have sometimes deliberately not indicated the author [...] I want them to give Plutarch a fillip on my nose and get burned insulting Seneca in me. (296–7)

With his agricultural metaphor, Montaigne is in standard georgic mode, drawing on the established humanist commonplace of the 'garden of letters'.[27] But the concern with flicking noses renders this garden and its gardener very small indeed: rather than tilling the fields and cultivating learning, Montaigne is eyeing up his neighbour on the adjoining allotment and waiting for him to say something about his cauliflowers.

This passage was substantially revised in the Bordeaux Copy. Prior editions had Cicero and Aristotle in place of Seneca and Plutarch, and spoke not of agricultural 'transplantation' but instead put the matter of judgement centre stage. '[A]Ce que je desrobe d'autruy', Montaigne wrote, 'ce n'est pas pour le faire mien' [What I steal from others, it is not to make it my own].[28] He claims only the 'part' of reasoning and judging ('de raisonner et de juger'), of selecting his material: 'le demeurant n'est pas de mon rolle' [the rest is beyond my role]. The reader is invited in turn to judge Montaigne on his judgements. He asks only that 'on voie si j'ay sceu choisir ce que joignoit justement à mon propos' [they see whether I have been able to choose something that fits appropriately with my discourse]. He sometimes conceals his authors' names ('je cache par fois le nom de l'autheur'), but only to 'tenir en bride la legiereté' [hold in check the carelessness] of readers who lack 'le nez capable de gouter les choses par elles mesmes, s'arrestant au nom de l'ouvrier et à son credit' [a nose for judging things on their own terms, stopping at the author's name and reputation]. 'Je veus', he declares, 'qu'ils s'eschaudent à condamner Ciceron ou Aristote en moy' [I want them to get burned criticising Cicero or Aristotle in me].

One might imagine that Montaigne's shift to Seneca and Plutarch reflected the reality of his book's reception, with readers variously recognising and not recognising these two authors in a book seen increasingly as the work of a new French Seneca or French Plutarch. But his original point – that in lifting a line from someone else he isn't looking to claim it but rather to exercise his judgement and invite us to apply our own – mutated into something much more directly antagonistic. Montaigne's imagined reader, or rather a certain sort of imagined

---

[27] On this masculine metaphor of 'humanist fieldwork' and its relation to a feminised paradigm of domestic labour, see Katie Kadue, *Domestic Georgic: Labors of Preservation* (Chicago: University of Chicago Press, 2021), esp. pp. 5–8.
[28] *Essais* 1580, II.10.96.

reader, is no longer careless, guilty of 'legiereté', but foolhardy in having 'la temerité' to throw around such 'sentences hastives'. And this shift from moderate correction to outright antagonism turns on a nose: where once the reader had a poor nose, not for sniffing out sources but for judging things 'par elles mesmes', on their own terms, now the nose, which is really Plutarch's, is on Montaigne's face and he is goading us to flick it.

In the 'Apologie', Montaigne again imagined the response his book and his borrowings were to receive and, while the relationship between author and reader remains antagonistic, the issue is inverted: '[B]j'en laisse plus librement aller mes caprices en public: d'autant que, bien qu'ils soyent nez chez moy et sans patron, je sçay qu'ils trouveront leur relation à quelque humeur ancienne; et ne faudra quelqu'un de dire: Voylà d'où il le print!' [I let my caprices fly all the more freely in public, inasmuch as, although they are born with me and without a model, I know that they will find their relation to some ancient notion; and someone will not fail to say: That's where he got it!] (II.12.546/408–9). Montaigne's 'caprices', like his book, are entirely his own, without a patron other than himself. And yet he knows he will find readers, source-hunting pedants, who go looking for ancient antecedents and will no doubt find them, though they miss the point: his opinions are born 'chez moy'.

If we compare these two antagonistic relationships, it seems that we are caught in a bind: we can stay on the lookout for Seneca and Plutarch, or Cicero and Aristotle, and avoid getting burned for having flicked the wrong nose, but, in doing so, we risk becoming the pedant who finds 'sources' that aren't really there. The solution to this quandary is, one might think, simply to judge the material on its own terms, to enact the principle Montaigne himself employs as an emblem of free-thinking: 'Ce n'est non plus selon Platon que selon moy, puis que luy et moi l'entendons et voyons de mesme' [It is not more according to Plato than according to me, since he and I understand and see it in the same way] (I.26.152/111). That this phrase is, as Richard Scholar has noted, based on an adage with a long history both complicates and proves Montaigne's point.[29] As Gisèle Mathieu-Castellani has argued, Montaigne's contradictory claims – to say, on the one hand, 'it is no more according to Plato than according to me' and, on the other, 'it is not me who says this but Plato, or Plutarch, or Seneca' – serve as a

---

[29] 'Amicus Plato sed magis amica veritas' [Plato is my friend but truth is a greater friend]. See Richard Scholar, '"J'aime Michel, mais j'aime mieux la verité": Creative Reading and Free-Thinking in Montaigne', *Nottingham French Studies*, 49 (2010), 39–51.

'caution' to the 'indiligent lecteur', prompting the reader to reflect on and examine statements without recourse to authority.[30]

But Montaigne would not have us disregard authority, let alone authors, *tout court*. Authorial association proves remarkably sticky: attributing a saying or idea to a given author seems impulsive and unavoidable. It is rhetorically helpful too. Montaigne regularly finds the habits of the pedant ripe for profitable subversion. For Montaigne, playing with authorship and attribution is a handy method of engaging not just antiquity but his contemporary readers. Take another example, again concerned with a nose: he imagines himself being asked ('Me demandez vous') why a sneeze is met with a 'bless you', but the two other sorts of wind we produce do not receive such an 'honneste recueil' [civil reception] (III.6.899/685). It is because a sneeze comes from the head and is blameless, we are told. But don't laugh at 'cette subtilité', he says, assuming we already have: 'elle est (dict-on) d'Aristote' [it is, they say, from Aristotle]. Withholding the author's identity and then revealing it, Montaigne teaches us that a name offers no guarantee of wisdom. But his critique of authority is not limited to Aristotle: the parenthetical 'dict-on' locates this free-thinking exercise in a culture of pedants sniffing out ancient sources. Montaigne may be poking fun at Aristotle, but principally he is mocking those who invoke him.

There are moments when Montaigne takes on the role of source hunter himself. In the margins of the Bordeaux Copy, immediately before the claim that his opinions are born 'chez moy et sans patron' (II.12.546/408–9), he included a line taken from Cicero's *De divinatione*: 'Nihil tam absurde dici potest quod non dicatur ab aliquo philosophorum' [Nothing so absurd can be said that it has not been said by some philosopher] (*De divinatione*, II.58.119). With this ironic quotation, Montaigne retrospectively introduces his claim to originality and independence as a gloss on a canonical author. But in citing Cicero, he is also making a more serious point, recording the experience of discovering that what he thought was properly his own was in fact already in circulation. In the same margin, he notes how his behaviour and opinions (though he crossed out 'opinions') 'sont naturelles', but, for propriety's sake, he dressed them up 'plus decemment' with quotations and examples lest they wander around underdressed 'en publiq' (II.12.546/409). It was a marvel, he writes, to bump into, as though by chance ('rencontrer, par cas d'adventure'), what he had hitherto been

---

[30] Gisèle Mathieu-Castellani, *Montaigne ou la vérité du mensonge* (Geneva: Droz, 2000), p. 129.

certain was entirely and originally his.³¹ Montaigne's game of recording these encounters serves as a wry means of pushing the reader to think for themselves without deferring to authority. But it also reveals the disquieting sense of alienation that Montaigne felt upon colliding with his own double and realising that his grasp on himself and his belongings was less sure than he had thought.

Montaigne's opinions are entirely his own, then, and the borrowings we encounter no more than embellishments and supports, included for decency's sake, or fortuitous encounters and coincidences recorded, as with the quotation from Cicero, as a matter of curiosity. It is all Montaigne. Except for when it isn't – when Seneca or Plutarch are deliberately kept just below the surface, concealed so that a hasty and intemperate reader will lash out and get stung. We ought to judge things on their own terms, 'par elles mesmes', but – like Montaigne – we cannot help but point and say, 'Voylà d'où il le print!' [That's where he got it!]

Montaigne's reflections on authorship are not simply a lesson in anti-authoritarian free-thinking. It always matters who is speaking in the *Essais*, especially when the answer to that question is unclear. In these moments of authorial ambiguity, we see Montaigne thinking with something like the author function, thinking – and encouraging his reader to think – with the effect of a sentence or idea seeming to have multiple, competing authors, or a shifting and insecure relationship with the name that authorises it. 'Cuius?' [Whose?] The question Seneca imagines Lucilius asking about the 'common property' being parcelled up and sent his way takes on a new significance when read alongside Montaigne's confrontational and contrarian approach to authorship. Our view of authorial association determines how we judge the thing itself, and when that association changes (or seems to), it casts new light not only on the thing being judged but on us, our preconceptions and prejudices. Authorship in the *Essais* is not authority but it retains a function, shaping our reading and determining the patterns of our judgement. Faced with Montaigne's borrowings, the reader is pressured to keep a close eye on the 'registre', the account book that is the *Essais*, and asked to judge the constant flow of textual exchange. Revealing an author lurking in the shadows, he springs the question on us and challenges us to give account of the negotiation of literary property. It is a transaction that is not so

---

³¹ See Guerrier, *Rencontre et reconnaissance*, pp. 123–6. For Guerrier, these chance encounters ('rencontres' that occur 'de façon aléatoire') are significant in their reversal of the logic of exemplarity. He argues that what emerges from Montaigne's account is in fact a greater sense of possession and ownership over what he found first in himself and later in his reading ('La superposition ne modifie donc rien; elle permet juste de parfaire la "possession" du déjà-là', p. 125).

much a done deal, set in stone as it is put into print, but rather a vital 'commerce', a movement that might yet slip out from under our noses.

'Cuius?' Even as Montaigne instructs us to judge things on their own terms, not to get stuck on an author's name and its 'credit', his book compels us to say who is speaking. He demands that we pick one nose to flick, waiting for us to get it wrong so that he might give a fillip in return. And even when we recognise a source, the question of property persists. Is he a horse thief or an industrious bee?[32] Perhaps, as La Croix du Maine thought, the *Essais* illustrate Montaigne's 'diverse leçon', his wide reading and erudition, and exemplify an ideal of successful, valuable imitation.[33] Perhaps, though, we ought to follow Malebranche and see in the *Essais* nothing but 'un tissu de traits d'histoire, de petits contes, de bons mots, de distiques et d'apophtegmes' [a patchwork of tales from history, anecdotes, witticisms, verse couplets and sayings].[34] Montaigne encourages his reader to adopt both of these views: the work – whether we mean the transformative labour or the *œuvre* – is his entirely and not his at all.

Perhaps we can cut the Gordian knot by swapping out a model of authorial ownership for one of patronage. Montaigne's opinions are, after all, 'sans patron'. As Warren Boutcher has shown, this claim to be his own patron and to be the patron of his book is strikingly original: the *Essais* are not published 'under the protection of named individuals', ancient or modern; they are instead modelled on and authorised by the 'pattern' (another early modern sense of *patron*) of his persona.[35] But the problem remains the same, albeit expressed in different terms: is Montaigne an authentic 'patron-author' who commissions and manages the work of others? Or is he a subordinate artisan, a lackey, a counterfeiter, a fraud? It is possible that Montaigne has made others speak and work for him. But it is just as possible that he is like the 'riche Romain' who had a man for everything – one to give him an argument, another to find an apt line from Homer, and

---

[32] For Montaigne's echo of Seneca's apian metaphor, see I.26.152/111. On the horse thief metaphor (III.12.1056/809, erased in the Bordeaux Copy, fol. 467r), see Stephen Rendall, *Distinguo: Reading Montaigne Differently* (Oxford: Clarendon Press, 1992), p. 56.
[33] 'Je diray que si Plutarque est tant estimé pour ses beaux œuvres, que cetui-cy le doibt estre pour l'avoir imité de si pres' [I would say that, if Plutarch is to be valued for his great works, then this one here ought to be valued for having imitated him so closely]. *Le premier volume de la bibliotheque du sieur de la Croix du Maine* (Paris: L'Angelier, 1584), p. 329.
[34] Nicolas Malebranche, *Recherche de la vérité* (1674), in *Œuvres*, ed. Geneviève Rodis-Lewis and Germain Malbreil (Paris: Gallimard, 1979), vol. 1, p. 275.
[35] Boutcher, *The School of Montaigne*, vol. 1, pp. 94–5.

so on – but no real 'science', no 'suffisance', and no authorship of his own: 'Autant en diroit bien un perroquet' [A parrot could well say as much] (I.25.137/100–1).

If we turn back to the conclusion of the 'Apologie', lifted wholesale from Plutarch, do we see Montaigne as a good, authentic patron, calling on the 'suffisance' of an ancient and employing it effectively, or do we see a parrot? An author digesting his reading or a copyist regurgitating his source? An artisan identifying what is good and true so that it might be put to proper use or a thief taking what he can? How are we to go about making such judgements amid Montaigne's provocations and open avowals of deception? How are we to judge when it seems ever more likely that someone's nose is going to get flicked?

Between Two Stools

In 'De l'art de conférer', Montaigne provides something of a model for how to respond to this problem:

> Le subject, selon qu'il est, peut faire trouver un homme sçavant et memorieux; mais *pour juger en luy les parties plus siennes* et plus dignes, la force et beauté de son ame, *il faut sçavoir ce qui est sien et ce qui ne l'est point*, et en ce qui n'est pas sien combien on luy doibt en consideration du chois, disposition, ornement et langage qu'il y a fourny. Quoy? s'il a emprunté la matiere et empiré la forme, comme il advient souvent. (III.8.940, my emphasis)

> The subject, according to what it is, may give a man a reputation for learning and a good memory; but *in order to judge the qualities that are most his own* and most worthy, the strength and beauty of his mind, *we must first know what is his and what is not*; and in what is not his, how much is due him in consideration of the choice, arrangement, embellishment and style that he has supplied. What if he has borrowed the matter and made the form worse, as often happens? (718, my emphasis)

The proper judgement of what is and is not the property of a given author is a serious matter. Talk of flicking noses might give the impression that Montaigne's contradictory provocations – everything is mine; nothing is mine – are no more than an erudite game aimed at scolding the amateur reader and amusing the expert. But there is a direct line connecting the judgement of literary and intellectual property and the judgement of character: to judge 'les parties plus siennes', to judge the force and beauty of someone's soul, one must first work out, quite literally, what is and is not theirs. That process of inventory begins on the page and begins in reading. Language, after all, and especially the language of Seneca (who says what he feels and feels what he says, *Ep.* 75.4) and of 'nostre Plutarque', is the medium by which we might know one another 'jusques dans l'ame' [right into his soul] (II.31.716/541).

This outline of a methodology for judging property, literary or otherwise, is prompted by an account of Montaigne's own reading. He recalls an encounter some years previously with a line he thought praiseworthy and remarkable, 'non vulgaire', in Philippe de Comines (III.8.940/718).[36] Later though, he came across precisely the same idea in Tacitus and, as he notes in a later addition, in Seneca and Quintus Cicero.

When Montaigne reads something, he judges it on its own terms. If he finds it to be elegant, true or otherwise remarkable, he takes that judgement as the foundation for a reading of the author's character. He is presenting himself as the opposite of those hasty readers who go about things back to front, their judgements being led by names and authority. The problem emerges only when Montaigne finds that the authorial relationship he had taken for granted is not what it seems to be. In recounting this experience, he is describing one familiar to readers of the *Essais*.

So how does Montaigne the reader judge what does and does not belong to an author? His response would surely serve as a guide for his own readers, finding themselves in a similar situation. Montaigne's proposed inventory, the 'registre' or balance sheet of how much one owes an author working with borrowed material for his work ('combien on luy doibt'), makes imitation a matter of rhetorical accountancy. We judge the imitator's choice ('chois', *inventio*), arrangement ('disposition', *dispositio*), style and eloquence ('ornement et langage', *elocutio*). If the rewriting is successful and all is in order – if the imitator takes the 'matiere' and, in repurposing it, improves it or, at least, doesn't make it worse – then it belongs to him, since it reveals his character and 'les parties plus siennes'.

The solution to the problem is thus far entirely conventional: we find exactly the same rationale set out by Lipsius, who argued that his cento, the *Politica*, made up almost entirely of quotations, belonged to him on account of his selection (*inventio*) and arrangement (*ordo*). But it is a solution that does not work for Montaigne:

---

[36] Appropriately, the line is about getting just reward and recompense for one's work: 'qu'il se faut bien garder de faire tant de service à son maistre, qu'on l'empesche d'en trouver la juste recompense' [that we must be careful not to serve a master so well that we keep him from finding a fair reward for our service].

> Nous autres, qui avons peu de practique avec les livres, sommes en cette peine que, quand nous voyons quelque belle invention en un poëte nouveau, quelque fort argument en un prescheur, nous n'osons pourtant les en louer que nous n'ayons prins instruction de quelque sçavant si cette piece leur est propre ou si elle est estrangere; *jusques lors je me tiens tousjours sur mes gardes*. (III.8.940, my emphasis)

> We, who have little contact with books, are in this strait that, when we see some fine piece of inventiveness in a new poet, some strong argument in a preacher, we dare not praise them for it until we have found out from some learned man whether this element is their own or someone else's. *Until then, I always stand on my guard*. (718, my emphasis)

We as readers, 'nous autres', are also 'en cette peine', incapable of the rhetorical accountancy practised by the anonymous 'on' and the unnamed 'sçavant'. Montaigne leads by example: when he does not know what parts of a text belong to whom, he holds himself 'tousjours sur [ses] gardes'. We might say that he suspends judgement. Without knowing whether something is or is not borrowed, he doesn't dare praise a 'belle invention' and is unable to even begin his 'consideration du chois, disposition, ornement et langage'.

This is not a disinterested or tranquil suspension of judgement though. What Montaigne describes is a state of alert, of struggle and anxiety rather than sublimation and *ataraxia* – a moment more of suspense than suspension. He opposes himself to the 'sçavant', capable of making judgements about literary property, but the antithesis he proposes has him not so much suspending judgement as fretting, unable to determine things definitively one way or another.[37]

It would seem, then, that Montaigne goads a certain sort of reader into making hasty judgements, encouraging parallel readings of his book as, on the one hand, a patchwork of gathered (and sometimes stolen) flowers and, on the other, as a work entirely his own. It is a strategy designed to teach such a reader to judge things on their own terms, without worrying about who authored them. Meanwhile, in his own reading, he takes an entirely different tack: one characterised not by cool, dispassionate assessment but by a vigilant, painful suspension of judgement in which he holds himself on guard. The 'temerité' of the hasty reader is inverted in Montaigne's own example, but not as we might expect.

The problem of reading a book and not knowing what belongs to whom is not resolved by having the author's name printed on the title

---

[37] It is unclear whether Montaigne thinks the *sçavant*'s ability to judge would be desirable: he seems to accept without consideration that this ability is beyond him.

page, even when that name is your own. In a passage from the 1580 edition of 'De la praesumption', Montaigne sketches himself leafing through books ('je feuillette les livres, je ne les estudie pas'), acquiring material casually as it becomes fodder for his faculty of judgement: 'l'autheur, le lieu, les mots et autres circonstances, je les oublie incontinent' [the author, the place, the words, and other circumstances, I immediately forget] (II.17.651/494). But when he returned to this passage in later additions, he noted how this carefree habit of accumulation entailed a reciprocal carelessness for what was once his:

> [B]Et suis si excellent en l'oubliance que mes escrits mesmes et compositions, je ne les oublie pas moins que le reste. On m'allegue tous les coups à moy-mesme sans que je le sente […] [C]Ce n'est pas grand merveille si mon livre suit la fortune des autres livres et si ma memoire desempare ce que j'escry comme ce que je ly, et ce que je donne comme ce que je reçoy.

> [B]And I am so good at forgetting that I forget even my own writings and compositions no less than the rest. People are all the time quoting me to myself without my knowing it […] [C]It is no great wonder if my book follows the fate of other books, and if my memory lets go of what I write as of what I read, and of what I give as of what I receive.

Montaigne deals with his own book as he deals with any other: he reads – and forgets – his 'compositions' as a reader rather than an author; he hears his words in the mouths of others ('on m'allegue') and fails to recognise them.

Montaigne's memory and the memorialising function of the *Essais* are subjects that have been pored over extensively. Andrea Frisch has asked how Montaigne's own tendency towards 'oubliance' resonated in a war-torn age conscious that some things are better off forgotten, while the genre and design of his book – whether as a self-image, preserving his memory for his descendants, or as a 'registre-journal', a radically public act of private record-keeping – have long been seen as working in response to the failures of human memory.[38] What is salient

---

[38] See Andrea Frisch's numerous studies of memory in and around the *Essais*: 'Montaigne and the Ethics of Memory', *L'Esprit créateur*, 46.1 (2006), 23–31; 'Montaigne on Memory', in Desan (ed.), *The Oxford Handbook of Montaigne*, pp. 648–62; *Forgetting Differences: Tragedy, Historiography, and the French Wars of Religion* (Edinburgh: Edinburgh University Press, 2017). See also Nicolas Russell, *Transformations of Memory and Forgetting in Sixteenth Century France: Marguerite de Navarre, Pierre de Ronsard, Michel de Montaigne* (Newark: University of Delaware Press, 2011), p. 105; Carlo Montaleone, 'Montaigne, pratique de l'oubli et erreurs de perspective', *Bulletin de la société internationale des amis de Montaigne*, 68 (2018), 117–30. On writing as a cognitive affordance and an extension of cognitive work including memory, see Clark and Chalmers, 'The Extended Mind', and Anderson, *The Renaissance Extended Mind*, pp. 116–44.

here in 'De la praesumption' is that Montaigne's memory is not aided by writing. Here at least, writing is not conceived as a vast, permanent *mémoire de papier* (III.13.1092/838), lightening the cognitive load of the author and discharging responsibilities for storage to a material archive. Indeed, it is an encounter with writing that reveals the disruption, the clean break between the author and the words that once were his but have since been lost and forgotten.

The bonds that tie Montaigne to his writing are curiously fragile. 'En mes escris mesmes', he writes, 'je ne retrouve pas tousjours l'air de ma premiere imagination: je ne sçay ce que j'ay voulu dire' [Even in my own writings I do not always find again the sense of my first thought; I do not know what I meant to say] (II.12.566/425–6). But, as he goes on to explain, he does often find himself tied firmly to ideas and opinions – just not ideas he thought were 'his'. He routinely ('Maintes-fois' [many times]) takes 'une contraire opinion à la mienne' [an opinion contrary to my own] and tries it on, adopting a position merely 'pour exercice et pour esbat' [as exercise and sport]. Having tried it on, though, he quickly finds it suits him well: 'mon esprit, s'applicant et tournant de ce costé là, m'y attache si bien que je ne trouve plus la raison de mon premier advis, et m'en despars' [my mind, applying itself and turning in that direction, attaches me to it so firmly that I can no longer find the reason for my former opinion, and I abandon it]. The shift in agency is telling: it is the 'esprit' that yokes Montaigne to an opinion that is not his and deprives him of that which was. The result – to paraphrase a passage I will return to in Chapter 6 – is that Montaigne believes what he believes entirely, in the moment, even though he knows that he once thought differently and might soon think something else again (II.12.563/423). Returning to his writing does not add another link to an unbroken chain of authorial moments. Often, it does precisely the opposite, underscoring the discontinuity of writing and authorial identity while bearing witness to the difficulties Montaigne experienced in distinguishing 'ce qui est sien et ce qui ne l'est point'.[39]

Montaigne presents the fragility and impermanence of authorial association as a rather commonplace curiosity. There are hints of 'peine' and 'merveille' as he reflects on his experience of not recognising himself, and not recognising others, though he remains remarkably casual and nonchalant. Even so, his attention to authorship's impermanence

---

[39] This discontinuity of authorial moments is a countercurrent to what André Tournon has seen as the act of 'profération' by which the *Essais* are authored and authorised under the single moment of authorship, the date given at the end of the 'Au lecteur'. See 'Les Marques de profération dans les *Essais*', cited above.

precipitates a striking, novel conception of our 'commerce' with books. Attending to authorial loss threatens to up-end the old models of imitation and textual transfer, in which Epicurus and Seneca and Montaigne and anyone else can be the 'author' of a true and elegant saying about old men leaving life as if they had just entered it. Out of the cornucopian abundance of literary communalism emerges a way of thinking alert to scarcity and deprivation. And Montaigne's attention to authorial loss is not simply an attention to plagiarism: he is not concerned (in the passages under discussion here, at any rate) that would-be thieves are out to deprive him of what is rightfully his. Rather, he marvels at how 'his' ideas cease to be his and couldn't be stolen even if someone wanted to steal them: he has already given them up when he imagines others quoting his own words back at him ('on m'allegue'). What is radical about this approach to authorship is not Montaigne's particular openness about literary fraud or impersonation; it is his description of the sense that authorial associations can be built and unbuilt, acquired and lost, materialise and fade away. As we saw at the end of the 'Apologie', in those words that seem to be spoken now by Plutarch, now by Montaigne, all things below the heavens dissipate and come back together: like everything else, authorship 'vient et puis s'en va' [comes and then goes]. So while Montaigne provokes a certain sort of reader, coaching them to judge things on their own terms without getting stuck on authorial credit, he depicts himself grappling with and marvelling at authorship's volatility and impermanence, watching authorship come and go, all the while holding himself on guard.

Moveable Goods: Using and Profiting from Literary Property

'Quicquid bene dictum est ab ullo, meum est' [Whatever is well said by anyone is mine] (*Ep.* 16.7). The idea of literary goods as common property, ready to be taken up and incorporated, put to work by imitating authors who draw as though from a cornucopia, was more than familiar to Montaigne. It structured his way of thinking and shaped the images with which he discussed his book of 'fleurs estrangeres' (III.12.1055/808). But this mode of accumulation, where Seneca's claim, 'meum est', sits comfortably alongside countless other, identical claims, is cast into doubt by Montaigne's sustained attention to loss and dispossession.

In place of the mythic cornucopia, we might instead foreground usufructuary possession as a model for literary ownership. This rather more mundane image of fruitfulness and productivity, defined in the Justinian Digest as 'the right to use and profit from another's property while preserving intact the substance of that property', was familiar to Montaigne not only on account of his career in the *parlement*.[40] Its trace is also felt, as Kathy Eden has shown, in his reflections on 'his enjoyment or *jouyssance*' of his household, his children, his coffers, his books: all of these were held by Montaigne not as properties he owned but as material goods he could use and profit from.[41]

Montaigne would have also encountered usufructs in Seneca. In the final book of the *De beneficiis*, Seneca, who in the letters so often stresses his ownership of other men's goods, takes up this notion to think again, from a different perspective, about the relationship between books and authors. Coming to the end of his book on gifts and services – a theme that returns us to the topic of *munuscula*, the tributes included at the end of his early letters to Lucilius – he tries to resolve a problem. The Stoics say that the wise man, having freed himself from mental disturbance (7.2.3), is alone in being able to say that all things are his ('omnia illius sunt'). Everything is his but not in the way that everything belonged to Alexander the Great. The sage, free from desire and covetousness, has everything because he wants nothing (7.2.5–6). Seneca imagines his interlocutor's objection (7.4.1): if everything belongs to the sage, how can someone give him a gift? How could anyone pay him a favour or do him a service? To live unable to receive a gift, incapable of establishing the bonds, connections and allegiances structured by them – that is surely to live a very impoverished life indeed.

The paradox allows Seneca to unpack the different ways goods might be held, possessed and owned. There is nothing, he replies, to prevent something belonging both to the wise man and to the person who actually possesses it ('et sapientis [...] et etiam eius, qui possidet', 7.4.2), though this is not the familiar argument that they hold things in common. Instead, he gives the example of the king to whom everything belongs according to the law. The king owns everything, but that does not prevent his subjects, who possess, use and enjoy that property, from giving him as a gift something that was in some way already his. And so the apparent contradiction has been resolved: 'Non ideo, quod habeo,

---

[40] 'jus alienis rebus utendi fruendi salva rerum substantia', *Dig.* 7, tit. 1, s. 1.
[41] Kathy Eden, *The Renaissance Rediscovery of Intimacy* (Chicago: University of Chicago Press, 2012), pp. 114–17. On Montaigne's understanding of 'le droit de l'usufruit', particularly as it relates to Stoic and Sceptical conceptions of natural law, see Katherine Almquist, 'Du prêt et de l'usufruit des images: le droit de la propriété dans la pensée sceptique de Montaigne', in Demonet and Legros (eds), *L'Ecriture du scepticisme chez Montaigne*, pp. 169–77.

meum non est, si meum tuum est; potest enim idem meum esse et tuum' [It is not necessarily true that what I have is not mine if what is mine is also yours; for it is possible that the same thing may be both mine and yours] (7.4.6).

The same applies to literary property, a point Seneca proves by taking us to the bookshop. We say that certain books belong to Cicero, but Dorus the bookseller says those same books belong to him ('suos vocat'). Both statements are true ('utrumque verum est'): one claims them because he wrote them and the other because he bought them ('Alter illos tamquam auctor sibi, alter tamquam emptor adserit'). And so it is obvious, declares Seneca, that both Cicero and Dorus own the same book – they just own it in different ways ('utriusque enim sunt, sed non eodem modo', 7.6.1).[42]

Echoing another Stoic, Montaigne turned to precisely this model of ownership to articulate the difference between the divine and the human. 'C'est ce que dit Epictete: que l'homme n'a rien proprement sien que l'usage de ses opinions' [This is what Epictetus says: that man has nothing properly his own but the use of his opinions] (II.12.489/360).[43] The gods hold health and other goods, 'en essence', in reality, and evils, sickness and so on, 'en intelligence', in thought. Man, on the contrary, 'possède ses biens par fantasie' [possesses his goods only in fancy] and has true possession only of the use of his opinions. Not even our thoughts belong to us, merely their 'usage': our one true possession is, as Katherine Almquist puts it, the 'capacité d'imaginer' [the capacity to imagine].[44]

Notably, Montaigne extends his discussion of Epictetus and our singular usufructuary possession to criticise Seneca, along with Cicero and a number of others, for their 'temerité' (the same quality he criticised in his own hasty readers). These ancients presume that their philosophies grant them access to the divine: in imagining their wise men, they dream up 'dieux mortels' (II.12.489–90/361). For Montaigne, all possession is

---

[42] See also Seneca's comments introducing his customary quotation from Epicurus in *Ep.* 14.17–18: he promises that the 'usus fructusque' of his gift will bring Lucilius pleasure, only for his apprentice-addressee to ask the author's name. Seneca replies that the name ought not to matter as the words were uttered for everyone ('omnibus dixit')'.

[43] This sentence is taken from the late classical collection of *sententiae* compiled by Stobaeus rather than from Epictetus' *Enchiridion*. On Epictetus' and Seneca's different responses to the Stoic paradox that 'the wise man owns everything', see Thomas Bénatouïl, 'Les possessions du sage et le dépouillement du philosophe: un paradoxe socratique et ses reprises stoïciennes', *Rursus: Poiétique, réception et réécriture des textes antiques*, 3 (2008), https://doi.org/10.4000/rursus.213.

[44] 'Toutes ses opinions, toutes ses imaginations, tout ce que l'homme possède, c'est leur *usage*'; Almquist, 'Du prêt et de l'usufruit des images', p. 176.

usufructuary: we are all owners of goods only insofar as we make use of them. There is no hierarchy of king and tenant-farmer, or of Cicero and the bookseller, the one being master ('dominus') and the other user (having only 'usus'), both of them owners but in different ways. Such a relationship exists only with God. Only God *is*; only God *has*. As with our being, our possessions are impermanent, insecure and subject to change.

Montaigne's correction of Seneca's 'temerité' recasts the relationships between Cicero, Dorus and the books they lay claim to. We might say that Cicero and Dorus *are* both owners of the same book at the same time and agree with Seneca that both claims are true. But it is a truth that we have no real 'communication' with. What matters for us, living beneath the firmament, is who *was* seen as the author and who *will be* seen as the author in a given moment.[45]

The notion that all property – material, intellectual, literary – is usufructuary illuminates Montaigne's account of 'peine' when judging what does and does not belong to an author ('ce qui est sien et ce qui ne l'est point'). Reading authorial association as an impermanent relationship brought about by 'usage' resolves the contradiction of the *Essais* being, at once, common stock, consubstantial with Montaigne, and something he no longer recognises. Departing from those familiar metaphors of acquisition and communalism, Montaigne's understanding of 'usage' as the sole basis for authorial ownership makes intellectual property a contingent quality, something that must be continually and repeatedly judged and which places judgement – Montaigne's and the reader's – at the forefront of reading and communication.

Making Use of Seneca

In 'De l'inequalité qui est entre nous', Montaigne returns to those questions of how to judge someone's character and how to judge what is theirs. It is a chapter that begins and ends with Plutarch, exemplifying the circular dialectic of the *Essais*, their movement from the familiar to the unusual and back again, only to find that the familiar now looks different.[46] We are all radically dissimilar, begins Montaigne, before

---

[45] This sense of ownership as dependent on 'usage' is reflected in Montaigne's anecdote about the 'riche Romain' discussed above. This Roman exemplifies 'owners' of books who do not know how to use them, thinking that 'la suffisance loge en leurs somptueuses librairies' [ability dwells in their sumptuous libraries] (I.25.137/100–1).

[46] On circular dialectic in the *Essais*, see Hartle, *Michel de Montaigne: Accidental Philosopher*, pp. 91–120.

suggesting that we look beyond material possessions to recognise a deeper ethical equality: 'tout ce qui s'appelle bien' [all that is called good] is the same for both king and pauper (I.42.263/192). And yet kingship is a burden rather than a reward and, as such, kings are worse off than the common man. Tracing a pattern of inequality–equality–inequality, the chapter ends where it started, but, having considered a different perspective, our original way of seeing things is changed.

Plutarch says 'en quelque lieu' [in some place] that 'il ne trouve point si grande distance de beste à beste, comme il trouve d'homme à homme' [he does not find so much difference between one animal and another as he does between one man and another] (I.42.258/189). Montaigne agrees, or at least seems to: he goes one further ('j'encherirois volontiers sur Plutarque') and says that more separates one man from another than a given man and a given animal. This comparison of man and beast provides Montaigne with a theme that will be developed at length: the custom of judging animals on their natural qualities but men on goods they have acquired.

> Mais, à propos de l'estimation des hommes, c'est merveille que, sauf nous, aucune chose ne s'estime que par ses propres qualitez.[47] Nous louons un cheval de ce qu'il est vigoureux et adroit,
>
> *volucrem*
> *Sic laudamus equum, facili cui plurima palma*
> *Fervet, et exultat rauco victoria circo,*
>
> non de son harnois;[48] un levrier de sa vitesse, non de son colier: un oyseau de son aile, non de ses longes et sonettes. Pourquoy de mesmes n'estimons nous un homme par ce qui est sien?[49] Il a un grand train, un beau palais, tant de credit, tant de rente: tout cela est autour de luy, non en luy.[50]

---

[47] Seneca, *Ep.* 76.6: 'Omnia suo bono constant' [everything is estimated by its own good]. Compare expressions of the same sentiment elsewhere: 76.14: 'Eo quidque laudatur, cui comparator, quod illi proprium est' [Each thing is praised in regard to that attribute which is taken as its standard, in regard to that which is its peculiar quality]; 41.6: 'quid enim est stultius quam in homine aliena laudare?' [for what is more foolish than to praise in a man the qualities which come from without?]

[48] *Ep.* 41.6: 'non faciunt meliorem equum aurei freni' [a golden rein does not make a better horse].

[49] A loose imitation of *Ep.* 124.22–3: 'Quid capillum ingenti diligentia comis? [...] in quolibet equo densior jactabitur iuba, horrebit in leonum cervice formonsior. Cum te ad velocitatem paraveris, par lepusculo non eris. Vis tu relictis [...] ad bonum reverti tuum?' [Why dress your hair with such unending attention? Yet you will see a mane of greater thickness tossing upon any horse you choose, and a mane of greater beauty bristling on the neck of any lion. And even after training yourself for speed, you will be no match for the hare. Are you not willing to abandon these details and come back to the good that is really yours?]

[50] *Ep.* 41.7: 'Familiam formosam habet et domum pulchram, multum serit, multum fenerat: nihil horum in ipso est sed circa ipsum' [Suppose he has a retinue of comely slaves

Vous n'achetez pas un chat en poche. <u>Si vous marchandez un cheval, vous lui ostez ses bardes, vous le voyez nud et à descouvert;</u>[51] ou, s'il est couvert, comme on les presentoit anciennement aux Princes à vandre, c'est par les parties moins necessaires, afin que vous ne vous amusez pas à la beauté de son poil ou largeur de sa croupe, et que vous vous arrestez principalement à considerer les jambes, les yeux et le pied, qui sont les membres les plus utiles,

Regibus hic mos est: ubi equos mercantur, opertos
Inspiciunt, ne, si facies, ut saepe, decora
Molli fulta pede est, emptorem inducat hiantem,
Quod pulchrae clunes, breve quod caput, ardua cervix.

<u>Pourquoy, estimant un homme, l'estimez vous tout enveloppé et empacqueté?</u>[52] Il ne nous faict montre que des parties qui ne sont aucunement siennes, et nous cache celles par lesquelles seules on peut vrayement juger de son estimation. <u>C'est le pris de l'espée que vous cherchez, non de la guaine: vous n'en donnerez à l'adventure pas un quatrain, si vous l'avez despouillé.</u>[53] <u>Il le faut juger par luy mesme, non par ses atours.</u>[54] Et, comme dit tres-plaisamment un ancien: <u>Sçavez vous pourquoy vous l'estimez grand? Vous y comptez la hauteur de ses patins. La base n'est pas de la statue. Mesurez le sans ses eschaces:</u>[55] <u>qu'il mette à part ses richesses et honneurs, qu'il se presente en chemise.</u>[56] A il le corps propre à ses functions, sain et allegre? <u>Quelle ame a il? est elle belle, capable et heureusement pourveue de toutes ses pieces?</u>[57]

and a beautiful house, that his farm is large and that he has a large income: none of these things is in the man himself; they are all on the outside].

[51] *Ep.* 80.9: 'Equum empturus solvi iubes stratum, detrahis vestimenta venalibus ne qua vitia corporis lateant' [When you buy a horse, you order its blanket to be removed; you pull off the garments from slaves that are advertised for sale, so that no bodily flaws may escape your notice].

[52] *Ep.* 80.9: 'hominem involutum aestimas?' [if you judge a man, do you judge him when he is wrapped in a disguise?].

[53] *Ep.* 76.14: 'gladium bonum dices non cui auratus est balteus nec cuius vagina gemmis distinguitur, sed cui et ad secandum subtilis acies est et mucro munimentum omne rupturus' [you will speak of a sword as good not when its sword-belt is of gold, or its scabbard studded with gems, but when its edge is fine for cutting and its point will pierce any armour].

[54] *Ep.* 41.7–8: 'Nemo gloriari nisi suo debet. [...] Lauda in illo, quod nec eripi potest nec dari' [No man ought to glory except in that which is his own. Praise the quality in him which cannot be given or snatched away.]

[55] *Ep.* 76.31: 'excalceantur et ad staturam suam redeunt. [...] Quare ergo magnus videtur? cum basi illum sua metiris. Non est magnus pumilio licet in monte constiterit; colossus magnitudinem suam servabit etiam si steterit in puteo' [They remove their shoes and return to their proper stature [...] Why then does he seem great to you? It is because you are measuring the pedestal along with the man. A dwarf is not tall, though he stand upon a mountain-top; a colossal statue will still be tall, though you place it in a well.]

[56] *Ep.* 76.32: 'Atqui cum voles veram hominis aestimationem inire et scire qualis sit, nudum inspice; ponat patrimonium, ponat honores et alia fortunae mendacia' [But when you wish to inquire into a man's true worth, and to know what manner of man he is, look at him when he is naked; make him lay aside his inherited estate, his titles, and the other deceptions of fortune].

[57] *Ep.* 76.16: 'Bonum autem est, si ratio eius explicata et recta est et ad naturae suae voluntatem accommodata' [He is good, however, if his reason is well-ordered and right and adapted to that which his nature has willed].

Est elle riche du sien, ou de l'autruy?⁵⁸ la fortune n'y a elle que voir? Si, les yeux ouverts, elle attend les espées traites; s'il ne luy chaut par où luy sorte la vie, par la bouche ou par le gosier; si elle est rassise, equable et contente: c'est ce qu'il faut veoir,⁵⁹ et juger par là les extremes differences qui sont entre nous. (I.42.259–60).

But apropos of judging men, it is a wonder that, ourselves excepted, nothing is valued except by its own qualities. We praise a horse because it is vigorous and skilful,

> Thus we praise the steed,
> Who wins the highest palms with easy speed,
> Amid the raucous plaudits of the Circus

not for its harness; a greyhound for its speed, not for his collar; a bird for its wing, not for his jesses and bells. Why do we not likewise judge a man by what is his own? He has a great retinue, a beautiful palace, so much influence, so much income: all that is around him, not in him. You don't buy a cat in a bag. If you are bargaining for a horse, you take off its trappings, you see him bare and uncovered. Or if he is covered, as in olden days they used to offer horses to princes for sale, the covering covers only the least important parts, and is there so that you may not waste time on the beauty of its coat or the breadth of its crupper, but linger principally over considering its legs, eyes, and feet, which are the most useful parts,

> When kings want to buy horses, this is ever their way,
> To see them covered up, lest they be led astray
> And buy a soft lame foot, paired with a handsome face,
> Fine cruppers, a short head, a neck of arching grace.

Why in judging a man do you judge him all wrapped up in a packet? He displays to us only parts that are not at all his own, and hides from us those by which alone one can truly judge of his value. It is the worth of the blade that you seek to know, not of the scabbard; perhaps you will not give a penny for it if you have unsheathed it. You must judge him by himself, not by his finery. And as an ancient says very comically, Do you know why you think him tall? You are counting in the height of his heels! The pedestal is not part of the statue. Measure him without his stilts; let him put aside his riches and honours, let him present himself in his shirtsleeves. Has he a body fit for its functions, healthy and lithe? What sort of soul has he? Is it rich of its own riches, or of others'? Has fortune nothing to do with it? If open-eyed he awaits the drawn swords; if he cares not whether his life expires by the mouth or the neck; if his soul is composed, equable, and content: this is what we must see, and by this judge the extreme differences that are between us.

---

⁵⁸ *Ep.* 76.32: 'Animum intuere, qualis quantusque sit, alieno an suo magnus' [Consider his soul, its quality and its stature, and thus learn whether its greatness is borrowed or its own].

⁵⁹ *Ep.* 76.33: 'Si rectis oculis gladios micantes videt et si scit sua nihil interesse, utrum anima per os an per iugulum exeat, beatum voca' [If a man can behold with unflinching eyes the flash of a sword, if he knows that it makes no difference to him whether his soul takes flight through his mouth or through a wound in his throat, you may call him happy].

If we are to judge men properly, we must judge them in the same way we judge a horse: the opening distinction proposed by Plutarch between man and beast collapses in Montaigne's long list of analogies. Except that the analogies are not, in fact, Montaigne's. Everything underlined is taken from Seneca, and for the most part from just one letter.

The two verse quotations, from Juvenal and Horace respectively, perform an explicit foreignness against which the French prose looks decidedly Montaignian. Similarly, the reference towards the end of this passage to 'un ancien' signals that what follows comes from elsewhere (even if it is not particularly clear where the borrowing ends). Montaigne cites his source only once the better part has been smuggled through undetected: pointing at the end to his debt to this 'ancien', he leads us to think the rest of it is all him, 'nez chez moy et sans patron' [born with me and without model] (II.12.546/409).

This is, then, an instance of Montaigne challenging the hasty, intemperate reader. He looks to deceive us, passing off Seneca's words as his own, but, at the same time, he encourages us to call out the deception. The nod to Seneca tips us off, acting as a prompt to look back over what came before and declare 'Voylà d'où il le print!' [That's where he got it!] (II.12.546/409). Having uncovered Montaigne's ruse, our perspective changes and we recognise Montaigne's borrowings as stolen goods – this is a clear case, it would seem, not of properly employed common stock, nor simply of excessive imitation bordering on parroting. It is a case of outright theft.

And yet the subject matter makes plain the irony that underpins Montaigne's imitative practices: he is using silently translated sayings taken from Seneca to criticise a tendency to judge men not on what is theirs but on what is borrowed, extrinsic and foreign. We read this passage thinking that we are reading Montaigne, judging him, his thoughts and his judgements, only to find – provided we recognise Seneca lurking in the shadows – that it isn't Montaigne at all. In concealing Seneca in this way, Montaigne writes Seneca's lesson into the form of his essay, teaching us to be alert in judging 'ce qui est sien et ce qui ne l'est point'. The words are Seneca's, then, and to learn this lesson – that we should judge a man on what is properly his and not on what he has merely borrowed – we have to recognise that the words are not Montaigne's. But for the joke to work, we also have to see that Montaigne has repurposed his stolen material: he has transformed these lines not to repeat a Stoic principle – that material goods do not reveal the man – but to stage a comic lesson in reading. In other words, to get the joke, we must see these words alternately now as Montaigne's and now as Seneca's. 'Est elle riche du sien, ou de l'autruy?' Is it rich with its own wealth, or that of others? Our response to this question hesitates between contradictory answers: Montaigne's riches here are really Seneca's, but recognising this reveals the transformative irony that makes them his, though the irony depends on them not being his.

We might think here of the image of boys playing with mercury, one of Montaigne's key metaphors: the tighter they grasp and squeeze this 'genereux metal', the more it escapes them (III.13.1067/816). The authorial doubleness of this extract reveals a similar vitality. We see different authorial associations, different 'usages' – we see that, in one sense at least, Seneca and Montaigne both 'are' the authors of these words, both have a claim to ownership of these words as revealing the work of their 'imaginations' – but our experience of reading and engaging with the material forces us to see now one 'visage', now another. To make sense of this passage, we have to establish what does and does not belong to each man ('ce qui est sien et ce qui ne l'est point'), we have to answer Seneca's question – 'cuius?', whose is it? But we cannot follow the model of the schoolmaster or the 'sçavant', judging *chois*, *disposition*, *ornement* and *langage*. Neither Montaigne nor, I suggest, his reader is able to tally up the balance sheet and settle the account: the matter remains undecided not because we suspend judgement entirely, stepping back from the matter and shrugging our shoulders, but because different and even contradictory authorial associations seem to come in and out of focus, one displacing the other. There is an authorial instability here that requires us to be on our guard, applying our judgement not to the transfer of text itself, not to the rhetorical categories that legitimise imitation (*dispositio*, *eloquentia* and so on), but to the shifting 'branloire perenne' of authorial association (III.2.804/610).

Thinking with Authors: On Weak and Temporary Judgements

Preferring *astheneia*, 'absence of strength', to the term listed among the *phonai skeptikai* – *isostheneia*, 'equal strength', 'equipollence' – Frédéric Brahami has argued that Montaigne's doubtful thought does not lead to *epoché*, an absolute suspension of judgement, but rather to weak and temporary judgements: there can be no equilibrium when the soul is in a state of flux. And if there is no *isostheneia*, no balancing of equal appearances, there can be no *epoché*.[60]

[60] Brahami, *Le Scepticisme de Montaigne*, pp. 68–9.

'La plus penible assiete pour moy', writes Montaigne, 'c'est estre suspens és choses qui pressent et agité entre la crainte et l'esperance' [the most painful situation for me to be sat in is to be in suspense about urgent matters, and tossed between fear and hope] (II.17.644/488). Even in trivial matters ('és choses plus legieres'), deliberation pains him ('m'importune'), such that he would rather commit himself at random to one course of action, whatever it might be, than 'souffrir le branle et les secousses diverses du doute et de la consultation' [endure the various shocks and ups and downs of doubt and deliberation]. Chance, not judgement, determines Montaigne's position, and suspense ('deliberation') leads not to *ataraxia* but 'trouble': 'Peu de passions m'ont troublé le sommeil; mais, des deliberations, la moindre me le trouble' [Few passions have troubled my sleep; but as for deliberations, the slightest troubles it].

The self-portrait Montaigne paints here could not be further from that of the classical Sceptic. Sylvia Giocanti has argued that this restlessness is ultimately compatible with Scepticism, and we might see in Montaigne's account of casting himself at the feet of chance an echo of Apelles throwing his sponge.[61] But Montaigne's rejection of suspense, along with his account of the affect and disposition that go with it, are entirely alien to both the theories and practices of the ancient Sceptics.

His habit of readily, desperately taking up whatever position he finds shapes his idiosyncratic mode of unresolved thought. In writing his *Essais*, Montaigne is not concerned with the ordered progression of a disinterested 'esprit' but, as Giocanti has shown, with the 'roulis', the swaying and tilting of discourse and judgement between contrary positions.[62] For Montaigne, Giocanti suggests, it is a matter not of suspending judgement but of learning how to go with the flow ('"apprendre à rouler" le mieux possible'), embracing and recognising the 'branloire perenne', the perennial movement, in which we live (III.2.804/610). Counterintuitively, what marks Montaigne's thought as doubtful is his inability to put up with suspense, his weakness that compels him to roll from one judgement to another, committing himself fully to his beliefs in the moment even though he knows that the moment will not last.[63] It is

---

[61] Sylvia Giocanti, 'Un scepticisme sans tranquillité?', *Bulletin de la société internationale des amis de Montaigne*, 55 (2012), 63–90. Giocanti addresses the relationship between Scepticism and restlessness more fully in *Scepticisme et inquiétude* (Paris: Hermann, 2019). On Apelles' sponge as a metaphor for Scepticism, see Cave, *Pré-histoires*, pp. 23–5.

[62] Giocanti, *Penser l'irrésolution*, pp. 19, 511.

[63] As noted above, Chapter 6 will discuss in detail a passage from the 'Apologie' in which Montaigne describes the experience of believing his beliefs fully while being fully aware that he has previously believed things he no longer believes, II.12.563/423. The fact that

not suspending judgement but committing constantly to a series of weak and temporary judgements that constitutes the essential characteristic of doubt in the *Essais*.

In 1576, Montaigne had made a run of 'jetons', medals imprinted with the image of a balance above the 'mot sacramental' of the Pyrrhonians, 'ΕΠΕΧω', that word Montaigne translated in the 'Apologie' as 'je soutiens, je ne bouge' [I hold back, I do not budge] (II.12.505/374).[64] But his account of being both unwilling and unable to suspend judgement mobilises this well-known image of equipollent fixity in new ways, recasting it in the mould of a novel form of doubtful thinking remarkably unlike that found among the ancient Sceptics. Seen in this light, the set of scales serves not as a symbol of constant, static *isostheneia*, the precursor to tranquil *ataraxia*. Instead, the balance seems to tip back and forth endlessly, without ever resting definitively one way or the other. Thus, when Montaigne holds his guard in judging 'ce qui est sien et ce qui ne l'est point', he does not stand back, disinterested and uninvolved; he sees the matter now one way, now another: this 'suspense' is not a passive suspension of judgement but an active, mobile adoption of multiple perspectives.

In the *Essais*, authorial association is insecure, temporary and inconstant. Suspense is, in all matters, 'la plus penible assiete' (literally 'the most painful seat') – here as elsewhere he is sitting with 'le cul entre deux selles', his rear end between two stools (I.54.313/227) – and this unsettled awkwardness translates into Montaigne's painful, uncomfortable posture of being on guard in his reading, unsure of what is or is not a given author's property. Together, Montaigne's habit of flitting between weak and temporary judgements and his notion of literary property as usufructuary govern his 'commerce' with his authors. His hesitations between French and Latin, his games of concealment and revelation, his contradictory provocations reflect a reimagining of authorship and its role in communicating thought. The relationship between a given author and their work is understood as an impermanent, insecure association – an association, based in usage, that is frequently contested by other authors making similar claims. It is for the reader to settle the dispute but, provided we read like Montaigne, any judgement will be made only in the moment and without any guarantee that it will last: 'Car en ce que je dy, je ne pleuvis autre certitude, sinon que c'est ce que

---

his judgements are weak and temporary does not prevent them from feeling strong in the moment.

[64] See Marie-Luce Demonet, 'Jeton', in Desan (ed.), *Dictionnaire de Montaigne*, pp. 988–92. Demonet notes the erroneous lower-case omega. One of these medals is extant and kept at the Château de Montaigne.

lors j'en avoy en ma pensée, pensée tumultuaire et vacillante' [For in what I say I guarantee no certainty except that it is what I had at the time in my mind, a tumultuous and vacillating mind] (III.9.1033/790).

'J'en attache quelque chose à ~~mon livre~~ ce papier; à moy, si peu que rien' [I stick some of it to ~~my book~~ this paper; to myself, next to nothing] (I.26.146/107). In attending to the ways literary property associates diversely with different author figures, Montaigne developed a means of thinking with authorship, thinking with authorial doubleness as he examined the subject under discussion, his relationship with it, his relationship with his own thoughts and with those of others. Attaching something to the paper, to the space between himself and a figure such as Seneca or Plutarch, became a means of examining it from multiple perspectives, asking whether it looks different in Montaignian or Senecan guise and asking how these different impressions might illuminate or reveal his thinking – how they might reveal that which is properly his own, which is to say 'l'usage de ses opinions'. Where Seneca and Plutarch show things now one way, now another ('tantost d'un visage, tantost d'un autre', II.12.509/377), Montaigne invites us to see in the *Essais* different authorial 'visages' depending on how we look.

Montaigne's habit of thinking with authorship is related to what Terence Cave has identified as a broader early modern mode of 'thinking with commonplaces'. Commonplaces, Cave argues, are not simply sentences expressing a particular view – to see them as such would be to miss the play, manipulation and handling of these discursive artefacts and, consequently, to miss the ways in which they make meaning. Commonplacing is one of the key tools that make up the early modern *outillage mental*. It is a way of thinking and not just a means of expressing thought. 'Thinking with commonplaces is not a philosophy', Cave argues. 'It is above all a practice, oriented towards experience.'[65] At the heart of this practice is a fluency that allowed early moderns to think with and through a 'commonplace lexis': 'once one knows the lexis, one becomes sensitive to all kinds of inflections and micro-variations'.[66]

Montaigne thinks with authorial association in a way that is similarly sensitive, alert to the shifts in effect, meaning and resonance that occur as he associates a given idea with himself or with an authorial interlocutor. This is a sensitivity evident not only in his hesitations between Latin and French, nor only in his use of borrowed material: it can be seen also

---

[65] Terence Cave, 'Thinking with Commonplaces: The Example of Rabelais', in *Retrospectives: Essays in Literature, Poetics, and Cultural History*, ed. Neil Kenny and Wes Williams (London: Legenda, 2009), pp. 38–47 (p. 45).
[66] Ibid., p. 39.

in his reading of ideas 'nez chez moy et sans patron', but which he no longer recognises. Thinking with authorship in this way forms part of a broader mode of doubtful writing: it allows Montaigne to consider ideas and sentences from multiple perspectives, surveying himself and his relationship with the words on the page in a way that is ongoing and unresolved, while at the same time tracing that survey in writing. It is in this sense that we might understand Montaigne's claim to be 'consubstantial' with his book: it is in and with his book that he examines his judgement – 'l'usage de ses opinions' – and he is consubstantial with his book for as long as he thinks with it and it reveals his thinking.

As well as supporting and communicating his ongoing, unfinished thinking, Montaigne's 'commerce' with authors and authorship calls for doubtful, unresolved reading. His provocations and contradictory claims of ownership and debt force the reader into a game of identifying 'ce qui est sien et ce qui ne l'est point', even as we, 'nous autres', are grouped among those unable to do so with any authority. We are instead led to follow Montaigne in making weak and temporary judgements; we are encouraged to recognise the instability, the 'coulante et fluante' nature of authorship, to see two authorial 'visages', now one, now the other, and, with each 'visage', to come to a different understanding of its place in the *Essais*. In making authorship a matter of judging usage, not definitively but temporarily, both authorship and its judgement become vital, mobile: 'et le jugeant et le jugé estans en continuelle mutation et branle' [both the judging and the judged being in continual change and motion] (II.12.601/455). The reader, goaded into flicking Plutarch's nose on Montaigne's face, finds that the faces themselves are flickering back and forth.

Writing a book in which a given line seems now to be authored by Montaigne, now by some ancient, is not just a metaliterary game. It is a mechanism with which to think through an idea from multiple perspectives; a means of asking himself what it is that he thinks, what opinions and judgements make up himself and his character. It is also an invitation to his reader, an invitation to recognise Montaigne in the shifting commerce of authorial exchange and, indeed, to ask what claims to ownership, what claims to 'usage', we might make ourselves. Thinking with authorship is a tool for self-reflection, asking what does and does not belong to us, and a tool for communication. This can be seen clearly in 'De la vanité'. In this chapter, overwhelmingly concerned with movement, precarity and 'vagabondage', with being away from home and being uprooted, Montaigne discussed his affinity for Rome and its ancient inhabitants: '[B]Or j'ay esté nourry dés mon enfance avec ceux icy; j'ay eu connoissance des affaires de Romme, long temps avant que je l'aye eue de ceux de ma maison' [Now I have been brought up from childhood with these dead. I was familiar with the affairs of Rome long before I was with those of my own house] (III.9.996/762).[67] After digressing briefly to talk of friendship, he returns, by way of Pompey and Brutus, to the ancient city, the city he threw himself into, having found himself 'inutile à ce siecle' [useless for this age].

A cluster of post-1588 additions to this passage give voice to the timeless lament of having been born in the wrong generation:

> [C]Est-ce par nature ou par erreur de fantasie que la veue des places que nous sçavons avoir esté hantées et habitées par personnes desquelles la memoire est en recommendation, nous esmeut aucunement plus qu'ouïr le recit de leur faicts ou lire leurs escrits? *Tanta vis admonitionis inest in locis. Et id quidem in hac urbe infinitum: quacunque enim ingredimur in aliquam historiam vestigium ponimus.* [B]Il me plaist de considerer leur visage, leur port et leurs vestements; je remache ces grands noms entre les dents et les faicts retentir à mes oreilles. [C]*Ego illos veneror et tantis nominibus semper assurgo.* (III.9.996–7)

> [C]Is it by nature or by an error of the imagination that the sight of the places we know were frequented and inhabited by people whose memory is held in honour, somehow stirs us more than hearing the story of their deeds or reading their writings? *Such is the power of places to call up memories. And in this city this is infinite; for wherever we walk we set our foot on history.* [B]I like to reflect on their faces, their bearing, and their clothes. I chew over those great names between my teeth and make them resound in my ears. [C]*I venerate them and always rise to honour such great names.* (763)

Modelling a Latinity that ought to prove Montaigne's membership of the ancient club he aspires to, he inserts a quotation first from Cicero and then from Seneca. If we recognise those quotations and know where they come from – if we can judge Montaigne on his fluency, on his feeling for the sense of his quotations – it becomes clear that something does not quite fit. Returning to the source, we see that, at this point in the *De finibus* (5.1–2), Cicero and his interlocutors are discussing Athens, while the 'tantis nominibus', the names Seneca venerates, are for the most part Greek.[68]

---

[67] On Montaigne in Rome, see Boutcher, *The School of Montaigne*, vol. 1, pp. 261–314, and Margaret M. McGowan, *Visions of Rome in Late Renaissance France* (New Haven, CT: Yale University Press, 2000), pp. 228–34. McGowan considers this passage, 'filled with yearning', to suggest that Montaigne, 'drawing on his direct experience of Rome and on phrases recollected from his reading', 'sees all the layers of the city at once, from its state when it was in its prime to its magnificent ruins', pp. 248–9.

[68] Montaigne's quotation from the *De finibus* is made up of two phrases, the second of which is slightly reworked. These phrases come from different parts of the text (5.1.2 and 5.2.5) and are spoken by different interlocutors, Marcus Piso and Lucius Cicero. Seneca's list of venerable wise men – Socrates, Plato, Zeno, Cleanthes – also includes Cato the Elder and Younger and Gaius Laelius Sapiens.

Montaigne repeats Seneca and Cicero while referring to something different. 'Hac urbe': those Latin words no longer mean what they meant in their original contexts. And yet, at the same time, they do refer to the same thing: the words borrowed from these ancients describe the feeling of intimate connection with a past culture still accessible through a geographical and literary connection. Both Montaigne and his ancient sources speak of that same sense of knowing those who have long since died by walking in their footsteps, speaking their names and repeating their words. What unites Montaigne with Seneca and Cicero, then, is a shared feeling of distance and disconnection bridged by culture and architecture. In Montaigne's hands, these Senecan and Ciceronian words become reflexive in a way that is productively unsuccessful: we feel this sense of difference; we recognise that Cicero's love of 'hac urbe', 'this city', is the same as Montaigne's, even if the city is different; we understand that Montaigne is different from Seneca and Cicero and, in seeing this difference, bridged by travel and literature, we see their similarity.

Both of these Latin quotations were added after 1588. In something of a trend in post-1588 additions, Montaigne combines quotation and translation when borrowing from the same text: the sentence in French immediately preceding the quotation from Cicero is a translation of a line from the same book of *De finibus* (5.1.2). Montaigne has, it would seem, only partially digested his source and, in leaving Cicero half-chewed, gives a new inflection to the 1588 text that follows: 'je remache ces grands noms entre les dents' [I chew over these great names between my teeth].

The Bordeaux Copy reveals Montaigne's attention to the interplay of translation and quotation: he began his marginal note by writing the Latin quotation ('Tanta vis admonitionis inest in locis') only to cross it out, replacing it with a translation, before crossing out the translation in turn, and reinstating the Latin. This hesitation shows Montaigne's care for how authorship will be perceived. Here, he is thinking with the *De finibus*, asking where it fits on the Montaigne/not-Montaigne spectrum, placing different sections along this continuum, asking how far his perspective overlaps with Cicero's, teasing out the similarity laced with difference that characterises their shared experience of reaching into a distant culture.

The work in progress evident in the Bordeaux Copy reveals more fully what is already legible in the printed text of the *Essais*. But whether we have access to these crossings out or read the passage as Montaigne would have expected it to be printed, it is clear that he is thinking with ambiguous, doubled-up authorial presences, sustaining the tension between difference and similarity so that we might feel, as he does, that complex combination of closeness and distance. And while authorship – in this passage and across the *Essais* – is indeed ambiguous, it is not blurry or imprecise. We might compare the experience of reading passages such as this one with having 'double vision' – we see Montaigne *and* Cicero, for example – but we see both figures clearly. The doubleness cannot be resolved by a 'sçavant' supplying a footnote: we cannot determine once and for all what belongs to whom, 'ce qui est sien et ce qui ne l'est point'. Senecan and Ciceronian descriptions of Athens overlap with Montaigne's reflections on Rome, with Seneca and Cicero at once Montaigne's analogue and stand-ins for the essayist's own list of venerable names. Montaigne speaks their words with shifting degrees of transparency, and in the process illuminates and reveals himself. Using words that have been used by others, he found in his approach to authorship a tool with which to understand and judge himself, to ask (continuously, repeatedly, without coming to a fixed conclusion) what is his and what is not.

Doubtful Authorship and Doubtful Thought

Thinking with authorial instability offered Montaigne a new way of examining his thoughts, their relationship with him, and their relationship with his reading. At the same time, it allowed him to engage his reader, to demand agility and alertness in the face of shifting authorial associations. It is a way of keeping us on our toes, making sure we keep our eyes on the ball:

> La parole est moitié à celuy qui parle, moitié à celuy qui l'escoute. Cettuy-cy se doibt preparer à la recevoir selon le branle qu'elle prend. Comme entre ceux qui jouent à la paume, celuy qui soustient se desmarche et s'apreste selon qu'il voit remuer celuy qui luy jette le coup et selon la forme du coup. (III.13.1088)

> Speech belongs half to the speaker, half to the listener. The latter must prepare to receive it according to the motion it takes. As among tennis players, the receiver moves and makes ready according to the motion of the striker and the nature of the stroke. (834)

As Hall Bjørnstad notes, the appearance of the tennis players is triggered by the word 'branle', motion.[69] In Montaigne's 'branloire perenne', it is

---

[69] Hall Bjørnstad, 'The Metaphors of Textual Transfer: From Indigestion to Early Modern Tennis', in Bjørnstad (ed.), *Borrowed Feathers*, pp. 215–28 (p. 227). For a contrary reading, see Richard Regosin, who has argued that Montaigne uses this metaphor 'not to elaborate on how the game can be viewed as exchange between equals, or how the

not only words and ideas that are on the move: authorial associations are inconstant too. If we want to keep up with this inconstancy, to go with the flow ('rouler au vent'), and read and write proficiently, we have to be agile, 'allegre': 'j'aymeroy aussi cher que mon escolier eut passé le temps à joüer à la paume; au moins le corps en seroit plus allegre' [I would like just as much that my student had passed his time playing tennis; at least his body would be more agile] (I.25.138/101). We saw in the previous chapter how Seneca and Plutarch were able to move Montaigne. Here again, the physicality of Montaigne's metaphors is significant: reading Seneca and Plutarch, reading the *Essais*, and reading the movement between them, we have to be able to move in turn.

The line from 'De l'experience' comparing conversation and tennis is itself lifted from Plutarch.[70] Here, then, precisely at the moment he is describing the movement between author figures, between writers, readers and rewriters, Montaigne engages in the act he describes, responding to Plutarch's volley and redirecting 'la balle', which is now in his court.

Reading – both in and of the *Essais* – is not passive reception. But neither is it appropriation or digestive transformation or any of those other familiar metaphors for textual transfer. Each of those ways of thinking recognises the movement of text that takes place between authors, but presents that transaction as acquisitive and resolved, moving in one direction through a chain of imitators. At each link in that chain, authorial ownership might be disputed – readers might disagree as to whether the transformative work of imitation is successful – but one can, typically, come to a conclusion and settle the account, deciding how much we owe an author for the material, its selection, its arrangement, its decoration. In the *Essais*, by contrast, ownership is pegged to the continuous assessment of ongoing and shifting 'usage' and the different, conflicting 'visages' it reveals. If this were not the case, the end of the

---

receiver is also always (potentially) the sender', but rather to describe a 'one-way process' in which 'the receiver is forced to adjust according to what is coming his way'; Richard Regosin, *Montaigne's Unruly Brood: Textual Engendering and the Challenge of Paternal Authority* (Berkeley: University of California Press, 1996), pp. 113–15.

[70] 'Et ceulx cy cuident que tout l'affaire soit en celuy qui dit, & rien en celuy qui escoute […] il est à moitié de la parole avec celuy qui dit […] Mais tout ainsi comme en jouant à la paulme, il fault que celuy qui reçoit la balle se remue dextrement, au pris qu'il voit remuer celuy qui luy renvoye: aussi au parler y a il quelque convenance de mouvement entre l'escoutant et le disant' [And they think that the whole business lies with the person who is speaking, and not at all with the listener. Half of speech is with the person who is speaking. But just as in a game of tennis, the person receiving the ball must move with agility, adapting to the movements he sees in the person who is serving, so also with speech there is a certain concordance between the person listening and the person speaking] ('Comment il fault ouïr', fol. 29r).

'Apologie', to return to an earlier example, would be seen as a straightforward transaction from one author figure, 'Plutarch', to another, 'Montaigne', and that would be the end of it. Montaigne's framing of his borrowings, coupled with the ambiguities inherent in their content and handling, prevents us from making such 'once and for all' judgements.

As among tennis players, authors and readers have to move together to keep the ball in play. In the *Essais*, we find Montaigne playing with Seneca or Plutarch or both of them or someone else. A given idea does not become definitively his by virtue of having passed into his half of the court, and neither does it cease (entirely) to be his once he sends it back. Rather, the text moves back and forth, taking on a particular characteristic – its 'spin' – 'selon la forme du coup', depending on how it is used. As readers of the *Essais*, we are more than spectators: we join in, playing with Montaigne and his own competitors, with the authors he reads and those who read him in turn, in an ever more complex, ever expanding game. Between Latin and French, between his and someone else's, currently his and his no longer: with these movements, and with the weak and temporary judgements that assess them, Montaigne used authorship to think and write doubtfully – to examine his unresolved thoughts and record this examination so that a reader might pick it up and carry on.

Montaigne's conception of authoring is grounded in the metaphors of digestive transformation, pillage and parroting, horticultural transplantation and common stock that dominated early modern literary culture. He draws from all these metaphors, combining them and repurposing them to suit his needs, often in ways that are not entirely compatible. But even as he uses these standard images, he works to express a novel, distinct conception of authorship, distinct from the traditions he invokes. What is significant for Montaigne is the mutability of authorial associations: they can be broken; he can encounter his words and fail to recognise them; he can read borrowed words and see them only as his.

It may be true that an idea is no more 'selon Montaigne' than 'selon Platon', given that they both see the matter in the same way (I.26.152/111). But Montaigne does not respond to the Sceptic's *ou mallon*, 'no more this way than that', by suspending judgement, nor does he follow his own instruction and judge things 'par elles mesmes', paying no heed to name and credit. Instead, he asks how things look when aligned with different *personae*. 'Cuius?', 'Whose is it?'; Montaigne seems to ask Seneca's question without expecting an answer, or at least knowing that the answer cannot stick, intrigued rather to see how different responses change how we see ourselves and the world.

Authorship in the *Essais* is ambiguous, not just in local moments of borrowing and not simply in the abstract. It is this tendency towards doubleness – the fact that the *Essais* seem regularly to be caught between different author figures – that makes Montaigne's mode of authoring a tool for seeing things now one way, now another. In displacing authorship onto the page ('à ce papier', I.26.146/107), he developed a 'forme d'escrire' that is 'douteuse et irresolue'; a way of writing in harmony with the erratic changeability of our thinking and the world towards which it is directed.

Chapter 3

Forming Thoughts I: Thinking About Form

De la forme de l'imagination

'Je peins principalement mes cogitations', wrote Montaigne, 'subject informe': 'A toute peine le puis je coucher en ce corps aerée de la voix' [What I chiefly portray is my cogitations, a shapeless subject [...] I have to struggle to couch it in this airy body of the voice] (II.6.379/274).[1] The metaphor of the literary self-portrait has long served as a guide for understanding the relationship between the 'forme' of the *Essais* and their formless subject, though the limitations of the analogy are now similarly well established.[2] In place of the painter and his painting, more recent studies have drawn connections to early modern 'registres', account books or ledgers, to read the *Essais* as a record of Montaigne, preserving his thoughts and character, ready to be consulted by friends, acquaintances, unknown readers and Montaigne himself.[3] The image of the 'registre' no doubt alters our image of the essayist, foregrounding the clerical over the aesthetic and placing the painter of 'crotesques' (I.28.183/135) somewhere in the background: front and centre is the work of book-keeping that occupied the supposed retiree, fit only

---

[1] Translation modified. Frame has 'It is all I can do to couch my thoughts in this airy medium of words.'

[2] On the inadequacy of the portrait metaphor, see Gérard Defaux, *Marot, Rabelais, Montaigne: L'Écriture comme présence* (Paris: Champion-Slatkine, 1987), p. 183; Terence Cave, 'Montaigne', *Proceedings of the British Academy*, 131 (2005), 183–203, and, by the same author, *How to Read Montaigne* (London: Granta, 2007). Vittoria Fallanca, by contrast, has argued that early modern conceptions of drawing as an 'accumulative and open-ended' practice of 'keeping track' collapse the implicit dichotomy between Montaigne's 'fluid and mobile writing' and portraiture as 'fixed and immutable'. See 'The Design of Montaigne's *Essais*', pp. 37–74 (p. 40).

[3] Most notably in Warren Boutcher's study of the *Essais* as a 'radically open' and 'public' form of the otherwise familiar practice of keeping a 'registre' or 'contrerolle', a 'personal journal' or 'account book'. See *The School of Montaigne*, esp. vol. 1, pp. 54–5, 318.

for a job that does not exist ('un office sans nom', III.13.1078/825). But swapping the painter for the clerk or the accountant leaves the essential relationship between 'forme d'écrire' and the 'forme' of the imagination unchanged: writing follows, imitates and records the thinking it transcribes; it reproduces the shape, or shapelessness, of thinking in the shape of the *Essais*.[4]

But the *Essais* are not shapeless. In the first edition, Montaigne closed his book by noting that it is in writing that he gives his thoughts 'un peu plus de forme' [a little more form], not so much tracing the shape of his thinking as providing it (II.37.785/597). In what follows, I suggest that the task of 'couching' – bedding in, planting – his mercurial subject in an airy (but solid enough) form of writing is a matter of forming thoughts. His 'forme d'escrire' gives thoughts shape, or at least shape enough so that they might not run straight through his hands, but drip through his leaky vessel, inherited from the Danaïdes, and stick to his 'papier'. This form responds to the shapelessness of thinking, but not by imitating it. Thinking in and with writing, his literary 'forme' communicates his thinking as it takes shape.

Montaigne repeatedly describes himself and his way of thinking as 'double'. His 'forme d'escrire' works doubly too. First, it communicates thought, tracing and recording the shape and feel of this liquid, shapeless subject. But it also sustains or promotes a 'double', unresolved way of thinking, both in Montaigne and in his reader (which includes Montaigne reading himself). The *Essais* serve, then, as a 'registre', recording judgements, and as an affordance, as a material resource that supports the activity of thinking. Montaigne's forms of writing and forms of thinking shape one another: the form of the *Essais* both responds to thinking's doubleness and produces it. It is in this light that we might consider Montaigne's 'commerce' with his book as neither mimetic imitation nor archival record-keeping, but instead as something concerned with 'usage', in which the *Essais* serve as a workbook,

---

[4] On 'forme' as keyword, with reference to generic form and philosophical 'Forms', see Philippe Desan, *Les Formes du monde et de l'esprit* (Paris: Presses Universitaires de Paris-Sorbonne, 2008), and, by the same author, 'Pour une théorie de la forme des *Essais*', in *Dix études sur Montaigne* (Paris: Garnier, 2020), pp. 133–45. See also Ian Winter, 'L'Emploi du mot *forme* dans les *Essais* de Montaigne', in *Montaigne et les Essais 1580–1980*, ed. François Moureau, Robert Granderoute and Claude Blum (Paris and Geneva: Slatkine Reprints, 1983), pp. 261–8; J.-Y. Pouilloux, 'La forme maîtresse', in *Montaigne: une vérité singulière* (Paris: Gallimard, 2012), pp. 71–91; Alberto Frigo, '"Un sujet bien mal formé": expérience de soi, forme et réformation dans les *Essais* de Montaigne', *Cahiers de philosophie de l'Université de Caen*, 52 (2015), 69–92.

an extension of his thinking.[5] In the previous chapter, I considered Montaigne's practice of thinking with authorship. In this chapter and its 'double' that follows, I ask how he thinks with form. I suggest that the task of forming thoughts might be understood not as a labour of preservation looking to the future, calcifying and recording thought's passage, but as the activity of materialising thought in the moment, giving it substance in order to think with thought extended onto the page.[6]

It is in this light that the distinction between Scepticism and doubtful writing can be seen most clearly. Classical Scepticism presented itself always in a self-consciously rhetorical mode, structured by arguments against a dogmatic opponent and relying on 'refreins' and set expressions (what Montaigne calls 'façons de parler', II.12.505/374) to perpetuate contradiction, enquiry and debate. Sextus defines Scepticism as a *dunamis*, a power or ability ('id est vis & facultas'), a skill that one practises in order to present an opponent with contradictions.[7] It is a rhetorical and philosophical ability (*dunamis*) to deal dynamically in potentials. As Stéphane Marchand has noted, Sextus uses the word *dunamis* 'mainly in a linguistic context', and most often in the adverbial form (where it means 'implicitly', 'virtually', 'potentially'), to argue that a given word, saying or proposition *might* mean one thing, but it *might* mean another.[8] Scepticism is this 'ability' to say what something *could* mean; the ability to counter an opponent's argument by revealing 'implicit', 'implied' or 'potential' meanings. The Sceptic serves the dogmatist as a doctor, employing arguments of varying strength to cure them, as best they can (*kata dunamin*, 'pro viribus'), of their rashness.[9] But the Sceptic is dynamic not just in their ability to change tack depending on circumstance. Their *dunamis*, their *facultas*, is 'dynamic' in that

---

[5] Alternatively, one might take the practices of thinking with form that are the focus of this chapter as a reminder that mimetic representation can serve as an affordance too, not 'merely' or 'simply' recording its subject – Montaigne's patterns of thinking – but serving as a material extension of thinking itself: representing his subject allows Montaigne to survey and interrogate it.

[6] On domestic labours of preservation – pickling, freezing and so on – see Kadue, *Domestic Georgic*, esp. ch. 3: 'Correcting Montaigne: Agitation and Care in the *Essais*', pp. 77–102.

[7] *Outlines of Pyrrhonism*, I.4.10.

[8] Marchand gives the following illustration: 'by *A* we say *dunamei* – i.e. implicitly or virtually – *B*'. See Stéphane Marchand, 'Sextus Empiricus' Use of *dunamis*', in *Sceptical Paths: Enquiry and Doubt from Antiquity to the Present*, ed. Giuseppe Veltri, Racheli Haliva, Stephan Schmid and Emidio Spinelli (Berlin: De Gruyter, 2019), pp. 23–41 (pp. 23, 28).

[9] *Outlines of Pyrrhonism*, III.32.199. Marchand also notes in Sextus' conclusion the use of *dunamis* to describe 'weighty arguments, capable of vigorously rebutting (*kai eutonōs anaskeuzein dunamenois*) the dogmatic affliction of conceit'; 'Sextus Empiricus' Use of *dunamis*', p. 37.

other sense too: antagonistic and combative. It is necessarily tied up with a rhetorical practice of refutation and argument. Scepticism is a *facultas* that employs language not to communicate the patterns of the author's thinking but to (re)shape and (re)direct that of the addressee: the Sceptic's arguments, style, tone and demeanour change in response to the patient, not the physician.

The *Essais* by contrast employ the formal techniques discussed here to guarantee a parrhesiastic harmony of doubtful thinking and doubtful style. Where Montaigne uses writing as a tool for doubtful thinking, the Sceptic is concerned with style, language and form only in so far as it persuades the addressee to abandon their dogmatism. The Sceptic is most concerned, in matters of language and style, not to fall into dogmatic expression themselves, which would undermine their persuasiveness. Hence their reliance on self-purging set expressions. Linguistic ambiguity plays a key part in Sceptical arguments, of course, but where the Sceptic uncovers the doubtfulness of a word or proposition (its 'potential' or 'implied' meanings) as a step towards *epoché* (itself a stepping stone to *ataraxia*), Montaigne's doubtful writing is instead directed ultimately at communication: at communicating a style of thinking that is itself facilitated by literary expression. I will return to Montaigne's *parrhesia* in subsequent chapters. In what follows, I aim to show that doubtful writing is not a rhetorical position (just as it is not simply a record or representation of thought), but a way of thinking in writing: an application of literary and compositional practices that form and communicate Montaigne's 'subject informe'.

In chapter 1, I considered the curious claim that Seneca and Plutarch, along with other dogmatists who make up the 'tiers genre' of philosophers, have 'une forme d'escrire douteuse' [a doubtful way of writing] (II.12.509/377). But in what sense is their form 'doubtful'? Does it describe a doubtful way of thinking or provoke a doubtful response from a reader? On what stylistic and compositional techniques do these twin aspects of doubtfulness depend? What is the relationship between a practice of writing doubtfully and a style of writing that seems doubtful or prompts a doubtful way of thinking, whoever that thinker might be?

These questions grapple with a cluster of related 'formes': the 'forme' of thought (Montaigne's 'subject informe'), the form of the *Essais*, and the forms of thought and writing found in Seneca and Plutarch. The literary techniques Montaigne adapted from these authors shaped his particular use of writing as a cognitive affordance. Reworking their 'formes d'écrire', he developed a means of doubling up perspectives and overlaying compositional moments not to represent or illustrate thought, but to materialise it, giving thought shape and substance but without pinning it down or setting it in concrete. He found in Seneca and Plutarch related but distinct forms of unresolved writing. Brought together, these forms became a mode of 'writing doubly'. But before considering these 'formes d'écrire', this chapter begins with Montaigne's accounts of thought's shape and shapelessness, its feel and its slipperiness, in order to ask what he means when he talks about 'forme' and what it might mean for that 'forme' to be 'double'.

'Sans terme, et sans forme': Getting a Feel for Form

Defining terms is, in the context of the *Essais* at least, likely to be a fool's errand. Everyone knows what a stone is, for instance, but ask a pedant and he will tell you that it is a type of body, and that a body is a type of substance: 'On eschange un mot pour un autre, et souvent plus incongeu' [We exchange one word for another word, often more unknown] (III.13.1069/819). One needs a light touch to escape the fate of the mouse stuck in pitch, caught in philology's stickiness, and to avoid finding oneself sitting among the children playing with mercury: 'Plus ils le pressent et pestrissent, et s'estudient à la contraindre à leur loy, plus ils irritent la liberté de ce genereux metal' [The more they press it and knead it and try to constrain it to their will, the more they provoke the independence of this spirited metal] (III.13.1067–8/816–17). Montaigne's liquid, fluid form, itself a product of his leaky commerce with Seneca and Plutarch, deals in shapeshifting terms, especially when handling the shape and form of thought and the imagination.

That image of the children playing with mercury morphs, over the course of a few pages, to describe the quicksilver quality of thought itself. 'Nul esprit genereux', Montaigne writes, 'ne s'arreste en soy' [A spirited mind never stops within itself] (III.13.1068/818):

> [B]ses poursuites sont sans terme, et sans forme; son aliment c'est admiration, chasse, ambiguité. Ce que declaroit assez Appollo, parlant tousjours à nous doublement, obscurement et obliquement, ne nous repaissant pas, mais nous amusant et embesongnant. C'est un mouvement [C]irregulier, [B]perpetuel, sans [C]patron, [B]et sans but. (III.13.1068)[10]

> Its pursuits are without limit and without form; its food is wonder, the chase, ambiguity. Apollo revealed this clearly enough, always speaking to us doubly, obscurely, obliquely, not satisfying us, but keeping our minds

---

[10] The [C] markers in the final sentence are absent in the Villey-Saulnier edition. Montaigne's imagery here echoes Seneca's discussion of the mind in a state of sublime, poetic frenzy in *De Tranquillitate animi*, 17.11. I will return to this parallel in Chapter 6.

interested and busy. It is an irregular, perpetual motion, without pattern and without aim. (818)[11]

André Tournon saw in this description of the mind's endless movement the emblematic 'zététique', the proclivity to enquiry, that defined the 'essai pyrrhonien'.[12] Montaigne's experience of thinking – for this is not a theory of cognition or a psychology so much as an account of what spirited, engaged thinking feels like – is marked by irresolution and open-endedness: it is 'sans terme', 'perpetuel', hunting and roaming 'sans but', without aim. In this regard at least, he is describing a way of thinking that places him in the company of Pyrrho and his followers, 'encore en queste', still hunting for the truth (II.12.502/371).

The *Essais*, like the cognitive 'poursuites' they track, are 'sans terme'. They record a never-ending series of revisions and second looks: there is always a 'route par ailleurs', a road not travelled (III.13.1068/818). But Montaigne did not write a philosophical diary. The movement of the 'esprit genereux' is not only 'sans terme' but 'sans forme', not only 'perpetuel' but 'sans patron'. Irresolution – open-endedness, 'la peinture du passage' – is only half of the picture Montaigne paints in describing the experience of thinking, and his gesture not to the ancient Sceptics but to Pythian Apollo and his strange, outlandish, 'double' way of speaking is indicative: couching thought's form (or formlessness) is not simply a matter of deferring conclusion; it is a matter of style.[13]

Montaigne's account of this double, shapeless way of thinking is particularly slippery, and his revisions in the Bordeaux Copy show him turning increasingly towards spatial, almost embodied terms, thinking haptically and visually to grasp his 'genereux' subject as though it were an object of perception. In 1588, the passage read: 'C'est un mouvement perpetuel, sans arrest, & sans but' [It is a perpetual movement, without stop and without aim]. In the Bordeaux Copy, this became 'un mouvement [C]irregulier [B]perpetual, sans arrest [C]regle patron, [B]& sans but' [an irregular, perpetual movement, without stop rule pattern, and without aim]. These edits introduce non-linearity into Montaigne's

---

[11] Translation modified. Frame translates 'sans terme' as 'boundless'; 'doublement' as 'equivocally'; 'patron' as 'model'.
[12] Tournon, *Route par ailleurs*, esp. pp. 7–31.
[13] Compare Plutarch's 'Pourquoy la prophetisse Pythie ne rend plus les oracles en vers', fol. 634v: 'Si ne m'esbahis pas s'il estoit aucunefois besoing aux anciens de double entente, de circunlocution & obscurité' [And I should not be surprised if there was a need among the ancients for *double entente*, circumlocution, and obscurity]. On Montaigne's reception of Plutarch's Apollo, see Raymond Esclapez, 'Le Dieu Apollon: des "Dialogues pythiques" de Plutarque aux *Essais* de Montaigne', in *Moralia et Œuvres morales à la Renaissance*, ed. Olivier Guerrier (Paris: Garnier, 2008), pp. 253–74.

characterisation of the movement of thought: it is 'irregulier'; not so much endless ('sans arrest') as something else, 'sans regle', perhaps, wild and unruly.¹⁴ Or perhaps not: he reconsiders, crossing out 'sans regle' and replacing it with 'sans patron'. It was in the same period of revision, after 1588, that he reworked his claim in the 'Apologie' that his 'imaginations' are born 'chez moy et sans ~~exemple~~ patron' (II.12.546/409).

Bernard Sève has suggested that Montaigne understood the spirit to be fundamentally, essentially 'déréglé', unruly: the rules that tame this endlessly productive monster have to come from elsewhere – custom, the rules of society, the demands of the body and so on.¹⁵ But it is not clear that Montaigne wished to straighten out, to rule or tame, his unruly 'esprit genereux'. With the shift to 'sans patron', he gestures towards a much broader, and less doctrinaire, response to the mind's patternless movement: a movement without a model or guide to follow, a movement that proceeds of its own accord.

The 'poursuites' of the mind are 'sans terme' but they are also, crucially, 'sans forme'. As Jean-Yves Pouilloux and Philippe Desan have both argued, 'forme' in the *Essais* says nothing of essential being.¹⁶ If Plato or Aristotle, 'monarque de la doctrine moderne' [monarch of modern learning] (I.26.146/107), are present in Montaigne's thinking here, their influence is lexical rather than theoretical. When he writes elsewhere of 'la maistresse forme de nature' (II.32.726/548) or his own 'maistresse forme' (which is, he says, 'ignorance', I.50.302/219), he is speaking only of general characteristics and the way these things appear: 'forme' is, in Montaigne's lexicon, a matter of aspect and appearance, of shape, quality and character as it is perceived. To say that thought's movement is 'sans patron' and 'sans forme' is not to say that thought is without essence, guiding principle or definition, but rather that it is, or at least appears to be, shapeless, unmoulded, liquid.

Montaigne imagines the imagination by giving substance and shape to a shapeless subject.¹⁷ He perceives his 'esprit' and recognises that his

---

[14] The revision of 'sans arrest' might be read as an effort to avoid juridical overtones: where 'sans arrest' might imply a lack of a final verdict, 'sans regle' and 'sans patron' point instead towards a wandering, vagabond open-endedness.

[15] Sève, *Montaigne: des règles pour l'esprit*, pp. 16–17, 28–31.

[16] Pouilloux, 'La forme maîtresse', pp. 71–91; Desan, *Les Formes du monde et de l'esprit*, p. 13.

[17] On the imagination – 'fantasie', 'phantasia' – as, in Descartes' terms, the 'façon de penser particulière pour les choses matérielles' [special way of thinking for material things], see John Lyons, *Before Imagination: Embodied Thought from Montaigne to Rousseau* (Stanford, CA: Stanford University Press, 2005), esp. p. xi for the quotation from Descartes, and Wes Williams, 'Montaigne on Imagination', in Desan (ed.), *The Oxford Handbook of Montaigne*, pp. 679–98.

thinking is not only open-ended or unresolved but 'sans forme', even as he sketches its outlines. Getting a feel for thought's formlessness, he insists on its doubleness, the quality that characterised doubtful, obscure Apollo. 'Nostre entendement', he writes elsewhere, 'est double et divers, et les matieres doubles et diverses' [our understanding [...] is double and diverse, and matters are double and diverse] (III.11.1034/792). 'Doubleness' is itself an obscure characteristic, butting up against and overlapping with diversity, with figures of parallelism, contradiction and inversion, with ambiguity, and with its more nefarious shades, dubiousness and duplicity. After all, Montaigne's comparison of the mind – 'double et divers', erratic – with the shoe of Theramenes, 'bon à tous pieds' [good for either foot], is not, or at least not straightforwardly, a celebration of its varied utility so much as a joke about its yielding flexibility (III.11.1034/792). What, then, might it mean to think and write 'doubly'?

'Double et divers'

Trouillogan, Rabelais' parody of the Sceptic, provides an illuminating parallel. His response to Panurge's question – whether or not he should marry – is marked, as we might expect of a Sceptic, by 'répugnance' and 'contradiction'.[18] In the course of their conversation, Trouillogan answers Panurge's question in at least two separate moments: 'Et premierement quand Panurge luy a demandé, me doibz je marier ou non? avoit respondu: Tous les deux ensemblement: à la seconde foys avoit dict: Ne l'un ne l'aultre' [When Panurge asked him, 'Should I marry or no?' Trouillogan had first replied, 'Both together,' and then, 'Neither.'][19]

Panurge then complains that they have been speaking in 'membres mal joinctz' [ill-joined clauses] and compels them both to speak 'sans disjunctives' [without logical disjunctives] and in an 'aultre style' [different style].[20] What follows is a rapid-fire exchange in which Trouillogan shifts 'dynamically' (in the multiple senses of Sextus' *dunamis*) between positions in response to Panurge's questions. What animates this slippery character is not his self-contradiction but rather his need to contradict

---

[18] Rabelais, *Tiers livre*, in *Œuvres complètes*, ed. Mireille Huchon (Paris: Gallimard, 1994), p. 463; *Gargantua and Pantagruel*, trans. M. A. Screech (London: Penguin, 2006), p. 545. On Trouillogan and Scepticism, see Emmanuel Naya, '"Ne sceptique ne dogmatique, et tous les deux ensemble": Rabelais "on Phrontistere et escholle des pyrrhoniens"', *Etudes Rabelaisiennes*, 35 (1998), 81–129.
[19] Rabelais, *Tiers livre*, p. 462; *Gargantua and Pantagruel*, p. 544.
[20] Rabelais, *Tiers livre*, p. 463; *Gargantua and Pantagruel*, p. 546.

his interlocutor. Trouillogan, 'le Philosophe perfaict' [an accomplished philosopher], 'respond assertivement de tous doubtes proposez' [replies affirmatively to all doubts expounded to him].[21] Amid this flurry of rebuttals, and after the call for disjunctives to be dropped, it is Panurge's use of 'ou' [or] that prompts Trouillogan's most contradictory response:

> Panurge: Estez vous marié ou non?
> Trouillogan: Ne l'un ne l'aultre, & tous les deux ensemble.[22]
>
> Panurge: Are you or are you not married?
> Trouillogan: Neither one nor the other, and both together.

As George Hoffmann has shown, Trouillogan is not simply a figure of ridicule mocking the wiliness of philosophers: these chapters constitute a lesson in logic and in expression, with Trouillogan teaching Panurge that he has been formulating his questions incorrectly.[23] The problem lies in his use of conjunctions, which are 'mal joinctz': 'Estez vous marié *ou non?*' (my emphasis). The disjunctive conjunction – 'ou non?', translating the logician's 'vel' – is seized upon by Trouillogan, and it is in response to this that he produces his own problematic conjunction: 'et'. The philosopher returns almost exactly to the answers he gave at the beginning, answers that he originally gave separately, but here he ceases his dynamic flitting from one position to another. Amid all the juggling of oppositional binaries, the ampersand works against the downward pull of logic to keep both options – or rather both pairs of options: not yes and not no; yes and no – up in the air at the same time.

It is here that the difference between what Montaigne calls 'diverse' thinking and the 'doubleness' of thinking can be discerned. The 'tiers genre' 'nous presente [...] diverses raisons, sans choisir celle que nous avons à suyvre' [present us with diverse reasons, without choosing the one that we should follow].[24] Montaigne himself 'parle diversement' [speaks diversely], precisely because 'je me regarde diversement' [I see myself diversely] (II.1.335/242). 'Combien diversement', he asks, 'jugeons nous des choses? Combien de fois changeons nous nos fantasies?' [How diversely we judge things! How many times we change our notions!] (II.12.563/423). At one point, Montaigne hesitates over this keyword as he reflects on his own habit of writing: 'Joint qu'à

---

[21] Rabelais, *Tiers livre*, p. 445; *Gargantua and Pantagruel*, p. 523.
[22] Rabelais, *Tiers livre*, p. 465; *Gargantua and Pantagruel*, p. 548.
[23] George Hoffmann, '"Neither one or the other and both together"', *Tiers livre*, 35: How Scholastic Logic Can Help Explain the Marriage Question', *Etudes rabelaisiennes*, 25 (Geneva: Droz, 1991), pp. 79–90.
[24] I am here quoting *Essais* 1580, II.12.268–9. The passage was revised in the Bordeaux Copy, fol. 213r. For the revised passage in Villey-Saulnier and Frame, see II.12.509/377.

l'adventure ay-je quelque obligation particuliere à ne dire qu'à demy, à dire confusément, à dire ~~diversement~~ discordamment' [Besides, perhaps I have some personal obligation to speak only by halves, to speak confusedly, to speak ~~diversely~~ discordantly] (III.9.995–6/762).

Diversity – variety, difference, unlikeness, to take some of the definitions provided by Cotgrave – is not doubleness. Nor, for that matter, is it especially or necessarily doubtful, though Sceptical thinking depends on it. 'Diverse' thinking lies at the heart of the Sceptic's *ou mallon*, 'no more this than that', and is key also to the Pyrrhonian 'universal' or 'general mode' of presenting dynamic counterarguments. It is, as Montaigne reminds us in the 'Apologie', the technique that allowed Anaxagoras to take up such a 'monstrueux et desordonné' [monstrous and disordered] (II.12.526/391) position as to say that snow is black.[25] But it is also a technique that would have found a much less monstrous, even commonplace, reflection in the schoolboy exercise of argument *in utramque partem*.

The *Essais* record Montaigne thinking 'diversement' on every page: he considers one 'visage' of a subject, then another, then another, and so on, moving through time – the time of thinking, reading, writing – such that each position or concept or perspective is taken separately and in sequence. It is a way of thinking that maintains shifting relations with its subject, moving through these relations 'sans terme'.

But thought is not just 'sans terme' and not just 'divers'. We are double, Montaigne tells us, even as he gestures towards the strangeness of this idea and our difficulty understanding it: 'nous sommes, *je ne sçay comment*, doubles en nous mesmes, qui faict que ce que nous croyons, nous ne le croyons pas, et nous ne pouvons deffaire de ce que nous condamnons' [we are, *I know not how*, double within ourselves, with the result that we do not believe what we believe, and we cannot rid ourselves of what we condemn] (II.16.619/469, my emphasis).

Montaigne recognised this doubleness by seeing himself in another. Addressing one of Epicurus' 'principaux dogmes' [principal doctrines], 'Cache ta vie' [Conceal your life], he invites us to consider the philosopher's 'dernieres paroles' [last words], recorded in a letter to his philosophical successor, Hermarchus.[26] Montaigne judges these last

---

[25] Anaxagoras' argument is found in Sextus Empiricus, *Outlines of Pyrrhonism*, I.13.411.

[26] Montaigne's is a double translation: he is quoting from Cicero's Latin (*De finibus*, 2.30.96). Plutarch's essay on Epicurus' saying is another key source for Montaigne, though one that barely mentions Epicurus at all: indeed, it begins by making a point of not naming this teacher who recommended obscurity all while wanting to be known as the person recommending it ('Voire mais celuy mesme qui l'a dit vouloit bien que lon

words to be 'grandes et dignes d'un tel philosophe' [great and worthy of such a philosopher], but catches in them 'quelque marque de la recommendation de son nom' [a certain mark of commending his name] (II.16.619–20/469). Epicurus has broken his own rule. In the letter, which Montaigne translates, he writes that his pain is eased 'par le plaisir qu'apportoit à mon ame la souvenance de mes inventions et de mes discours' [by the pleasure which the remembrance of my discoveries and my teachings brought to my soul]. Epicurus then implores Hermarchus to honour the affection he has hitherto shown him by caring for Metrodorus' children. Montaigne teases out the subtext: Epicurus is asking his friend to make sure that his intellectual and legal heirs have sufficient funds to pay for monthly philosophical meetings in his memory, along with an annual celebration to be held on his birthday. So much for the injunction to reject glory and 'cache ta vie'. The pleasure Epicurus speaks of, the pleasure he says comes from the memory of his philosophical teachings, 'regarde aucunement la reputation qu'il en esperoit acquerir apres sa mort' [concerns the reputation that he hoped to acquire from them after his death] (II.16.620/469–70). As Cicero, Montaigne's source, puts it, this 'praiseworthy' ('laudandam') letter is Epicurus' own refutation.[27]

For Montaigne, though, this is not evidence of insincerity, of saying one thing but thinking another. It is a sign of our doubleness: Epicurus believes and thinks two things at once. Montaigne does not argue that Epicurus believed his precept about rejecting glory while healthy, and then stopped believing it when death was at hand; nor does he argue that Epicurus claimed to believe one thing while actually believing something else. Rather, 'ce que nous croyons, nous ne le croyons pas' [what we believe, we do not believe]. Our understanding ('entendement') is 'double' precisely because it is capable of thinking this *and* that, regardless of contradiction, at the same time. That doubleness is not the product of logic having gone astray: the experience of what might be called cognitive dissonance is entirely natural, entirely normal.[28]

sçeust, que c'estoit luy qui l'avoit dit: car il le disoit expressement à fin qu'il ne demourast incogneu', 'Si ce mot commun, Cache ta vie, est bien dit', *Œuvres morales et meslées*, fol. 291v).

[27] 'Ea cum summa eius philosophia nulla modo congruebat' [this is entirely inconsistent with the chief tenets of his philosophy]; 'Ita redarguitur ipse a sese' [Hence he is his own refutation] (*De finibus*, II.31.99).

[28] Montaigne's form works to reveal and capture this experience of doubleness that we might call cognitive dissonance. For a recent exploration of the ways literature interacts with cognitive dissonance, see Cave, *Live Artefacts: Literature in a Cognitive Environment*, ch. 7: 'Capturing Cognitive Dissonance', pp. 146–62. I will return to cognitive dissonance in Chapters 4 and 6.

Provided we look closely enough, we all find, in different ways, that the disjunctive 'ou' simply doesn't apply.

Montaigne's rejection of the Aristotelian principle of non-contradiction – 'it is impossible for the same attribute at once to belong and not to belong to the same thing and in the same relation' – is, as Ian Maclean has noted, 'l'abandon d'un concept rigoureux de vérité' [the abandonment of a rigorous concept of truth].[29] But it is not a rejection of truth itself, nor a *politique* equation of truth with appearance, in which the only truth that matters is the one people can be persuaded to believe. Subsequent chapters in this book will consider the potential for truth-telling given Montaigne's diagnosis of doubleness not only in himself but in us ('nous'), though it should be clear that doubleness is not a synonym for hypocrisy: Epicurus is not an actor, a fraud or a liar; he is 'double', wanting and thinking two things at once. Nor is the doubleness of thinking the same as the dynamic, antagonistic diversity of the Sceptics. The presentation of our doubleness as universal and natural makes it clear that this is no *dunamis* or *facultas*, no learned technique or practised philosophical position.

Montaigne's ability to diagnose people's doubleness is what qualifies him for a job that doesn't exist. In 'De l'experience', he imagines for himself an 'office sans nom' [an office without a name], one that would draw on his long experience of studying himself relationally, seeing himself reflected in the lives of others (III.13.1076/824).[30] In this imaginary role, he would serve as a truthful, honest counsellor to a prince, telling him his truths just as he 'uncovers' ('decouvre') his friends ('j'eusse dict ses veritez à mon maistre' [I would have told my master home truths]) (III.13.1076–7/824–5). But where 'les sçavans' [the learned] and other 'artistes' who study human nature work to find patterns, gathering 'en bandes cette infinie diversité de visages' [in bands this infinite diversity of aspects] (III.13.1076/824), Montaigne finds doubleness no matter how hard he looks:

> Non seulement je trouve mal-aisé d'attacher nos actions les unes aux autres, mais chacune à part soy je trouve mal-aysé de la designer proprement par quelque qualité principalle, tant elles sont doubles et bigarrées à divers lustres. (III.13.1076–7)

---

[29] Ian Maclean, *Montaigne philosophe* (Paris: Presses Universitaires de France, 1996), pp. 33–4, 50. The interpolated quotation is from Aristotle, *Metaphysics*, 1005b.
[30] 'Pour m'estre, dés mon enfance, dressé à mirer ma vie dans celle d'autruy, j'ay acquis une complexion studieuse en cela' [By training myself from my youth to see my own life mirrored in that of others, I have acquired a studious bent in that subject]. On this passage and its illustration of Montaigne's 'connaissance pratique de soi, orientée vers l'action' [practical knowledge of the self, oriented towards action], see Alain Legros, 'Montaigne, son livre, et son roi', *Studi francesi*, 41.2 (1997), 259–74.

> Not only do I find it hard to link our actions with one another, but each one on their own I find hard to designate properly by some principal characteristic, so double and motley do they seem in different lights. (824–5)

Doubleness is not a synonym for diversity. They are related characteristics and both essential to Montaigne's conception of himself and of human experience; but noting that we – and our infinite, diverse 'actions' and 'visages' – are 'double' distinguishes Montaigne's way of thinking from more commonplace moral assessments of human variability, inconstancy and flightiness. We are 'double' all the way down and in every moment. This doubleness is not the courtier's duplicity, nor the sophist's dubiousness, nor the diversity of parts and aspects catalogued by 'sçavans': it is, as Montaigne's invention of a new, unprecedented job suggests, something novel, something 'sans patron'.

Writing in a way that responds to our doubleness requires a new form. We might draw comparisons with rhetorical and philosophical paradoxes – with Trouillogan's 'répugnantes et contradictoires responses', for instance.[31] But writing doubly is not a skilful trick, a temporary illusion intended to correct or rebut an interlocutor. It is a way of writing that deals not in potentials (*dunamis*), but in how we really, actually, naturally think.

Writing doubly demands not just the endlessness of the 'flux de caquet' [flow of babble] (III.5.897/684) but its oozing, shapeless liquidity too.[32] It requires that outlandish conjunction used by Trouillogan: '&'. In response to Panurge, Trouillogan's '&' works ultimately to show up the sloppiness of his interlocutor's speech. It says little, if anything, of Trouillogan and what he really thinks. Beguiling in its contradiction, it marks the dizzying high point of this strange discourse, though it is not clear that anyone – least of all Panurge – learns much at all. Montaigne likewise was grappling with a *casus perplexus* ('Nous sommes, *je ne sçay comment*, doubles'), though his relationship with language couldn't be more different. It is telling that Trouillogan introduces his '&' at the moment Panurge shifts focus away from his own predicament and

---

[31] 'Repugnant' or contradictory propositions are, in Jacques Lefevre d'Estaples' definition, 'those which cannot be true together' ('simul esse non vera possunt'). See Hoffmann, 'Neither one nor the other and both together', p. 81. These are not related to the Renaissance genre of the 'paradox', in which a contrarian argument is made against prevailing *doxa*. On the word 'paradoxe' and the early modern genre of the mock encomium, see Chapter 6.

[32] On this phrase, and on excessive speech and endless talk in the *Essais* more broadly, see Emily Butterworth, '"Un flux de caquet": Excès et éthique de la parole à la Renaissance (le cas de Montaigne, "Sur des vers de Virgile")', in *Mauvaises Langues!*, ed. Florence Cabaret and Nathalie Vienne-Guerrin (Mont-Saint-Aignan: Presses des Universités de Rouen et du Havre, 2013), pp. 327–40.

asks the philosopher about himself. Trouillogan tells us nothing. In the *Essais*, by contrast, it is in writing doubly that Montaigne attempts to reveal himself as he is and communicate his mercurial spirit in all of its vitality.

Detached Pieces: Senecan and Plutarchan Forms of Irresolution

Montaigne identified in Seneca and Plutarch two distinct forms of unresolved writing: ways of writing that express the movement and diversity of thought without freezing it, without pinning it down. But the *Essais* do not reproduce these old styles: Montaigne remakes his models – his 'patrons' – as he thinks and writes with them. It is in relation to these modes of writing, disarticulated and reformed, that his own practice of writing doubly takes shape.

Plutarchan Perspectives

Plutarch's style, in Montaigne's account, might best be characterised as a way of studying diverse perspectives, revealing different, even contradictory aspects of the same thing by reading and judging 'à pieces décousues' [by detached pieces] (II.10.413/300). Consider the example of Charilaus, king of Sparta, whom Montaigne takes as a mirror (albeit a rather grand one) for himself. On a number of occasions, Plutarch notes how Charilaus, praised as an 'homme fort doulx et debonnaire' [most gentle and courteous man], was criticised for his goodness: as Montaigne puts it, 'Il ne sçauroit estre bon, puisqu'il n'est pas mauvais aux meschants' [He could not possibly be good, since he is not bad to the wicked] (III.12.1063/814).[33] And yet elsewhere, Plutarch presents the opposite case: 'Et comment ne seroit il bon, dit il, quand il ne sçauroit estre mauvais non pas aux meschans mesmes?' [And how could he not be good, he said, since he cannot be bad even to the wicked?][34] Charilaus, like Montaigne, is characterised by doubleness, double in

---

[33] For Charilaus as 'homme fort doulx et debonnaire', see 'Les Dicts notables des Lacedemoniens', fol. 215r. Compare Plutarch's version (in Amyot's translation) of the judgement paraphrased by Montaigne: 'Et comment seroit il bon, quand il n'est pas mauvais aux meschans?' For near-identical versions of this saying, see 'Comment on peut discerner le flatteur d'avecq l'amy', fol. 44r, and 'De l'envie et de la haine', fol. 108r.
[34] 'Lycurgus', *Vies des hommes illustres*, fol. 29r. Compare Montaigne's version: 'il faut bien qu'il soit bon, puisqu'il l'est aux meschants mesme' [He must certainly be good, since he is good even to the wicked] (III.12.1063/814).

a way similar to but not quite the same as Epicurus: double not in having competing, contradictory thoughts or feelings but double in our judgement of him. Plutarch approaches this doubleness by presenting different perspectives: 'Plutarque le presente en ces deux visages sortes, comme mille autres choses, diversement et contrairement' [Plutarch presents it in these two ways, as he does a thousand other things, diversely and contrarily] (III.12.1063/814).[35]

In the 'Apologie', Montaigne highlighted the exception that proves the rule. Some people, he notes, think that devils have their origin in the souls of the damned, while 'Plutarque pense qu'il se face des dieux de celles qui sont sauvées' [Plutarch thinks that gods are made of those that are saved]. Plutarch's boldness, his certainty and assurance in this matter, is remarkably uncharacteristic: he is usually so moderate and restrained ('des plus retenus pourtant et moderez de la bande'):

> il est peu de choses que cet autheur là establisse d'une façon de parler si resolue qu'il faict cette-cy, maintenant par tout ailleurs une maniere dubitatrice et ambigue. (II.12.556)
>
> there are few things that that author asserts in such decisive words as he does this, maintaining everywhere else a doubting and ambiguous manner. (417)

Notably, it is as this point in the 'Apologie' that Montaigne is doing precisely what Plutarch typically does and what Plutarch does not do in this instance: he is compiling a lengthy doxography, a list of different opinions, on 'le subject de nostre ame' (II.12.554–6). Surveying the diversity of approaches to this abstruse topic, Montaigne is miming the habits he identified with Plutarch earlier in the chapter, providing his reader with 'causes contraires de mesme subject et diverses raisons, sans choisir celle que nous avons à suivre' [contrary causes for the same subject and diverse reasons, without choosing which we have to follow].[36]

But Plutarch's writing is not just a survey of different opinions. The work of this 'maistre ouvrier' [master workman] is deft rather than laborious or exhaustive, and, while it might be full of 'discours estandus, tres-dignes d'estre sceus' [extensive discussions, well worth knowing], what captures Montaigne's attention is Plutarch's ability to point to a seemingly endless supply of routes one might take and perspectives one might consider:

---

[35] Translation modified. Frame translates 'diversement et contrairement' as 'variously and contrastingly'.
[36] *Essais* 1580, II.12.568–9. For the revised version of this passage in Villey-Saulnier and Frame, see II.12.509/377.

> il y en a mille qu'il n'a que touché simplement: il guigne seulement du doigt par où nous irons, s'il nous plaist, et se contente quelquefois de ne donner qu'une attainte dans le plus vif d'un propos. (I.26.156)
>
> there are a thousand that he has only just touched on; he merely points out with his finger where we are to go, if we like, and sometimes is content to make only a stab at the heart of a subject. (115)

Gesturing in this way, Plutarch leaves his work open and invites his reader to take up where he left off. Indeed, Montaigne imagines himself not only continuing Plutarch's work but working alongside him, looking at what he looked at and seeing it differently, from another perspective: 'J'ay leu en Tite-Live cent choses que tel n'y a pas leu. Plutarque en y a leu cent, outre ce que j'y ay sceu lire, et, à l'adventure, outre ce que l'autheur y avoit mis' [I have read in Livy a hundred things that another man has not read in him. Plutarch has read in him a hundred besides the ones I could read, and perhaps besides what the author had put in] (I.26.156/115). In Montaigne's account, then, the defining quality of Plutarch's writing, that 'livre solide' from which he draws with his leaky colander, is its 'genereux' production of an endlessly diverse way of seeing things.

Diversity takes many forms in Plutarch's writing. Some of his opuscules are explicitly doxographic, such as 'Les Opinions des philosophes', while his dialogues have a tendency to wander. The discussion of the inscription at the Temple of Apollo in Delphi finds a number of dead ends before reaching the conclusion that would end up in Montaigne's 'Apologie', while the dialogue on Socrates' 'daemon' is, as Montaigne puts it, 'tout estouffé en matière estrangere' [quite smothered in foreign matter] (III.9.994/761). But Plutarch's manner of writing 'diversely', from different perspectives, is not limited only to dialogues, doxographic surveys and other similarly multivocal genres. 'Du premier froid', for instance, is a work of natural philosophy written with a single, unified voice that nonetheless provides a clear model of doubtful (perhaps specifically Sceptical) irresolution. If the first principal of heat ('la premiere puissance du chaud') is fire, then what, asks Plutarch, is the 'premier froid' [principle of cold]?[37] Plutarch argues first that it is air, then water, and finally earth, before providing a brief conclusion that is, in fact, not a conclusion at all:

> Compare [...] ces arguments la avec les raisons des autres, & si tu trouves que les unes ne cedent ny ne surpassent gueres les autres en probable verissimilitude, laisse moy là l'opiniastreté d'espouser aucunes particulieres opinions,

---

[37] Plutarch, 'Du premier froid', fol. 529r.

estimant que le surseoir et retenir son jugement en choses obscures & incertaines, est fait en plus sage philosophe, que non pas de prester & adjuster à l'une ou à l'autre partie son consentement.[38]

Compare [...] these arguments with the reasons given by others, and if you find they neither yield to nor overcome those others in probability, abandon the stubbornness of espousing any particular view, and consider that to suspend and withhold one's judgement in obscure and uncertain matters, rather than offering one's support to one party or another, makes for a wiser philosopher.

As in his surveys and dialogues, Plutarch writes in a way that is unresolved, exploratory and doubtful.[39] In Sceptical terms, he practises *epoché* (the suspension of judgement) and identifies *isostheneia* (the equilibrium of arguments of equal strength): he presents his various arguments separately and in sequence before announcing his uncertainty and challenging the reader to see things differently.

'Hic et nunc' in Seneca's Letters

To identify Seneca as a writer whose work is 'unresolved' or 'diverse', let alone doubtful, would seem to fly in the face of all evidence. He has a habit, as Montaigne notes, of hectoring his reader, hammering home the same old talking points time and again:

Je me desplais de l'inculcation, voire aux choses utiles, comme en Seneque, et l'usage de son escole stoïque me desplait, de redire sur chaque matiere tout au long et au large les principes et presuppositions qui servent en general, et realleguer tousjours de nouveau les argumens et raisons communes et universelles. (III.9.962)

I dislike inculcation, even of useful things, as in Seneca, and I dislike the practice of his Stoical school of repeating, in connection with every subject, in full length and breadth, the principles and premises for general use, and restating ever anew their common and universal arguments and reasons. (734–5)

---

[38] Ibid., fol. 534v.
[39] Noting that it 'consists of a debate marshalled along overtly sceptical lines', George Boys-Stones has argued for a more nuanced approach to the 'scepticism' of this text, suggesting that 'this interpretation glosses over too quickly what Plutarch actually says [...] [H]e says that *if* no one position emerges as more plausible than the others [...] *then* we should consider the matter unclear and suspend judgement.' See George Boys-Stones, 'Plutarch and the Probable Principle of Cold: Epistemology and the *De Primo Frigido*', *The Classical Quarterly*, 47 (1997), 227–38 (pp. 227–8). Jan Opsomer has identified a similar practice in Plutarch's *Questions Platoniciennes*. See Jan Opsomer, 'Arguments non linéaires et pensée en cercles: forme et argumentation dans les *Questions Platoniciennes* de Plutarque', in *Les Dialogues platoniciens chez Plutarque*, ed. X. Brouillette and A. Giavatto (Leuven: Leuven University Press, 2011), pp. 93–116 (p. 114).

And yet the letters in particular, which constantly retread the same path, provided Montaigne with a model for thinking about diversity. In letter writing, and especially the genre of the philosophical letter, Montaigne found a form of writing irresolution that hinged not on shifting opinions but on time.

Montaigne describes Plutarch's 'manière' in much more detail and much more explicitly than he describes the style of Seneca. But we can join up the dots, seeing what he says about Seneca, what he writes about the epistolary form, and how his views on these fit together. His comments on his own letter-writing habits have typically been read as a sprezzatura-laden expression of anti-Ciceronianism and a rejection of flattering sycophancy and its concomitant obligations.[40] 'J'escris mes lettres tousjours en poste' [I always write my letters poste-haste], he boasts, 'si precipiteusement' [so precipitously] that even 'les grands' with whom he maintains a correspondence have learned to put up with letters covered in 'litures' [scratchings] and 'trassures' [crossings out] (I.40.253/186). His hasty scribbling is itself a clear signal of his frank countenance, his disregard for 'paroles courteoises' in favour of an anti-artificial, natural aesthetic.

> Je commence volontiers sans project; le premier traict produict le second [...] Comme j'ayme mieux composer deux lettres que d'en clorre et plier une, et resigne tousjours cette commission à quelque autre: de mesme, quand la matiere est achevée, je donrois volontiers à quelqu'un la charge d'y adjouster ces longues harengues, offres et prieres que nous logeons sur la fin. (I.40.253–4)
>
> I begin without a plan; the first remark brings on the second [...] Just as I would rather compose two letters than close and fold one and always resign that job to someone else; so, when the substance is finished, I would gladly give someone else the charge of adding those long harangues, offers, and prayers that we place at the end. (186–7)

Montaigne places letter writing within a temporal framework: he writes quickly, throwing himself precipitously into the act of writing; his hurried hand bears the trace of the elliptical progression of thought

---

[40] Eric MacPhail, for instance, considers the anti-Ciceronianism of I.40 'part of a larger challenge to the prevailing values of rhetorical humanism'; Eric MacPhail, 'Montaigne and the Theatre of Conscience', *French Studies*, 68.4, (2014), 465–76 (p. 465). Natalie Zemon Davis has sited Montaigne's 'unwillingness even to write in the prostituted language of courtesy and compliments' within a broader cultural anxiety concerning gift-giving. See Natalie Zemon Davis, *The Gift in Sixteenth-Century France* (Madison: University of Wisconsin Press, 2000), pp. 74–5. See also Michel Magnien, 'Montaigne (re)lecteur des *Tusculanes*', in *La Librairie de Montaigne*, ed. Philip Ford and Neil Kenny (Cambridge: Cambridge French Colloquia, 2012), pp. 157–82.

and writing, falling back in on itself as he composes his text. He begins without a plan, allowing composition and thought to develop as one. This is an engaged mode of writing, a way of writing in the here and now, and it is one that is conceived as presence: as soon as the writing starts to drag ('depuis que je les traine'), 'c'est signe que je n'y suis pas' [it is a sign that I am not there].[41]

Letter writing is temporally *fixed*. It is not just that letter writing takes place in time. Rather, what distinguishes the epistle from other types of writing is that it is tied to distinct and discrete compositional moments. Letter writing, as Montaigne sees it at least, is so temporally fixed that he struggles to shift from writing in and for a specific moment to the more formulaic material that he would rather delegate to someone else – the 'longues harengues, offres et prieres' that could be written by anyone, to anyone, at any time. He would rather write two letters than 'close and fold' one – a 'closing up' that is figurative but also literal and material (a necessary part of epistolography before the advent of the envelope). That association of signing off and sealing up demonstrates Montaigne's point: there is a difference between epistolography proper (writing in the moment) and the formulaic activities, textual and material, that enclose it.

Montaigne's approach to letter writing is, in his view, 'bien loing de l'usage present' [very far from current practice] (I.40.253/186). Under the title of this chapter, 'Consideration sur Cicéron', he is inviting his reader to recognise the gulf between, on the one hand, his own 'old-fashioned' style, which does without the fireworks of Ciceronianism, and, on the other, letters that weigh their words carefully, letters that conceal their motives. At the same time, it is a claim that draws a line connecting old-fashioned Montaigne and that other great model of Latin epistolography, Seneca's *Epistulae ad Lucilium*. The preceding chapter sets up and encourages this comparison: it centres on a discussion of two pairs of letter writers – Cicero and Pliny; Seneca and Epicurus.[42]

---

[41] Presence has long been recognised as a motif in early modern reflections on writing (see, for example, Defaux, *Marot, Rabelais, Montaigne: L'Écriture comme présence*) though Nathalie Oddy's recent study has shown how Montaigne's understanding of this notion is illuminated by cognitive approaches to literature. See Nathalie Oddy, 'Presence of Mind: Consubstantiality and Extended Cognition in Montaigne's *Essais*', unpublished DPhil dissertation, University of Oxford, 2022.

[42] On this comparison of pairs, see O'Sullivan, '"Un traict à la comparaison de ces couples"', pp. 223–42. On the relationships between Epicurus' and Seneca's letter writing, see Brad Inwood, 'The Importance of Form in Seneca's Philosophical Letters', in *Ancient Letters: Classical and Late Antique Epistolography*, ed. A. D. Morrison and Ruth Morello (Oxford: Oxford University Press, 2007), pp. 133–48, and Tischer, '*Nostra faciamus*: Quoting in Horace and Seneca', pp. 292–313.

Montaigne's letter writing is presented, then, not only as anti-Ciceronian but, implicitly, as Senecan: as frank, direct, practical, without ceremony or flattery, written in and for the moment, addressing present concerns.

Seneca and letter writing are discussed again in the conclusion to 'De trois bonnes femmes' (II.35). Here, Montaigne translates at length Seneca's 104th epistle and, in introducing this letter, further emphasises the temporal and spatial grounding – the presence of the here and now – characteristic of this 'usage ancien':

> En l'une des lettres qu'il escrit à Lucilius, apres qu'il luy a fait entendre comme, la fiebvre l'ayant pris à Rome, il monta soudain en coche pour s'en aller à une sienne maison aux champs, contre l'opinion de sa femme qui le vouloit arrester, et qu'il luy avoit respondu que la fiebvre qu'il avoit, ce n'estoit pas fiebvre du corps, mais du lieu, il suit ainsin[.] (II.35.750)

> In one of the letters he writes to Lucilius, after giving him to understand that since he had been seized by fever in Rome, he promptly got in a coach to go off to a house of his in the country, against the advice of his wife, who wanted to stop him; and that he had replied to her that the fever he had was not a fever of the body but of the place, he goes on thus[.] (568)

In the 'excellens' words that Montaigne proceeds to translate, Seneca expresses his affection for Paulina and resolves to live not for his own sake but for hers, worrying not 'combien resoluement je pourrois mourir' [with how much resoluteness I could die] but 'combien irresoluement elle le pourroit souffrir' [with how little resoluteness she could bear my death]: 'Ainsi ma Pauline m'a chargé non seulement sa crainte, mais encore la mienne' [Thus my Paulina has given me not only her fear to bear, but also my own] (II.35.750/568–9). Notably, this extended translation of Seneca's commitment to living is included as a parallel, a double, to the account of double suicide (Seneca's being successful, Paulina's not, though no less virtuous for that) which Montaigne takes as the third of his 'contes' in this chapter detailing 'trois bonnes femmes' (II.35.747–9/566–7). Seneca's paradoxical affirmation that 'c'est quelquefois magnanimité que vivre' [it is sometimes magnanimity to live] (II.35.750/569) is, like the more famous combination of speech, action and will that emerges in his suicide, a 'dict', a notable saying, that must be situated within its 'histoire' for it to have any weight.

This 'tesmoignage de grandeur de courage' recorded in Seneca's letter and translated by Montaigne must be read, as the essayist's framing makes clear, in its temporal context. Seneca writes in and for the moment: despite the tendency towards repetition and 'inculcation', each letter is fixed to a historical point, a moment of writing, and could not have been written at any other time.

The philosophical epistle – at least as it is found in Seneca – is an occasional genre. Seneca and his school might have a habit of restating, 'tousjours de nouveau, les argumens et raisons communes et universelles' [ever anew their common and universal arguments and reasons] (III.9.962/734–5), but each letter restates the case from a fixed temporal moment. This temporal fixity lies at the heart of the relationship between Seneca's epistles and Montaigne's *Essais*.

It is a point of connection that runs parallel with – if not against – a more familiar view that sees Seneca's epistles as proto-essays. As Marcus Wilson has noted, the claim that the *Epistles* are 'really essays' is a 'reclassification' that has had a 'remarkably good run', and one that might be explained by their having been 'gratuitously endowed with Baconian titles' and thus processed 'for modern (or at least mid-twentieth century) consumption'. The result, Wilson argues, is that they are 'converted into the genre they are said to resemble'.[43] The problem with this conversion is that it 'discourages the reading of the collection sequentially':

> Each new epistle resituates the author differently in a new time, a new mood, sometimes in a new place. Neither the author's self nor the context in which he writes is fixed. He offers a record of his temporary accords with the world and, as it were, rediscovers his philosophy through different situations.[44]

Seneca's epistolography is unresolved in its tracking of the linear and sequential progression of time: whatever might be said in one letter can always be reconsidered in the one that follows. This combination of temporal and temporary writing shapes what Bernard Sève has seen as Montaigne's great innovation, the 'temporalisation' not of a given opinion or description – opinions change, and so does the world – but of philosophical discourse itself.[45] In tying philosophy to the here and now, Seneca provided Montaigne with a means of replacing the timeless, impersonal and reproducible functions of philosophical argument with something more fluid. In the *Essais* (which, to be clear, are no more 'really epistles' than the *Epistles* are essays, though in this they are similar), philosophy must be done again and again. What distinguishes

---

[43] Marcus Wilson, 'Seneca's Epistles Reclassified', in *Texts, Ideas, and the Classics*, ed. S. J. Harrison (Oxford: Oxford University Press, 2001), pp. 164–87 (pp. 164–5).
[44] Ibid., pp. 167–8.
[45] Sève, *Montaigne: des règles pour l'esprit*, p. 293. See also Maclean, *Montaigne philosophe*, pp. 34, 55. As Maclean has shown, conventional Scholastic philosophy employs temporal markers to resolve contradictions – the contradiction 'Peter is prodigal', 'Peter is not prodigal' is resolved by time (Peter is prodigal in the morning, a miser in the evening) – though this temporality is situated within the world being described and not in the atemporal, logical operations of philosophical discourse.

the *Essais* from the *Epistles* is that, with Montaigne, one does not always find the same answers, the same 'argumens et raisons communes et universelles', even when one asks the same questions.

Seneca's *Epistles* modelled for Montaigne a way of writing philosophy not in the *semper et ubique* of the Scholastic treatise – timeless, impersonal, reproducible – but in the *hic et nunc* of daily life. They illustrate a way of writing philosophy capable of change and progression across time.[46] Indeed, as a collection of letters advocating day-to-day Stoic labour, tracing the work of 'Seneca proficiens' and his apprentice, the *Epistulae* seem as much a journal and record of *ars vivendi*, the art of living, as a guide or textbook. Moving through the letters is to move through time and, in doing so, to see the multiple facets of the subjects and ideas discussed within. The letter is particularly suited to this sort of philosophical project. As A. D. Morrison and Ruth Morello have noted, letters – usually used to deliver news – have a 'sense of urgency', 'a sense of development and change': 'Ethics needs to be done every day – hence letters.'[47] With a letter, Seneca can say one thing today and something else tomorrow: his writing is always unresolved, constantly awaiting the next temporary instalment in the sequence.

The reframing of the *Epistles* as proto-essays obscures the importance of this chronological sequence. Nearly every letter begins by announcing the event that occasioned it, locating the act of writing – along with the ideas and opinions it expresses – in space and time.[48] As Wilson argues, Seneca's letters 'don't carry dates', but much of their effect 'depends on their sequence'.[49] This temporal and temporary fixity is the key to Seneca's form, and we might follow Wilson in reconceiving the *Epistles*

---

[46] This is not to say, however, that Seneca's philosophy does change substantially but simply that his form stands as an exemplar to Montaigne of a philosophical discourse capable of writing change and philosophical 'movement'.

[47] 'Editors' Preface', in Morrison and Morello (eds), *Ancient Letters*, p. ix.

[48] Consider the following examples which locate each letter variously with reference to the time of year, local events, personal events and so on: 'December est mensis; cum maxime civitas sudat' [It is the month of December, and yet the city is at this very moment in a sweat] (*Ep.* 28.1); 'Sollicitum esse te scribis de iudicii eventu, quod tibi furor inimici denuntiat, existimas me suasurum, ut meliora tibi ipse proponas et adquiescas spei blandae' [You write me that you are anxious about the result of a lawsuit, with which an angry opponent is threatening you; and you expect me to advise you to picture to yourself a happier issue, and to rest in the allurements of hope] (*Ep.* 24.1); 'Librum tuum, quem mihi promiseras, accepi et tamquam lecturus ex commodo adaperui ac tantum degustare volui' [I received the book of yours which you promised me. I opened it hastily with the idea of glancing over it at leisure; for I meant only to taste the volume] (*Ep.* 46.1); 'Moleste fero decessisse Flaccum, amicum tuum, plus tamen aequo dolere te nolo' [I am grieved to hear that your friend Flaccus is dead, but I would not have you sorrow more than is fitting] (*Ep.* 63.1).

[49] Wilson, 'Seneca's Epistles Reclassified', p. 184.

not as proto-essays, nor as miniature moral dialogues ('the "dialogue" model') but as 'serial epistolography'.⁵⁰

Unlike Plutarch, Seneca does not present the reader with diversity of opinion – his message is typically constant and steadfast – but rather with multiple moments, snapshots of his perspective and place in time. The philosophical letter as it is found in Seneca can always be modified, contradicted or supplemented by the one that follows: it is fixed to the moment, but in being fixed, unbinds the philosophical project and permits a range of different and even competing perspectives to be maintained across time. As Seneca's editor (and Montaigne's correspondent) Justus Lipsius put it, letters should flow freely, keeping up with the flow of time: 'bis non scribo, bis vix eas lego' [I do not rewrite them, and I hardly re-read them]. His point was that letters should be written without affectation – a point that Montaigne made too, when boasting of his bad handwriting – though the liquid metaphor that follows points to an affinity between this form and its all-but-unformed matter: 'Profluunt mihi ex liquido quodam canali aperti pectoris: et ut animus aut corpus meum est cum scribo, ita illae' [They pour forth from me out of some flowing channel of my open heart, and however my spirit or my body is while I am writing, so are my letters].⁵¹

In only writing 'once', the letter writer puts afterthoughts, reviews and reservations in the letter still to be written: the chronology of thought becomes the chronology of writing and, in returning as Seneca does to his central ideas, the letter writer does write 'twice', but separately. It is a form that ties thought and writing to the here and now in a series of individual testaments, fixed temporally and temporarily. But reading them in context and reading them together, they are infinitely diverse, looking again and again from different perspectives in an endless series of 'décousus' textual moments.

Seneca and Plutarch: Generic Models?

Focusing on Montaigne's comment that he would have 'prins plus volontiers ceste forme' – the epistle – 'à publier mes verves, si j'eusse eu à qui parler' [preferred to adopt this form to publish my sallies, if I had had someone to talk to] (I.40.252/185–6), there has been a tendency to suggest that the *Essais* take the Senecan epistle and make it 'Plutarchan'

---

⁵⁰ Ibid., p. 185.
⁵¹ *Justii Lipsii Epistolarum selectarum centuria prima* (Antwerp: Plantin, 1586), fol. *5v.

in the absence of an addressee.⁵² This reading, which goes back at least as far as Friedrich's influential study, has focused on the epistle's dialogic qualities to the exclusion of other salient features: its situation in time; its ability to construct and maintain different perspectives.⁵³ Seneca's letters are important to Montaigne not simply because they are addressed to an individual, engaged in informal dialogue, and not only as an early model destined to be marginalised as Montaigne found his voice (his late inclusion alongside Plutarch as a key author among the 'tiers genre' makes abundantly clear his continued importance). In Seneca's philosophical letters, Montaigne found a guide, a model for philosophical writing made up of 'diverses pieces' [disparate pieces] set down 'à diverses poses' [at diverse interruptions] (II.37.758/574).

This reframing of Seneca and Plutarch has so far been concerned with drawing out the latent irresolution of their ways of writing. It is a quality not typically associated with either author: Seneca is usually seen to be constant in his teaching of *constantia*, and while Plutarch might be known for his parallels, they end in a *synchresis* that pulls everything together. It is Montaigne's reading of these authors that uncovers their unexpected inclination towards diversity and open-endedness. But to return to the account of the 'esprit genereux', along with the question of how writing might communicate it, the sort of unresolved writing seen in Seneca and Plutarch – 'sans terme' in its survey of diverse perspectives – seems incapable of grasping thought's doubleness. In both cases, the single epistle or isolated 'opinion' is dogmatic rather than doubtful: theirs is a 'forme d'escrire douteuse' made up of 'cadances dogmatistes' (II.12.509/377). For all their irresolution, these doubtful dogmatists present their 'divers visages' one at a time. It is in the reading, in the movement between these moments, that their doubtfulness emerges.

Montaigne's commerce with these forms goes beyond a straightforward combination of Senecan temporality with Plutarchan perspectives. Central to the *Essais* and their distinct mode of forming thought is the disruption of their linear, serial ways of writing. 'Ils ont tous deux', he wrote, 'cette notable commodité pour mon humeur, que la science que j'y cherche, y est traictée à pieces décousues' [They both have this notable advantage for my humour, that the knowledge I seek is there

---

⁵² See, for instance, Alain Legros, 'Autant la forme que la substance', *Montaigne Studies*, 26 (2014), 79–86 (p. 83).
⁵³ Hugo Friedrich, *Montaigne*, trans. Robert Rovini (Paris: Gallimard, 1968), pp. 368–75. See also Richard Sayce, *The Essays of Montaigne: A Critical Exploration* (London: Weidenfeld and Nicolson, 1972), p. 263. More recently, see the preface to the 2009 Gallimard edition of the *Essais* edited by Emmanuel Naya, Delphine Reguig and Alexandre Tarrête: 'son livre est comme une correspondance sans correspondent' (p. 13).

treated in detached pieces] (II.10.413/300). These detached pieces, like the 'marqueterie' of the *Essais*, are predisposed to a certain leakiness. But it is the leakiness that allows Montaigne to catch hold of his subject, grasping loosely the shapeless patterns of the 'esprit' he hoped to communicate. In the *Essais*, Senecan and Plutarchan modes of irresolution are collapsed and transposed, giving depth to linear irresolution: in Montaigne's hands, the habit of writing 'à pieces décousues' becomes a habit of overlaying perspectives and moments in time. This, I suggest, constitutes a new mode of thinking about doubt, in which irresolution is conceived not as a suspension of judgement nor as an ongoing enquiry, but as a natural condition of thinking in doubles. Reworking Seneca and Plutarch to capture thought's doubleness, Montaigne found a form fit for thinking in.

Transposing 'chronologie'

Montaigne's declaration that his book is 'tousjours un' [always one] makes up some of the most famous lines of the *Essais*. In a particularly scrappy moment of redaction and revision, the sentences that follow this claim look to reconcile the clear assertion of unity with the 'marqueterie mal jointe' of a book written in disconnected snatches – a book whose 'premiere impression forme' [first edition form] was increasingly supplemented with additional 'surpoids' [overweights] (III.9.964/736).

Montaigne's concerns, to begin with at least, are commercial, reassuring 'les imprimeurs' ('printers', crossed out in the Bordeaux Copy) and 'l'acheteur' [the buyer] that they will not leave empty-handed should they pick up a new edition of the always singular book.[54] But his focus then turns to something else: 'la chronologie', the only instance of this word in the *Essais*. Anachronism is clearly something that troubles Montaigne or, at least, something that he expects will trouble his reader. The 'litures' and 'trassures' that cover this page in the Bordeaux Copy demonstrate his difficulty in setting things straight. A first attempt – 'Et en peut avenir que la chronologie se trouble' [And it might happen that the chronology is muddled] – is replaced with a second and then a third,

---

[54] George Hoffmann's argument in *Montaigne's Career* (Oxford: Clarendon Press, 1998) that the additions were required to renew the *privilege* and were thus commercially motivated does not account for the systematic revision of punctuation. André Tournon has suggested that these minor edits are to be seen within the established, codified practice of 'profération', whereby a legal scribe updates and reaffirms a written account. See Tournon, 'Les Marques de profération dans les *Essais*', pp. 163–72.

each expressing the point in similar terms.⁵⁵ Eventually, he settled on a version that went further: his disordered, achronological writing is not only to be excused; it is to be expected. Writing achronologically does not place Montaigne outside time. Quite the opposite: 'De là toutesfois il adviendra facilement qu'il s'y mesle quelque transposition de chronologie, mes contes prenans place selon leur opportunité, non tousjours selon leur aage' [Thence, however, it will easily happen that some transposition of chronology may slip in, for my stories take their place according to their timeliness, not always according to their age].

In the printed text that follows but which, in terms of compositional chronology, came before, Montaigne notes that his refusal to correct his earlier work stems from a fear of losing something good ('je crains de perdre au change' [I fear to lose by the change]), since there is no guarantee that his understanding improves with time: '[B]mon entendement ne va pas tousjours avant, il va à reculons aussi' [my understanding does not always go forwards, it goes backwards too]. But the addition made in the margins, discussing his habit of overwriting and the 'transposition de chronologie', effects its own change. It recasts the humility topos as a reflection on the spatial wandering of thought through the space and temporalities afforded by the book: sometimes his mind skips back a page or two, or jumps from one end of the book to the other, not always forwards, but backwards too.

Another passage, again involving a post-1588 revision to a comment on his reluctance to 'correct' himself, seems to confirm this shift in (or duplication of) meaning. He often fails to grasp '[B]l'air de ma premiere imagination' [the sense of my first thought], he notes, and just as often scolds himself for correcting and inserting 'un nouveau sens' in place of 'le premier, qui valloit mieux' [the first one, which was better] (II.12.566/425–6). '[B]Je ne fay qu'aller et venir: mon jugement ne ~~va~~ [C]tire [B]pas tousjours ~~en mieux~~ [C]avant, [B]il ~~va flottant et roulant~~ [C]flotte, il vague' [I do nothing more than come and go: my judgement does not always go ~~better~~ forwards, it ~~goes floating and rolling~~ floats, it strays]. What was in 1588 a comment on the improvement, the linear progression (or otherwise) of his capacity for judgement, becomes, in light of these later interventions, a spatial image of thinking as double. Thinking, as Montaigne conceives it, does not just march along a path stretching from ignorance to understanding. It wanders back and forth across the space of the material text and the timeline of its composition.

---

⁵⁵ 'Par où il s'y pourra trouver quelque transposition de chronologie' [From which might be found some transposition of the chronology]; 'D'où il y peut eschoir quelque praeoccupation de chronology' [From which might emerge some trouble with the chronology].

Both thinking and writing go backwards as well as forwards, moving across the text and jumping back in time to consider again a thought from years earlier. It is the singular book that supports and makes legible these movements. Montaigne's material, compositional practices both trace and make possible his elliptical thinking, this habit of thinking across temporal moments and taking a second look from a different perspective.

Alongside an increasingly spatial conception of how thought and understanding move, there is a related shift in thinking about the double (or plural) temporalities of the activity of writing. This also is seen most clearly in revisions made in the Bordeaux Copy. Montaigne's discussion of his 'transpositions de chronologie' was a manuscript addition to a printed passage that was already concerned with the temporal composition of his book. It is in the printed text that he excuses himself and entreats his reader to 'laisse [...] courir encore ce coup d'essay et ce troisieme allongeail' [let this essay and this third extension run on] (III.9.963/736).[56] If his thought were only to go 'avant' and never 'à reculons', we might expect his third book to be followed by a fourth, a fifth, a sixth – to follow the pattern of a private diary or 'registre', or to follow the advice Montaigne gives to others: to start up afresh and write new thoughts elsewhere ('Qu'il die, s'il peut, mieux ailleurs') or to think before rushing to print ('Qu'ils pensent bien avant que de se produire'). Such a pattern would no doubt better serve to track the daily work of thought and judgement just as Seneca's serial epistolography recorded his.

'[A]Ce fagotage de tant de diverses pieces', Montaigne writes, 's'est basty à diverses poses et intervalles' [This bundle of so many disparate parts [...] is built up with diverse interruptions and intervals]. The activity of writing is tied to the activity of thinking so that he might 'representer le progrez de mes humeurs' [represent the course of my humours] and, in tracing this progress, 'reconnoistre le trein de mes mutations' [trace the course of my mutations] (II.37.758/574). But this account of the relationship between time and essaying, so familiar to readers of the *Essais*, is yet another instance in which a serial, linear conception of thought's movement is supplanted with a sense – spatial, imagined as an object of perception – that thought is prone to doubling. That shift from

---

[56] It is unclear as to what exactly constitutes this 'troisieme allongeail': the third book is surely the *first* 'allongeail' and is, in any case, not obviously analogous to the process of addition practised upon the first two books. The 1588 edition, where this phrase was introduced, was the third printed edition (after 1580 and 1582, both printed by Simon Millanges in Bordeaux), though a third edition would be a *second* 'allongeail'. On this, see André Tournon, *Essais de Montaigne, Livre III* (Paris: Atlande, 2002), pp. 21–4.

open-endedness to doubleness is one that takes hold as the chronology of the *Essais* becomes ever more transposed. Montaigne's account of gathering up his bundle of diverse pieces was first printed in the 1580 edition and, while he no doubt revised his work before publication, his use of the 'fagotage' metaphor has more to do with humility than with justifying (or excusing) a work that is patently disordered. Montaigne's edits and revisions were at this stage a private affair and, in presenting his work as a disparate bundle, he asks us to accept the *Essais* as a collection of thoughts accumulated over the years. They are unworked, unpolished, unfinished; simple reflections (rather than a planned-out treatise) recorded on different topics and now brought to the printer to be sent out into the world. Diverse, certainly, and the product of nearly a decade's worth of private study, but chronologically and compositionally all rather straightforward.[57]

Montaigne goes on to note that he chooses not to correct '[A]mes premieres imaginations par les secondes' [my first imaginings by my second] (II.37.758/574). This claim, which is itself corrected in the Bordeaux Copy (fol. 327v), was, in 1580 at least, one entirely in keeping with Lipsius' summary of letter writing: 'bis non scribo, bis vix eas lego' [I do not rewrite them, and I hardly re-read them]. It is only once these 'imaginations' are placed in order that the image of the 'fagotage' takes on a different sense, no longer evoking merely an ever-growing, unordered bundle but a disordered one. That sense of disorder depends on the publication of the *Essais* and its subsequent revision; it depends on Montaigne returning to the printed book and overwriting it; it depends on the interaction between Montaigne as reader and Montaigne as author, between print and manuscript, between then and now.[58] It is by disrupting and disordering the *Essais* that Montaigne

---

[57] It is in this light that we might consider a chapter with almost no 'transposition de chronologie': 'Observations sur les moyens de faire la guerre de Julius Caesar' (II.34). Montaigne inserted a number of Latin verse quotations in the 1588 edition and added two passages in the Bordeaux Copy, but this chapter is otherwise tied to a specific moment of writing prompted by his reading of Caesar in spring 1578. As he notes at the head of the chapter, 'Je veux icy enregistrer certains traicts particuliers et rares, sur le faict de ses guerres, qui me sont demeurez en memoire' [I want to record here certain individual and unusual features, on the subject of his wars, that have remained in my memory] (II.34.736/556). For Montaigne's marginal comments in his edition of Caesar, see Legros, *Montaigne manuscrit*, pp. 489–620. On the relationship between Montaigne's private notes on Caesar and the 'print version' published in this chapter of the *Essais*, see John O'Brien, 'All Outward and On Show: Montaigne's External Glosses', in *Self-Commentary in Early Modern European Literature, 1400–1700*, ed. Francesco Venturi (Leiden: Brill, 2019), pp. 165–88.

[58] Montaigne's early readers did not, of course, have access to critical editions indicating the different 'couches'. But he is more than aware that his reader might be conscious of the changes he made to his book. Once the 'registre' went out into the world in the 1580

recognises 'le trein de mes mutations', not by following the journey 'en avant' of his thinking, but by using his book as a witness to his multiple perspectives and 'imaginations', his contradictory but coexisting ways of seeing.

Montaigne's 'transposition de chronologie' is presented as something innocuous, as something that slips in easily ('il adviendra facilement qu'il s'y mesle quelque transposition de chronologie'). But it is this transposition that allows him to write in the *hic et nunc* of thinking and to pursue its doubleness. Transposing temporal moments does not only reveal a shifting opinion – it does not only allow him to juxtapose contrasting judgements made in different compositional moments and notice their dissimilarity. It also produces ambiguities and forges connections, remoulding extant material such that it seems to take on a new aspect. The multiple senses of Montaigne's claims that his understanding goes backwards as well as forwards – claims that mean different things, depending on how alert our own reading is to the compositional 'marqueterie' – are as much an illustration as an explanation of his mode of writing doubly. His disruption of chronology in these passages rewrites earlier comments on the chronology of essay writing. But to rewrite is not to erase: Montaigne produces an account of chronology that is itself double, shifting and acquiring new meanings as he returns to his key images of 'fagotage', 'marqueterie' and movement. Even where the words themselves remain unchanged, inflected only by their new surroundings, they seem at once to imagine the onward march of thinking and writing and, at the same time, its disordered, irregular movement, a movement that is 'double', 'sans forme' and 'sans patron'; a movement not only reflected in writing but made possible by thinking with and across the material book.

Montaigne's writing progresses non-chronologically while being grounded in the here and now of composition. Where other writers smooth over the cracks and hide the seams, he leaves the chronology of composition, like the chronology of thinking, plain to see, running through and against the flow of prose and reading. 'Essaying', writes Richard Scholar, 'is caught in the flow of time.' Temporal markers – signals of shifts from one age to another, from one moment to another – structure Montaigne's prose such that 'the passing of time is woven into the fabric of the passage'.[59] The *Essais*, like Seneca's epistles, are

---

edition, it was 'hypothequé', mortgaged to the public, and could no longer be understood purely as a sequence of disconnected 'pieces': it had taken 'form' in such a way as to change his understanding of how he thinks with and relates to his now-public book.

[59] Scholar, *Montaigne and the Art of Free-Thinking*, p. 76.

composed in such a way that they are inextricable from the *hic et nunc* in which they are produced. In both texts, this temporality is necessarily open-ended. Even when their author ceases to add further instalments, the sense of a sequential continuation remains: this endlessness is ingrained in the form such that the reader, engaging with the text, can posit their own addendums.

For Montaigne, though, this open-endedness is not, as it was for Seneca, a linear passage in which the movement through time mirrors the movement through text: in the *Essais*, compositional chronology 'va à reculons aussi' [goes backwards too]. Working with the public record of his 'imaginations', returning to the printed text and rewriting it, allowed him to subvert that key principle of letter writing: rather than writing once, he writes again and again, making serial epistolography not only unresolved and diverse but double. Most importantly, Montaigne transposes this chronology while calling attention to the temporality of writing: not only does he inform the reader directly with references to 'surpoids' and 'allongeails', or with claims not to correct first thoughts with second thoughts. This temporality is embedded in Montaigne's prose with its recurring references to 'tantost', 'hier', 'à cette heure' [sometimes, yesterday, at this moment]. All authors edit and revise their texts. Even Lipsius admits that he casts an eye over his letters: he hardly rereads them ('bis vix eas lego'), but he does reread them. Moving non-chronologically while reminding us constantly of the temporality of writing, Montaigne marks his distance from the everyday reality of writing 'à diverses poses et intervalles'. What in most authors is made invisible and concealed from the reader is in the *Essais* brought to the surface, seized upon by Montaigne as a tool with which to recognise himself and to make himself known.

'[A]Je ne corrige point mes premieres imaginations par les secondes; [C]ouy à l'aventure quelque mot, mais pour diversifier, non pour oster' [I do not correct my first imaginings by my second – well, yes, perhaps a word or so, but only to vary, not to delete] (II.37.758/574). Montaigne, seeing things differently, offers his reader two contradictory assertions: he does not correct himself; he does correct himself. They are maintained and asserted equally: the irony of this correction ensures that we read it not as a change of heart but as a consequence of that strange doubleness Montaigne recognised – even if he couldn't explain it – in Epicurus, in himself, in understanding and in everything else. The 'mutations' of his thought mean that he has different opinions depending on how he looks at things. Presenting them together rather than in sequence, he doubles up, disorders and makes more doubtful the sort of thinking that is done with the *Essais* – thinking done both by Montaigne, looking at himself differently, and by his reader, encountering Montaigne and recognising complexity.

Encouraging a mode of reading that mirrors his composition – disordered, non-linear – Montaigne directs us towards an associative way of thinking, finding connections and 'rencontres' between the 'pieces décousues' of the *Essais*. His writing traces shifting perspectives over time, but he pushes the reader to see those perspectives side by side, collapsing the temporal distance even as it insists on the temporality of writing. Writing twice – 'bis scribere' – not to correct but to look again, Montaigne's 'transposition de chronologie' has an effect not unlike Trouillogan's shift from dynamic disagreement to disruptive conjunction. It is not the 'ou' that is troubling: a bundle of diverse perspectives might be in want of structure or a conclusion, but it is quite conventional. It is the 'et' that causes problems.

Perhaps the clearest example of this counterintuitive way of thinking is Montaigne's backdating of the 'Au lecteur'. Where the 1588 edition had revised the original date, 'ce premier de Mars. 1580.', to read 'ce 12. Juin. 1588.', the Bordeaux Copy restores the original timestamp, 'ce premier de Mars ~~1580~~ mille cinq cens quattre vins'.[60] In the *Essais*, especially as they developed after their original publication, the reader is presented with discrete textual moments in chronological disorder and encouraged to read them as being written concurrently, even as Montaigne highlights the temporal leaps, the 'sauts et gambades' [leaps and gambols], between them (III.9.994/761).

The *Essais* are not a straightforward 'registre' of Montaigne's thoughts, tracing the 'trein' of their 'mutation' over time. Collapsing his compositional chronology, Montaigne makes diverse, even contradictory moments of thinking simultaneously available to the reader (which includes Montaigne reading his own book). Seneca's serial epistolography takes a series of snapshots, keeping track of the philosopher's progression in his daily labour. With Montaigne, we see something more like a double exposure. Transposing chronology, he records his thoughts wherever and whenever they occur to him: it may be that he writes only when he is at home ('non ailleurs que chez moy', II.37.758/574) but, in the space of the book, his thoughts find their place wherever they fit ('selon leur opportunité, non tousjours selon leur aage', III.9.964/736). The resulting tensions reflect the contradictions of his double 'esprit',

---

[60] Bordeaux Copy, fol. Aiir. There are other extant copies of the 1588 edition that record the same restoration of the original date written in Montaigne's hand: these are the Lambiotte copy, held in Bordeaux, and the Solvay copy, held in Brussels. See Alain Legros, '*Essais* de 1588 et l'Exemplaire de Bordeaux' (2015), https://montaigne.univ-tours.fr/essais-1588-exemplaire-bordeaux/ [accessed 6 November 2023].

communicating and revealing a doubleness that all too easily slips between our fingers, a doubleness Montaigne recognised without understanding ('je ne sçay comment'). Writing doubly, he invites us to recognise it too.

'Je m'estalle entier … d'une veue': Perspectives on Montaigne's 'skeletos'

The analogy of the double exposure finds a less anachronistic analogue in Montaigne's long post-1588 coda to 'De l'exercitation'. It is here that he describes how he tries to couch in the 'corps aerée de la voix' [airy body of the voice] his 'cogitations', that 'subject informe' 'qui ne peut tomber en production ouvragere' [that does not lend itself to expression in actions] (II.6.379/274). Giving account of a man by what he has done is more straightforward, though he notes that the wise (and the devout) have avoided living remarkable lives. The events of his own life, he continues, tell more of Fortune and circumstance than anything proper to himself. Repeating a point he would make in 'Du dementir' (II.18.663/503), he is explicit in distinguishing his *Essais* from the genre of life writing: even if he were presumptuous enough to write an account of his 'life', his 'gestes' would show only partial glimpses of the man he really is, 'eschantillons d'une montre particuliere' [samples which display a particular perspective] (II.6.379/274).[61]

> Je m'estalle entier: c'est un Skeletos où, d'une veue, les veines, les muscles, les tendons paroissent, chaque piece en son siege. L'effect de la toux en produisoit une partie; l'effect de la palleur ou battement de coeur, un'autre, et doubteusement. (II.6.379)
>
> I am *all* on display, like a mummy on which at a glance you can see the veins, the muscles, and the tendons, each piece in its place. Part of me is revealed – but only ambiguously – by the act of coughing; another by my turning pale or by my palpitations.[62]

From the semi-corporeal image of the spectral voice, a container for a shapeless but vital thinking spirit, Montaigne ends up, by way of association, at an unusual image lifted from anatomy, an image that similarly

---

[61] Translation modified. Frame has 'samples which display only details'. The relationship between the *Essais* and life writing will be discussed more fully in Chapter 5.
[62] The translation is taken from Screech, p. 426. Frame has 'I expose myself entire: my portrait is a cadaver on which the veins, the muscles, and the tendons appear at a glance, each part in its place. One part of what I am was produced by a cough, another by a pallor or a palpitation of the heart – in any case dubiously' (p. 274).

blurs the living and the dead, the material and the spiritual. It is a body on the cusp of death that recalls, in its coughing and spluttering and its exposure of taut musculature, the sweating, labouring Seneca steeling himself 'contre la mort' (III.12.1040/795). It is an image that would be echoed again when Montaigne imagines his own agonising labours as others watch him battling with the stone, that foreign body ('corps') inside his own (III.13.1091/836).[63]

This 'skeletos' is surprisingly alive. But it is not a 'life': it is not an account of Montaigne's actions or circumstances, nor a personal history ('ce ne sont mes gestes que j'escris, c'est moy, c'est mon essence' [It is not my deeds that I write down; it is myself, it is my essence]). Montaigne, then, intends to present himself 'entier', privileging a moral, intellectual and cognitive identity that is not interior so much as concomitant with himself.

And yet he uses 'skeletos', a peculiar word in sixteenth-century French, loaded with foreignising Greekness, and one that seems to exclude precisely those cognitive, affective and psychological aspects he prioritises. 'Squelette' was a recent coinage: Marie-Luce Demonet has traced its emergence to a flurry of uses in the 1570s and 1580s, principally in medical texts – notably Ambroise Paré's *Monstres et prodigues* (1573) – though it also turns up in Ronsard, in the first sonnet of his *Derniers vers* (1586).[64] In Greek, *skeletos*, related to *skello*, meaning 'to dry up, to wither', refers not to what we would call a skeleton but to a mummy. In the context of Renaissance French, though, Demonet suggests that the meaning of this newly incorporated word was quickly established, referring specifically to 'anatomie sèche', bones stripped of flesh.[65] Ronsard's sonnet leaves little ambiguity: 'Je n'ay plus que les os, un squelette je semble, | Decharné, denervé, demusclé, depoulpé' [I have nothing now but my bones, I look like a skeleton, without flesh, nerves, muscles, pulp].[66] Clearly, though, Montaigne's use of the term to describe his project of exposing himself entirely ('je m'estalle entier')

---

[63] On this passage, see Chapter 6 and Luke O'Sullivan, '"Feuilletant ces petits brevets descousus": consolations fausses et l'écriture de la vérité', *Bulletin de la société internationale des amies et amis de Montaigne*, 74 (2022), 187–205.

[64] Marie-Luce Demonet, 'Le Skeletos de Montaigne ou la leçon de l'anatomie', in *Théâtres de l'anatomie et corps en spectacle*, ed. I. Zinguer and L. Van Delft (Berne: Peter Lang, 2006), pp. 63–88 (p. 68). See also Jean Balsamo, 'Skeletos', in Desan (ed.), *Dictionnaire de Montaigne*, pp. 1742–3. Both Demonet and Jean Balsamo have noted that Montaigne may have encountered this term in the Greek text of Plutarch. Amyot translates it as 'un corps mort'. See, for instance, 'Antonius', *Vies des hommes illustres*, fol. 654r.

[65] Demonet, 'Le Skeletos de Montaigne ou la leçon de l'anatomie', p. 69.

[66] 'Je n'ay plus que les os', ll. 1–2, in *Œuvres complètes*, ed. Jean Céard, Daniel Menager and Michel Simonin, 2 vols (Paris: Gallimard, 1993–94), vol. 2, p. 1102.

is much more inclusive and seems to imagine something more like a cadaver – albeit one that is alive.[67] Between these different meanings, Demonet reads Montaigne's 'skeletos' as an image of nakedness and transparency: 'le livre est un corps nu comme une "anatomie", un corps total […] sans la peau de l'apparence' [the book is a naked body like an 'anatomy', a complete body, without an outer skin of appearance].[68] Presenting us with his 'skeletos', then, Montaigne reveals all.

Montaigne had some first-hand experience of the anatomy theatre: he had seen skeletons during his visit to Basel, both in the university and at the home of Felix Platter, the anatomist and professor of medicine.[69] But Jean Balsamo has suggested that Montaigne is also thinking, once again, with books: what Montaigne has in mind, Balsamo argues, are the anatomical drawings made famous by Vesalius and Charles Estienne – drawings that reveal the body's separate layers, peeling back the skin, then the muscles, then the nerves, and so on with each illustration.[70] These printed anatomies depict their cadavers propped up and positioned in lifelike poses, flayed and skinned to varying degrees. In one drawing might be depicted a skeleton, but in another, a human figure made entirely from muscles and, in another, the full network of tendons.

Montaigne's image seems a spectacularly poor choice. These anatomical drawings depict precisely what he does not want to show, which is to say only 'eschantillons d'une montre particuliere' [samples which display a particular perspective] – only, in Balsamo's terms, 'couches successives', successive layers.[71] The 'skeletos' imagined in the

---

[67] Based on Montaigne's comment in 1.20.87/60 ('Ainsi faisoyent les Egyptiens, qui, au milieu de leurs festins et parmy leur meilleure chere, faisoient aporter l'Anatomie seche d'un corps d'homme mort'), Philippe Desan has suggested that, for Montaigne, 'anatomie' is synonymous with 'corps mort' or 'cadavre' (*Les Formes du monde et de l'esprit*, p. 44). 'Skeletos' similarly seems to be understood to refer specifically to a dead body. On 'anatomie seche, qui est un corps où il ne reste que les os', see Pierre de la Primaudaye, *Suite de l'academie française* (Paris: Chaudière, 1580), fol. 23r.

[68] Demonet, 'Le Skeletos de Montaigne ou la leçon de l'anatomie', p. 66.

[69] Montaigne's account in the *Journal de voyage* is brief: 'Nous vîmes aussi et chez lui [Félix Platerus, médicin] et en l'école publique des anatomies entières d'hommes morts qui se tiennent' [We also saw, both at his house and in the public school, some entire skeletons of men that stand up by themselves]; *Journal de voyage*, ed. Fausta Garavini (Paris: Gallimard, 1983), p. 90. The English translation is Frame's: *The Complete Works of Montaigne: Essays, Travel Journal, Letters*, trans. Donald M. Frame (Stanford, CA: Stanford University Press, 1957), p. 878.

[70] Balsamo, 'Skeletos', p. 1742: 'un dessin ou une représentation anatomique du corps découpé en couches successives'.

[71] See, for instance, Estienne's *La Dissection des parties du corps humain* (Paris: Simon de Colines, 1546), pp. 96–7. These facing pages present two illustrations, both of a full-length cadaver: the first is constituted solely of bones, the second of muscles.

Essais is, as Jean Céard has noted, an impossible drawing: Montaigne places himself on the dissection table and proposes to make everything visible 'd'une veue', but also, at the same time, wants to keep everything in its proper place ('chaque piece en son siège'), 'comme si ce corps pourrait découvrir toutes ses pieces sans pourtant être désassemblée' [as though this body could reveal all its parts without being disassembled].[72]

Céard argues that Montaigne's scriptural dissection preserves 'l'unité du vivant' [the unity of the living individual].[73] But it is a unity made up of disparate parts: Montaigne's unity is not homogeneity. Similarly, if we are to read Montaigne's attempt at presenting these different parts 'd'une veue' as indicating a desire for transparency, as Demonet suggests, this is not a transparency in which we look 'through' the skin to some deeper, inner self.[74] Instead, it describes a desire to make multiple perspectives available simultaneously. Montaigne no doubt wants to reveal what lies beneath 'la peau de l'apparence', but he wants to show what is only skin deep too, even as he encourages his reader to recognise its shallowness.

With this bundle of quasi-defective metaphors – the vital cadaver, the dissection ('anatomie') that abandons the scalpel, the airy body of the voice that lets us 'see' the thoughts it contains – Montaigne describes a new way of looking: a way of seeing multiple layers, perspectives, connections, effects and causes all at once. In contrast to the dead body cut up into 'pieces décousues', and unlike its representation in printed images, his 'skeletos' is alive with movement: 'd'une veue', we see 'l'effect de la toux' [the effect of a cough] and the 'battement de cœur' [beating of the heart]. We see each layer of Montaigne's anatomy, each 'couche' of his 'cogitations', separately and together at once: we see these thoughts in motion along with their causes and their consequences. We see the whole of Montaigne *and*, at a glance, each layer and each part.[75] But recognising this complex, vital, shapeshifting cadaver is not to understand it. Just as Montaigne recognised his doubleness without being able to explain it ('je ne sçay comment'), so too does the reader

---

[72] Jean Céard, 'Montaigne Anatomiste', *Cahiers de l'Association internationale des études françaises*, 55 (2003), 299–315 (p. 313).
[73] Ibid., pp. 313–14.
[74] Demonet, 'Le Skeletos de Montaigne ou la leçon de l'anatomie', pp. 63–6.
[75] While Montaigne presents himself 'entier', this does not require him to have a global understanding of himself, a view of himself 'en gros' [as a whole] (II.1.337/243). It is rather his form and the compositional techniques discussed in this chapter that allow these diverse parts to be seen 'd'une veue'. On the relationship between parts and wholes, see Chapter 6.

encounter this figure and see its connections doubtfully ('doubteusement', II.6.379/274).

Montaigne's 'skeletos', the revenant body that gives form to his 'informe' thoughts, a body that is at once the 'airy' body of the voice, the body of the *Essais*, and the ailing, ageing body of the man who wrote them, offers the reader a new way of seeing Montaigne. The *Essais* reveal multiple perspectives, 'eschantillons d'une montre particuliere', all at once. This conception of his book as a multi-perspectival depiction of all his constituent parts is the corollary to his disordered chronology. He pieces together his 'skeletos' (here again the image is defective: the work of 'marqueterie', the addition and inclusion of 'surpoids', works counter to the excisions of the anatomist's scalpel) by overlaying diverse perspectives or opinions, building up the text, writing a bit here and a bit there, 'diverses pieces [...] à diverses poses'. Accumulating and transposing moments of writing and their respective ways of seeing, Montaigne found a form with which to make his book, like his 'entendement', not only 'divers' but 'double'.

The Shape of Thinking

This chapter has traced some of the metaphors, images and ways of thinking about form that structured Montaigne's conception of how thought might be couched in writing. It began by highlighting his emphasis on two qualities, doubleness ('double') and shapelessness ('sans forme'), that distinguish the *Essais* as 'sans patron', unlike other forms of doubtful, unresolved writing, whether those be taken from the Sceptical camp of philosophers or from the 'tiers genre' of dogmatists.

These images and metaphors show Montaigne getting a feel for form. But it is in their limitations and contradictions that they are most revealing. The 'corps aerée de la voix' holds on to its liquid subject to produce a body of writing that might be held more securely, a body that is half-living and half-dead, a body that is entirely opaque and solid (and perhaps also, like Apollo's double speech, 'obscure' and 'oblique'), but transparent enough that we might peer into its subcutaneous layers. His muddled 'chronologie' records the passage of time and reveals (to Montaigne as much as to anyone else) his shifting perspectives and opinions, not by piling up instances of diversity but by doubling moments of thought and composition. The 'cheval eschappé' [runaway horse] (I.8.33/21) of the imagination does not charge in a straight line. If thinking can go backwards as well as forwards, 'avant et à reculons aussi', that is in no small part because Montaigne thinks with and through his book, across its sequence of pages and chapters, and across the muddled 'fagotage' of *hic et nunc* moments that it inscribes.

Reading these formal and compositional practices in light of a doubtful Seneca and Plutarch recasts familiar understandings of the role played in the *Essais* by revision, editing, 'adding but not correcting'. Montaigne draws from both Seneca's serial epistolography and Plutarch's ability to point towards endlessly diverse perspectives. Bringing them together, the *Essais* develop a form of writing made up of multiple 'here and nows' that call on the reader to look in multiple directions at once. Rewriting is not only a matter of updating or adding to the 'registre': it is a way of making singular moments of composition reflect and communicate the doubleness of the 'esprit'. This is not the Sceptic's *ou mallon*, 'no more this than that', and nor is it *epoché*, that mental state ('status mentis') in which nothing is given or taken ('per que neque ponimus quicquam neque tollimus').[76] Nor still is it the withholding of assent (*retentio assentionis*). Montaigne's doubt is not that of the slippery philosopher, always offering another option. The slipperiness of the *Essais* stems not from the disjunctive 'or' – Panurge's 'ou', the logician's 'vel' – but from an attempt to sustain, over the course of the book and its years of writing, Trouillogan's disruptive conjunction, 'et'.

The effects of these compositional habits are seen most clearly in the additions and insertions made across the three main strata of the *Essais*. But they are not limited to shifts 'd'aage en autre' [from one age to another] (III.2.805/611). 'De minute en minute', perspectives are doubled up and overlain: '[C]Semant icy un mot icy un autre: eschantillons despris de leur piece: escartez', as Montaigne put it [Scattering a word here, there another: samples separated from their context: dispersed] (I.50.302/219, punctuation following the Bordeaux Copy, fol. 126r). As Richard Scholar has noted, 'each segment' in this sentence 'corresponds to a separate thought', holding together a cluster of similar yet different ways of imagining scattered, diverse, non-linear writing.[77] The prose enacts in microcosm the form it describes. At the same time, though, we also see, provided we mirror Montaigne's scattered composition with a similar flightiness, a parallel operating at a completely different scale. Samples, 'eschantillons', taken out of context look radically different when seen from a different perspective. Consider another passage, from the same period of composition but separated in the Bordeaux Copy by dozens of pages: Montaigne's claim that his 'skeletos' does not

---

[76] *Outlines of Pyrrhonism*, I.4.11.
[77] Scholar, *Montaigne and the Art of Free-Thinking*, p. 84.

show 'eschantillons d'une montre particuliere' [samples which display a particular perspective] (II.6.379/274). The *Essais* are and are not made up of dislocated, partial 'eschantillons'; his 'pieces' are disordered and yet always find their proper place; his book is 'tousjours un' even as it reflects an understanding that is 'double'.

Chapter 4

Forming Thoughts II: Writing Doubly

Montaigne reminds his reader constantly of the need to look closely, to 'regarder de pres', in order to uncover the diversity and doubleness latent in oneself, in others, in ways of writing and in the world. The doubleness of the *Essais* has been brought to the surface in a number of the passages discussed already in this study: in Montaigne's shuffling of the uncertain categories of the three 'genres' of philosophers in Chapter 1; in the doubling up of authorial associations, of what is 'mine' and 'not mine', in Chapter 2; in his shifting relationships with 'chronologie', 'fagotage', 'eschantillons' and the direction of understanding in Chapter 3.

But as well as telling his reader to look closely, Montaigne also stressed the importance of taking one's time. A reader has to sit with his writing long enough, and consider a sufficiently large portion of his fragmentary text, for thought – his own and his reader's – to get moving. In his own reading of Plutarch, Montaigne found himself unable to resist snatching up a 'cuisse ou aile' [drumstick or wing] (III.5.875/666) – portions, certainly, but not meagre ones. This chapter traces the effect of Montaigne's thoughts about form on the practice of writing doubly. It takes three draughts from his liquid 'commerce' to show him both thinking with Seneca and Plutarch – engaging explicitly with them and their writing – and thinking with their modes of irresolution, with their 'manière' though not necessarily with their 'matière'. Montaigne's doubtful, unresolved form emerged in his dealings with these authors, though this chapter shows that it is not limited to moments of direct engagement. My aim is not to provide an exhaustive survey of the different ways Montaigne used Seneca and Plutarch, but rather to take three samples, 'eschantillons', that show the relationship between these 'formes' in diverse lights.

Seams, 'Seems' and Themes

'Quo diversus abis?' [Whither do you leave the course?] (III.9.994/760). With this line taken from Virgil, Montaigne announces that he is 'hors de [son] theme' [outside of his subject].[1] He had been discussing the divisions and tumults that gripped France, as well as his own fortune in weathering the storm, though really it might be said that he had lost his theme quite a bit earlier. The quotation from Virgil, breaking one digression and opening another, leads into a strange passage in which Montaigne engages in a process of seeing and describing his writing from multiple perspectives, performing his formal practices as he attempts to describe them.

'Je m'esgare:; mais plustost par licence, que par mesgarde: mMes fantasies, se suyvent:; mais parfois c'est de loing: & Et se regardent; mais d'une veuë oblique' [I lose myself, but rather by licence than carelessness: My ideas follow one another; but sometimes it is from a distance, And look at each other, but with a side-long glance].[2] Montaigne's prose pushes and pulls at once, turning on doubles and repetitions as it sustains opposition. Remoulding what was a flowing sentence of moderation and compromise, the graphic markers – what André Tournon called 'majuscules de scansion' – repackage this sentence as a series of antagonistic, dynamic '*x* but *y*' statements.[3] This is not a moment of paradiastole, repackaging vice as moderate virtue, but a moment of sustained tension. With his pun on 'm'esgare' and 'mesgarde', Montaigne seems to be saying that he loses himself but not by getting lost; that his 'licence' – his outlandish boldness – is licensed and permitted.[4] Looking

---

[1] The line from Virgil is taken from the *Aeneid*, book 5, line 166: Gyas, during the boat race which forms the first part of the funeral games for Anchises, is addressing Menoetes who, fearing rocks lurking beneath the waves, takes the ship further out to sea when cornering and, in doing so, loses the race. That this is part of a game – a simulation – and a competition between antagonists may be significant when we come to consider Montaigne's use of 'sembler' to describe the ways in which he and other writers get lost.

[2] Translation modified. Frame's translation obscures the wordplay, giving 'I go out of my way' for 'je m'esgare'. Unless otherwise stated, quotations from the *Essais* in this section refer to III.9.994–5/760–2, though I have restored the punctuation and spelling as it is seen on fol. 447v of the Bordeaux Copy.

[3] In addition to Tournon's edition of the *Essais*, see Tournon's numerous studies of Montaigne's punctuation, and most notably an early article on this passage from III.9, 'Montaigne et l'"alleure poétique": pour une nouvelle lecture d'une page des *Essais*', *Bibliothèque d'Humanisme et Renaissance*, 33 (1971), pp. 155–62.

[4] Cotgrave defines 'licence' as 'permission, leave', while Antoine Fouquelin described it as an excessive freedom that 'montre quelque audace & hardiesse de dire ce qui sembloit dangereux à dire' [shows some boldness and bravery in saying what would seem to be dangerous to say]; *La Rhétorique françoise* (Paris: Wechel, 1555), p. 111.

in two directions at once, looking sidelong, 'd'une veue oblique', this sentence sets up a long and involved reflection on form, particularly on Montaigne's form as it relates to that of Plutarch and Plato. Thinking on the page and thinking with a complex cluster of shifting resemblances, Montaigne asks how literary form works to capture and lose 'fantasie' or attention, how it tracks a cognitive itinerary and drops breadcrumbs, some more and some less obviously pertinent, that let a reader follow in his footsteps or perhaps just let him retrace his own.[5]

It is a passage that has been seen as a celebration of 'l'alleure poetique', in which a roaming, vagabond style of 'sauts et gambades' [leaps and gambols] declares Montaigne's freedom of thought (III.9.994/761).[6] But it is also, as Emma Claussen has shown, a reflection on vagrancy: Montaigne's enthusiasm for poetic inspiration takes shape in the context of the very real experiences of wandering and refuge-seeking that are the focus of key parts of his chapter.[7] In rereading this passage, my own focus lies with the anxieties and doubts that percolate through the prose as he tries to get his bearings. Asking himself where he is, Montaigne is seen here thinking with appearance and resemblance, those staples of doubtful enquiry, stitching together not only multiple ways of seeing but multiple ways of seeming too.

Claiming that 'les noms de mes chapitres n'en embrassent pas tousjours la matiere' [the titles of my chapters do not always embrace their matter] – his titles are also leaky, with 'matière' once again proving slippery, prone to escaping one's grasp – Montaigne's 1588 text characterises his own writing as especially poetic: some poets 'languissent à la prosaïque' [languish prosaically], while the best prose 'reluit par tout de la vigueur et hardiesse poetique' [shines throughout with the vigour and boldness of poetry]. The poet's fury, that hint of inspired madness (*furor poeticus* or *enthousiasmos*), is what wins poetry 'la maistrise, & preeminence en la parlerie' [mastery and pre-eminence in speech].[8] Montaigne's focus, in this first version, is on establishing a link between

---

[5] On pertinence considered from a cognitive perspective, see Neil Kenny, '"A propos, ou hors de propos, il n'importe": Relevance Theory and Montaigne', in *Lucidity: Essays in Honour of Alison Finch*, ed. Ian James and Emma Wilson (Cambridge: Legenda, 2016), pp. 20–32, and Terence Cave and Kirsti Sellevold, '"Or, ces exemples me semblent plus à propos": une phrase inaugurale dans les *Essais* de Montaigne', in *Eveils: études en l'honneur de J.-Y. Pouilloux*, ed. Valérie Fasseur, Olivier Guerrier, Laurent Jenny and André Tournon (Paris: Garnier, 2010), pp. 64–75.

[6] See, for instance, Desan, *Les Formes du monde et de l'esprit*, p. 169.

[7] Emma Claussen, 'Montaigne's Vagabond Styles: Political Homelessness in the Sixteenth Century', *Forum for Modern Language Studies*, 57.3 (2021), 273–90 (p. 279).

[8] On *furor poeticus* in this passage, see André Tournon, *Montaigne: la glose et l'essai – édition revue et corrigée* (Paris: Champion, 2000), pp. 136–41.

prose and poetry that licenses his own digressive, associative way of writing. 'Il faut avoir un peu de folie', he writes, 'qui ne veut avoir plus de sottise' [a man must be a little mad if he does not want to be even more stupid].

At a point after 1588, Montaigne returned to these commonplaces and refashioned them as part of an extended reflection on how, if at all, he gets lost in his writing. The pun on *m'esgare–mesgarde* spirals out of control as he attempts to write and think through a series of oppositions. Rewriting and overwriting this passage, Montaigne made half a dozen major additions and numerous smaller changes, and it is with these that I am most concerned. Tournon's analysis of these additions, half a century ago, established an approach to the Bordeaux Copy as a material text that traces the movement of Montaigne's thought.[9] But in returning to this reflection on form and digression, we might pay closer attention not only to thought's 'leaps and gambols', but to moments of stitching and fastening too: it is certainly the case that Montaigne imagined his thought as itinerant, but it follows an itinerary in which plotted positions are transplanted, transposed and overlapped. Montaigne opened the digression by asking, in Virgil's voice, where he is, but it would seem that he is in many places at once. These additions, stitched together but with loose, visible, leaky seams (the 'marqueterie' remains 'mal jointe'), show Montaigne collapsing time and perspective as he forms his thought, giving it shape while, at the same time, preserving its double, liquid formlessness.

His approach to his own way of writing is mediated through textual and authorial doubles. The first addition we encounter (and one of the first to be written) introduces Plato, a figure who, at first glance, seems to stand as an analogue for Montaigne himself. 'J'ay passé les yeux sur tel dialogue de Platon mi party d'une fantastique bigarrure, le devant à l'amour, tout le bas à la rhetorique' [I have run my eyes over a certain dialogue of Plato, a fantastic motley in two parts, the beginning about love, all the rest about rhetoric]. He is describing the *Phaedrus*, a text that is, as Montaigne notes, split in half. Plato allows Montaigne to examine, even legitimise, his own style, with its 'fantasies' that move and shift from one sentence to the next: 'Ils ne creignent point ces muances', he writes, 'Et ont une merveilleuse grace à se laisser ainsi rouler au vent, ou à le sembler' [They do not fear these changes, and with wonderful

---

[9] Tournon, 'Montaigne et l'"alleure poétique"', pp. 155–62. Tracing the various symbols indicating points of insertion – I, ± and X, among others – Tournon has suggested an alternative reading to the commonly accepted order found in modern editions of the *Essais*. It is Tournon's sequencing, which is followed in his Imprimerie Nationale edition, that is used here.

grace they let themselves thus be tossed in the wind, or seem to].[10] This final phrase – 'ou à le sembler' – is key, not just in this comment on Plato, but in the passage more generally: the whole of this digression turns, as will become clear, on this slippery notion of semblance and its ability to stitch together different ways of 'seeming', depending on where the stress is placed.

The first addition prompts a second: a lengthy reflection on Plutarch (a second authorial double for Montaigne), on Plutarch's essay about Socrates and his 'daemonic' double, and on Montaigne's account of his own relationship with the 'indiligent lecteur' [inattentive reader]. It is a passage full of doubles, 'fantasies' that 'se suyvent', albeit 'de loing' and 'd'une veue oblique'. Indeed, the allusion to Socrates' 'daemon' sends Montaigne's thinking straight back to Plato. Written after the reference to Plutarch but placed before it in the text, he squeezes in a line, full of hesitation and written in a particularly small hand: 'c'est un art come dict Platon legere volage ~~sacrée daemoniacle sacrée~~ daemoniacle' [it is an art, as Plato says, that is light, flighty, ~~holy, daemonic, holy~~, daemonic]. In passing from 'daemon' to 'daemon', from Plato to Plutarch and back again, Montaigne draws connections that are neither linear nor argumentative but associative, pulling both thought and writing in multiple, distinct directions, simultaneously following diverse 'fantasies' that look obliquely at each other across the space of the page.[11]

The intermingling of Plato and Plutarch, as well as the hesitation between 'sacrée' and 'daemoniacle', shows again Montaigne's habit of thinking in pairs and thinking with authors, not holding them up as stable points of reference but drawing implied points of connection between them. He juxtaposes authors who themselves engage in the sort of textual juxtaposition he is interested in, all the while comparing this juxtaposed pair with himself. Editing his text and putting these diverse ideas and interlocutors next to each other, Montaigne allows multiple, unstable points of connection, resemblance and difference to become legible on the page.

Montaigne revised his comments on Plutarch substantially: drafts fill the whole of the right-hand margin. His first effort employs that key

---

[10] Translation modified. Frame pins down Montaigne's underspecified 'Ils', which he translates as 'The ancients'.

[11] Olivier Guerrier has noted that both the *Phaedrus* and Plutarch's essay on Socrates' 'daemon' are concerned with 'l'enthousiasme du philosophe', with divinely inspired, raving speech, and with 'paroles [...] conduites par une force extérieure' [words [...] guided by an exterior force]. See Olivier Guerrier, *Quand les poètes feignent: 'fantasie' et fiction dans les Essais de Montaigne* (Paris: Champion, 2002), pp. 86–96 (pp. 88–9). Montaigne's own thinking here is similarly enraptured in its non-linear, associative progression. For further discussion of *enthousiasmos*, see Chapter 6.

term 'sembler' twice in quick succession: 'Il me semble qu'il y a ouvrage en Plutarche ~~qui de~~ dedié à Socrates qui ~~et~~ a peine en parle il un mot sur la fin tout le corps estant d'Epaminondas. Ces escartemants sont d'autant plus ingenieus qu'ils semblent estres fortuites' [There is, I think, a work in Plutarch dedicated to Socrates that hardly says a word about him until the end, the body being about Epaminondas. These gaps are all the more ingenious as they seem to be accidental.] The ingenuity of these 'escartements' reflects the mercurial leakiness of the 'esprit genereux', the *ingenium* characterised by overabundance and *débordement*.[12] As well as gaps, Montaigne finds lines of connection joining Plutarch to both Plato and himself: Plutarch's lacunae *seem* to be accidental ('ils semblent estres fortuites'), just as Plato's dialogues seem to 'rouler au vent'; both point back to Montaigne, who seems to lose himself, 'mais plustost par licence'. Are we to understand 'sembler' in the same way for both Plutarch and Plato? Is Montaigne saying 'This seems to be the case' or is he saying, 'They seem to lose themselves, go with the flow, and this all seems to be accidental and inartificial, but it is not really'? Montaigne invites both senses of semblance and stitches them together. The resulting seam affords two ways of reading and thinking that are overlain: we read this complex set of connections and see the different ways these authors 'seem' to lose themselves at once, 'd'une veue'.

Montaigne's edits do not resolve these ambiguities: the 'escartements', the leaps and gaps, in his own writing remain. In a further addition, he introduces a comment of direct self-assessment before the reference to Plutarch and the 'daemon', thereby rendering more explicit – though not necessarily more clear – the comparison of his own digressive qualities with those of Plutarch: 'Ils [mes chapitres] en disent tousjours en quelque coin un mot bien serré[.] l'autheur ne la [la matière] pert pas c'est l'indiligent lector' [They [my chapters] speak [of the matter] always, in some corner, some succinct word. The author does not lose it; it is the inattentive reader.][13] This is the first of a number of attempts to write the paradoxical statement – echoing and expanding upon the

---

[12] On *ingenium* as 'esprit' in early modern French, see Raphaële Garrod, 'La Politesse de l'esprit: Cartesian Pedagogy and the Ethics of Scholarly Exchange', in *Descartes and the Ingenium: The Embodied Soul in Cartesianism*, ed. Raphaële Garrod and Alexander Marr (Leiden: Brill, 2021), pp. 184–203.

[13] The spatial mapping of the *Essais* is salient here, not least for its ambiguity. One might suppose that this 'coin', along with the reference to 'en arriere', draws on the painterly metaphors familiar to readers of the *Essais* (a reading supported by the echo of the Horatian image of the monstrous chimera, Ars poetica, ll. 4–5, used to describe Plutarch's essay on Socrates, the body of which is about Epaminondas). Equally, the 'coin' might suggest a more domestic space such as the 'coin d'une librairie' in which Montaigne imagines his *Essais* being placed (II.18.664/503).

1588 claim, 'Je m'esgare, mais plustost par licence' – that he both loses and does not lose his subject. In writing this double idea, Montaigne positions himself as both author and reader: he aligns himself with the subtlety of Plato and Plutarch, imagining himself a 'diligent' reader of their works and, at the same time, sees himself as an author in his own right who might be read by someone less attentive than him.

His next attempt goes as follows: 'Au demurant, encore la que la montre soit autre et autre le gros du corps, si ne la [la matière] laisse je pas en arriere, et en laisse en un coin tousjours quelque mot, et bien serré. C'est l'indiligent lectur qui la pert non pas moi' [Nevertheless, though the face may be one thing and the rest of the body another, still I do not leave the matter behind, and always leave some succinct word of it in a corner. It is the inattentive reader who loses it, not me.] Amid all the leaks, Montaigne's form is certain to hold on to something, some well-grasped, concise material, something of substance. Here, there is a significant shift from 'l'autheur' to 'moi': the forthright claim that opened this digression, 'Je m'esgare' [I lose myself], even with its 'licence', has been entirely contradicted. Though we cannot say how long, a significant amount of time separated Montaigne's claim to lose himself ('Je m'esgare', printed in the 1588 edition) from his accusation that it is the reader who gets lost (seen in the manuscript revision). Modern editions make it easy to resolve this contradiction and to imagine Montaigne revising or correcting a passage that had become outdated. But such a reading would not have been available to Montaigne's imagined reader, nor to a reader (no matter how 'diligent') of early modern editions in which these temporal gaps are made invisible. Beyond these practical considerations, Montaigne is clear that his jumps and shifts, his 'escartements', are not to be read as corrections: 'je ne corrige point mes premieres imaginations par les secondes' [I do not correct my first imaginings by my second] (II.37.758/574). Reading this passage, we do not see a narrative of his changing opinions but a double image of different ways of thinking. For the reader, it is not the case that Montaigne thought he had a tendency to lose himself and his 'theme' in 1588, and then realised, while making his changes in the Bordeaux Copy, that it is the reader who gets lost. As readers, we encounter both moments at once: he loses himself and does not lose himself.

This version is still, in any case, inadequate and Montaigne rewrites his idea a final time:

> Il est des ouvrages en Plutarque où il oublie son promesse theme, où le propos desseigné de son argument ne se trouve que par incident, tout estouffé en matiere estrangere: voyez ses alleures au Daemon de Socrates. O Dieu, que ces escartemans gaillardes escapades, que cette variation a de grace beauté, et

plus lors qu'elle semble nonchalante et fortuite que plus elle retire au nonchalant et fortuite. C'est l'indiligent lecteur qui pert mon subject, non pas moy[:] il s'en trouvera tousjours en un coing quelque mot bien serré, il qui ne laisse pas d'estre pertinent et suffisant quoi qu'il ne soit estendu bastant, quoy qu'il ne soit estendu serré.

There are works of Plutarch's in which he forgets his promise theme, in which the designated matter of his subject is found only incidentally, quite smothered in foreign matter: see his movements in 'The Demon of Socrates'. Lord, what grace beauty there is in these gaps lusty sallies and this variation, and more so the more casual and accidental they seem. It is the inattentive reader who loses my subject, not I. Some succinct word about it will always be found off in a corner, which will not fail to be pertinent and sufficient though it might not be long sufficient, though it takes little room.

Across these different versions, Montaigne juggles the order in which he sets out his implied comparison with Plutarch, a modulation that works in concert with a movement away from the impersonal and generic 'autheur' to an insistence on 'moi'. There's a shift also from a more neutral view of 'escartements' to an exuberant celebration of 'gaillardes escapades'.

There is a central question, though, that remains unclear at all stages of composition: who loses whom? Montaigne began the passage by losing himself but only 'par licence'; Plato's dialogues 'roulent au vent' or at least seem to; Plutarch's variation, in the final version, almost 'semble nonchalante' [seems nonchalant], but is judged ultimately to 'retire', to resemble, 'au nonchalant et fortuite'; at the very end of the passage, Montaigne states in plain terms, seemingly contradicting his opening point, that 'c'est l'indiligent lecteur qui pert mon subject, non pas moy'.[14] What, then, is the difference between losing the subject and seeming to lose the subject? And what is the purpose of these difficult and fluctuating distinctions, stitched together over one another in one of the most heavily revised pages of the Bordeaux Copy? What, in short, are we to make of all this seeming and seaming?

Plutarch's role in this passage is to stand as a mirror for Montaigne: the laudatory description of Plutarch's digressive qualities and the 'beauté' of his variation maps congruently onto what we – and, I think, Montaigne himself – think about the *Essais*. It echoes the preceding

---

[14] For Guerrier, the 'seeming' seen among the ancients is only superficial: Montaigne invites his reader to 'ressaisir l'unité sous le désordre apparent, bref à ne pas être dupe du hasard qui semble le régir, de même que lui n'était pas dupe des errances des dialogues de Platon […] ou de la feinte nonchalance de Plutarque' [grasp the unity beneath the apparent disorder; in short, not to fall for the randomness that seems to hold sway, just as he did not fall for the wandering of Plato's dialogues or Plutarch's feigned nonchalance]; Guerrier, *Quand les poètes feignent*, p. 92.

comments about being 'hors de [son] theme' and having titles that 'n'en embrassent pas tousjours la matiere' [do not always embrace their matter]. And yet, in his final version, Montaigne has arranged his ideas – evident in the earlier drafts though without drawing this direct parallel – to draw a clear and distinct line of difference separating Plutarch and himself: Plutarch 'oublie son theme', writes Montaigne, 'non pas moy'.

These layers of revision after revision are a clear indication, should one be needed, of the weight given to style, 'forme' and 'manière', in setting out this ambiguous symmetry between Montaigne and Plutarch, a symmetry in which the essayist and his patron are stitched together, though in a way that serves principally to highlight the 'escartements' in this 'marqueterie'. Style at the level of the sentence and sub-clause allows Montaigne to place his 'pieces décousues' next to one another the better to reveal the contrast: his comments on Plutarch and his comments on himself are written in styles so different that they do not quite fit. The 'couppé', 'serré' quality of Montaigne's self-assessment – 'c'est l'indiligent lecteur qui pert mon subject, non pas moy' – inverts and reverses its structure around 'mon subject', dropping the verb in the second clause. It is tightly wrought and delicately balanced, abrupt and haughty to the point of being defensive. Taken in context, it punctuates the preceding description of Plutarch, a description that begins in apostrophe, invoking the divine ('O Dieu, que ces gaillardes escapades [...]'), and swells with amplification, with its repetition of 'où [...] où' and 'que [...] que [...] plus lors que'. Comparing this version with Montaigne's first attempt reveals how far he has taken what was originally a simple observation and overloaded it with a rush of rhetorical effects that break off suddenly into stark *brevitas* as his attention turns towards himself.[15]

The stylistic shift is what structures Montaigne's complex, 'double' resemblance to Plutarch. It allows him to pick at the seams of this bond even as he ties himself to his patron: as he notes elsewhere, 'La ressemblance ne faict pas tant un comme la difference faict autre' [Resemblance does not make things so much alike as difference makes them unlike] (III.13.1065/815). In expressing these ideas in two radically different styles, he displaces his own exuberant enthusiasm for Plutarch's style

---

[15] The first version reads as follows: 'Il me semble qu'il y a ouvrage en Plutarche dedié à Socrates qui a peine en parle il un mot sur la fin tout le corps estant d'Epaminondas. Ces escartemants sont d'autant plus ingenieus qu'ils semblent estres fortuites' [There is, I think, a work in Plutarch dedicated to Socrates in which he hardly speaks a word about him until the end, the body being about Epaminondas. These gaps are all the more ingenious since they seem to be accidental.]

onto Plutarch himself, while reserving a succinct, curt point for his self-assessment, troubling the easy association of Plutarch's 'gaillardes escapades' [lusty sallies] with his own wandering digressions. What he writes about Plutarch implies that they are similar; how he writes it suggests that they are not.

In this passage and its layers of revision, we see Montaigne thinking 'doubly' as he attempts to express his intuitive idea about how he loses and yet does not lose his subject. After a number of abortive attempts, his idea finds expression once he attaches his self-description to his description of Plutarch – that is, once he thinks through his doubled-up thoughts with his own double, a double who seems just like him and who seems 'nonchalant', subject to fortune. He thinks about and describes himself and Plutarch simultaneously, keeping both of their manners of writing in mind at once, to see that they are both the same and not the same on precisely this point about whether or not they 'really' digress and lose the thread of their writing. Montaigne's writing, then, is just like Plutarch's. Except that it is not.[16]

It is at the meeting point between writing and rewriting, reading himself and reading Plutarch or Plato, that Montaigne thinks through these paradoxical thoughts: it is with these textual practices of sticking together different ways of seeing that this thinking is done. At the very bottom of this heavily revised page, he adds a further qualification: 'Joint qu'à l'adventure ay-je quelque obligation particuliere à ne dire qu'à demy, à dire confusément, à dire diversement discordamment' [Besides, perhaps I have some personal obligation to speak only by halves, to speak confusedly, to speak diversely discordantly]. Montaigne's thinking and writing sustain a plurality of opinion and perspective – he loses his theme, he doesn't; he is like Plutarch, he isn't. It is a way of writing that makes connections that go 'avant et à reculons aussi' [forwards and backwards], 'à sauts et à gambades' [in leaps and gambols], pushing us to read across the passage, non-linearly, finding links and comparisons that seem to rupture under scrutiny, only for another set of connections to emerge. This is a doubtful passage and we do not need to reduce its doubleness, its contradictions, in an attempt to find its definitive, stable meaning. Engaging with Montaigne's prose, entering into 'commerce' with it, using it as he uses Plutarch, we see him now one way, now another.

---

[16] As Montaigne notes in his final chapter, 'La ressemblance ne faict pas tant un comme la difference faict autre' [Resemblance does not make things so much alike as difference makes them unlike] (III.13.1065/814).

This page contains one further manuscript addition that casts some light on the complex relationship between thinking and writing. In the bottom margin, written before the section on 'l'indiligent lecteur' – the later section is shaped to fit around it – and written, apparently, with much greater ease, Montaigne noted the following:

> Par ce que la coupure si frequente des chapitres de quoy j'usoy au commencement m'a semblé rompre l'attention avant qu'elle soit née: et la dissoudre, dedeignant s'y coucher pour si peu, et se recueillir: je me suis mis à les faire plus longs, qui requierent de la proposition et du loisir assigné.

> Because such frequent breaks into chapters as I used at the beginning seemed to me to disrupt and dissolve attention before it was aroused, making it disdain to settle and collect for so little, I have begun making them longer, requiring fixed purpose and assigned leisure.

Montaigne's chapters, made up like those he found in Seneca and Plutarch of 'pieces décousues' but stitched together, serve as a repository for liquid thinking. But the *Essais* are not just a vessel for thoughts themselves, a reservoir in which miscellaneous ideas might be collected, a 'registre' keeping a record of each changing fancy. The form of the *Essais* captures thinking rather than thoughts: they give their reader as well as their author – anyone who uses them – a leaky vessel that holds on to thinking long enough to reveal its mobility, shapelessness and doubleness. In making his chapters longer, Montaigne was not looking to make his 'registre' more comprehensive, increasingly rich or diverse. Lengthening his chapters is a matter not only of making them 'sans terme', endless and unresolved; it is about making them more spacious, giving the attention room to wander without letting it dissolve ('dissoudre') completely. To see this lengthening as linear open-endedness is to see Montaigne's form only 'à demy': the other half lies in its capacity to give form and space to thinking that is 'sans forme'. Montaigne's leaky prose, full of seams, doubles and 'escartements', holds our attention without squeezing too tight. For both the author and the reader – 'indiligent' or otherwise, provided they give him enough time to get (half) lost – the *Essais* prompt as well as record uncertain thinking. Between these loose seams and dropped stitches, Montaigne's writing seems at once to have caught hold of his thinking, with something ('quelque chose') stuck to 'ce papier', and, at the same time, to serve as a resource with which to think, inviting us as readers to imitate Montaigne just as he imitated the Danaïdes, 'remplissant et versant sans cesse' (I.26.146/107).

Present and Future Concerns

Montaigne went back to his early chapters so that he could make them longer: he wanted to give his reader's imagination the time and space to make connections, find gaps and get lost. 'Nos affections s'emportent au-delà de nous' (I.3), almost at the very beginning of the first book, is a chapter concerned explicitly with time, with reaching from the present into the past and the future. This concern is reflected in Montaigne's revisions, in which interpolations bring into contact remote moments of writing, interweaving distinct perspectival threads. In both the 'matière' and its handling, Montaigne collapses chronologies to piece together a chapter that thinks doubtfully, recording multiple, plural ways of seeing, and prompting the reader to attend to ideas and perspectives that point in two directions at once. The first sentence, introduced in the 1588 edition, captures these characteristics in microcosm:

> [B]Ceux qui accusent les hommes d'aller tousjours beant apres les choses futures, & [C]Et [B]nous aprennent à nous saisir des biens presens, & nous rassoir en ceux-là, comme n'ayant aucune prise sur ce qui est à venir; voire assez moins que nous n'avons sur ce qui est passé, touchent la plus commune des humaines erreurs: s'ils [C]S'ils [B]osent appeller erreur, chose à quoy nature mesme nous achemine, pour le service de la continuation de son ouvrage. (I.3.15, punctuation following the Bordeaux Copy, fol. 4r).[17]

> Those who accuse men of always gaping after future things, and teach us to lay hold of present goods and settle ourselves in them, since we have no grip on what is to come, indeed a good deal less than we have on what is past, put their finger on the commonest of human errors, if they dare to call an error something to which Nature herself leads us in serving the continuation of her work. (8)

This is a long sentence and one that would be extended further in the Bordeaux Copy. It is structurally complex too, not simply bounding along from clause to clause, always looking ahead, but looking backwards, looking askance 'd'une veue oblique'. As André Tournon has noted, the shift to a capital letter halfway through – from 's'il' to 'S'il' – confirms that this is 'un retour critique' that holds two equal parts 'en concurrence', balancing two opposing perspectives.[18] With this subtle change, Montaigne presents two clauses as though they were side by side: if the Sceptic is prone to seeing things first 'on one hand' and then on the other, here Montaigne is trying to extend both hands

---

[17] I have provided the [C] markers which are not present in the Villey-Saulnier edition.
[18] Tournon, *Route par ailleurs*, p. 404.

together, encouraging the reader to consider his clauses as simultaneous and yet separate perspectives on our tendency to get ahead of ourselves.

Looking closer still, we can take Tournon's point further. Montaigne's underspecified first clause introduces his anonymous judges, but he leaves his point hanging, suspended in a complex cluster of branching sub-clauses. An age seems to pass before he reaches his main verb ('touchent') and comes to a verdict on their judgement: they ('ceux') put their finger on the commonest of human errors ('touchent la plus commune des humaines erreurs'). This first 'half' of the sentence is itself governed by parallels, comparisons and other balancing techniques: the anonymous 'ceux' are opposed to the equally generic 'les hommes'; 'choses futures' balances 'biens presens' while being doubled by 'ce qui est à venir'. This in turn opens up its own pairing, opposing and balancing 'ce qui est passé'. And so on.

Doubles, pairs, parallels and counterweights are seemingly everywhere, even in just half a sentence. Indeed, they proliferate at such a pace that they make Montaigne's point: grasping 'biens presens', what is in front of us, is enough to be getting on with, without worrying about 'choses futures'. We ought to resist this tendency to let the mind race ahead of itself. Or at least we might come to this conclusion if – 'si' – those who judge such things are right to call something so natural an 'error': perhaps we ought rather to recognise and accept this tendency, knowing that we cannot correct our nature. Where the first half of the sentence pursues its fractal, Hydra-like series of oppositions and balances, this qualification, signalled by the shift to the upper case (from 's'ils' to 'S'ils'), is, it would seem, the principal counterweight that balances everything that comes before it, establishing order and equipollence in a stylistic manifestation of Sceptical even-handedness.[19]

But it is a balancing act that does not quite work: the spinning plates that have been set up in each successive clause and sub-clause come crashing down.[20] The diligent reader, looking closely (able to 'regarde[r] de prez', just as Montaigne looks closely at the doubtful form of Seneca, Plutarch and the rest of the *tiers genre*, II.12.509/377), sees that it is Montaigne, not the anonymous 'ceux', who dares call this natural tendency an 'erreur'. '[B]eant apres les choses futures' – his antithesis, his sub-clauses, his rich and diverse exposition of his argument – Montaigne

---

[19] On the Hydra as a figure of recursive, endless enquiry, see his critique of pedantic philologists who define 'stone' as a type of body, 'body' as a type of substance: 'Pour satisfaire à un doubte, ils m'en donnent trois: c'est la teste de Hydra' [To satisfy a doubt, they give me three: it is the Hydra's head] (III.13.1069/819). See also II.20.675/511, discussed below.
[20] On Montaigne as a 'juggler' of clauses, see Chapter 1.

has struggled to grasp ('saisir') his first premise: it has got away from him and slipped between his fingers. The first half of the sentence, if we cut through its copiousness, contains two judgements: the judgement of 'ceux' who criticise 'les hommes' for chasing after future concerns, and the judgement of Montaigne that this accusation touches on man's most common error. In accumulating his diverse perspectives, he loses his thread, elides these two judgements, and displaces his own judgement onto 'ceux', disowning it and arguing against it. It is a sentence that reveals Montaigne shifting his perspective 'de minute en minute' (III.2.805/611).

Montaigne equivocates in his judgement of these anonymous judges: they are both correct – they 'touchent la plus commune des humaines erreurs' – and incorrect: to err in living according to Nature is surely a contradiction. It is in the shape and movement of Montaigne's prose that this unstable doubleness emerges. His balancing qualification ('S'ils osent appeller') is wrong: it draws an inference without foundation, with the result that Montaigne is arguing with himself. But at the same time, it proves him right: his error testifies to his assertion that 'les hommes' are 'tousjours beant apres les choses futures' [men always go gaping after future things], that Nature (as Montaigne notes in a post-1588 extension) 'nous imprim[e] cette imagination fausse' [imprints in us this false idea], pushing us to race ahead without grasping what is at hand. Importantly, he does not describe this doubleness, nor does he say that the anonymous accusers are *somewhat* right, or right given a certain set of circumstances. Rather, it is the network of clauses, perspectives and caveats that reveals the pattern of Montaigne's thinking and calls on the attention and judgement of the reader to both follow this pattern and go beyond it.

This one sentence, included at the beginning of the chapter for the 1588 edition, shows the cross-currents, the doubleness, of Montaigne's thought in the moment. It introduces a chapter that is concerned explicitly with movement across time: with yearning after an ungraspable future and reaching back towards a time we have left; with transporting oneself into historical moments, ancient and modern; with jumps from one moment of thought and writing to another.

Between the first edition and the version in the Bordeaux Copy, the chapter quintupled in size, overloading the original five hundred words with layers of addition and reflection. In the 1580 text, Montaigne told five stories, all taken from modern history, about military men caring in different ways for their bodily remains and their posthumous 'fortune': Bertrand du Guesclin, who died commanding a siege, ultimately served as a platter on which his defeated enemy placed the keys to the fortress;

Edward I of England had his son swear to boil his bones and carry them as a totem whenever his army fought the Scots, and so on. The chapter ends with something of a volte-face: a story about Maximilian I and his coy, bashful concern not to be seen naked (indeed, not to be seen at all) after his death. But even with the concluding twist, this collection of stories offers a coherent reflection on the proper degree of care a nobleman ought to have for his mortal remains.[21] There are no great leaps, no 'escartements' for stray thoughts for drip through, and it all comes to an end rather abruptly.

The subsequent additions change that. What was a neat arrangement of examples concerning material presence after death bubbles up, percolating with diverse thoughts about the New World, about Plato and his '[C]grande precepte', 'Fay ton faict and te cognoy' [Do thy job and know thyself] (I.3.15/8), about the difference between esteem and affection, about servitude and obligation to princes, about the tendency to flatter and speak sycophantically even after a king has died, about frank judgements against tyrants from critics who sometimes find their voice even when tyrants are still living.[22] The chapter is stuffed with anecdotes, references and tangents. And that accounts only for the material inserted before the first of those five original stories.

'[B]Nous ne sommes jamais chez nous, nous sommes tousjours au-delà' [We are never at home, we are always beyond], wrote Montaigne immediately after the long, complex opening sentence (I.3.15/8). In his writing as much as his thought, Montaigne is always on the move, always somewhere else. Following this movement from one compositional moment to another, tracing the 'transposition de chronologie', uncovers the 'poursuites [...] sans terme, et sans forme' of his 'esprit' (III.13.1068/818). Across the different scales of this chapter, within a single sentence and across the chapter as a whole, in one moment of writing and across the decades of composition, Montaigne's perspective is seen always to be doubled up in its vagabond wandering, retracing his steps to look again, look a little closer, and see things from a different perspective. His is a 'vagabondage' that is affective, cognitive and stylistic, operating through spatial movement, mapping a journey of the heart and mind across the space of the page and by way of Rome, Paris, the battlefields of Europe, the New World and Antiquity.

---

[21] On early modern conceptions of death, afterlives and the power of language (and particularly tense and grammar) to shape these afterlives, see Neil Kenny, *Death and Tenses: Posthumous Presence in Early Modern France* (Oxford: Oxford University Press, 2015).
[22] On frank speech and future concerns about servitude and obligation, see Luke O'Sullivan, 'On Being Tongue-Tied: *Franchise*, Fluency, and Precarity in Montaigne's "De la vanité"', *Forum for Modern Language Studies*, 59.4 (2023), 616–35.

Montaigne's revisions to this chapter illustrate the effects of his transposed chronology: in rewriting it – that is, making it longer and more diverse – he has written a series of Senecan epistles on this central theme of present and future concerns, but, rather than presenting them sequentially, he overlaps them, collapsing the chronology of thinking and writing so that we, as readers, think of and through these diverse but associated ideas at once. The work to make these chapters longer does not plug gaps so much as uncover them, letting them make their presence felt. 'Béant après les choses futures', reaching for connections between the words he has written and those he is about to, Montaigne overlays a study of noble manliness in confronting death with a series of thoughts not on martial but on political and ethical power, redirecting attention from the battlefield to the forum or the prince's court. These different arenas inflect each other at a distance, inviting diverse assessments of '[C]vertu' and 'posterité' (I.3.16/9) to imagine the various origins of the power exhibited by these men and their bodies, a power that is a product, variously, of noble character, servitude, frank judgement, and mortal, material, almost magical remains. There is no clear argument structuring these reflections but, thinking through different forms of the '[A]soing que nous avons de nous au delà cette vie' [the concerns we have for ourselves beyond this life] (I.3.17–18/10), Montaigne moves between different perspectives, surveying diverse 'visages' and exploring the gaps between them.

Mixed Feelings

'Nous ne goustons rien de pur' is another of Montaigne's chapters that swelled with each edition. It began as a straightforward account of the 'foiblesse', the weakness, of the human condition: nothing we encounter can 'tomber en nostre usage' [come into our experience] without losing its 'simplicité et pureté naturelle' (II.20.673/510). Nature's 'elemens' have to be changed, 'alterez', for us to handle them, just as we debase gold and other metals ('il le faut empirer par quelque autre matiere pour l'accommoder à nostre service'). 'Usage', as was seen in Montaigne's dealings with authorship, is all that truly belongs to us, and it transforms the material to which it is applied. Montaigne's focus, in this first version, remains fixed on the debasement of supposed goods. The 'voluptez, plaisirs, et biens' that we experience are all tinged with 'quelque melange de mal et d'incommodité' [some mixture of pain and discomfort], and even 'les loix mesmes de la justice' [the very laws of justice] cannot exist without some 'injustice' creeping in. Montaigne calls on a paraphrased line of Greek verse ('Les dieux nous vendent tous les biens qu'ils nous donnent' [The gods sell us all the good things they give us]), along with a quotation from Tacitus and a reference to Plato, to show that we cannot remove these 'incommodités': those who try find themselves hacking away at 'la teste de Hydra' [the Hydra's head]. With that, this short chapter comes to a neat and uncomplicated close (II.20.673–5/510–12).[23]

For a chapter on admixture and alloys, it strikes a remarkably singular, unified tone. It is, one might say, an expression of a Sceptical line of thinking, marked by doubt in one's ability to apprehend the world as it truly is, but the chapter itself is not doubtful, nor enquiring, double or any other epithet we might associate with a way of thinking that is 'sans terme' and 'sans forme'.[24] By 1588, however, this had changed. The shift to thinking doubly can be seen in the way Montaigne introduces two of his later reflections. First, he introduces Metrodorus, who speaks 'pareillement' [likewise] to the line of Greek that precedes him (or, perhaps, to another 1588 insertion on 'morbidezza' and 'mollesse', those 'maladifves et douloureuses' [sickly and painful] qualities that characterise the 'extreme volupté' of sexual pleasure).[25] Second, in a relatively long passage that is included after the Tacitus quotation, Montaigne declares that 'Il est pareillement vray, que pour l'usage de la vie et service du commerce public, il y peut avoir de l'excez en la pureté et perspicacité de nos esprits' [It is likewise true that for the uses of life and for the service of public business there may be excess in the purity and perspicacity of our minds] (II.20.675/511).

This chapter became increasingly multifaceted with Montaigne's numerous additions and second thoughts. But across these different moments and perspectives, what emerges is a way of thinking concerned not only with admixture but with disagreement, especially disagreement with oneself. Thinking 'pareillement', Montaigne is caught between two contradictory assessments of what he is doing. On the one hand, he finds his theme an opportunity to indulge in the pleasurable pastime of finding curious admixtures, a *divertissement* not unlike the game of

---

[23] Cf. *Essais* 1580, II.20.486–7.
[24] As Sextus notes in the *Outlines of Pyrrhonism*, the Sceptics adhere to 'appearances' ('phaenomena, id est apparentia') while doubting whether the underlying object is such as it appears ('an tale sit ipsum subjectum quale apparet') (I.10.13–14). On 'phantasies' or appearances as 'passive impressions' and thus 'not disputed by Sextus Empiricus, who instead focuses his attack on the dogmatic claim that representations are true reflections of things', see Jan Miernowski, 'Montaigne on Truth and Skepticism', in Desan (ed.), *The Oxford Handbook of Montaigne*, pp. 544–61 (esp. pp. 553–8).
[25] 'Pareillement' in this clause introducing Metrodorus would ultimately be crossed out in the Bordeaux Copy, fol. 289r.

hunting out 'subtilitez frivoles et vaines' that are the focus of another chapter (I.54).[26] Equally, though, he finds such thinking to be a stultifying, impractical obsession with overfine distinctions – an obsession that ought to be avoided; a hindrance that impedes ('empesche') the execution of anything at all ('aux executions de grand et de petit pois') (II.20.675/512). The chapter presents a series of developments in which Montaigne engages with his own contradictory approaches to admixture but without zooming out to reflect on, explain or gloss his self-contradiction. In short, it is a chapter in which the formal practices of overlaying different ways of looking reveal – for Montaigne as much as his reader – that he is not entirely sure of himself: that he is uncertain of his thinking and of the whole enterprise of looking closely that forms the essential core not only of this chapter but of the *Essais*.

This uncertainty and self-disagreement is reflected in Montaigne's relationship with his interlocutors, of which there are many.[27] In the 1588 text, having quoted a line and a half from Lucretius on the resemblance of pain and sexual pleasure (a pleasure so consubstantial with pain that it is called 'langueur, mollesse, foiblesse, defaillance, *morbidezza*' [languor, softness, weakness, faintness, *morbidezza*]), Montaigne changes tack: 'Metrodorus ~~pareillement~~ disoit qu'en la tristesse il y a quelque alliage de plaisir' [Metrodorus ~~likewise~~ used to say that in sadness there is some alloy of pleasure] (II.20.673–4/510).[28] As Terence Cave has argued, one of the 'lignes de force majeures' of the *Essais* consists in resolving cognitive dissonances (social as well as intrapersonal dissonances) through a continual process of attunement ('travail

---

[26] His attraction to such admixtures in sex – the resemblance of pain and '[le] plaisir [...] de la generation en son poinct plus excessif' [the pleasure [...] of generation at its most excessive point] (II.20.674/511) – heightens the sense that this accumulation of contraries is itself directed not only by curiosity but also by pleasure. On subtlety, see Ian Maclean, 'Montaigne/Cardano: The Reading of Subtlety/The Subtlety of Reading', *French Studies*, 37.2 (1982), 144–56, and Raphaële Garrod, 'Subtle Democritus: Natural Philosophy, Ethics, and Poetics in Montaigne's "De Democritus et Heraclitus" (I, 50)', *Montaigne Studies*, 34 (2022), 59–72.

[27] The chapter accumulates 'dicts', sayings, which are included in each stage of composition: '[A]C'est ce que dit un verset Grec ancien'; '[C]Socrates dict que'; '[B]Metrodorus disoit'; '[C]Et dict un Attalus en Seneque'; '[C]C'est ce que les anciens disent de Simonides' (II.20.673–5/510–12).

[28] On Renaissance conceptions of 'mollesse' [softness] as gendered, see Freya Baur and Teodoro Patera (eds), *Mollesses renaissantes: défaillances et assouplissement du masculin* (Geneva: Droz, 2021). The shift to a more sexually explicit mingling of pain and pleasure appears to be prompted – rather than simply illustrated – by Montaigne's reading of Lucretius: in his reading, he highlighted the lines quoted in this chapter (IV.1133–4), along with dozens of others in the second half of Book 4 of *De Rerum natura*, which focuses on love, lust and its associated disappointments. See Screech, *Montaigne's Annotated Copy of Lucretius*, p. 356.

continuel d'ajustement' or 'de réglage').²⁹ The *Essais*, Cave suggests, attend to moments of difference and disjunction and accommodate them in a 'dialogue communicatif' between different ideas or ways of seeing, between author and book, or between thought and body, between Montaigne and the authors he reads, between Montaigne and his reader.³⁰ The introduction of Metrodorus seems to be a further instance of this sort of calibration: within a broader reflection on tension and admixture in thought, feeling and perception, it marks a shift from thinking about pain in pleasure to pleasure in pain, a shift from thinking with one Epicurean, Lucretius, to another, Metrodorus.³¹

What follows, though, is not a moment of attunement but of dissonance:

> Je ne sçay s'il vouloit dire autre chose; mais moy, j'imagine bien qu'il y a du dessein, du consentement et de la complaisance à se nourrir en la melancholie; je dis outre l'ambition, qui s'y peut encore mesler. (II.20.674)
>
> I do not know whether he meant something else, but for my part I indeed imagine that there is design, consent, and pleasure in feeding one's melancholy; I mean beyond the ambition that can also be involved. (510)

Montaigne's 'je ne sçay' marks a moment of strangely acute uncertainty, a collapse in the routine work of mind-reading that runs untroubled through his engagement with numerous other 'dicts' [sayings] in this chapter. At the same time, this uncertainty leaves him more confident of himself and of what he thinks: 'but for my part', he cuts in, resolute.

Montaigne is thinking here not only with Metrodorus but with Seneca. He encountered this Epicurean saying in Seneca's 99th epistle which is itself a letter-within-a-letter, and this prompts in Montaigne's chapter a flurry of Senecan borrowings.³² In this 99th letter to Lucilius, Seneca transcribes a copy of a letter he had sent to their mutual friend, Marullus,

---

²⁹ Terence Cave, 'Un demi-tour de cheville: Pour une lecture cognitive des *Essais*', *Bulletin de la société internationale des amis de Montaigne*, 74.1 (2022), 109–27 (pp. 116–17). Cave alludes to 'Nous ne goutons rien de pur' briefly in his conclusion, which he takes as a reflection on the 'voisinage *imperceptible*' [imperceptible closeness] of 'états qui passent habituellement pour être opposés' [states that are typically understood as opposed] (p. 127).
³⁰ Ibid., p. 119.
³¹ It was in response to Epicurus' dying words, in which he entreated his inheritors to honour 'la memoire de luy et de Metrodorus', that Montaigne noted how 'nous sommes, je ne sçay comment, doubles' [we are, I know not how, double] (II.16.619–20/469). On Epicurus' dying words, see Chapter 3.
³² On this letter and the letter that precedes it, see Marcus Wilson, 'The Subjugation of Grief in Seneca's *Epistles*', in *The Passions in Roman Thought and Literature*, ed. Susan Morton Braund and Christopher Gill (Cambridge: Cambridge University Press, 1997), pp. 48–67.

when the latter's son had died and Marullus had been said to have become 'soft', 'molliter', in his grief (*Ep.* 99.1). It is that softness that finds its echo in the sexual 'mollesse' and 'morbidezza' Montaigne has just been discussing, albeit in quite a different context. In his letter, Seneca quotes from another letter, that of Metrodorus to his sister, in which he says that there is a pleasure related to sadness that ought to be sought out in trying times. Seneca cites him directly, quoting him in Greek: 'Ipsa Metrodori verba subscripsi' [I have appended the very words of Metrodorus] (*Ep.* 99.25). But he is not making use of Epicurean 'common property': he cites Metrodorus not to agree with him, not to console Marullus and excuse his softness, but to disapprove of the Epicurean's lesson and to hold Marullus to an imagined response: 'Illud nullo modo probo, quod ait Metrodorus'; 'De quibus non dubito quid sis sensurus' [And in no wise do I approve of the remark of Metrodorus'; 'I have no doubt what your feelings will be in these matters] (*Ep.* 99.25–6).

Metrodorus is introduced by Seneca not as an authority to be agreed with but as an analogue of Marullus, subject to the same reproach: both have found pleasure in grief, and both have gone looking for it. Seeing his own softness reflected in Metrodorus, Marullus is supposed to be able to recognise it as a moral failing and correct himself. In Montaigne's use of Metrodorus, this context has been erased entirely. Montaigne's doubt in his interpretation of Metrodorus ('Je ne sçay s'il vouloit dire autre chose') mirrors Seneca's emphatic, imposing certainty in reading the thoughts and feelings of his interlocutor. Here, in engaging with a nested trio of letters, Montaigne stumbles not in establishing what he thinks but in establishing communication: Seneca, with whom he so often agrees, is here on the other side of the argument; that opposition, silently erased, leaves him imagining that Metrodorus, with whom he does agree, might have meant something altogether entirely different.

The dialogue with Seneca continues, but uncomfortably: Montaigne's qualification – 'je dis outre l'ambition' [I mean beyond ambition] – is a direct response to his unnamed interlocutor who, in another letter, seems to entirely contradict his refutation of Metrodorus: 'Est aliqua et doloris ambitio' [There is an element of self-seeking even in our sorrow] (*Ep.* 63.2). Montaigne would quote from this letter directly, in translation, in a post-1588 addition to this passage:

[C]Et dict un Attalus en Seneque que la memoire de nos amis perdus nous agrée comme l'amer au vin trop vieux,
  Minister vetuli, puer, falerni,
  Ingere mi calices amariores;
et comme des pommes doucement aigres. ~~Etiam retinentibus animum levant lachrimae profusae.~~

[C]And one Attalus, in Seneca, says that the memory of our lost friends is agreeable to us like the bitterness in a wine that is too old,
   Boy, that serve old Falernian wine,
   Pour me a bitterer cup for mine,
and like apples sweetly tart. ~~Though we try to hold them in check, tears, having fallen, ease the soul.~~

This quotation of Seneca's Attalus is a further instance of Montaigne agreeing with an interlocutor dismissed by Seneca: Seneca introduces his words with a note of derision ('Si illi credimus' [If we believe him]) before stating that he sees things differently ('Ego non idem sentio') (*Ep.* 63.6–7). Montaigne returns to Seneca again with a quotation in Latin taken from *Ep.* 99.16, and though this was ultimately crossed out, a similar line from another letter would be added slightly later: '[C]Nullum sine auctoramento malum est' [There is no evil without its compensation] (II.20.674/511; *Ep.* 69.4). In both cases, Montaigne shows Seneca disagreeing with himself (or at least seeming to: he ignores Seneca's detailed explanation of the distinction between letting natural tears fall and the Epicurean model of consolation which imagines that 'joy and grief can be mingled').[33]

One might take this as an instance of Montaigne lifting material indiscriminately from his reading, finding something he agrees with and can use without caring too much about what Seneca made of it. But it is not the only instance of intertextual tension here: the couplet from Catullus quoted above (27.1–2) is from a poem about demanding pure, unwatered, unmixed wine, wine that is 'merus' (27.7): 'abite, lymphae | vini pernicies' [begone, away with you, water, destruction of wine] (27.5–6). In a chapter on mixture, Montaigne's choice of poetic illustration could hardly be less apt.

In Seneca, Montaigne encounters the Stoic arguing for emotional purity: 'Quid tu dicis', he says to an imagined Metrodorus, 'miscendam ipsi dolori voluptatem?' [But what do you mean, by saying that with our very grief there should be a blending of pleasure?] (*Ep.* 99.27). For the Stoic, we should add nothing ('Nihil [...] adiciamus', *Ep.* 99.16) to our natural grief; our emotions – joy and grief – are and ought to be

---

[33] For a detailed analysis of these theories of consolation and the relationship between joy and grief, see Margaret Graver, 'The Weeping Wise: Stoic and Epicurean Consolations in Seneca's 99th Epistle', in *Tears in the Graeco-Roman World*, ed. Thorsten Fögen (Berlin: De Gruyter, 2009), pp. 235–52 (p. 250). Graver goes on to note that, for Seneca, 'there can be no such comparison' between joy and grief, 'and no counteracting. The joy experienced by the wise person in the memory of his friend is unalloyed' (p. 250). Though Seneca does not use this metallurgical term in this letter, one might note its salience, given Montaigne's theme.

unalloyed. But in reading these letters-within-letters, Montaigne finds himself uncertain: uncertain of what his interlocutors mean, uncertain of where his allegiances lie. Reading letters structured by disagreement, he produces a reflection on admixture marked by the 'confusion' that 'Nature nous descouvre' [Nature reveals to us] (II.20.674/511). Seneca is, at least as Montaigne reads him, a figure of admixture, capable of disagreeing with Metrodorus while espousing virtually identical points elsewhere in his letters. Montaigne is not sure what Metrodorus might have meant, and it seems that he is similarly uncertain of Seneca, but he knows himself: 'mais moy, j'imagine bien qu'il y a du dessein, consentement et de la complaisance à se nourrir en la melancholie' [but for my part I indeed imagine that there is design, consent, and pleasure in feeding one's melancholy].

This moment of certainty is counterbalanced by another. In the same period of revision as the passage discussing Metrodorus, Montaigne added a conclusion to this chapter, similarly presented as a moment of parallel, 'likewise' thinking, and one that echoes the introduction's discussion of 'usage': '[B]Il est pareillement vray que, pour l'usage de la vie et service du commerce public, il y peut avoir de l'excez en la pureté et perspicacité de nos esprits' [It is likewise true that for the uses of life and for the service of public business there may be excess in the purity and perspicacity of our minds] (II.20.675/511). The 'subtilité' of this 'clarté penetrante' [penetrating clarity] is entirely unsuited to 'cette vie tenebreuse et terreste' [this shadowy and earthy life]. We should manage human affairs 'plus grossierement et superficiellement', he declares: 'Il n'est pas besoin d'esclairer les affaires si profondement et si subtilement' [There is no need to light up affairs so deeply and so subtly]. Montaigne makes this point repeatedly before concluding with a reference to two men of his acquaintance who, for all their intellect, were entirely lost when dealing with practical matters: 'Je sçay un grand diseur et tresexcellent peintre de toute sorte de mesnage, qui a laissé bien piteusement couler par ses mains cent milles livres de rente'; 'J'en sçay un autre qui dict, qui consulte, mieux qu'un homme de son conseil [...] toutesfois, aux effects, ses serviteurs trouvent qu'il est tout autre' [I know one great talker and very excellent portrayer of every sort of managing, who has very pitifully let the revenue of a hundred thousand francs slip through his hands'; 'I know another who speaks and gives advice better than any man in his council [...] in practice, his servants find him quite different] (II.20.675/512).

This critique of subtlety and curiosity takes direct aim at the modes of attention Montaigne has been engaged in. '[B]On s'y perd', he writes, drawing on Livy, 'à la consideration de tant de lustres contraires et formes diverses. [C]*Voluntantibus res inter se pugnantes obtorperant animi*' [You get lost considering so many contrasting aspects and diverse shapes. *In revolving mutually contradictory things, their minds had become stupefied.*] Where Montaigne had been picking away at contradictions and tensions, not only in the world but also, I suggest, within an individual, in Seneca's complicated and seemingly contradictory account of grief and joy, here the chapter reveals a similar cognitive dissonance in his own thinking. In turning on 'les opinions de la philosophie eslevées' [the lofty ideas of philosophy] and finding them 'ineptes à l'exercice' [inept in practice], the conclusion added in 1588 offers not so much a Sceptical counterargument to the subtle uncovering of admixture that had been Montaigne's focus, but rather a moment of self-doubt and self-awareness. It is a moment of self-critique in which he tries to distinguish himself from an imagined pedant such as Simonides, who would be included in a post-1588 addition: 'par ce que son imagination luy presentoit [...] diverses considerations aigües et subtiles, doubtant laquelle estoit la plus vraysemblable, il desespera du tout de la verité' [because his imagination presented him [...] with diverse acute and subtle considerations, being in doubt which was the most probable, he totally despaired of the truth] (II.20.675/512). Simonides' attention to subtle differences offers no illumination, no advantage at all, and what once had the glimmer of *divertissement* seems now a pit of despair.

In these two moments of parallel, 'likewise' ('pareillement') thinking, Montaigne examined himself, his interlocutors and the relationship between them. At the same time, it is in thinking 'pareillement' that Montaigne interrogates the cognitive and intellectual habits that structure his *Essais*. Seneca's letters (and letters-within-letters) show the Stoic to be mixed and contradictory: he disagrees with Metrodorus and Marullus while saying much the same himself in another letter. Montaigne's own chapter, in which moments of writing are piled up and overlain, reveals a similar cognitive dissonance. On the one hand, he indulges his curiosity, teasing out pleasingly subtle admixtures, and, on the other, he criticises the vanity and uselessness of this pastime. He does not correct his earlier indulgence: in fact, he continues in later editions to apply a 'clarté penetrante' that, in the 1588 conclusion, would be judged excessive and in need of tempering. Like gold, he says, this 'pointue vivacité d'ame' [acute vivacity of mind] needs to be debased if it is not to 'trouble nos negotiations' [disturb our negotiations]. This is a chapter that develops competing lines of argument: we cannot perceive anything purely or clearly *and* we see things too clearly; notice this admixture that surrounds you since you cannot avoid it *and* do not pay it any heed as it will prevent you from doing anything. It is a chapter that inverts Lipsius' summary of letter writing – 'bis non scribo', 'I do not rewrite them': Montaigne writes twice and writes doubly, 'pareillement', to examine the admixture present even in his reflections on and responses to admixture.

Montaigne concludes his chapter by suggesting that this sort of subtle enquiry is no more than a road to stupefaction and that we would do better to get on with practical matters 'grossierement'. It is a conclusion that seems to offer a way through the tensions and ambiguities that run through this chapter. But Montaigne's call for simplicity and dullness is complicated by the fact that he disregarded it: he continued, after 1588, to gather his curiosities. Perhaps we should read the chapter as a demonstration – a clever, subtle, curious one at that – showing how mixture runs through everything. Perhaps we should read in the structure of the chapter a moral lesson, starting with one 'foiblesse' – our inability to perceive things purely – and ending with another – our tendency to see things too clearly, or more clearly than is useful; our vain efforts to grasp 'choses' too tightly. Perhaps we should seek out Montaigne's subtle, subterranean shifts and isolate the conflicting lines of argument at work in this compact chapter. And perhaps we shouldn't. Perhaps the message is, in fact, quite simple: 'L'homme en tout et par tout, n'est que rapiessement et bigarrure' [Man, in all things and throughout, is but patchwork and motley] (II.20.675/511). Whether we look closely or 'grossierement', doubleness, admixture and dissonance run through not only the subject of this chapter, and not only through its form and style, but through the thinking it communicates and the contradictory responses it demands.

'Bis scribo'

'Bis non scribo, bis vix eas lego' [I do not rewrite them, and I hardly re-read them]: Lipsius' account of letter writing, discussed in the previous chapter, takes writing once to be a clear sign, as well as a promise, of frank sincerity. Writing twice – writing doubly – threatens to break this contract maintained between the simple letter writer and the addressee, especially when writing twice is more about getting lost and letting one's thoughts wander than it is about correcting the record.

This chapter has taken three 'eschantillons' [samples] of Montaigne's doubtful, double form to show how it not only traces a roving, vagabond mind, but serves as a tool supporting contradictory, dissonant thought. He was not writing only for himself though: his attention to the reading and misreading of what Metrodorus might have meant, his forewarning to an 'indiligent lecteur', serve as pertinent reminders that his doubtful, double writing is concerned always with successful communication. For all of his doubleness, he remains a straight talker: he is the author of a 'livre de bonne foy' in which we find him 'en [s]a façon simple' ('Au lecteur', p. 3/2). Montaigne's doubtful writing depends on the admixture, the harmony, of these dissonant qualities: double and simple, both at the same time.

Chapter 5

Simple Truths

The *Essais* are a work in which Montaigne developed a new form of writing doubtfully and doubly. But to be 'double' in how one speaks or writes, to have 'une langue double', is to be a liar, a spreader of rumour, a 'susurrateur' whispering one thing to this person and another to that, and, in doing so, undermining not only houses but 'villes fortes' and 'nations puissantes'.[1] As Augustine explained in his two treatises on lying, it is not only the *intentio fallendi*, the intention to deceive, that makes the liar; it is their *duplex cor*, their double heart, and their *duplex cogitatio*, their double thought.[2] To be 'double' is, for Montaigne's contemporaries at least, tantamount to hypocrisy. Take, for instance, Antoine du Val's pleonastic pairing in his argument that Calvin's theory of predestination makes God 'double & hypocrite: car commander le contraire de ce qu'on veult, c'est l'hypocrisie, & faulx semblant' [double and hypocritical, because commanding the opposite of what one wishes is hypocrisy and dissemblance].[3]

---

[1] See, for instance, Erasmus, *Lingua* (Antwerp: Michael Hillenius, 1525), esp. fol. L5iiiv, drawing on Ecclesiasticus 28:15–30. For a French imitation of this text, translating 'bilinguis' as 'une langue double', see Jean de Marconville, *Traicté de la bonne & mauvaise langue* (Paris: Jean Dalier, 1573). My French quotations are from Marconville's paraphrase of Ecclesiasticus, fol. 19v. On rumour, gossip and the figure of the wandering or double tongue, see Emily Butterworth, *The Unbridled Tongue: Babble and Gossip in Renaissance France* (Oxford: Oxford University Press, 2016).

[2] 'Duplex cor dicitur esse mentientis, id est, duplex cogitatio' [A liar is said to have a double heart, which is to say a double thought]; Augustine of Hippo, *De mendacio*, in *Operum D. Aurelii Augustini Hipponensis episcopi*, 11 vols (Antwerp: Plantin, 1576), vol. 4, p. 3. For early modern French responses to Augustinian conceptions of lying, see James Helgeson, *The Lying Mirror: The First-Person Stance and Sixteenth-Century Writing* (Geneva: Droz, 2012), pp. 110–18.

[3] Antoine du Val, *Les Contrarietez et contredits qui se trouvent en la doctrine de Jean Calvin, Luter, et autres nouveaux Evangelistes de nostre temps* (Paris: Chesneau, 1567), fol. 44v.

'Doubte' and 'double' differ only by a letter, and Montaigne's doubleness points just as readily to dissemblance as to philosophical enquiry. It is a quality that leaves him exposed to accusations not only of hypocrisy but of dubious reasoning and wily sophistry. Indeed, one of Aristotle's *Sophistical Refutations* (*De Sophisticis Elenchis*) concerns precisely this word and the sophist's trick of making 'le defendeur ridicule, en luy faisant repeter plusieurs fois un mesme mot' [the defender ridiculous by making him repeat the same word many times]. The sophist 'entreprendra de prouver qu'une mesme chose est le double, & n'est pas le double: & dira ainsi, *Le deux est le double de l'unité. Le deux n'est pas le double de trois. Donc une mesme chose est le double et n'est pas le double*' [tries to prove that one single thing is both double and not double, and will say as follows: *Two is double one. Two is not double three. Therefore one single thing is double and not double.*][4] The decision to exemplify the sophist's dubious, doubtful reasoning with this basic computational function is itself illustrative. The sophist, who aspires only to vanquish ('vaincre') their opponent, is characterised by a double way of speaking: they use words without considering their relation to the thing they describe, entangling their interlocutor in 'tromperie' [tricks], 'menterie' [lying] and 'repetition ridicule' [ridiculous repetition].[5]

In the intellectual and political climate of late sixteenth-century France, the matter of truth and dissemblance was a serious one. Montaigne's opening moves establish his persona not only as someone acting in good faith, author of a 'livre de bonne foy' ('Au lecteur', p. 3/2), but as something of an expert in navigating this particularly thorny issue. An early reader picking up a 1580 copy of the *Essais* and turning through its opening chapters would have encountered a book directed predominantly at questions of how and when to speak and how to judge the speech of someone else: those early chapters variously consider liars, whether to beg for mercy when bested in battle, how to go about dangerous negotiations, and the difference between people who weigh their words carefully and those who have a talent for improvisation. In beginning his project, Montaigne presented himself as an authority on matters of political, military and ethical prudence, and, across these different areas of reflection, his expertise lies with speech.[6]

---

[4] Aristotle, 'Second livre des elenches sophistique', in *L'Organe, c'est à dire l'instrument du discours*, trans. Philippe Canaye ([Geneva]: Jean de Tournes, 1589), p. 712.
[5] Ibid., pp. 706–7, 746.
[6] Montaigne's seventeenth-century Italian translator, Girolamo Canini, expanded his title to reflect these areas of expertise: *Saggi di Michel sig. di Montagna, overo Discorsi naturali, politici, e morali* (Venice: Marco Ginammi, 1633). On this edition, see Boutcher, *The School of Montaigne*, vol. 2, pp. 152–64.

Despite this framing, Montaigne gives his readers more than a few reasons to doubt his 'bonne foy' and to be suspicious of his self-presentation as a plain, free and frank speaker.[7] His doubleness seems to be entirely at odds with such claims, bearing a striking similarity to dissemblance. What's more, his whole project of self-presentation is itself suspect: 'Mais, à qui croyrons nous parlant de soy, en une saison si gastée? veu qu'il en est peu, ou point, à qui nous puissions croire, parlant d'autruy, où il y a moins d'interest à mentir' [But whom shall we believe when he talks about himself, in so corrupt an age, seeing that there are few or none whom we can believe when they speak of others, where there is less incentive for lying?] (II.18.666/505). In an age characterised by flattery and vanity, by civil war breeding distrust between neighbours and corrupting the simple honesty of civil society, there is always something to be gained by being duplicitous, something to be won by speaking falsely, positively or negatively, about someone else, and all the more when speaking about oneself. Who, then, should be taken at their word? Who should be believed in such a corrupted age? Not, it would seem, Montaigne, writing 'doublement, obscurement, obliquement' and, worse still, 'parlant de soy' [speaking about himself].

Critical assessments of truth in the *Essais* have tended to distinguish between different sorts of truth. There is 'the truth of the schools', the sort of truth Scepticism might be concerned with: truth about things in the world, which – for the Sceptics and other doubters, at least – requires a clarity of perception and a degree of knowledge beyond our capacity. In its place, Montaigne is seen to embrace a 'vérité du mensonge', a truth analogous only to that of legal fictions (*fictiones legis*) or of 'tesmoignages fabuleux' [fabulous testimonies] that serve as true ones, provided they are possible (I.21.105/75). This is a truth of pure possibility, limited to speculation and exploration at the level of the hypothetical.[8]

---

[7] Jan Miernowski has read in the 'Au lecteur' 'des propositions contradictoires et autodestructrices' akin to the Sceptical use of self-purging formulae, introducing 'un livre de mauvaise foi' while playing on the modesty topos with a 'cascade' of negatives ('aucune fin', 'nulle consideration' and so on). See Miernowski, *L'Ontologie de la contradiction sceptique*, pp. 22–3. For a similar reading of the 'Au lecteur' as a 'double jeu de la provocation et de la séduction' characterised by 'ruses', see Yves Delègue, *Montaigne et la mauvaise foi* (Paris: Garnier, 1998), ch. 1: 'La "bonne foy" en question: l'avis "au lecteur"', pp. 15–33 (p. 33).

[8] On truth operating at a 'niveau hypothétique, de pure possibilité', see Prat, *Constance et inconstance chez Montaigne*, p. 257. On 'la vérité judiciaire' as made up of 'spéculations intellectuelles', 'exercices de virtuoses, libres et peut-être plaisants', see André Tournon, 'La Question du préteur', in Demonet and Legros (eds), *L'Ecriture du scepticisme chez Montaigne*, pp. 265–72 (p. 272). See also Olivier Guerrier, 'Le Champ du "possible": de la jurisprudence aux *Essais*', in Demonet and Legros (eds), *L'Ecriture du scepticisme chez Montaigne*, pp. 159–68.

Alongside this limited truth is an understanding of truth as sincerity, in which Montaigne's opening invocation of *bona fides* calls for a truce with a reader willing to supply their own good faith. This contract is a surrogate for certainty, requiring both parties to act on trust.[9] Between Montaigne's philosophical doubt and his assessment of his political context, there seems to be little place for truth-proper; even less so given his attachment to the form of doubtful, double writing that has been my focus.

Recent scholarship has paid significant attention to Montaigne's 'franchise', his free and frank speech characterised by openness, simplicity and naivety, to read the *Essais* as an exercise in truth-telling.[10] These studies align the 'rhétorique naturalisée' of the *Essais* – their simple, seemingly artless style – with *parrhesia*, the Greek notion of plain speaking in which *logos* and *bios* accord with *ethos*.[11] This is the harmony of speech, life and character that underpins Montaigne's sense that he could see Plutarch 'jusques dans l'ame' [even into his soul] (II.31.716/541). It is this same harmony that is at work in Seneca's own contract with his reader: 'quod sentimus loquamur, quod loquimur sentiamus' [let us say what we feel and feel what we say] (*Ep.* 75.4).[12]

This chapter and the one that follows build on these studies of *parrhesia* in the *Essais* by asking how this aesthetic and ethics of open simplicity – 'Le parler que j'ayme, c'est un parler simple et naif, tel sur le papier qu'à la bouche' [The speech I love is a simple, natural speech, the same on paper as in the mouth] (I.26.171/127) – is troubled and complicated by the doubleness, which is similarly stylistic and

---

[9] See Jan Miernowski, 'Montaigne on Truth and Skepticism', in Desan (ed.), *The Oxford Handbook of Montaigne*, pp. 544–61 (pp. 558–61). André Tournon has read Montaigne's scepticism in light of a legal, judicial framework to present this contract as one of 'véracité', 'bonne foi' and 'confiance' (*Route par ailleurs*, pp. 276–86).

[10] Reinier Leushuis, 'Montaigne *Parrhesiastes*: Foucault's Fearless Speech and Truth-Telling in the *Essays*', pp. 100–21 and Virginia Krause, 'Confession or *Parrhesia*? Foucault after Montaigne', pp. 142–60, both in Zalloua (ed.), *Montaigne after Theory/Theory after Montaigne*; Olivier Guerrier, '*Parrêsia*, de Socrate à Montaigne', in *Rencontre et reconnaissance*, pp. 180–92; John O'Brien, 'Slavery and Freedom in a Time of Civil War: La Boétie, L'Hospital, and Montaigne', *Early Modern French Studies*, 44.1 (2022), 53–68; O'Sullivan, 'On Being Tongue-Tied'.

[11] On Montaigne's 'natural' rhetoric, see Philippe Desan, Déborah Knop and Blandine Perona (eds), *Montaigne: une rhétorique naturalisée?* (Paris: Champion, 2019). In her introduction, Blandine Perona notes that, in spite of the 'opposition entre art et nature, entre rhétorique et sincérité', Montaigne valorises and practises a rhetorical form of doubt and ignorance (pp. 11–13).

[12] On this letter as a model of *parrhesia*, see Michel Foucault, *L'Herméneutique du sujet. Cours au Collège de France, 1981–1982* (Paris: Gallimard, 2001), pp. 384–91; *The Hermeneutics of the Subject*, ed. Frédéric Gros, trans. Graham Burchell (Basingstoke: Palgrave Macmillan, 2005), pp. 401–9.

ethical, that runs through Montaigne's sense of himself, the world and his book. His doubtful truth-telling is not a case of simply 'saying it how it is', speaking sincerely or making a full and accurate record of his judgements, but is concerned rather with developing a form that extends and makes legible the experience of thinking: it is a mode of truthful communication that depends upon the literary and textual practices, indebted to readings of Seneca and Plutarch, that are the subject of this study.

Seneca and Plutarch are key sources for early modern understandings of the social and discursive practices that can be grouped under the name 'parrhesia': they are sources for theoretical outlines of frank truthfulness and they provide practical advice on how to give and receive counsel. They also give expression to concerns and anxieties about the vulnerabilities that proliferate when one enters into a parrhesiastic bargain.[13] My aim in these chapters is not only to highlight their role as models for Montaigne's own sketch of simple truth-telling. Alongside their promotion of an ethical-discursive simplicity, these authors shape his understanding of doubleness and inconstancy. The *parrhesiastes* tells it how it is, but it is with Seneca and Plutarch that Montaigne pulls at the relationship between truth-telling and self-knowledge. It is with this pair and the tensions that emerge from his reading that he forged a paradoxical conception of truth-telling that is both simple and double.

Placing Seneca and Plutarch at the centre of an analysis of truth-telling in the *Essais* reveals at once Montaigne's debt to classical parrhesiastic traditions and his dramatic reversal of their key characteristics and assumptions. Foregrounding these authors uncovers the tensions at the heart of Montaigne's style and illuminates the ethical and communicative problem his form looks to resolve. Writing doubly is not simply an antagonistic rhetorical strategy, aimed at wrong-footing a reader and encouraging critical reassessment, nor only a transcription of cognitive activities, publishing a private record of the author's doubtful reflections, but rather an effort to communicate truthfully and authentically.[14]

---

[13] For a discussion of the early modern reception of Plutarch's essay on flattery and frank speech (*parrhesia*), see Luke O'Sullivan, '"Des responses et rencontres": Frank Speech and Self-Knowledge in Guillaume Bouchet's *Serées*', *Renaissance and Reformation/ Renaissance et réforme*, 43.3 (2020), 167–94. See also David Colclough, *Freedom of Speech in Early Stuart England* (Cambridge: Cambridge University Press, 2005), and Annalisa Ceron, 'How to Advise the Prince: Three Renaissance Forms of Plutarchan Parrhesia', *History of Political Thought*, 38.2 (2017), 239–66.

[14] This is not to suggest that truthful, even friendly communication is incompatible with antagonism. See Scott Francis, 'The Discussion as Joust: *Parrhesia* and Friendly Antagonism in Plutarch and Montaigne', *The Comparatist*, 37 (2013), 122–37.

Seneca and Plutarch, both of whom might readily be seen as advocates of a 'simple' mode of truth-telling, are seen in combination to provide the building blocks that complicate and contradict that central principle of simplicity: here too, it is Montaigne's habit of thinking with – through and against – these doubtful dogmatists that allows him to produce something distinct from the 'patrons' he borrows from. Recent studies have approached truth in the *Essais* as an ethical rather than a strictly epistemological problem, more concerned with veridiction and sincerity than knowledge. Reading Montaigne's truth-telling through his engagement with Seneca and Plutarch brings these different strands together, aligning ethical truth-telling with doubt – with philosophical doubt and self-knowledge but also with suspicion and mistrust.

Over the course of this study, I have traced doubtful thought and writing through a series of doubles. Here, I aim to show how the *Essais* make of doubt and truth a further interlocking couple. In presenting his work as one of truthfulness, Montaigne rewrote conventional understandings of what truth-telling looks like. In the *Essais*, truth-telling's defining characteristics were no longer constancy or fixity but doubt, doubleness and contradiction. Reconsidering his relationship with a number of dominant conceptions of truth – the truth of the schools, a historian's truth, *parrhesia* – these two chapters argue for the doubtfulness of truth-telling as it is reimagined by Montaigne. The first focuses on simplicity and self-knowledge with reference to Plutarch, before turning in the chapter that follows to consider Seneca's influence on Montaigne's 'paradoxe' form of truth-telling.

Montaigne's simple, straight-talking *ethos* served him well. It saved his life and his freedom more than once, when he relied on the 'simple credit' of his 'presence' and 'air' as a conciliatory tool with which to navigate conflict.[15] Here, though, I argue that the *Essais*' combination of Senecan and Plutarchan ideas, their combination of truth as 'telling it how it is' with a knowledge that 'how it is' is double and inconstant, produces a strange, paradoxical reconciliation of simplicity and doubleness: one in which good faith bears all the hallmarks of dissemblance, or rather seems to, if one is not looking closely enough.

---

[15] See Valerie M. Dionne, *Montaigne: écrivain de la conciliation* (Paris: Garnier, 2014), esp. pp. 35–66, 165–77. For Montaigne's accounts of two occasions, once at home, once while travelling, when his 'franchise' saved him from being attacked, see III.12.1060–2/812–14.

Truth and Lies: 'Une façon de parler'

To write doubtfully is not to say 'je doubte'. Nor, for that matter, is it to follow the Pyrrhonians, constantly falling back on their 'refreins' – *epecho*, *ou mallon* and so on. Montaigne's truth-telling is not simply a matter of recording or confessing his uncertainty, nor the work of fashioning his *persona* as a free or non-dogmatic or uncertain thinker. If the *Essais* are, as Montaigne describes Pyrrhonism, 'une perpetuelle confession d'ignorance' [a perpetual confession of ignorance] (II.12.505/374), the truth of this confession, shaped by the discursive and ethical techniques that produce it, depends as much on the form as the content.

Montaigne's truth is not the truth of the philosopher, logician or theologian. It is not, as Ian Maclean has shown, the truth of the schools. Their correspondence theory of truth, in which truth depends on a proposition corresponding with both the thing in the world (*convenientia rei*) and the image of it in the mind (*convenientia mens*), demands a knowledge that we cannot secure.[16] For Montaigne, that sort of truth, which is 'uniforme et constante', becomes corrupted whenever it is placed in our hands (II.12.553/415), and any access we do have to this truth is given to us by God.[17] 'Aussi ne fay-je pas profession de sçavoir la verité', he notes: 'J'ouvre les choses plus que je ne les descouvre' [Nor do I profess to know the truth [...] I uncover things more than I discover them] (II.12.501/370).[18] Montaigne identifies the problems with a correspondence theory of truth when he discusses the liar paradox and shows how its 'logique' is undone by self-reference:

---

[16] On Montaigne's scholastic inheritance and his engagement with this theory of truth, see two studies by Ian Maclean: 'Montaigne and the Truth of the Schools', in *The Cambridge Companion to Montaigne*, ed. Ullrich Langer (Cambridge: Cambridge University Press, 2005), pp. 142–62, and *Montaigne philosophe*, esp. 'Montaigne devant la philosophie de son temps', pp. 17–58.

[17] 'La participation que nous avons à la connaissance de la verité, quelle qu'elle soit, ce n'est pas par nos propres forces que nous l'avons acquise' [The participation that we have in the knowledge of truth, whatever it may be, has not been acquired by our own powers] (II.12.500/369).

[18] In saying this, he aligns himself with Socrates, 'le plus sage homme qui fut onques, [qui] quand on luy demanda ce qu'il sçavoit, respondit qu'il sçavait cela, qu'il ne sçavoit rien' [the wisest man that ever was, when they asked him what he knew, answered that he knew this much, that he knew nothing] (II.12.501/370). See also III.13.1067/817: 'Je ne sçay qu'en dire, mais il se sent par experience que tant d'interprétations dissipent la verité et la rompent [...] Nous ouvrons la matiere et l'espandons en la destrempant' [I do not know what to say about it, but it is evident from experience that so many interpretations disperse the truth and shatter it [...] By diluting the substance, we allow it to escape and spill all over the place.]

> Si vous dictes: Il faict beau temps, et que vous disiez verité, il fait donc beau temps. Voylà pas une forme certaine? Encore nous trompera elle [...] Si vous dictes: Je ments, et que vous dissiez vray, vous mentez donc. L'art, la raison, la force de la conclusion de cette cy sont pareilles à l'autre; toutes fois nous voylà embourbez. (II.12.527)
>
> If you say 'It is fine weather', and if you are speaking the truth, then it is fine weather. Isn't that a sure way of speaking? Still it will deceive us [...] If you say 'I lie', and if you are speaking the truth, then you lie. The art, the reason, the force of the conclusion of this one are the same as in the other; yet there we are stuck in the mud. (392)

In saying 'je ments', we are just a stone's throw from 'je doubte'. The problem is underscored by Montaigne's direct address to his imagined reader. 'Si vous dictes', he says: it matters who that 'vous' refers to, how what they say relates to and reflects their thoughts, intention and character. If we are to avoid getting stuck in the quagmire ('embourbez'), we have to be able to read our interlocutors 'jusques dans l'ame', peering into their souls. Disregarding that link between speech and speaker, we find ourselves deceived not only by the apparent simplicity of these sample sentences, but by the idea that truth-telling is itself a simple matter of checking a proposition against a referent. The logic is straightforward, and the 'force de la conclusion' seems to hold, but it crumbles as soon as the context becomes one of real-world communication between real people.

Montaigne's ambivalence regarding historical truth is well known: 'Advenu ou non advenu, à Paris ou à Rome, à Jean ou à Pierre, c'est toujours un tour de l'humaine capacité, duquel je suis utilement advisé par ce recit' [Whether they have happened or no, in Paris or Rome, to John or Peter, they exemplify, at all events, some human potentiality, and thus their telling imparts useful information to me] (I.21.105/75). But this nonchalance about the facts should not be taken as a carelessness with the truth: Montaigne is no politician, for whom the truth is whatever is most expedient.[19]

For Montaigne, we cannot know the truth – that knowledge belongs only 'à une plus grande puissance' [to a greater power] (III.8.928/708) – but we can speak truthfully. The social, communicative aspect of veridiction is addressed at length in 'Du dementir'. It is a chapter that draws attention to itself: midway through the middle book, it is (uncharacteristically) a direct continuation of the chapter that it follows, 'De la praesumption', which is in turn a continuation of the one before that,

---

[19] On 'nonchalance' and the politicking courtier's sprezzatura, see Green, *Montaigne and the Life of Freedom*, p. 151.

'De la gloire'.²⁰ Reaffirming his claim in the 'Au lecteur' that his is a private book intended only for 'mes parens et amis' (p. 3), Montaigne is concerned in this chapter with defending his project against accusations of vanity and presumption: the *Essais* are not a statue to be erected in a public square but something for the corner of a library, 'pour en amuser un voisin, un parent, un amy, qui aura plaisir à me racointer et repratiquer en cett'image' [to amuse a neighbour, a relative, a friend, who may take pleasure in associating and conversing with me again in this image] (II.18.664/503). A post-1588 addition, echoing a line from Seneca, takes this further: 'Et quand personne ne me lira, ay-je perdu mon temps de m'estre entretenu tant d'heures oisives à pensements si utiles et aggreables?' [And if no one reads me, have I wasted my time, entertaining myself for so many idle hours with such useful and agreeable thoughts?] (II.17.665/504).²¹ Montaigne's point, in opening this chapter, is to dispel any illusion that he is writing a 'life', an account of himself following the model of great men such as Caesar and Xenophon, or those names – familiar from Plutarch's *Lives* – who wrote memoirs that are now lost: 'les papiers journaux du grand Alexandre, les commentaires qu'Auguste, Caton, Sylla, Brutus et autres avoyent laissé de leurs gestes' [the journals of Alexander the Great, and the commentaries that Augustus, Cato, Sulla, Brutus, and others left about their deeds] (II.18.663/503).²² Far from writing a 'life' or a 'mémoire' – a record of things worthy of remembrance, to be kept for posterity – Montaigne portrays himself as writing for no one at all besides himself.

Montaigne is not, for reasons that I will develop later in this chapter, only defending himself from accusations of vanity. Nor does his distinction turn purely on the difference between life writing as a history of 'gestes' [deeds] and his own writing of that 'subject informe', his

---

²⁰ 'De la praesumption' begins 'Il y a une autre sorte de gloire' [There is another kind of vainglory] (II.17.631/478) while 'Du dementir' starts with 'Voire mais on me dira que [...]' [Yes, but someone will tell me that...] (II.18.663/503).
²¹ See Seneca, *Ep.* 7.11: 'Bene et ille, quisquis fuit, ambigitur enim de auctore, cum quaereretur ab illo, quo tanta diligentia artis spectaret ad paucissimos perventurae, "Satis sunt," inquit, "mihi pauci, satis est unus, satis est nullus"' [The following was also nobly spoken by someone or other, for it is doubtful who the author was; they asked him what was the object of all this study applied to an art that would reach but very few. He replied: 'I am content with few, content with one, content with none at all.'] Montaigne translates this passage more closely at I.39.247/182.
²² On ancient 'autobiographies' and their relationship to other classical genres of life writing, see Christopher Smith and Anton Powell (eds), *The Lost Memoirs of Augustus and the Development of Roman Autobiography* (Swansea: Classical Press of Wales, 2009), esp. Christopher Pelling, 'Was There an Ancient Genre of Autobiography?', pp. 41–64. Pelling notes the 'dangers of setting oneself in a tradition that has Caesar and Sulla as its prime examples (p. 45). It might be suggested that Montaigne is following in this tradition of differentiating one's own writing from these problematic precursors.

'cogitations' (II.6.379/274). What distinguishes Montaigne's 'dessein' from these genres of life writing is a difference in how they conceive truth: where the historian or memoirist provides an accurate account or record, Montaigne's own 'registre' guarantees veridiction by appealing to authenticity – an authenticity that is characterised by precisely those qualities of simplicity that are contradicted by his doubtful, double form.[23]

Montaigne turns to this mode of veridiction as authenticity in the final third of 'Du dementir', abandoning his original concerns about presumptuous vanity to address a problem that is more pressing, more troubling for his project of writing about himself. As he does so, he breaks out of the isolated interior space of private reflection – the space in which he might write not even for his friends, family and neighbours but for no one at all – and returns to the matter of social communication and its corruption in this rotten age: 'Mais, à qui croyrons nous parlant de soy, en une saison si gastée?' [But whom shall we believe when he talks about himself, in so corrupt an age?] (II.18.666/505). The issue is one that cuts to the heart of the *Essais* and it is notable that Montaigne shifts at this point from using the first person singular to the first person plural, a move that reveals the universality of this problem, but one that is itself suspicious: he slips out of his role as singular defendant in favour of a much more comfortable position as member of the jury precisely when the case turns to this more pernicious accusation.

Citing Pindar and Plato, he notes that 'le premier traict de la corruption des mœurs, c'est le bannissement de la verité' [the first stage in the corruption of morals is the banishment of truth] and that 'l'estre veritable est le commencement d'une grande vertu' [to be truthful is the beginning of a great virtue]. Montaigne's focus here is not the truth of the schools, nor a historian's truth, but an ethical truthfulness, or rather its loss; a truth that might be seen as concomitant with sincerity or honesty, though it is significant that the language used here is that of 'vérité' rather than simple 'bonne foi'. 'Nostre verité de maintenant', he writes, 'ce n'est pas ce qui est, mais ce qui se persuade à autruy: comme nous appellons monnoye non celle qui est loyalle seulement, mais la fauce aussi qui a mise' [Our truth of nowadays is not what is, but what others can be convinced of; just as we call money not only that which is legal, but also any counterfeit that will pass] (II.18.666/505). Inverting famous definitions of truth from Aristotle and Augustine – it was the latter who

---

[23] To write an accurate (as opposed to authentic) account would require a clarity of self-perception and a degree of self-knowledge that Montaigne, for his own part at least, senses to be beyond him. See 'Parrhesiastic Lives', below.

most clearly defined truth as 'that which is' – Montaigne decries his state in which truth has become partial and partisan: what passes as true these days is precisely that, 'la fauce qui a mise' [the counterfeit that will pass], while truth itself is no longer 'uniforme et constante' but contingent on whose truth we are talking about.[24]

The French are notorious liars, writes Montaigne, and have been for centuries: 'aux François le mentir et se perjurer n'est pas vice, mais une façon de parler' [to the French, lying and perjury are not a vice but a manner of speaking] (II.18.666/505). And yet we are more affronted by accusations of this offence, 'qui nous est si ordinaire' [which is so common among us], than any other. It is, he says, invoking Plutarch's life of Lysander, 'un vilein vice', 'car que peut on imaginer plus vilain que d'estre couart à l'endroit des hommes et brave à l'endroit de Dieu?' [for what can you imagine uglier than being a coward towards men and bold towards God?][25] It is a vice so ubiquitous that it threatens to tear apart society itself, dependent as it is on its foundation of truth-telling:

> Nostre intelligence se conduisant par la seule voye de la parolle, celuy qui la fauce, trahit la société publique. C'est le seul util par le moien duquel se communiquent nos volontez et nos pensées, c'est le truchement de nostre ame: s'il nous faut, nous ne nous tenons plus, nous ne nous entreconnoissons plus. S'il nous trompe, il rompt tout nostre commerce et dissoult toutes les liaisons de nostre police. (II.18.667)

> Since mutual understanding is brought about solely by way of words, he who breaks his word betrays human society. It is the only instrument by which our wills and thoughts communicate, it is the interpreter of our soul. If it fails us, we have no more hold on each other, no more knowledge of each other. If it deceives us, it breaks up all our relations and dissolves all the bonds of our society. (505)

---

[24] See Augustine's *Soliloquia*, II.5.8: 'nam verum mihi videtur esse id quod est' [for it seems to me that the true is that which is], a definition considered at the very beginning of Aquinas' *Quaestiones disputatae de veritate*. On Montaigne's echo of Augustine, see Yves Delègue, 'L'Imitation de la vérité', in Fasseur et al. (eds), *Eveils: études en l'honneur de J.-Y. Pouilloux*, pp. 29–43 (esp. p. 37). In William of Moerbeke's scholastic Latin, Aristotle writes that 'Dicere namque ens non esse aut hoc esse falsum, ens autem esse et non ens non esse verum; quare et dicens esse aut non verum dicet aut mentietur' [To say that what is is not, or that what is not is, is false; but to say that what is is, and what is not is not, is true; and therefore also he who says that a thing is or is not will say either what is true or what is false] (*Metaphysics*, 1011b25). For William of Moerbeke's translation, see *Metaphysica, lib. I-XIV. Recensio et Translatio Guillelmi de Moerbeka* (Leiden: Brill, 1995).

[25] Montaigne's association of lying with lower social status ('villainy') resonates with a conventional understanding of *parrhesia* as a 'noble' practice entangled with socio-economic and ethical freedom (*franchise* or *liberté*). On 'villainy', see Jonathan Patterson, *Villainy in France, 1463–1610: A Transcultural Study of Law and Literature* (Oxford: Oxford University Press, 2021), esp. ch. 2: 'The Villain: Morality and Status', pp. 42–54.

Bristling with internal rhymes and waves of repeating vowels, Montaigne's prose performs the 'liaisons' it describes, though the effect is less to underscore the mutual upholding effected by social good faith than it is to evoke the toppling of a long run of dominoes. 'Tournons les yeux par tout', Montaigne wrote elsewhere, 'tout crolle autour de nous' [Let us turn our eyes in all directions: everything is crumbling around us] (III.9.961/734).

In serving as the 'truchement de nostre ame', truthful speech allows us to hold on to each other, providing us – plural – with a means of moving beyond the distrust of the individual 'parlant de soy'. As he says in 'Des menteurs', a chapter that works in parallel with 'Du dementir', 'Nous ne sommes hommes, et ne nous tenons les uns aux autres que par la parole' [We are men, and hold together, only by our word] (I.9.36/23), restating in similar terms the essential connection between language, social interaction and truthfulness.

'La parole' is the 'truchement', the interpreter, not only of thoughts but of the soul. It is a tool ('util') that we work with, interpreting ourselves, our desires and thoughts, and that work of interpretation is transformative rather than transparent.[26] Montaigne's reflexive verbs – 'se conduisant', 'se communiquent' – dislodge the singular self reaching out into the world with language. In its place, he underscores a process of knowing oneself in language that is remarkably close to making oneself known in language. Community, 'nostre police', lies at the heart of Montaigne's sense of this interpretative tool, but this account of 'nostre intelligence' 'se conduisant' – conducting itself – solely, purely through language places communication at the heart not only of his relationship with others but also with himself. Where his earlier argument in 'Du dementir' had enclosed him in a private space of reflection, his account here renders authentic expression and self-reflection aspects of the same practice, both centred on interpreting the soul authentically and truthfully with the 'util' of 'la parole'. To put that another way, where one might expect the truthfulness of the *Essais* to reside in their publication of private practices of reflection or to depend on a mapping of a public

---

[26] In noting that 'la parole' interprets 'l'ame' in a way that is not 'transparent', I mean that language cannot look into the mind and make its movements visible without effecting some sort of change: if language is an 'imago animi', an image of the soul, the translation into 'sermo' is transformative. But language can be used 'transparently' in the sense outlined by Andy Clark in his account of 'transparent technologies': 'tools that become so well fitted to, and integrated with, our own lives and projects that they are [...] pretty much invisible-in-use. These tools or resources are usually no more the object of our conscious thought and reason than is the pen with which we write, the hand that holds it while writing, or the various neural subsystems that form the grip and guide the fingers'; Andy Clark. *Natural-born Cyborgs: Minds, Technologies, and the Future of Human Intelligence* (Oxford: Oxford University Press, 2003), pp. 28–9.

persona onto a natural, authentic, private disposition, here it is public, social communication that takes precedence and serves as a model for understanding a relationship with oneself.[27]

The sort of truth that Montaigne outlines in 'Du dementir' is one that is recognised not in the correspondence of the thing said and the thing described (not, to repeat the example from the 'Apologie', in the correspondence between 'il fait beau temps' and the weather outside), but in the relationship between speech and the speaker, their thoughts and their soul. This conception of truth as a 'façon de parler', a style or way of speaking, is not a lax, second-rate surrogate standing in for a more robust, more rigorous, more elusive truth. Truth-telling as Montaigne imagines it may indeed be 'simple', but it is not easy, and while language serves as an essential 'util', it is a tool prone to failure and abuse. This difficulty can be seen almost everywhere Montaigne looks. Indeed, it is not only truth-telling's rarity (these days at least) that he points to. It is the danger that comes with it: gone are the days, he says, in which 'on appelle Caesar tantost voleur, tantost yvrongne à sa barbe' [Caesar is at one moment called a robber, now a drunkard to his face] (II.18.667/506). Planning a chapter that he would never write, he wonders 'en quel temps print commencement cette coustume de si exactement poiser et mesurer les paroles, et d'y attacher nostre honneur' [at what time the custom began of weighing and measuring words so exactly, and attaching our honour to them]. No longer, Montaigne laments, are words avenged merely with words ('les paroles se revenchent seulement par les parolles') and no longer can men speak frankly and freely 'sans entrer en querelle' [without having a quarrel over it].

His complaint is no doubt nostalgic for a peace that never existed. Foucault's study of *parrhesia* in Greek and Roman texts identified danger and risk at the heart of ancient conceptions of truth-telling as speaking openly and fully, saying everything.[28] That danger is most

---

[27] I use 'public' and 'private' here in their modern senses. On the early modern sense of 'privé', which 'was not yet quite "private"; rather, it connoted familiarity, intimacy, and – crucially – secrecy', see Butterworth, *The Unbridled Tongue*, pp. 89–100. See also Kathy Eden, 'Reading and Writing Intimately in Montaigne's *Essais*', in *The Renaissance Rediscovery of Intimacy*, pp. 96–118.

[28] Foucault, *L'Herméneutique du sujet*, p. 348; *The Hermeneutics of the Subject*, p. 366. The etymological root of *parrhesia* is, as Foucault reminds us, *pan*, 'everything', and *rhêma*, 'that which is said'. Foucault goes on to consider the ambiguity of this absoluteness, noting a pejorative sense, found in Aristophanes and in the Church Fathers, in which *parrhesia* consists in saying anything, as well as the more positive form of speaking 'sans dissimulation ni reserve ni clause de style ni ornement rhétorique' [without concealment, reserve, empty manner of speech, or rhetorical ornament]; Michel Foucault, *Le Courage de la vérité* (Paris: Gallimard, 2009), p. 11; *The Courage of Truth*, ed. Frédéric Gros, trans. Graham Burchell (Basingstoke: Palgrave Macmillan, 2011), p. 10.

explicit in the counselling of a king, prince or tyrant, where the truth-teller risks their life (Montaigne gives the examples of Asinius Pollo and Favorinus, both of whom knew to hold their tongue when debating with Augustus and Hadrian respectively), but it is present also in speaking truthfully to a friend, risking friendship, or to oneself, threatening a positive self-image that one might find comforting.[29]

The role of the *parrhesiastes* is the one job Montaigne imagined he would have been good at, an 'office sans nom' [nameless office] in which he would have counselled a prince:

> J'eusse dict ses veritez à mon maistre, et eusse contrerrolé ses meurs, s'il eust voulu. Non en gros, par leçons scholastiques, que je ne sçay point [...] mais les observant pas à pas, à toute opportunité, et en jugeant à l'œil piece à piece, simplement et naturellement, luy faisant voyr quel il est en l'opinion commune, m'opposant à ses flateurs. (III.13.1077)
>
> I would have told my master home truths, and watched over his conduct, if he had been willing. Not in general, by schoolmasterly lessons, which I do not know [...] but by observing his conduct step by step, at every opportunity, judging it with my own eyes, piece by piece, simply and naturally, making him see how he stands in public opinion, and opposing his flatterers. (825)

Parrhesia is not the truth of the 'technician' professing the truths of a *tekhnê* (this is not, in other words, the truth of the pedagogue instructing a student), nor that of the sage speaking truths of nature and being.[30] It is rather a truth grounded in *ethos*, character, and its relationships with *logos*, what someone says, and *bios*, their life. Embodying this parrhesiastic role, Montaigne gives his qualifications for this position, qualifications that depend not on knowledge but character: 'J'eusse eu assez de fidelité, de jugement et de liberté pour cela' [I should have had enough fidelity, judgement, and independence for that] (III.13.1078/825). As he says in 'De l'art de conférer', 'autant peut faire le sot celuy qui dict vray,

---

[29] On Asinius Pollo and Favorinus, see the conclusion to 'De l'art de conferer', III.7.920/702–3. On *parrhesia* as defined by risk, see Michel Foucault, *Le Gouvernement de soi et des autres* (Paris: Gallimard, 2008), pp. 59–70; *The Government of Self and Others*, ed. Frédéric Gros, trans. Graham Burchell (Basingstoke: Palgrave Macmillan, 2010), pp. 61–73. We might see Montaigne's comment on the 'interest à mentir' [incentive for lying] (II.18.666/505) as describing the corollary to the danger accepted by the *parrhesiastes*.

[30] Foucault, *Le Courage de la vérité*, p. 25; *The Courage of Truth*, p. 25. While the relationship between teacher and student is not typically parrhesiastic, instruction in ethics and philosophy often is, as we see in the relationship between Seneca and Lucilius, for instance. In understanding *parrhesia* as a truth distinct from those of the technician, the sage and the prophet, we might recall Montaigne's claim in 'Du repentir' to speak in the voice not of someone holding the office of 'grammarien ou poëte ou jurisconsulte', but 'comme Michel de Montaigne' (III.2.805/611).

que celuy qui dict faux: car nous sommes sur la maniere, non sur la matiere du dire' [he who speaks true can speak as foolishly as he who speaks false; for we are concerned with the manner, not the matter, of speaking] (III.8.928/708). If we are to judge truthfulness in this corrupted age, we have to follow Montaigne's 'humeur' and look 'autant à la forme qu'à la substance, autant à l'advocat qu'à la cause' [at the form as much as the substance, the advocate as much as the cause] (III.8.928/708).[31]

It is from this perspective that we can look again at Montaigne's fascination with Seneca's life and death, his exaltation of Cato, his meditation on Socrates and his 'superbe' 'voix' – 'sec et sain' [sober, sane], 'veritable, franc et juste' [truthful, frank, and just] – in Plato's *Apology* (III.12.1054/807).[32] We might look back also to his habit of thinking with and through different authorial associations: 'Ce n'est non plus selon Platon que selon moy' [It is no more according to Plato than according to me], but it matters who is speaking, and who is seen to be speaking, if we are to hear a truth-defining harmony between words, borrowed or otherwise, and the movements of the soul (I.26.152/111). Truth-telling requires this harmony of *bios*, *ethos* and *logos*; it demands that we look at the 'forme' as much as the 'substance' and see in that form a character brought to life.[33]

Parrhesiastic Lives

Given Montaigne's comments on the sort of writing that reveals men's souls, one might expect the *Essais* to embrace more readily the genre he is so clearly at pains to reject in the opening movements of 'Du dementir'. Here and elsewhere, he sets up significant barriers between

---

[31] Compare the opening to Plutarch's 'Les Contredicts des Philosophes Stoiques', fol. 561r: 'En premier lieu je voudrais que lon veist une conformité & accord entre les opinions & les vies des hommes: car il n'est pas tant necessaire que l'Orateur & la Loy, comme dit Aeschines, sonnent une mesme choses, comme il est requis que la vie d'un philosophe soit conforme & consonante avec sa doctrine & sa parole' [In the first place, I would want us to see a conformity and accord between men's opinions and their lives: because it is not as necessary for an orator and the law to be in harmony, as Aeschines said, as it is for the doctrine and teachings of a philosopher to conform and be consonant with his life].

[32] On *parrhesia* in Montaigne's account of Socrates' last words, see Guerrier, *Rencontre et reconnaissance*, pp. 180–92.

[33] Montaigne describes himself 'ayant à m'y pourtraire au vif' [having here to portray myself to the life] (II.8.386/278) and notes that his 'defauts s'y liront au vif' [will be read here to the life] (p. 3/2). See George Hoffmann, 'Portrayal from Life, or to Life? The Essays's Living Effigy', *French Forum*, 25.2 (2000), 145–63.

the *Essais* and the broad, somewhat amorphous category of life writing exemplified by Plutarch's *Vies des hommes illustres*, Diogenes Laertius' *Lives of the Ancient Philosophers*, the similarly psychological histories of Tacitus, and the (now largely lost) autobiographies and memoirs that Montaigne alluded to explicitly. The effort to which he goes to distinguish his *Essais* from a 'vie' or a memoir is itself salient. If the distinction is obvious to us, he clearly thought it might not be. In what follows, I consider his relationships with these genres to ask how life writing functions parrhesiastically and whose soul it reveals, suggesting that the *Essais* recuperate from these 'patrons' not their ability to accurately portray or record a life in harmony with character, but their capacity to reveal the activity of judgement, functioning as 'util' and 'truchement' as much as 'registre', 'mémoire' or 'contrerolle'.

Two well-known passages, found in 'Des livres' and 'De l'art de conférer' respectively, point to Montaigne's sense that it is in this particular form of history that the parrhesiastic harmony is most legible. Echoing Jacques Amyot's distinction between 'histoire' and 'vie', Montaigne declares that those who 'escrivent les vies' [write lives] are most suited to him precisely because 'ils s'amusent plus aux conseils qu'aux evenemens, plus à ce qui part du dedans qu'à ce qui arrive au dehors' [they spend more time on plans than on events, more on what comes from within than on what happens without]: 'Voylà pourquoy, en toutes sortes, c'est mon homme que Plutarque' [That is why in every way Plutarch is my man] (II.10.416/303).[34] In the same passage, and in terms echoing the 'skeletos' metaphor used to describe his own project in 'De l'exercitation', he notes how it is among the historians and life writers that man 'paroist plus vif et plus entier qu'en nul autre lieu, la diversité et verité de ses conditions internes en gros et en destail, la varieté des moyens de son assemblage et des accidents qui le menacent' [appears more alive and entire than in any other place, the diversity and truth of his inner qualities in the mass and in detail, the variety of ways he is put together, and the accidents that threaten him] (II.10.416/303).

---

[34] For Amyot's distinction between 'histoire' and 'vie', see 'Aux lecteurs', *Vies des hommes illustres*, fol. A7r: 'l'une concerne plus ce qui est au dehors de l'homme, l'autre ce qui procede du dedans: l'une les evenemens, & l'autre les conseils' [one is more concerned with what is outside of a man, the other with what comes from within; one with events, the other with plans]. See also the opening passage of 'Alexandre le Grand': 'je n'ay pas pris à escrire des histoires, ains des vies seulement' [I have not written histories but only lives] (fols. 464r–v). Noting that the distinction between history proper and the minor genre of life writing was made already by Cicero (*De Oratore*, II.63), Sébastien Prat argues that Amyot places them on an equal footing and that Montaigne goes one further, arguing for the superiority of 'lives'. See Prat, *Constance et inconstance chez Montaigne*, pp. 245–7.

Montaigne praises Tacitus and his 'utile' history, attentive to the private sphere, in similar terms: 'Cette forme d'Histoire est de beaucoup la plus utile. Les mouvemens publics dependent plus de la conduicte de la fortune, les privez de la nostre. C'est plustost un jugement que deduction d'Histoire' [This form of history is by far the most useful. Public movements depend more upon the guidance of fortune, private ones on our own. This is rather a judgement of history than a recital of it] (III.8.941/719). Montaigne quoted extensively from Tacitus' history in his judgement of Seneca's own parrhesiastic life, in which the Stoic's dying words and deeds served as 'l'image de mes [i.e. Sénèque] meurs et de ma vie' [the picture of my [i.e. Seneca's] character and my life], guarantor and evidence of 'ces beaux preceptes de la philosophie' [those fine precepts of philosophy] (II.35.748/566). Like Plutarch, Tacitus records opinion and thought, both at the level of the individual and the community: 'ils tiennent registre des evenemens d'importance; parmy les accidens publics sont aussi les bruits et opinions populaires. C'est leur rolle de reciter les communes creances, non pas de les regler' [they keep a record of important events; among public incidents are also popular rumours and opinions. It is their part to relate common beliefs, not to regulate them] (III.8.942/720).[35] But these histories and lives work doubly in their uncovering of thought, character and judgement: not only do they record the thought and judgements of their historical subjects; they also reveal the judgement ('C'est plustost un jugement') and, in the case of Plutarch at least, the soul of the historian.

This is a form of life writing that reveals the beliefs ('creances'), the interior ('dedans') of an individual – whether the historical subject or the author – and consequently allows the reader to assess relationships between *bios* and *logos*. It is a genre, one might think, that is well suited to Montaigne's own project of truthfully communicating his 'imaginations'. The fact that Montaigne was writing about himself was, in this regard at least, no great impediment: the distinction between biography and autobiography was subtle to the point of being non-existent, as seen in numerous classical and early modern examples in which lives are written in the third person, irrespective of authorship.[36]

---

[35] Here too we might see a parallel with Montaigne's own form as he describes it in 'Du repentir': 'Les autres forment l'homme; je le recite' [Others form man; I tell of him] (III.2.804/610).
[36] The classical example that would have been most familiar to Montaigne is Caesar, whose writings ought to be, according to the essayist, 'le breviaire de tout homme de guerre' [the breviary of every warrior] (II.34.736/556). D'Aubigné's *Vie à ses enfants*, written around 1629, continues this tradition of writing in the third person.

But writing about yourself risks being seen to imagine yourself a second Caesar. Even he had the humility to be 'espargnant à parler de soy' [sparing in speaking of himself] (II.10.416–17/303). And yet in reading Caesar, the essayist finds 'tant de syncerité en ses jugemens' [so much sincerity in his judgements] (II.10.416/303). Montaigne constantly anticipates a reader who might mistake the repeated juxtaposition of life writing and the *Essais* as vanity – he reminds his reader constantly of his difference in degree and status and rejects accusations of presumption or ambition. Instead, he points to the capacity of those 'excellens' historians to not only record and depict parrhesiastic lives ('de la condition des Princes et de leurs humeurs, ils en concluent les conseils' [from the nature and humours of Princes they infer their intentions]), but to reveal their own judgement and shape that of the reader: they have the 'suffisance de choisir ce qui est digne d'estre sçeu' [the capacity to choose what is worth knowing] (II.10.417/304).

In short, it seems that the sort of truth-telling Montaigne aspires to is one closely aligned with the genre of life writing not on account of its historical truthfulness, nor its depiction of frank truth-tellers, but because of the genre's ability to communicate the thinking and judgement of the author. As Alison Calhoun suggests, Montaigne found in Plutarch 'an early prototype for how to construct the transverse self'; a way of 'using others to demarcate what the self is not', a way of expressing his own interior space by reflecting and engaging with that of others.[37] Montaigne would take this further, Calhoun suggests, placing this 'indirect self-portrait' or 'transverse self' at the centre, positioning this 'self' as subject as well as authorial judge.[38]

Montaigne regrets that we lack a 'Life of Plutarch' or some 'memoires de sa vie' (II.31.716/541) and laments that Tacitus did not dare 'parler rondement de soy' [to speak roundly of himself]. But in plotting his own course, breaking 'ces regles populaires de la civilité en faveur de la verité et de la liberté' [these common rules of civility in favour of truth and liberty], daring 'non seulement parler de moy, mais parler seulement de moy' [not only to speak of myself, but to speak only of myself], Montaigne did not aspire to produce a historian's account of his 'conseils' (III.8.942/720). He reveals himself not as Plutarch and Tacitus revealed the minds of the historical actors they bring to life, but in the same way that they revealed themselves, by thinking in writing such that his judgement, his character, becomes legible on the page. It is, then, by drawing a conspicuous contrast between his own mode of writing

[37] Calhoun, *Montaigne and the Lives of the Philosophers*, p. 16.
[38] Ibid., p. 16.

and that of the historians that he delimits the connection between them, anticipating that this connection will be misread: it isn't Montaigne's vanity but his desire to communicate his character that leads him towards life writing.

The potential parallels between life writing and the *Essais*, detailed carefully by Calhoun, invite us to read in Montaigne's 'registre' or 'contrerolle' a private, domestic mode of historical record-keeping that aspires to the parrhesiastic harmony of expression and character found in Plutarch or Tacitus.[39] Seen in this light, it would be precisely when Montaigne is not himself 'la matière de [son] livre' (p. 3/2) that this generic approximation would be most clear. And yet, if we identify in the *Essais* a truth-telling modelled on and related to the 'registres' he found in his historians – 'ils tiennent registre des evenements d'importance' [they keep a record of important events] (III.8.942/720) – we will have landed on a point of connection that he seeks almost constantly to undermine: he speaks only of himself, he tells us; his is no history, no 'life'; and though the historians could or might have written more about themselves, we are reminded that they did not. Montaigne forges these connections with historians and their modes of writing judgement as much through points of contrast as similarity: they are recast in his own image as he stresses what could have been had they been able, in spite of chronology, to follow his example. Aligning himself – awkwardly – with historians, life writers and memoirists, he points not to their historically accurate records, their inventories of lives, 'conseils' and so on, but to the way these record-keepers communicate and reveal themselves in the process: 'C'est plustost un jugement que deduction d'Histoire' [This is rather a judgement of history than a recital of it] (III.8.941/719).

Montaigne saw this project of writing about himself and writing himself out truthfully as novel and unusual. We do not have to take him at his word – which in itself renders problematic his efforts to present himself as an authentic truth-teller – and neither do we have to agree with his self-assessment. What is clear, though, is that he looks repeatedly to pre-empt and qualify the perceived relationship between his *Essais* and the related genres of life writing, history and record-keeping. When he described his 'office sans nom', that imagined role as *parrhesiastes* to a prince, he noted that 'toute cette fricassée que je

---

[39] Noting that a 'registre' is 'a paper roll or codex in which records of acts and judgements are kept by a *greffier* or clerk on a daily basis, or into which separate notes and memoirs are copied', Warren Boutcher interprets Montaigne's description of his book to mean that he 'keeps a written record – a history of sorts – of his changing ideas in order to "check" them, like an administrator verifying accounts'. See Boutcher, *The School of Montaigne*, vol. 1, p. 106.

barbouille icy n'est qu'un registre des essais de ma vie' [all this fricassee that I am scribbling here is nothing but a record of the essays of my life] (III.13.1078/826). This record is not a 'mémoire' or a *historia sui temporis* or a *vita propria*.[40] Montaigne's 'registre-journal' is not a summative account of himself or his life. It is rather, as Warren Boutcher puts it, a 'private practice of continuous archival record-keeping'; what Terence Cave has described as a 'continuous record' that allows Montaigne to 'review and assess his thought-processes over time'.[41] That continuous, everyday activity is key: the 'registre', in being put to use, reveals Montaigne not by stockpiling his thoughts but by serving as a tool in and with which to think.

Montaigne's 'scribbling' records his thoughts not as an account of the thinking that has been done, not in a way that is after the fact, but as the trace of thought as it is conducted in writing. In short, the point of connection between the *Essais* and these forms of life writing lies not in the historians' truthful records or depictions of 'conseils' and parrhesiastic lives, but in their ability to translate the activity of judgement truthfully and authentically into writing – to employ writing as 'le seul util par le moien duquel se communiquent nos volontez et nos pensées' [the only instrument by which our wills and thoughts communicate] (II.18.667/505). This distinction is important in that it presupposes a different conception of the relationship between 'conseils' and their presentation on paper: one rooted in authenticity rather than accuracy; in employing writing as an extension of thinking rather than as a representation of it.

Between the 'registre' and the 'vie', Montaigne presents his novel form as a tool, an 'util', with which to interpret the soul; not to record his thoughts but to reveal them, writing in such a way that his thoughts and his soul 'se conduisent' [conduct themselves] on the page. It is a way of writing truthfully that makes his way of thinking legible to himself and to his reader: it is not a record of what was apparent to him but in need

---

[40] Montaigne notes that he was encouraged by friends to write a history of 'les affaires de mon temps' on account of his 'veue moins blessée de passion', but rejected the idea: calling himself a 'sworn enemy' ('ennemy juré') of obligation and perseverance ('constance'), he notes how his breathless style is unfit for extended narration before suggesting that his 'freedom' ('ma liberté, estant si libre') would lead him to publish dangerous and punishable material ('jugemens [...] illegitimes et punissables') (I.21.106/76).

[41] Boutcher, *The School of Montaigne*, vol. 2, pp. 439–40; Cave, 'Montaigne', p. 192. Cave notes that the 'registre' metaphor is more useful, more accurate than the commonplace portrait metaphor. My aim here is to show that, for Montaigne, the key feature of the 'registre' depends on it being more than an account or a storehouse of judgements: its points of connection with the writing of lives, of *ethos*, and the soul, seat of judgement, ensure that it communicates the activity of thinking as much as it records its outputs.

of being made public, so much as a technology with which to recognise and know himself in writing. To put that another way, the *Essais* draw on both the 'registre' and the 'vie' because the truthfulness Montaigne aspires to demands more than exhaustive, continuous record-keeping. His 'flux de caquet' [flow of babble] (III.5.897/684) requires a leaky, double form of writing and not simply an open-ended one, as previous chapters in this study have shown. It is in this light that the distinction between Montaigne's truthful writing and another key generic neighbour, confession, can be seen more clearly. As Virginia Krause has noted, reading Montaigne's account of religious and judicial confession in light of Foucault's analysis of veridiction and power, 'the self cannot naively discover in confession a voluntary and authentic form of expression outside of networks of institutional practices'.[42] Montaigne's distrust of the 'complicity of confession with the institutions mandating it' produces an understanding of confession haunted by force, extraction and imposition opposed not only to the aesthetic and ethical ideals of 'franc' openness, but to his experience of self-knowledge and its lacunae. We might say, along similar lines, that Montaigne does not know himself, his character, his judgement without the discursive and social practices that reveal them.

He repeatedly makes plain the difficulty inherent in attempting to uncover or to gain access to the 'interior' world of thought. 'Ceci m'advient aussi', he writes, 'que je ne me trouve pas où je me cherche; et me trouve plus par rencontre que par l'inquisition de mon jugement' [This also happens to me: that I do not find myself in the place where I look; and I find myself more by chance encounter than by searching my judgement] (I.10.40/26–7). As Jean-Yves Pouilloux argues, the account given of Montaigne's fall from his horse in 'De l'exercitation' – a passage that traces the slipping in and out of what we might call 'consciousness' – 'se fonde non exactement sur l'expérience intime de soi, mais se reconstruit sur les regards des assistants et sur leurs récits' [is based not exactly on an intimate experience of the self but is reconstructed through the perspective of witnesses and based on their accounts]: it is 'par définition marquée de blancs, d'absences, que la narration à soi seule, quelle que soit l'honnêteté de Montaigne, par un mouvement autonome, comble' [by definition marked by blanks, absences, that are filled in independently by the narrative itself, irrespective of Montaigne's sincerity].[43] The 'life', in combination with the 'registre', affords those 'rencontres', those moments in which Montaigne

---

[42] Krause, 'Confession or *Parrhesia*? Foucault after Montaigne', p. 146.
[43] Pouilloux, *Montaigne: une vérité singulière*, pp. 64–5.

encounters and recognises himself: these two genres come to bear on the *Essais*, then, not (only) in their memorialising function or in their claims to accuracy and exhaustiveness, but in their ability to communicate and reveal the workings of judgement and the soul. It is in their combined ways of writing – their 'façons de parler', their *logos* – that one discerns the *ethos* of the author.

'Un registre des essais de ma vie' [A record of the essays of my life] (III.13.1078/826). The *Essais* sit between these two genres, drawing from them a conception of writing as a tool that reveals the soul. The image of domestic management encapsulated by the 'registre' might well be read in parallel to the more illustrious genre of the life, and seen to translate it into something more fitting for a man of Montaigne's standing and reputation.[44] But that domestic management of his 'subject informe' is the work of forming thought, giving it sufficient shape to be communicated authentically on the page. Between the 'vie' and the 'registre', the *Essais* interpret their shifting 'subject', drawing on these 'patrons' as a framework within which to devise their own distinct parrhesiastic bargain: one in which Montaigne communicates judgement authentically rather than accurately, not only by recording 'volontez' and 'pensées' but by using writing as an 'util' with which to think, a 'truchement de l'ame' [interpreter of the soul].

Telling It How It Is: Plutarch's Simple Truth-Telling

When, at the end of 'Du dementir', Montaigne turns his focus from accusations of pride to the more troubling matter of untruth, his discussion of the 'liberté des invectives' found among the ancients draws freely from the countless examples to be found in Plutarch's *Lives* (II.18.667/506).[45] The twin activities of practising and recognising this form of frank speaking are given more sustained treatment in Plutarch's 'Comment on

---

[44] Katie Kadue's argument paints the contrast in even starker terms: Montaigne's bookkeeping is 'domestic drudgery' but, 'like the modern housewife conjured by Simone de Beauvoir, Montaigne is painfully aware that no matter how boring keeping a household running may be, "even in this area, things are capricious": even in the most tedious domestic operations, predictable results are not guaranteed'; Kadue, *Domestic Georgic*, pp. 79–80.

[45] In the life of *Pompeius*, Montaigne found 'Marcellus le Consul' 'appellant Caesar un brigand' [calling Caesar a brigand] (fol. 455r). In *Caton d'Utique*, Cato, upon finding a love letter written to Caesar by his half-sister Servilia, 'la rejetta à Caesar en luy disant, Tiens yvrongne' [threw it at Caesar, saying to him, 'keep it, you drunkard'] (fol. 534v). For these references and broader discussion, see Konstantinovic, *Montaigne et Plutarque*, pp. 390–1.

pourra discerner le flatteur d'avec l'amy'. Among the most frequently cited of Plutarch's works in the *Essais*, it was widely read and often translated in early modern Europe, having a significant impact on contemporary discussions of how to navigate between flattery and offence when giving counsel.[46]

Plutarch's essay is concerned principally with the reading of character, with the task of identifying a parrhesiastic harmony between *bios* and *logos* in order to distinguish the flatterer from the 'true friend', the *parrhesiastes* who speaks even uncomfortable truths. For Plutarch, this is a task that is both difficult and important, not only because we struggle to see into men's minds, and therefore struggle to determine who is and is not truthful, but because we struggle to read ourselves: we are blind to our own faults, and the true nature of our character is obscured by 'l'Amour de soy-mesme'. 'Nul ne peult estre juste & non favorable juge de soy-mesme', he writes at the beginning, 'car l'amant est ordinairement aveugle à l'endroit de ce qu'il aime' [No one can be a just and non-partial judge of himself, because the lover is typically blind with regard to the beloved].[47]

This essay on how to identify a truth-teller is introduced, then, as a response to the greater problems of self-knowledge: 'Or si c'est chose divine que la verité & la source de tous biens aux Dieux & aux hommes [...] il fault estimer, que le flatteur doncques est ennemy des Dieux, & principalement d'Apollo, pource qu'il est tousjours contraire à cestuy sien precepte, Cognoy toy mesme' [Now, if the truth is a divine thing and the source of all goods to both gods and men [...] we must judge the flatterer to be the enemy of the gods and principally of Apollo, because he stands always in opposition to that god's precept,

---

[46] Konstantinovic, *Montaigne et Plutarque*, pp. 26–7. Konstantinovic has recorded 22 allusions to the essay on flattery, compared with 21 to the much longer (and much more varied and thus more diversely applicable) 'Propos de table'. These are exceeded only by the two volumes of 'Dicts notables' – 33 allusions to the 'Dicts notables des roys anciens', 38 to the 'Dicts notables des Lacedaemoniens' – and 46 allusions to 'Quels animaux sont les plus advisez', all of which are from the 1580 text and confined to the 'Apologie'. For the wider reception of Plutarch's treatise, see Joanne Paul, *Counsel and Command in Early Modern English Thought* (Cambridge: Cambridge University Press, 2020). Paul traces Plutarch's influence on a range of key figures in sixteenth-century political thought, including Erasmus (pp. 17–21), More (pp. 21, 27) and Castiglione (p. 36), among others.

[47] 'Comment on pourra discerner le flatteur d'avec l'amy', fol. 40r, hereafter cited parenthetically. On *parrhesia* as a form of frank speech that directs and improves the recipient's relationship with themselves, see Foucault, *Le Gouvernement de soi et des autres*, p. 43; *The Government of Self and Others*, p. 43: 'la *parrêsia* est une vertu, devoir et technique que l'on doit rencontrer chez celui qui dirige la conscience des autres et les aide à constituer leur rapport à soi' [*parrhesia* is a virtue, duty, and technique which should be found in the person who spiritually directs others and helps them to constitute their relationship to self].

Know thyself] (fol. 40r). It is here that we might note Montaigne's own invocation of this precept in the closing lines of 'De la vanité', a passage to which I will return in the next chapter: he ventriloquises 'ce Dieu à Delphes' – this god who, as we saw in Chapter 3, speaks 'doublement, obscurement, obliquement' (III.13.1068/818) – to lament our vanity that leaves us blind to ourselves. Man alone, says Montaigne's Apollo, has his gaze turned always outwards and never back on himself: 'C'estoit un commandement paradoxe que nous faisoit anciennement ce Dieu à Delphes: Regardez dans vous, reconnoissez vous, tenez vous à vous' [It was a paradoxical command that was given us of old by that god at Delphi: Look into yourself, know yourself, keep to yourself] (III.9.1001/766).[48]

Speaking frankly, the true friend allows us to overcome our vain self-flattery and lets us recognise ourselves as we truly are. *Parrhesia* and, indeed, the *parrhesiastes* serve the listener as a tool, an 'util', that works in service of self-knowledge. And as Plutarch's recurrent medical metaphors make plain, it is a tool that is both diagnostic and curative.[49] As Foucault put it, '*We* are our own flatterers, and it is in order to disconnect this spontaneous relation we have to ourselves, to rid ourselves of our *philautia*, that we need a *parrhesiastes*.'[50] What we need is a 'vray amy': someone who will praise us for what ought to be praised and who will criticise what ought to be criticised. The *parrhesiastes*, then, speaking truly and truthfully, uses *parrhesia* to puncture our self-blindness and let us see ourselves from another perspective.

Parrhesia as it is framed in Plutarch's essay on flattery and frank speech is not, or not only, a matter of speaking openly, accurately recording or letting loose a self that is otherwise apparent. What is at

---

[48] I will return to the relationship between doubtful, double speaking and Apollo's 'commandement paradoxe' later in Chapter 6.

[49] 'Ne plus ne moins que le medecin' [No more nor less than the doctor], the 'vray amy' must, Plutarch instructs, mix 'du saffran ou de la lavende dedans ses compositions de medecin' [some saffron or lavender in his medicines], 'conduisant son malade par diverses voies à un mesme but' [leading his patient by varied means to one objective], which is to say 'sa santé' [his health] (fol. 43v).

[50] Michel Foucault, *Fearless Speech*, ed. Joseph Pearson (Los Angeles: Semiotext(e), 2001), p. 135. This volume, publishing Foucault's lectures on *parrhesia* delivered at the University of California at Berkeley in 1983, contains his most extensive discussion of this Plutarchan opuscule, though Plutarch is a major figure in his lectures delivered at the Collège de France and elsewhere between 1980 and his death in 1984. See, for instance, his lecture at Grenoble in 1982, published in *Discours et vérité, précéde de La parrêsia* (Paris: Vrin, 2016). On Foucault as a reader of Plutarch, and the choice of this 'eclectic' philosopher in conjunction with the Stoics (Epictetus and Seneca), see Edouardo Machado, 'Foucault, lecteur de Plutarque: de la notion de savoir "éthopoétique" à la construction d'une "esthétique de l'existence"', *Le Télémaque*, 47.1 (2015), 109–20.

stake here is precisely the intersection of a particular style of speech and its capacity to reveal and give form to an elusive self-knowledge. Here, the frank speaker and the listener falling out of *philautia* are distinct persons – the *Essais* trouble this, with implications that will be considered in due course – but for both participants in this interaction, it is the reading of character, the ability to see 'jusques dans l'ame' as afforded by frank speech, that structures this truthful communication.

Plutarch's account of this relationship is fundamentally adversarial, with the *parrhesiastes* working against the listener's vanity and the responses it triggers when challenged, while at the same time being subject to doubt, scrutiny and suspicion. The problem, as Plutarch explains, is that both the form and content of frank speech can be dissimulated easily. He is alert to the danger of over-correction too, warning us against reading all praise as flattery and anything dressed up as correction as evidence of fidelity:

> Pourtant ne fault pas souspeçonner universellement, que tous ceulx qui louënt autruy soient incontinent flatteurs: car le louër quelquefois, en temps & lieu, ne convient pas moins à l'amitié, que le reprendre & le blasmer: & à l'opposite, il n'y a rien si contraire à l'amitié, ne si mal accointable, que l'estre fascheux, chagrin, toujours reprenant, et tousjours se plaignant. (fol. 40v).
>
> However, we must not suspect in all circumstances that all those who praise another are flatterers: because to offer praise sometimes, in the right moment and circumstances, belongs no less to friendship than correction and blame. And, inversely, there is nothing so contrary to friendship, nor so unsociable, as being disagreeable, melancholy, always criticising and always complaining.

Self-knowledge, moral improvement and practical, prudential dealings with those who surround us depend on distinguishing the 'vray amy' from the 'flatteur', 'chose bien fort mal-aisee [...] puis qu'il n'y a difference entre eulx' [a very difficult matter [...] since there is hardly any difference between them]. It is especially difficult in the case of the flatterer against whom we must most diligently 'se garder' [guard ourselves]: 'celuy qui ne semble pas flatter, & ne confesse pas estre flatteur' [the one that doesn't seem to flatter, and claims not to] (fol. 41r). This flatterer imitates the truth-teller, feigning *franchise*, and the result is that both speak in the same way. 'Le flatteur', Plutarch notes, 'se compose comme une matiere propre à recevoir toutes sortes d'impressions, s'estudiant à se conformer & s'accommoder à tout ce qu'il entreprent de ressembler par imitation' [shapes himself as though made of some material fit for being moulded to any shape, working to conform and accommodate himself to those whom he seeks to resemble by imitation]. His greatest trick ('la plus grande ruze & plus fine malice qui soit en luy') is his imitation of frankness in speaking freely ('la franchise de parler librement'), his ability to borrow 'la propre voix & parole de l'amitié' (fol. 41v).

If the flatterer can imitate the parrhesiastic or truth-telling qualities of the friend, how are we to determine who is a true truth-teller? How are we to recognise truth-telling when both have the same 'maniere de dire'? For Plutarch, the tell-tale sign of true *parrhesia* is personal constancy: if someone's speech and actions are consistent across an axis of time, we can infer a similar consistency across a different axis, between thought and action.

> Premierement il fault considerer s'il y a egalité uniforme en ses intentions & actions, s'il continue de prendre plaisir à mesmes choses, & s'il les loue de mesme en tout temps, s'il dresse & compose sa vie à un mesme moule, ainsi comme il convient à homme libre amateur de semblables meurs & semblables conditions à la siene. (fol. 41v).

> First we must consider whether there is a uniform equality in his intentions and actions, whether he continues to take pleasure in the same things, and whether he commends them in the same way at all times, whether he directs and structures his life according to one pattern, as is proper for a freeman and lover of similar customs and conditions as his own.

Constancy defines the truth-teller, whose constant *ethos* can be read reflected in a similarly singular moulding of 'sa vie'. The contrast with the 'flatteur' is explicit:

> car tel est le vray amy, là où le flatteur au contraire, comme celuy qui n'a pas un seul domicile en ses meurs, & qui ne vit pas d'une vie qu'il ait elevé à son gré, mais qui se forme & compose au moule d'autruy, n'est jamais simple, uniforme, ne semblable à soy-mesme, ains variable & changeant tousjours d'une forme en une autre, comme l'eau courante qui tousjours coule sans cesse. (fols. 41v–42r).

> Because this is how the true friend is, while the flatterer, since he has no abiding-place within his character, and since he lives a life that is not as he has chosen it but which is formed and structured in the mould of another, is never simple, uniform, nor similar to himself, but variable and changing always from one form into another, like running water that flows incessantly.

Plutarch's 'vray amy' is characterised by simplicity, uniformity, constancy, and these qualities describe simultaneously both their 'intentions' and 'actions': consistent action mirrors an internal constancy of 'meurs', and this double constancy results in the 'egalité' required of the truth-teller. For Plutarch, then, we need a truth-teller because we do not know ourselves. We need a simple, honest, authentic friend who will tell us our truths as Montaigne would have told truths to a prince. But the problem of reading 'conseils' threatens to proliferate. How can our 'vrays amys' read our souls so clearly when theirs are, to us, so obscure, so patently vulnerable to imitation and dissimulation? In Plutarch's essay, the solution to this problem is simple: it is to demand of the *parrhesiastes* a constancy and transparency that we cannot have regarding ourselves.

Retooling *Parrhesia*

We can recognise in Plutarch's imagery some of the metaphors and 'refreins' that were to be picked up and exploited by Montaigne: the reference to moulds ('un mesme moule') recalls the leakiness, the overflowing *débordement* of Montaigne's 'caprices' and of his 'esprit genereux', both of which are described as 'sans patron' [without model or mould] (II.12.546/409 and III.13.1068/818). The comparison of the flatterer's character to 'eau courante qui tousjours coule sans cesse' echoes another passage indebted to Plutarch: the allusion, at the end of the 'Apologie', to Heraclitus' river, symbol of the 'coulante et fluante' nature of time and being ('estre') (II.12.602–3/455–7). The image of domiciliary retreat, of having 'un seul domicile en ses meurs', is both reflected in Montaigne's countless evocations of the domestic and inverted in his self-assessment as a vagabond spirit – indeed, in the *Essais*, the domestic space of 'retraite' is itself characterised by a movement and flightiness that Montaigne cannot suppress: 'Tout lieu retiré requiert un proumenoir. Mes pensées dorment, si je les assis. Mon esprit ne va, si les jambes ne l'agitent' [Every space of retirement requires a place to walk. My thoughts fall asleep if I make them sit down. My mind will not budge unless my legs move it] (III.3.828/629).

Plutarch's language of simplicity, stillness and retreat, opposed to doubleness and inconstancy, is a language shared by Montaigne. Montaigne's own 'refrein' – 'non un refrein de ceremonie, mais de naifve et essentielle submission: que je parle enquerant et ignorant, me rapportant de la resolution, purement et simplement, aux creances communes et legitimes' [not a ritual refrain but a naïve and complete submission: that I speak as an ignorant inquirer, referring the decision purely and simply to the common and authorized beliefs] (III.2.806/612) – declares his 'bonne foi' by appealing to precisely this language of simplicity, sincerity and consistency. Montaigne's 'parler simple et naif' [simple, natural speech] (I.26.171/127) is seen to guarantee 'une verité simple et naifve' [a simple, natural truth] (I.26.169/125). It is a parrhesiastic truth that is far more valuable than the 'truth of the schools' proffered by some 'maistre és arts' [Master of Arts] (I.26.169/125). In making these claims, Montaigne draws on the nexus of associated terms yoking truthfulness to qualities that can be performed in speech and recognised by the interlocutor: *simplicitas* and *libertas*. This pairing of truth and simplicity was equally important for Seneca, for Erasmus, whose familiar style opposes 'mentiri' [lying] with 'vere et simpliciter loqui' [speaking truthfully and simply], and for a host of other classical and early modern reflections on frank, plain speaking.[51]

It is a commonplace ethical aesthetic built on the belief that neutral, unaltered speech reveals fully the heart and mind of the speaker and that we have to do something – apply rhetorical figures or conceal what we think or misrepresent what we know to be the case – in order to pervert, change or distort this otherwise clear and transparent medium. Plain speaking is defined as truthful in its opposition to rhetoric (though claims to abandon rhetoric and to speak from the heart are themselves, of course, a rhetorical commonplace). As James Helgeson has noted, the belief in truth's simplicity is a product of a culture in which language was equated with presence, serving as a transparent 'image' of the mind.[52] 'Imago animi sermo est', as a proverb attributed to Seneca put it, 'qualis vir, talis oratio' [speech is the image of the soul: so the man, so his speech]. Seneca is, as we have already seen, his own example: his dying words, along with his death itself, will serve, he says (in Montaigne's translation of Tacitus' account), as 'l'image de mes meurs et de ma vie' [the picture of my character and my life] (II.35.748/566).[53] Translating and communicating the soul, using 'la parolle' as 'truchement de l'ame', ought to be the simplest thing in the world: one need only not stand in the way.

Montaigne's handling of these commonplace images places him at odds with his contemporaries. For the essayist, truth-telling is not a case of simply saying it how it is, revealing the 'inner world' of thought without interfering with or distorting its transparent linguistic medium.

---

[51] See Seneca, *Ep.* 40.4: 'quae veritati operam dat oratio incomposita esse debet et simplex' [speech that deals with truth ought to be simple and plain]. On Erasmus' 'familiar' style, see Eden, *The Renaissance Rediscovery of Intimacy*, pp. 73–95. For Montaigne's engagement with Erasmus on these ideas, see Bérengère Basset, 'Erreur/vérité, mensonge/sincérité, d'Erasme à Montaigne', *Bulletin de la société internationale des amis de Montaigne*, 63 (2016), 73–92. See also Gérard Milhe Poutingon, 'Le Style du parler simple et naïf des *Essais*', *Bulletin de la société internationale des amis de Montaigne*, 67 (2018), 175–90.

[52] Helgeson, *The Lying Mirror*, pp. 19–20, 118–25.

[53] Tacitus, *Annals* 15.62: 'imaginem vitae suae'. On the 'imago' metaphor and its afterlife, see James Ker, 'Passing into Memory: Seneca's *imago* and its Reproduction', in *The Deaths of Seneca*, pp. 281–324.

The commonplace concept of simple truth-telling relies on a belief not only that simple speech can communicate and reveal to someone else the inner world of 'conseils' and 'cogitations', but that this inner world is apparent and accessible to the person speaking. It also assumes that, barring some moral failing (a sycophantic streak or some other motivation for chameleon-like concealment), the inner world will be more or less constant. But to Montaigne it was clear that we do not know ourselves. It is an insight latent in Plutarch's framing of *parrhesia* and his discussion of why it is necessary, but one that is not brought out in the discussion of how to speak frankly and how to know who to listen to. There is not, for Montaigne, an interior 'self' that is immediately accessible to us, awaiting our introspection and ready to be translated into words. It is not even apparent that thought or the soul is properly 'interior' in Montaigne's view as it so clearly was for Plutarch. It is for this reason that he could not have taken the 'vie' genre and made it reflexive: to do so would require the sort of introspective clarity he so frequently refutes.

'Ainsin en cette-cy de se cognoistre soy-mesme', he writes, 'ce que chacun se voit si resolu et satisfaict, ce que chacun y pense estre suffisament entendu, signifie que chacun n'y entend rien du tout' [Thus in this matter of knowing oneself, the fact that everyone is seen to be so cocksure and self-satisfied, that everyone thinks he understands enough about himself, signifies that everyone understands nothing about it] (III.13.1075/823). As the insistence on 'chacun' makes clear, self-ignorance is a universal not limited just to those who think too highly of themselves: there is vanity in self-flagellation too. As Plutarch put it, no one can be a just and non-partial judge of himself: our 'selves' are elusive, blurry and other than they seem even to us.[54] One of the implications of this is that the 'vie' genre, which both Montaigne and Amyot laud for its ability to see into men's minds and to perceive their 'conseils', fails precisely when we would expect it to succeed. The *Essais* are not an account of Montaigne's 'inner' cogitations: for them to be so would require an introspective capacity greater than that which he recognises. If 'la parole' is a 'truchement', it does not simply 'translate' thoughts into language, allowing Montaigne to describe what he has thought and allowing us to see what he was thinking. Truthfulness requires, as he suggests in 'Du démentir', some sort of equivalence between thought and writing, but this equivalency cannot be conceived in terms of imitation, representation or mimesis: if language and writing were to come after thought, they would be incapable of expressing it.

---

[54] 'Comment on pourra discerner le flatteur', fol. 40r.

The 'truchement' does not recount his thoughts; it is instead an 'util' which forms part of his cognitive process. It does not translate thoughts; it is a 'truchement *de nostre ame*': it serves, facilitates and makes communicable the activities of thinking.

Foucault noted that when

> we raise the question of how can we know whether someone is a truth-teller, we raise two questions. First, how is it that we can know whether some particular individual is a truth-teller; and secondly, how it is that the alleged *parrhesiastes* can be certain that what he believes is, in fact, the truth.[55]

That first question, he suggested, was central to classical reflections on this topic, while the second 'sceptical' question 'is a particularly modern one'.[56] In his chronological division, Foucault has in mind a broad narrative in the history of philosophy, in which modern philosophy emerges a little after the age of the *Essais*, around the 'moment cartésien' in which access to the truth was no longer seen to depend on character but on 'connaissance', knowledge.[57] Plutarch's way of thinking is decidedly pre-modern: his argument – that consistency of action reflects consistency of intention, which equates to true and sincere belief – is not concerned with the possibility that a consistently held belief might be objectively false. Montaigne, anticipating Foucault's cartesian moment, does approach that second question, turning the problem of identifying *parrhesia* onto himself by making the enquiry reflexive: we might see this, for instance, in the 'Que sçay-je?' of the 'Apologie', that interrogative form that he holds as a 'devise' in response to the difficulties encountered by the Pyrrhonians (II.12.527/393).

But Montaigne goes beyond this second question, asking a third, concerned not with knowledge but with that central relationship between character and language. He approaches *parrhesia* according to the terms and rationale established by Plutarch, while seeing it from a different angle, drawing out a problem that is otherwise overlooked. How, Montaigne asks, am I to speak truthfully – that is, to communicate my 'intentions' and 'cogitations' in 'action' and 'parole' – when this world of thought is characterised by the qualities that Plutarch insists define the false friend and the lying 'flatteur'? Rather than engaging with

---

[55] Foucault, *Fearless Speech*, p. 15.
[56] Ibid., p. 15.
[57] Foucault, *L'Herméneutique du sujet*, pp. 15–20; *Hermeneutics of the Subject*, pp. 14–19. Foucault stresses that this shift is neither definitive nor sudden: 'tout l'intérêt de la chose, c'est que les liens n'ont pas été brusquement rompus comme par un coup de couteau' [what is interesting is precisely that the links were not broken abruptly as if by the slice of a knife] (p. 27/26).

what Foucault calls the 'second sceptical question' – is what I know the truth? – he asks how he can be a truth-teller when he speaks from a position of inconstancy: his 'esprit' is moving and double; his character is directly opposed to that of Plutarch's 'vray amy' who is 'simple, uniforme [...] semblable à soy-mesme'. Having turned the question back on himself, asking not if someone else is telling the truth but how he might speak truthfully, Montaigne cannot easily tally his experience of personal flux with this classical model of what truth-telling looks like. 'Nulle qualité nous embrasse purement et universellement', he writes. 'Qui pour me voir une mine tantost froide, tantost amoureuse envers ma femme, estime que l'une ou l'autre soit feinte, il est un sot' [No quality embraces us purely and universally [...] Whoever supposes, to see me look sometimes coldly, sometimes lovingly, on my wife, that either look is feigned, is a fool] (I.38.234–5/173). The interrogator who looks for constancy as a marker of truth is unable to recognise Montaigne as he truly is and, in expecting constancy, takes one of these dispositions as false. In opposition to these idiot interlocutors, he recognises and declares himself to be diverse, changing and multiple, while at the same time knowing that this is not the result of lying or pretence.

Montaigne inherited from Plutarch not only the commonplace classical association of *simplicitas* and authenticity but the framing of *parrhesia* as a tool that works in service of an ethical project. That project is one of self-knowledge, of recognising yourself as you truly are. For Plutarch and for Montaigne, we must avoid the flatterer and embrace the truth-teller, not only because they speak the truth, but because they speak the truth about us. In attending to himself, though, Montaigne encountered diversity, discord and vicissitude. The problem, then, is not – or not only – one of recognising the truth-teller so that we might recognise ourselves; rather, recognising our inconstancy, the question becomes one of asking how we are to speak, and be seen to speak, truthfully. Montaigne adopts but also adapts *parrhesia*, upending its conceptual apparatus such that the *parrhesiastes* employs frank, sincere and 'simple' speech not so that they might counsel another to know themselves better, but so that this mode of speech might reveal the doubleness and inconstancy that is concealed by a self-image that vainly and presumptuously stakes a claim to constancy. In truth, we have, as Montaigne and Plutarch declare at the end of the 'Apologie', no 'communication' with 'estre' [being] (II.12.601/455), and to speak truthfully is to speak in accordance with this inconstant *ethos*, bringing 'manière' into harmony with 'matière' not by changing who or what we are but by reflecting ourselves fully and authentically in language.

This is a version of *parrhesia* that is doubly inverted, with the ethical diagnosis and revelation turned back on the speaker and its defining characteristics – ethical and discursive, moral and oral – rewritten to be at once 'simple' and double, ambiguous, inconstant. The question asked by Plutarch – how to tell a flatterer from a true friend, a friend who will allow me to recognise myself as I am – remains salient, but it becomes compounded by a new problem: how, knowing myself to be double, can I speak the truth and speak the truth in ways that will be recognised as truthful?

Montaigne's Third Question

While we have in recent years paid close attention to Montaigne's performance as a *parrhesiastes*, to his avowed preference for the simple speech of the honest truth-teller, there is, it seems, a foundational set of questions raised by this appeal to simplicity: how can I speak truthfully when I am defined by inconstancy? What might it mean to speak 'simply' when 'nostre entendement', along with everything else, is 'double et divers' (III.11.1034/792)? If *parrhesia* is a tool that brings about self-knowledge, whose self-knowledge are we talking about? Plutarch underscored the diagnostic and curative roles played by the 'vray amy' in service of his friend, but in the *Essais* those interpersonal problems of recognising truth in another and proving oneself sincere are themselves seen to rest precariously on the assumption that the self we come to know, either through introspection or frank speech, is likely to be constant, 'semblable à soy mesme'.

In asking this third set of questions, not the classical conundrum of identifying the *parrhesiastes* nor the set of self-interrogations, centred on knowledge rather than character, that emerged with the 'moment cartésien', Montaigne established a framework within which 'simple' truth-telling could sit alongside ethical and discursive doubleness. They sit together uncomfortably – Montaigne's efforts to justify and reconcile these two, contradictory characteristics run throughout the *Essais* – and produce a form of truth-telling that is self-consciously paradoxical. The paradoxical nature of doubtful truth-telling will be the focus of the next chapter, which considers Seneca's role as influence and interlocutor informing Montaigne's efforts to know himself in writing, to know himself to be inconstant, and to write a book that truthfully communicates that inconstancy.

In this chapter though, it is Plutarch who has been seen to play a key role in providing the conceptual tools and apparatus with which

Montaigne imagined his own mode of *parrhesia* and his novel, distinct form of writing, caught somewhere between the 'life', the 'registre' and the moral treatise. Montaigne's understanding of truth-telling as a 'façon de parler' that reveals the soul resonates not only with the illustrious lives and examples that fill Plutarch's history (and which he found elsewhere too, of course, not least in Tacitus' account of Seneca's life). Plutarch, along with a number of other 'excellens' historians, was able to write in ways that not only provide a comprehensive account (whether of events, *res gestae*, 'conseils' or judgements on them), but that communicate the work of judgement itself. In reading lives, he read the *ethos* not only of Cato, Augustus, Alexander and so on, but of the historian too.[58]

The *Essais* are not simply a record of Montaigne's judgements, just as they are not a record of his actions.[59] His 'registre' records his 'fantasies' mid-flow; it serves as the tool ('util') that communicates the spirit, serving as a 'truchement de l'ame' [interpreter of the soul] that works to reveal Montaigne to himself as much as to externalise any already-apparent private self-knowledge. Here too it is Plutarch, and specifically his framing of *parrhesia* as a tool in service of self-knowledge, who shapes Montaigne's 'forme' and 'façon'. Expanding the empire of self-blindness, recognising that the *parrhesiastes* is just as blind to himself as his interlocutor, Montaigne retools *parrhesia*, grappling with the problem of how to recognise a soul that cannot be seen but that can be read, and that can be discerned in speech, writing and everyday behaviour. With his daily writing, his 'registre', he invents a parrhesiastic tool with which his true, authentic doubleness can be read plainly and simply: a tool with which to know himself and with which to make himself known.

---

[58] Montaigne's summary of his reading of Quintus Curtius, written on the last page of his copy of the *Historia Alexandri Magni* (Basel: Froben, 1545), notes how he reads in the 'parler brusque' [abrupt way of speaking] of this 'bon auteur' his 'esprit vif, pointu, gentil' [lively, sharp, refined spirit]. See Alain Legros' edition of Montaigne's extant manuscript notes and letters, *Montaigne manuscrit* (Paris: Garnier, 2010), pp. 650–1.

[59] Which is not to say that the *Essais* do not record Montaigne's thoughts: 'Je ne puis tenir registre de ma vie par mes actions: fortune les met trop bas; je le tiens par mes fantasies' [I cannot keep a record of my life by my actions; fortune places them too low. I keep it by my thoughts] (III.9.945–6/721). This record is the product of Montaigne's habit of thinking in and with writing: it does not record thought that exists outside of the formal, textual and compositional habits that produce it.

Chapter 6

Paradoxical Truth-Telling

'Nous flottons entre divers advis', wrote Montaigne, 'nous ne voulons rien librement, rien absoluëment, rien constamment' [We float between different states of mind; we wish nothing freely, nothing absolutely, nothing constantly] (II.1.333/240). It is a line that was introduced in the Bordeaux Copy, a marginal note summarising a string of Latin verse quotations – Horace, Lucretius and Homer (by way of Cicero and St Augustine) – all pointing to 'nostre façon ordinaire'. Our only constant is change: we are like 'cet animal qui prend la couleur du lieu où on le couche' [like that animal which takes the colour of the place you set it on] (II.1.333/240). Imagine a man, writes Montaigne, who could prescribe certain laws for himself and keep to them: there you would find a shining beacon of evenness, 'un ordre et une relation infaillible' between principle and practice. But such a man is not to be found among us ('nous'). Even in our thoughts and desires, we fall short not only of the constancy but even of the *liberté* that ought to define a noble, frank *ethos*.

Those words written in the margin were borrowed silently from Seneca: 'Fluctuamur inter varia consilia. Nihil libere volumus, nihil absolute, nihil semper' (*Ep.* 52.1). Seneca continues by ventriloquising the voice of Lucilius, or some other imagined interlocutor, protesting that fickleness is common enough but ought to be read as the mark of a fool: '"Stultitia", inquis, "est, cui nihil constat, nihil diu placet"' ['But it is the fool', you say, 'who is inconstant; nothing suits him for long']. Seneca's reply punctures his reader's vanity: 'Sed quomodo nos aut quando ab illa revellemus? Nemo per se satis valet ut emergat; oportet manum aliquis porrigat, aliquis educat' [But how or when can we tear ourselves away from this folly? No man by himself has sufficient strength to rise above it; he needs a helping hand, and someone to extricate him] (*Ep.* 52.2). He counts us ('nos') among those who are endlessly dragged away from themselves ('alio trahit') and who find their souls always tussling with some unknown force ('Quid conluctatur cum animo nostro[?]', 'What is it that wrestles with our spirit?', *Ep.* 52.1). Seneca's reader, identifying inconstancy with *stultitia* but not with themselves, is the mirror of Montaigne's idiot acquaintance who sees his changing disposition towards his wife, 'tantost froide, tantost amoureuse' [sometimes cold, sometimes loving] and concludes that one of them must be feigned: 'il est un sot' [he is a fool] (I.38.234–5/173). The worst sort of 'sot', for Montaigne at least, is the one who is blind to his own *sottise* and fails to recognise the inconstancy that runs through everything, himself included.

The helping hand ('manum aliquis'), and knowing whose hand to take, is the focus of the rest of Seneca's letter. He details the varying needs of different sorts of fools, some more and some less foolish, and goes through what they should look for when choosing a guide, a teacher, a *parrhesiastes*: 'qualis quisque sit, scies, si quemadmodum laudet, quemadmodum laudetur, aspexeris' [you can tell the character of every man when you see how he gives and receives praise] (*Ep.* 52.12). What we need is a guide who will teach us not only with words but by practising what they preach: we need truth-tellers 'qui vita docent' [who teach us by their lives] (*Ep.* 52.8).

With his silent quotation and the chapter into which it was inserted, Montaigne limited himself only to a diagnosis of the inconstancy that permeates our soul and splits it in two: 'Cette variation et contradiction', he added, 'a faict qu'aucuns nous songent deux ames [...] une si brusque diversité ne se pouvant bien assortir à un subjet simple' [These variations and contradictions [...] have made some imagine that we have two souls [...] for such sudden diversity cannot well be reconciled with a simple subject] (II.1.335/242). As seen in the previous chapter of this study, Montaigne focused principally not on the task of identifying a parrhesiastic other but on responding to the novel, unprecedented set of questions that arose from his reconciliation of simple truth-telling with a sense of himself as double. In this chapter, I consider Seneca's role in the development of this form of truthful communication. Attending to Seneca's influence illuminates a new conception of truth-telling as inconstant, as 'partial', both fragmentary and partisan. Truth-telling as it emerges in dialogue with Seneca continues to be parrhesiastic, understood as saying what one means, but it is defined also by a habit of attending to those strange moments of cognitive dissonance in which we believe and disbelieve all at once.[1]

---

[1] 'Nous sommes, je ne sçay comment, doubles en nous mesmes, qui faict que ce que nous croyons, nous ne le croyons pas, et nous ne pouvons deffaire de ce que nous condamnons'

Montaigne's is a paradoxical understanding of truth, shaped by dispute not only with received ideas (the contradiction of *dogma* and *doxa*) and not only within Montaigne (self-contradiction): it is not only that his truth-telling engages in paradoxes; his strange, contrarian reimagination of truth-telling's defining features is itself paradoxical. The previous chapter took as its starting point Montaigne's efforts to present a credible *ethos* in a 'saison gastée' [corrupted age] (II.18.666/505) and argued for doubtful writing as a tool ('util') with which to interpret and communicate the soul. This chapter unravels the paradoxes that emerge from truly and truthfully 'telling it how it is' when how it is seems incompatible with conventional ideas about ourselves. Montaigne's is a 'discours paradoxe', a way of thinking and writing that runs counter to common, good sense (III.5.875/667). In writing paradoxically, he is responding to a 'commandement paradoxe', the imperative to 'know thyself' (III.9.1001/766). These are the only two instances of the word 'paradoxe' in the *Essais*. Reading them against one another, this chapter will show how Montaigne's doubtful truth-telling is entangled with his reading of Seneca. It is with this figure – a figure of constancy and resolve, always harping on the same old maxims – that Montaigne wrote not only a paradoxical discourse but a paradoxical sort of truth. Overturning all received wisdom about what truth-telling looks like, he developed a way of writing that recognises and communicates his folly and his ignorance, a way of writing that reveals the true colours of his chameleon-like 'façon ordinaire'.

Diagnosing Inconstancy and Letting Loose the Mind

Seneca examined personal inconstancy and the proper response to it at length in his treatise on the tranquillity of the soul (*De Tranquillitate animi*). Along with his letters and his essay on the constancy of the sage (*De Constantia sapientis*), it occupied a key role in the intellectual climate of the late sixteenth century, informing the work of Lipsius, Guillaume Du Vair and other neo-Stoics as they stretched constancy to the point of being indistinguishable from virtue itself.[2] It is, at the

---

[we are, I don't know how, double within ourselves, with the result that we do not believe what we believe, and we cannot rid ourselves of what we condemn] (II.16.619/469). For a discussion of this phrase in context, see Chapter 3.

[2] See Prat, *Constance et inconstance chez Montaigne*, pp. 9, 129–30. On Lipsius' conception of *constantia* as part of a 'new secular ethics', see Jan Papy, 'Lipsius' (Neo-)Stoicism: Constancy between Christian Faith and Stoic Virtue', *Grotiana*, 22.1 (2001), 47–71 (p. 52).

same time, an essay in which Seneca is not as we might expect to find him, nor as monotone as Montaigne would have us believe. Here, contrary to expectation, Seneca declares inconstancy to be quite normal and both he and his interlocutor describe the alluring pull of sibylline, raving ecstasy. Seneca even recommends it.

The treatise opens with a letter he received from his friend, Annaeus Serenus, in which the author, anything but serene, appeals to Seneca as though to a doctor.[3] He asks his friend and mentor to offer the sort of helping hand Seneca had described in his letter to Lucilius (*Ep.* 52.2) and to diagnose and help cure his 'bonae mentis infirmitas' [weakness of good intention] (*De Tranquillitate animi*, 1.15). In terms that Montaigne would later echo, Serenus situates himself squarely in the middle of things, in the in-between spaces. He is caught in his ethical and philosophical progression between health and sickness, between blissful ignorance and the self-mastery that would permit him to live as he knows he ought:

> Illum tamen habitum in me maxime deprendo [...] nec bona fide liberatum me iis [i.e. vitia sua], quae timebam et oderam, nec rursus obnoxium; in statu ut non pessimo, ita maxime querulo et moroso positus sum: nec aegroto nec valeo. (1.2–3)
>
> Nevertheless the state in which I find myself most of all [...] is that I have neither been honestly set free from these vices that I hated and feared, nor, on the other hand, am I in bondage to them; while the condition in which I am placed is not the worst, yet I am complaining and fretful – I am neither sick nor well.

His mind hesitates between two things ('animi inter utrumque dubii', 1.4), knowing the lessons and principles of Stoicism – knowing them too well if anything (he can 'inculcate', to use Montaigne's word, as well as Seneca himself) – and yet he finds that this knowledge seems not to be enough.[4]

Serenus struggles to give a full account of this state of inner conflict and so determines to break things up and tackle the matter piecemeal: 'non tam semel tibi possum quam per partes ostendere' [I cannot show you so well all at once as a part at a time] (1.4). What follows is a tour

---

[3] On the irony of this cognomen, see Anna Lydia Motto and John R. Clark, *Essays on Seneca* (Frankfurt: Lang, 1993), p. 244.

[4] For Montaigne's comment on the tendency towards 'inculcation' among Seneca and the Stoics, see III.9.962/734. On Serenus as a fool ('stultus'), see Foucault, *L'Herméneutique du sujet*, pp. 126–31; *Hermeneutics of the Subject*, pp. 130–6. For Foucault, the fool 'n'a pas souci de soi-même' [has no care for himself], is open ('ouvert') to the outside world, and allows its representations to 'entrer dans son esprit' [enter into his mind] without examining them (pp. 126–7/131).

through three contexts – private life, public life, afterlife – and, in each, Serenus finds his resolutions and plans, his knowledge of what he ought to do, undone by his *animus*. As Foucault put it, 'Serenus knows the theoretical principles and practical rules of Stoicism, is usually able to put them into operation, yet he still feels that these rules are not a permanent matrix for his behaviour, his feelings, and his thoughts.'[5]

His first two examples detail his resolution to live a frugal, simple life at home and his intention to gain a public office and serve the common good: in each case, his mind is pulled away towards luxury and glory. In his third example, he turns to his literary ambitions:

> in studiis puto mehercules melius esse res ipsas intueri et harum causa loqui, ceterum verba rebus permittere, ut qua duxerint hac inelaborata sequatur oratio: 'quid opus est saeculis duratura componere? vis tu non id agere ne te posteri taceant? morti natus es, minus molestiarum habet funus tacitum. itaque occupandi temporis causa in usum tuum, non in praeconium aliquid simplici stilo scribe: minore labore opus est studentibus in diem.' (17.2)

> And in my studies I think that it is – by Hercules! – better to fix my eyes on the theme itself and to speak for it, entrusting the words to the theme so that unstudied language may follow wherever the theme may lead. I say: 'What need is there to compose something that will last for centuries? Will you not give up striving to keep posterity from being silent about you? You were born for death; a silent funeral is less troublesome! And so, to pass the time, write something in simple style, for your own use, not for publication; those who study for the day have less need for labour.'

As Elena Giusti has shown, this is a complaint that traces in its style a subversion of the Stoic precepts Serenus knows all too well: 'the interjection *mehercules*, the swift and abrupt reduplication of Serenus as the actor and addressee in his own prosopopoeia, the hurried direct questions, the dramatic oxymoron *morti natus es* [you were born for death]', all, Giusti argues, transform this expression of a desire for *inelaborata oratio*, simple speech, into its opposite.[6] Even before he describes his *animus* aspiring to big ideas ('se animus cogitationum magnitudine levavit') and becoming ambitious in speech ('ambitiosus in verba'), Serenus' prose reveals him already to have been swept away towards something more sublime, speaking in a voice that is not properly his

---

[5] Foucault, *Fearless Speech*, pp. 159–60.
[6] Elena Giusti, 'The Metapoetics of Liber-ty: Horace's Bacchic Ship in Seneca's *De tranquillitate animi*', in *Horace and Seneca: Interactions, Intertexts, Interpretations*, ed. Martin Stöckinger, Kathrin Winter and Andreas T. Zanker (Berlin: De Gruyter, 2017), pp. 239–64 (pp. 245–6). The translation given above follows Giusti's adaptation of Basore's Loeb.

own ('sublimius feror et ore iam non meo' [I am swept to loftier heights by an utterance that is no longer my own], 1.14).

When Seneca steps in and takes up the role of interlocutor, he does not, as one might expect, repeat the lessons that Serenus, in his prosopopoeia, had been repeating to himself. He begins in the familiar guise of the physician, reassuring his friend and patient that he is on the right path ('recta via', 2.2): his 'infirmitas' has left him in a condition like those who have long been ill and, having recovered, fear even the slightest sign of sickness. 'Horum non parum sanum est corpus', he explains, 'sed sanitati parum adsuevit' [It is not that they are not quite well in body, but that they are not quite used to being well] (2.1). As his counsel develops, though, Seneca becomes increasingly accepting – enthusiastic, even – of Serenus' natural inconstancy, encouraging not a flat tranquillity of mind but a certain degree of *enthousiasmos*, that state of elation and inspiration presented elsewhere by Seneca in resolutely negative terms and seen as a threat to the progress of the *proficiens*.[7] 'Quod desideras', he writes, 'autem magnum et summum est deoque vicinum, non concuti' [What you desire is something great and supreme and very near to being a god – to be unshaken] (2.3); 'Natura enim humanus animus agilis est et pronus ad motus' [For it is the nature of the human mind to be active and prone to movement] (2.11). This is a far cry from the Seneca of the *De Constantia*, which opens with him insisting that, no matter how steep and rugged the path ('ardua [...] et confragosa'), one must commit to reaching these highest of standards. Where other philosophers treat their patients softly ('molliter'), acting as a kindly family physician ('domestici [...] medici'), the Stoics hear their patients' complaints and say 'so what?' ('Quid enim?') (*De Constantia*, 1.1–2).

By the end of his essay on tranquillity, Seneca seems to be contradicting himself almost entirely, occupying a position at odds with that of the teacher of constancy Serenus himself was so able to ventriloquise. His conclusion takes up again the idea of the parrhesiastic life, noting that you can never be at peace without openly revealing yourself ('simpliciter ostendas'): living a false life made up for show ('ostentationi parata', 17.1) will lead only to anxieties. There is pleasure to be had in embracing a simplicity that is sincere and unadorned ('voluptatis sincera et per se inornata simplicitas', 17.2). But pleasure, plain speaking and even constancy should be held in moderation ('modum tamen rei adhibeamus', 17.2) and, in life, we require admixture ('Miscenda tamen ista

---

[7] See ibid., pp. 240–4. On the negative connotations of *enthousiasmos*, and particularly its sense not as divine poetic *furor* but a fascination with the sound of empty words ('verborum inanium sonitus', *Ep.* 108.6), see Seneca's epistles 28 and 108.

et alternanda sunt', 'Nevertheless the two things must be combined and resorted to alternately', as Seneca says of solitude and public life, 17.3).

'Tamen', 'nevertheless', is Seneca's watchword here: his conclusions on tranquillity are structured by a contrary, perhaps even contradictory, way of thinking; one that inclines towards a moderate acceptance of diversity more than its flattening out into strict constancy. He ends with the liberating power of wine – liberating not because it loosens the tongue but because it frees the mind of care ('liberat servitio curarum animum', 17.8) – before embracing the enraptured flightiness of language that Serenus tried, and failed, to hold at arm's length. Invoking Plato, Aristotle and (under cover of an anonymous 'Greek poet') Horace, he celebrates madness ('dementia'), raving ('insanire'), and declares, in a rush of polysyndeton that proves his point, that speech cannot rise to lofty heights unless the mind is excited and in motion ('nisi mota mens', 17.10).

> Non potest sublime quicquam et in arduo positum contingere, quam diu apud se est; desciscat oportet a solito et efferatur et mordeat frenos et rectorem rapiat suum eoque ferat, quo per se timuisset escendere. (17.11)
>
> So long as [the mind] is left to itself, it is impossible for it to reach any sublime and difficult height; it must forsake the common track and be driven to frenzy and champ the bit and run away with its rider and rush to a height that it would have feared to climb by itself.

Seneca's imagery here of the mind champing at the bit, threatening to unseat its rider, is recalled strongly in Montaigne's account of the 'esprit genereux' which 'va outre ses forces' [goes beyond its strength] (III.13.1068/818). It is echoed even more clearly in the image from 'De l'oysiveté' of the 'cheval eschappé' [runaway horse] – though in the *Essais*, it is precisely when Montaigne leaves the 'esprit' 'en pleine oysiveté' [in full idleness] (I.8.33/21) that its movement becomes most frenetic.[8] That the discussion of the 'esprit genereux' invokes Apollonian

---

[8] Compare Montaigne's account in I.8 with Seneca's description in epistle 56: 'Otiosi videmur, et non sumus. Nam si bona fide sumus, si receptui cecinimus, si speciosa contemnimus [...] nulla res nos avocabit, nullus hominum aviumque concentus interrumpet cogitationes bonas, solidasque iam et certas. Leve illud ingenium est nec sese adhuc reduxit introrsus, quod ad vocem et accidentia erigitur' [Men think we are in retirement, and yet we are not. For if we have sincerely retired, and have sounded the signal for retreat, and have scorned outward attractions, then [...] no outward thing will distract us, no music of men or of birds can interrupt good thoughts, when they have once become steadfast and sure. The mind which starts at words or at chance sounds is unstable and has not yet withdrawn into itself] (*Ep.* 56.11–12). Both recognise that adopting the life and circumstances of a retiree does not in itself produce a stable, tranquil mind, though the crucial difference is that, while Montaigne recognises that the spiritual 'horse' has already bolted, Seneca exhorts us to 'esse conpositum' (*Ep.* 56.14).

speech – double, obscure, oblique – further entangles these reflections on sublime, sibylline frenzy, and draws Seneca into the frame for Montaigne's reception of this god of self-knowledge and doubtful discourse. Seneca's argument that we need to let the spirit loose finds a further parallel in Montaigne's own complex, shifting argument – an argument that moves through its own shifting assessment of Plutarch's 'daemonic' style – about letting yourself get (half-)lost: 'Je m'esgare, mais plustost par licence que par mesgarde' [I lose myself, but rather by licence than carelessness] (III.9.994/761).[9]

To find in Seneca an advocate for frenzied raving and a lesson in self-care that accepts and even embraces inconstancy is to uncover a 'visage' quite different from the familiar portrait Montaigne often presents.[10] Serenus had been looking for his friend to repeat the lessons he had been telling himself but instead found his Stoic tutor-physician recommending a little looseness, a touch of madness and just enough inconstancy. Seneca begins his response to Serenus by determining constancy to be a quality achievable only by what Montaigne would later call 'dieux mortels' (II.12.489–90/361).[11] But by the time he has reached his peroration, Seneca is speaking in a very different divine register: one that recognises our flightiness, our need for movement, and embraces it, all in a language inflected by the imagery of the raving Sibyl, speaking madly in a mode that promises truth and self-knowledge.

Both Serenus' letter and the response he receives are marked by contradiction – Serenus grappling with his *animus*, Seneca contradicting his interlocutor but also overturning the lessons he gives elsewhere (or at least seeming to, speaking against the caricature that Serenus creates in his prosopopoeia). Both reject a totalising view governed by universal maxims and instead break up their material, studying themselves a part at a time: 'tamen', 'and yet', repeats Seneca, seeing now one 'visage', now another. In what follows, I attend to the echoes of these ways of thinking and writing – contradiction, prosopopoeia, multiperspectival approaches to the 'totality' of the soul – in Montaigne's inconstant, paradoxical truth-telling, reading in the *Essais* the trace of Serenus'

---

[9] On this passage, see Chapter 4. For Plutarch's influence on early modern understandings of sibylline or otherwise enraptured speech, see Anthony Ossa-Richardson, *The Devil's Tabernacle: The Pagan Oracles in Early Modern Thought* (Princeton, NJ: Princeton University Press, 2013), pp. 26–9.
[10] But it does not come entirely out of the blue: Seneca's ability to stir his reader, sending us into somersaults, was highlighted in Montaigne's parallel judgement on the respective styles of Seneca and Plutarch (III.12.1040/795). See Chapter 1.
[11] Montaigne is here echoing the Seneca of *De Tranquillitate animi*, declaring that to be unshaken is something 'deo vicinum' [close to being a god] (2.3), even as he counts the Stoic among the philosophers who set such unreasonable expectations.

cognitive dissonance along with Seneca's instruction to accept it, at least in part. 'Si on y regarde, on trouvera que j'ay tout dict, ou tout designé' [if you look, you will find that I have said everything or suggested everything] (III.9.983/751). With Seneca, Montaigne developed a mode of communicating himself fully in terms that accommodate inconstancy, contradiction and partialness. Indeed, in the *Essais* and the 'discours paradoxe' they develop, it is precisely these qualities that constitute the hallmark of the truth-teller.

'La forme du total'

'Ceux qui s'exercent à contreroller les actions humaines', writes Montaigne, 'ne se trouvent en aucune partie si empeschez, qu'à les r'appiesser et mettre à mesme lustre' [Those who make a practice of comparing human actions are never so perplexed as when they try to see them as a whole and in the same light] (II.1.331/239). As Warren Boutcher and others have shown, the 'contrerolle', a sort of written record closely related to the 'registre', is a key metaphor in Montaigne's conception of his literary project.[12] What is notable here, at the start of his chapter on inconstancy, is the curious, counterintuitive suggestion that the activity of keeping a 'contrerolle' does not facilitate ready comparison. Human actions, a category that includes the actions of the 'esprit', seem always to insist on being seen separately and considered in their own light.

In Chapter 3, I argued that Montaigne's 'double' form, writing a 'skeletos' in the 'corps aerée de la voix' [the airy body of the voice] (II.6.379/274), worked to reveal his diverse parts 'd'une veue' [at a glance] (II.6.379/274). Here, I suggest that Montaigne achieves this end not by presenting an overview but by recording in writing his inconstancy, as he sees (and wears) now one 'visage', now another. Speaking fully – another of *parrhesia*'s defining characteristics – is reworked in Montaigne's response to Seneca in such a way as to make it depend on partialness.

---

[12] On different types of 'contrerolle' or 'registre', from the public to the domestic to the private, see especially Boutcher, *The School of Montaigne*, vol. 1, p. 106, and vol. 2, pp. 350–3. See also Cave, 'Montaigne', p. 196. Hugo Friedrich similarly drew attention to this nexus of terms ('mettre en registre, enregistrer, mettre en rolle, enroller, contreroller'), though understood this 'registre de soi-même' as ultimately a private act ('Ecrire, pour Montaigne, ne signifie que secondairement se communiquer à autrui'); Friedrich, *Montaigne*, pp. 341–2. Boutcher's analysis stresses Montaigne's innovation in making public a private mode of record-keeping.

Human actions 'se contredisent communément de si estrange façon, qu'il semble impossible qu'elles soient parties de mesme boutique' [commonly contradict each other so strangely that it seems impossible that they have come from the same shop] (II.1.331/239). Montaigne's word choices here point insistently towards the realm of the paradoxical. 'Paradoxe' was still a relatively new word in sixteenth-century French. In his translation of Plutarch's essays on Stoic paradoxes, Amyot felt the need to define it for his readers: 'c'est à dire estranges opinions, advouons eulx mesmes facilement qu'elles sont estranges & exorbitantes' [which is to say unusual opinions, for they themselves accept that they are unusual and outlandish].[13] To say that human actions 'contradict' one another both 'commonly' and in a way that is 'estrange' – strange, uncommon, outlandish – is to domesticate and normalise paradox and contradiction. Like 'paradoxe', the early modern sense of 'contredire' was, as Neil Kenny has shown, particularly alert to 'la part du dire': 'contradiction' is something one typically does to someone else, and something done by speaking.[14] This discursive aspect is brought to the fore in Cotgrave's definition: 'contredire' is 'to contradict, to gainesay, thwart, crosse, contrarie in words; also to refell, convince, refute'. Montaigne's location of contradiction within the individual – his attention to contradictory opinions emerging from 'la mesme boutique' – renders each of us not only a source of changing, inconstant opinions but a site of dialogue and dispute.

Having established his thesis, Montaigne begins to set out his stall, only to find that he need not bother. He presents a couple of ancient examples and a modern illustration, writing in a way that seems to accord with the tradition of 'diverses leçons' gathered on a theme, though he quickly distances himself from this familiar sort of commonplacing: 'Tout est si plein de tels exemples, voire chacun en peut tant fournir à soy-mesme, que je trouve estrange de voir quelquefois des gens d'entendement se mettre en peine d'assortir ces pieces' [Everything

---

[13] 'Des communes conceptions contre les stoiques', fol. 574v. On early modern understandings of paradox, see Rosalie L. Colie, *Paradoxia Epidemica: The Renaissance Tradition of Paradox* (Princeton, NJ: Princeton University Press, 1966); Agnieszka Steczowicz, 'The Defence of Contraries: Paradox in the Late Renaissance Disciplines', unpublished DPhil dissertation, University of Oxford, 2004; Vincent Robert-Nicoud, *The World Turned Upside Down in 16th-Century French Literature and Visual Culture* (Leiden: Brill, 2018), pp. 30–3.

[14] Neil Kenny, 'La Part du dire dans le contredire, ou l'inconstance des paroles humaines: Léry, Montaigne, Colletet', *Seizième Siècle*, 4 (2008), 255–87 (p. 268). Kenny goes on to note parallels between Montaignian contradiction and Pyrrhonian *antithesis* (p. 274). In 'De l'art de conferer', Montaigne describes himself seeking out contradiction from his interlocutors: 'je m'avance vers celuy qui me contredit, qui m'instruit' [I go towards a man who contradicts me, who instructs me] (III.8.924/705).

is so full of such examples, each man, in fact, can supply himself with so many, that I find it strange to see intelligent men sometimes going to great pains to match these pieces] (II.1.332/239). Montaigne seems ready to abandon his 'contrerolle': inconstancy and self-contradiction are so abundant that they need no further exemplification – we are each our own example – and what is 'estrange' is not the paradox that we all contradict ourselves but the effort expended in illustrating and piecing together these contradictions.

He continues, nonetheless, to provide examples, sayings and quotations taken from his reading, though, in the pages that follow, he employs again and again the language of 'nous' and 'nostre': 'Nostre façon ordinaire, c'est d'aller apres les inclinations de nostre apetit, à gauche, à dextre, contre-mont, contre-bas [...] Nous ne pensons ce que nous voulons, qu'à l'instant que nous le voulons [...] Ce que nous avons à cett'heure proposé, nous le changeons tantost, et tantost encore retournons sur nos pas' [Our ordinary practice is to follow the inclinations of our appetite, to the left, to the right, uphill and down [...] We think of what we want only at the moment we want it [...] What we have just now planned, we presently change, and presently again we retrace our steps] (II.1.333/240).

Montaigne is again echoing words borrowed from Seneca's letters.[15] But in recycling old images and Senecan sentences, he is, I suggest, not only digesting and reproducing an established conviction that man is inconstant. He is instead rewriting the response to 'infirmitas' that he found in Seneca's letters to Lucilius by following the contradictory lessons taught by Seneca in his response to Serenus. Here, quoting Seneca's diagnosis of inconstancy, he expunges the corollary instruction to seek a cure and instead finds an account – plain and simple – of our 'façon ordinaire'.

Montaigne draws from Seneca throughout this chapter, though there are moments where the intertextual interaction rises to the surface and presents itself more explicitly.[16] After noting that 'Nous sommes

---

[15] 'Nesciunt ergo homines, quid velint, nisi illo momento, quo volunt' (*Ep.* 20.6); 'nemo proponit sibi, quid velit, nec si proposuit, perseverat in eo, sed transilit; nec tantum mutat, sed redit et in ea, quae deseruit ac damnavit, revolvitur' (*Ep.* 20.4).

[16] See Prat, *Constance et inconstance chez Montaigne*, pp. 41–4. There is a further point in this intertextual network: in *De Tranquillitate animi*, 2.14, Seneca quotes Lucretius, 'Hoc se quisque modo semper fugit' [Thus ever from himself doth each man flee] (*De Rerum natura*, III.1068). Montaigne does not quote this line anywhere in the *Essais*, though if we look at his copy of Lucretius (p. 269), we see that he highlighted this line and those surrounding it along with a summary gloss: 'l'inconstance de nos actions'; Screech, *Montaigne's Annotated Copy of Lucretius*, p. 324. Montaigne quotes from this highlighted section (III.1057–9) on p. 333/240 of 'De l'inconstance de nos actions'.

tous de lopins' [We are all patchwork] (II.1.337/244), he quotes one of Seneca's final epistles: 'Magnam rem puta unum hominem agere' [Consider that it is a great thing to play the role of one man] (II.1.337/244; *Ep.* 120.22). The context here is significant. As Catherine Edwards has noted, it is in this letter that Seneca outlines the 'ideal' of 'making oneself in harmony with oneself', embracing *constantia* and *aequabilitas*. But, as Seneca makes plain in the surrounding lines, this is an ideal that even the would-be philosopher, 'made up of a mass of contradictory roles', struggles to achieve.[17] Only the sage, the wise man, is uniform ('unum'): the rest of us are 'multiformes'. And so we suffer this intractable inconsistancy, which Seneca describes in terms reminiscent of Plutarch's account of the flatterer who is always 'dissemblable à soy mesme': 'sic maxime coarguitur animus imprudens; alius prodit atque alius et, quo turpius nihil iudico, impar sibi est' [this is how a foolish mind is most clearly demonstrated: it shows first in this shape and then in that, and is never like itself, which is, in my opinion, the most shameful of qualities] (*Ep.* 120.22).

Montaigne incorporates the diagnosis, but rejects the cure. He notes that 'il faut sonder jusqu'au dedans, et voir par quels ressors se donne le branle' [we must probe the inside and discover what springs set men in motion], but asserts that this work of self-study – which aspires to understand rather than still, to 'contreroller' but not to control – ought to be left to those who can handle it: 'c'est une hazardeuse et haute entreprinse, je voudrois que moins de gens s'en meslassent' [it is an arduous and hazardous undertaking, I wish fewer people would meddle with it] (II.1.338/244).

It is from this same 'ancien' that Montaigne takes his definition of 'sagesse': 'c'est vouloir et ne vouloir pas, tousjours, mesme chose' [it is always to will the same things, and always to oppose the same things] (II.1.332/240), which is taken from an early epistle.[18] In introducing this ideal, though, Montaigne points to its near-impossibility: 'En toute l'ancienneté, il est malaisé de choisir une douzaine d'hommes qui ayent dressé leur vie à un certain et asseuré plan, qui est le principal but de la sagesse' [In all antiquity it is hard to pick out a dozen men who set

---

[17] Catherine Edwards, 'Self-Scrutiny and Self-Transformation in Seneca's Letters', in *Seneca: Oxford Readings in Classical Studies*, ed. John G. Fitch (Oxford: Oxford University Press, 2008), pp. 84–101 (p. 98). Edwards sees Seneca's writings as 'part of a larger turn in the first and second centuries AD towards interiorization', studying the tensions that Seneca traces within himself in light of broader tensions between a public self demanded by the pressures of the Neronian court and an aspiration towards a private, interior self appropriate to the Stoic sage.

[18] 'Quid est sapientia? Semper idem velle atque idem nolle', *Ep.* 20.5.

their lives to a certain and constant course, which is the principal goal of wisdom] (II.1.332/240).

A second reference to 'un ancien' – 'Ce n'est pas merveille, dict un ancien, que le hazard puisse tant sur nous, puis que nous vivons par hazard' [It is no wonder, says an ancient, that chance has so much power over us, since we live by chance] (II.1.337/243) – introduces a whole series of images that identify inconstancy as a consequence of not being able to see the big picture. These are again all lifted from Seneca's *Epistles*.[19]

> [A]A qui n'a dressé en gros sa vie à une certaine fin, il est impossible de disposer les actions particulieres. Il est impossible de renger les pieces, à qui n'a une forme du tout [C]total [A]en sa teste. A quoy faire la provision des couleurs à qui ne sçait ce qu'il a à peindre? Aucun ne fait certain dessein de sa vie, et n'en deliberons qu'à parcelles. L'archier doit premierement sçavoir où il vise, et puis y accommoder la main, l'arc, la corde, la flesche et les mouvemens. (II.1.337)

> [A]A man who has not directed his life as a whole toward a definite goal cannot possibly set his particular actions in order. A man who does not have a picture of the whole [C]total [A]in his head cannot possibly arrange the pieces. What good does it do a man to lay in a supply of paints if he does not know what he is to paint? No one makes a definite plan of his life; we think about it only piecemeal. The archer must first know what he is aiming at, and then set his hand, his bow, his string, his arrow, and his movements for that goal. (243)

We are, Seneca and Montaigne tell us, at the mercy of chance and Fortune and, without taking a look at the bigger picture – without looking at our life 'en gros', holding the 'forme du total' in our mind – we are destined to live lives of discord. The whole of this passage, gathering a cluster of images and metaphors comparing the art of living to practical *technai*, is translated from epistle 71.[20] Montaigne's post-1588 correction clarifies his point – it is seeing the big picture, the relationships that make up the

---

[19] This passage serves as a further example of the sort of authorial ambiguity studied in Chapter 2: it is not immediately clear that any of the examples illustrating the *sententia* attributed to 'un ancien' are taken from Seneca.

[20] 'Necesse est multum in vita nostra casus possit, quia vivimus casu' [Chance must necessarily have great influence over our lives, because we live by chance] (*Ep.* 71.3); 'non disponet singulam nisi cui iam vitae suae summa proposita est' [no man can set in order the details unless he has already set before himself the chief purpose of his life] (*Ep.* 71.2); 'Nemo, quamvis paratos habeat colores, similitudinem reddet, nisi iam constat, quid velit pingere' [The artist may have his colours all prepared, but he cannot produce a likeness unless he has already decided what he wishes to paint] (*Ep.* 71.2); 'Scire debet quid petat ille, qui sagittam vult mittere, et tunc derigere ac moderari manu telum. Errant consilia nostra, quia non habent, quo derigantur' [The archer must know what he is seeking to hit; then he must aim and control the weapon by his skill. Our plans miscarry because they have no aim] (*Ep.* 71.3).

whole (rather than seeing the shape of each and every thing) that would allow us to piece things together – but it is an edit that works also to bring the text into closer alignment with Seneca's Latin: 'peccamus, quia de partibus vitae omnes deliberamus, de tota nemo deliberat' [the reason we make mistakes is because we all consider the parts of life, but never life as a whole] (*Ep.* 71.2).

Most significant, though, is not the fact that Montaigne borrows these images; it is that he extracts them from their broader philosophical lesson. The language of sin and error – Seneca's *peccamus* – is not picked up in the 'commerce' between these two 'boutiques', nor is the sense that either correction or cure might be possible. In Seneca's epistle, the insistent illustrations of the need to see things, including oneself, in the round are marshalled to show that such a unified approach is not only possible but closer to hand than we might think. To make sense of every 'part' we encounter – to know how to respond to this or that, what to seek out and what to ward off – you need only consider its relation to the Supreme Good: you should consider it in relation to the purpose of your whole life ('ad summum bonum, propositum totius vitae tuae, respice', *Ep.* 71.2). Here again Seneca stresses the importance of parrhesiastic harmony ('Illi enim consentire debet, quicquid agimus' [For whatever we do ought to be in harmony with the Supreme Good], *Ep.* 71.2) before providing us with a further everyday analogy: 'Quemadmodum quaerimus saepe eos, cum quibus stamus, ita plerumque finem summi boni ignoramus adpositum' [Just as we often go searching for those who stand beside us, so we are apt to forget that the goal of the Supreme Good lies near us] (*Ep.* 71.4). The Supreme Good needs no philosophical or rhetorical exposition: we can point to it with ease ('digito [...] demonstrandum est'). It is simply that which is 'honestum'; breaking it up into pieces ('in particulas') gets us nowhere (*Ep.* 71.4).

In the *Essais*, by contrast, we find only the illustrations of inconstancy and contradiction. The harmony that Seneca instructs us to adopt is found wanting. Similarly, where Seneca's pointing finger indicates the unifying principle close at hand, Montaigne's gestures point instead to difference and discontinuity, to things hitherto unseen and to things left unsaid. It is with these gestures that the essayist reveals himself fully even as he writes partially: 'on trouvera que j'ay tout dict, ou tout designé. Ce que je ne puis exprimer, je le montre au doigt' [you will find that I have said everything or suggested everything. What I cannot express, I point to with my finger] (III.9.983/751).[21] We are, Montaigne writes,

---

[21] On Plutarch as another author who points, see I.26.156/115, discussed in Chapter 3. Marina Perkins has drawn on relevance theory to provide a cognitive reading of

'si informe et diverse' that 'chaque piece, chaque moment faict son jeu' [each bit, each moment, plays its own game] (II.1.337/244). Writing fully is not a matter of compiling these pieces – such a presentation of ourselves 'en gros' is beyond us. It is instead a matter of writing in a way that records the act of looking closely and scrutinising diverse parts. The 'contrerolle', the 'memoires' in which he says or at least points at everything, reveals Montaigne in his daily 'commerce' with his book, and it is that 'commerce' that records his double, inconstant, contradictory 'contrarietez'. His accounts are neither full nor resolved: his 'contrerolle' does not add up. But Montaigne is not trying to 'r'appiesser et mettre en mesme lustre' [see as a whole and in the same light] his contradictory parts (II.1.331/239). Instead, it is in reflecting partially on himself in writing, using his book as a tool ('util'), that he communicates and reveals himself and his character fully.

In an especially well-known passage from 'De l'inconstance de nos actions', Montaigne notes how he speaks of himself 'diversement' because 'je me regarde diversement' [I look at myself in different ways]: 'je donne à mon ame tantost un visage, tantost un autre, selon le costé où je le couche' [I give my soul now one face, now another, according to which direction I turn it]. 'Distingo', he says, is the 'plus universel membre de ma Logique' [the most universal member of my logic] (II.1.335/242). Montaigne's invocation of scholastic logic is undoubtedly playful: 'distingo' ought to prevent equivocation, and yet 'Je n'ay rien à dire de moy, entierement, simplement, et solidement sans confusion et sans meslange, ny en un mot' [I have nothing to say about myself absolutely, simply, and solidly, without confusion and without mixture, or in one word] (II.1.335/242).[22]

But as Sébastien Prat has noted, Montaigne's use of this term, which also signifies the dyeing of textiles in different colours, recalls another of Seneca's practical images for recognising the relationship between part and whole.[23] In an early letter on the need to live according to

Montaigne's habits of pointing and leaving things unsaid. See Marina Perkins, '"Il guigne seulement du doigt par où nous irons": Underspecification in Montaigne's *Essais*', *Modern Language Review*, 118.3 (2023), 328–48.

[22] On 'distingo' or 'distinguer' as 'oster l'équivoque' [to remove equivocation], see Antoine Furetière's *Dictionnaire universel* (La Haye and Rotterdam: Arnoud et Reinier Leers, 1690), 'Distinguer'.

[23] Prat, *Constance et inconstance chez Montaigne*, p. 224. For an early modern witness to this sense, see Robert Estienne's *Dictionarium latinogallicum* (Paris: Charles Estienne, 1552), 'Distinguo', which cites Pliny and Ovid: '*Marqueter, Tacheter, Moucheter, Esteler, ou Estinceler de diverses couleurs, Taveler, Grivoler, Peincturer, Bigarrer, Piquoter. Colore vario distinguere aliquid. Ovid*' [*To pattern, to mottle, to fleck, to spread, or scatter with diverse colours, to blotch, to speckle, to paint, to make motley, to dot.* To pattern something with different colours, Ovid.]

one's own standard, to ensure that one's life does not contradict one's words ('ne orationi vita dissentiat'), Seneca declares that one's inner life should be one colour ('sine dissensione coloris') (*Ep.* 20.2). For Prat, it is this textile sense of 'distingo', corresponding with Montaigne's use elsewhere of 'bigarrure' [patchwork], that uncovers his subversion of Senecan lessons calling for harmony and constancy.[24] Notably, Montaigne gives his soul its different colours by looking at it differently ('je donne à mon ame tantost un visage, tantost un autre, selon le costé où je me couche'). His 'distingo', his act of couching the soul differently and in different hues, is concomitant with the keeping of a 'contrerolle': not to 'r'appiesser' his diverse pieces and '[les] mettre à mesme lustre' [to see them as a whole and in the same light] (II.1.331/239) but to see himself partially and, in doing so, to see his contradictions.

Montaigne's sense that he is presenting himself 'fully' but without seeing or presenting himself 'en gros' complicates the parrhesiastic traditions with which he is working. His book reveals his diverse parts 'd'une veue' but not by compiling them, sorting them into a structured workbook or ledger that might simplify or rationalise that diversity: if Montaigne counts himself among those who 's'exercent à contreroller les actions humaines', it should be clear that he did not see in his work the activity of tallying, accounting, piecing together his parts into a whole. Rather, it is in working with his book, thinking with the 'forme' that has been the focus of previous chapters in this study, the 'forme' that acts as a 'truchement de l'ame', that he recognises his contradictory parts. His book is always one, as indeed is he, but his perception and presentation of that whole is one glanced at and pointed to in the spaces between his detached pieces of writing, his 'pieces décousues'. *Parrhesia*, in Montaigne's hands, becomes a matter of writing 'diversement' as well as 'doublement': speaking fully, he finds himself under the 'obligation particuliere à ne dire qu'à demy' [personal obligation to speak only by halves] (III.9.995–6/762).[25]

Montaigne's partial truth-telling depends on a partial reading of Seneca – one that reads Seneca selectively and draws out the contradictions in the Stoic that reflect those that Montaigne found in himself and, indeed, in everything and everyone else. It was Serenus, caught between 'infirmitas' and wisdom, who struggled to see things 'en gros' and found himself compelled to tackle the matter piecemeal. In the *Essais*, it is Montaigne who not only advocates the necessity of seeing himself 'à parcelles' but whose view of Seneca is equally skewed and fragmentary.

---

[24] Prat, *Constance et inconstance chez Montaigne*, pp. 223–6.
[25] On this line from 'De la vanité', see Chapter 3.

In quoting Seneca's diagnosis while extracting it from the broader therapy, he makes the Seneca of the *Epistles* contradict himself, just as the Seneca writing to Serenus had contradicted the lessons he gives elsewhere. Montaigne's reworking of Senecan inconstancy is not an exercise in paradiastole, redescribing inconstancy as an ethical good: as Neil Kenny and others have shown, Montaigne dismisses the matter of moral judgement about constancy and inconstancy altogether.[26] It is simply the case that we are inconstant and a truthful account of that state must be one that attends to and reveals that inconstancy without resolving it. In Seneca, along with Plutarch and others, Montaigne found a clear account of parrhesiastic truth-telling as speech functioning in harmony with the movements of the soul, revealing fully the character of the speaker. But, by reading Seneca partially, he also found a language with which to recognise the soul's fragmentation and incoherence. With his fractured, contradictory Seneca, Montaigne recast *parrhesia* to accommodate these qualities without trying to cure them, giving an account of truth-telling, and not only a truthful account of himself, that is strange, outlandish, 'paradoxe'.

Inconstant Truths

Montaigne's conception of truth-telling is one in which the 'contrerolle' does not reveal the big picture but serves rather to show, 'd'une veue', a cluster of changing, contradictory parts. His relationship to these parts is 'partial' in another sense too. His habit of giving his soul 'tantost un visage, tantost un autre' – a habit that reflects the many faces he found in the 'forme d'escrire' of the 'tiers genre' – does not allow him to establish any critical distance from the opinions he tries on, at least not in the moment.[27] 'Ce que je tiens aujourd'huy et ce que je croy', he writes, 'je le tiens et le croy de toute ma croyance; tous mes utils et tous mes ressorts empoignent cette opinion et m'en respondent sur tout ce qu'ils peuvent' [What I hold today and what I believe, I hold and believe with all my belief; all my tools and all my springs of action grip this opinion and sponsor it for me in every way they can] (II.12.563/423).

The editions published in Montaigne's lifetime gave 'saisissent cette opinion' [seize this opinion] for 'empoignent cette opinion'. This change,

---

[26] Kenny, 'La Part du dire dans le contredire', p. 267. See also Prat, *Constance et inconstance chez Montaigne*, pp. 143–54.
[27] On Seneca and Plutarch speaking 'tantost d'un visage, tantost d'un autre, pour ceux qui y regardent de prez', see II.12.509/377.

made in the Bordeaux Copy, chimes with the passage at the end of the 'Apologie' describing the individual who tries to 'empoigner l'eau: car tant plus il serrera et pressera ce qui de sa nature coule par tout, tant plus il perdra ce qu'il vouloit tenir et empoigner' [grasp water: for the more he squeezes and presses what by its nature flows all over, the more he will lose what he was trying to hold and grasp] (II.12.601/455). A further watery metaphor follows shortly afterwards, recalling the endless filling up and pouring out that characterised Montaigne's commerce with Seneca and Plutarch: 'que la fortune nous remue cinq cens fois de place, qu'elle ne face que vuyder et remplir sans cesse, comme dans un vaisseau, dans nostre croyance autres et autres opinions, tousjours la presente et derniere c'est la certaine et l'infaillible' [whether fortune moves us five hundred times from our position, whether it does nothing but empty and pour back incessantly into our belief, as into a vessel, more and more different opinions, always the present and the latest one is the certain and infallible one] (II.12.563/423).[28] Montaigne may not be able to hold on to his opinions for long but, in the moment, their grip on him is unshakeable.

His expression of sincerity defines him as a *parrhesiastes*: his 'utils' – his intellect, his critical self-reflection, the 'contrerolle' that supports it – bind him to what he believes, and he in turn holds fast to an opinion that cannot be seen as anything other than true.[29] 'Je ne sçaurois ambrasser aucune verité ny conserver avec plus de force que je fay cette cy', he continues. 'J'y suis tout entier, j'y suis voyrement' [I could not embrace or preserve any truth with more strength than this one. I belong to it entirely, I belong to it truly.] And yet he knows, not least because of the 'contrerolle' that records these hard-and-fast beliefs, how often he has changed his mind: 'mais ne m'est il pas advenu, non une fois, mais cent, mais mille, et tous les jours, d'avoir ambrassé quelqu'autre chose à tout ces mesmes instruments, en cette mesme condition, que depuis j'aye jugée fauce?' [But has it not happened to me, not once, but a hundred times, a thousand times, and every day, to have embraced with these same instruments, in this same condition, something else that I have since judged false?]

As Emma Gilby has noted, Montaigne here 'embodies, in the most vigorous terms, a form of "croyance"' entirely at odds with the

---

[28] Compare I.26.146/107: 'où je puyse comme les Danaïdes, remplissant et versant sans cesse' [from whom I draw like the Danaïdes, incessantly filling up and pouring out].
[29] Compare Seneca, *Ep*. 75.3: 'Hoc unum plane tibi adprobare vellem, omnia me illa sentire quae dicerem, nec tantum sentire sed amare' [I should like to convice you entirely of this one fact: that I feel whatever I say, that I not only feel it, but am wedded to it].

'indifference' of Sceptical suspension.[30] He had just been discussing, dismissively, the absolute suspension of judgement that compels the Pyrrhonians, 'ceux qui doutent de tout', to doubt even that the sky is above them (II.12.563/423). Montaigne does not 'dout[e] de tout' and, crucially, he does not experience a suspension of judgement. Rather, he believes what he believes absolutely. In writing his *Essais*, he produces an account that focuses on the affective experience of thinking rather than on detached calculation or second-order reflection on the beliefs he variously holds.[31] It does not matter for Montaigne that his beliefs are inconstant, inconsistent or incoherent: when he believes something, 'j'y suis tout entier, j'y suis voyrement'. Even the 'utils' of self-study are shown here to work against any presumed critical distance or detachment. Montaigne's 'contrerolle' recognises and records his attachment to 'opinions' in a form that is incompatible with *epoché* and unable, therefore, to guide him towards tranquillity or constancy of the soul (*ataraxia*).

Though Montaigne recognises that he will almost certainly hold a different opinion in the future, he cannot use this knowledge to distance himself from what he currently believes: his awareness of the infirmity of 'raison' has no purchase on the actual experience of belief. As Jean-Yves Pouilloux put it, we cannot escape the belief that we are seeing things as they really are: 'cette considération rétrospective ne me délivre en aucune façon de ce que je crois aujourd'hui' [this retrospective awareness does not free me in any way from what I believe today].[32] To write truthfully, then, Montaigne writes his partialness – both his state of being made up of 'contrarietez' and his attachment to those parts as they grip him. The 'contrerolle' cannot afford a perspective 'en gros' without breaking those bonds and, in doing so, breaking the parrhesiastic harmony of speech and thought.

Looking back to Montaigne's doubtful, double form as discussed in Chapters 3 and 4, we might say, then, that the compositional habits of collapsing 'chronologie' and layering perspectives are formal techniques applied so that Montaigne might reveal his diverse parts 'd'une veue',

---

[30] Emma Gilby, *Sublime Worlds: Early Modern French Literature* (Oxford: Legenda, 2006), p. 108. For a reading of this passage as influenced by Academic Scepticism, detailing the 'processus psychologique du doute académicien', see Sébastien Prat, 'La réception des *Académiques* dans les *Essais*: une manière voisine et inavouée de faire usage du doute sceptique', in *Academic Scepticism in the Development of Early Modern Philosophy*, ed. Plínio Junqueira Smith and Sébastien Charles (Cham: Springer, 2017), pp. 25–44 (p. 41).

[31] On the opposition in this passage between thinking and 'science or calculation', see Lawrence D. Kritzman, *The Fabulous Imagination: On Montaigne's Essais* (New York: Columbia University Press, 2009), p. 157.

[32] Pouilloux, *Montaigne: une vérité singulière*, p. 182.

at a glance. But in the writing of those 'pieces décousues', his 'forme', his 'util', cannot do anything but grasp ('empoigner') his 'opinions' fully and completely, even in the knowledge that his grip will no doubt slacken and his opinions will be swapped for different, even contradictory beliefs. We might look back also to the discussion of authorial association and weak and temporary judgements in Chapter 2. The fact that Montaigne's attachment to his 'opinions' is weak does not prevent him from feeling them, in the moment, to be strong. The 'contrerolle' reveals not only the inconstancy of Montaigne's opinions, their tendency to change over time, but also the doubleness and cognitive dissonance he found reflected in Epicurus: 'nous sommes, je ne sçay comment, doubles en nous mesmes, qui faict que ce que nous croyons, nous ne le croyons pas, et nous ne pouvons deffaire de ce que nous condamnons' [we are, I know not how, double within ourselves, with the result that we do not believe what we believe, and we cannot rid ourselves of what we condemn] (II.16.619/469). Montaigne both believes what he believes fully, writing it authentically and sincerely, with full conviction, and knows not to believe that those convictions are stable or fixed. Crucially, though, this is a doubleness that emerges in Montaigne's 'commerce' with a doubtful, double form rather than in a detached, 'en gros' assessment of contradiction.

Montaigne describes his 'utils' grasping these opinions as an experience of embracing truth ('Je ne sçaurois ambrasser *aucune verité* ny conserver avec plus de force que je fay cette cy', emphasis added). He holds on to and reveals his beliefs as a *parrhesiastes*, and the inconstancy not only of his 'opinions' but of their expression is, counterintuitively, what guarantees his truthfulness. It is with a line misquoted from Plutarch that he articulates this paradox most clearly: 'Tant y a que je me contredits bien à l'adventure, mais la verité, comme disoit Demades, je ne la contredy point' [So, all in all, I may indeed contradict myself now and then; but truth, as Demades said, I do not contradict] (III.2.805/611). Montaigne has been reading the life of Demosthenes, in which Plutarch responds to the view that the Athenian orator 'estoit homme inconstant & variable de nature' [was an inconstant man and variable in his character]. Plutarch thought these accusations were unfair: Demosthenes never changed political parties and his policies remained constant; indeed, he 'laissa la vie pour ne se vouloir point changer' [gave up his life because he didn't want to change].[33] 'Il ne feit point comme Demades', Plutarch continues, 'lequel se voulant justifier de ce qu'il avoit tourné sa robbe en matiere de gouvernement de la chose

---

[33] 'Demosthenes', *Vies des hommes illustres*, fol. 586v.

publique, dit qu'il s'estoit bien contredit à soy-mesme assez de fois selon les occurrences des affaires, mais contre le bien de la chose, jamais' [He was not like Demades who, wanting to justify having changed his mind in the government of the republic, said that he had indeed contradicted himself many times as events occurred, but he had never contradicted the interests of the commonwealth]. In context, Demades is a figure of *politique* inconstancy, excusing his flip-flopping with an ancient version of 'when the facts change, I change my mind'. Plutarch's judgement of these men is clear: Demosthenes, not Demades, is the moral *exemplum* to be imitated.

In Montaigne's telling, the phrase attributed to Demades becomes much more pointed in its paradoxical nature, and much more pointedly to do with truth-telling (in Plutarch, Demades says nothing of 'la verité'). Montaigne may, of course, simply be joking, comparing himself with the unscrupulous politician and acknowledging, with a wry smile, his own slipperiness. The casual, off-hand 'à l'adventure' certainly points in this direction. But 'niaiser et fantastiquer' [playing the fool and fantasticating] lay at the heart of Montaigne's doubt and, by extension, his philosophising (II.3.350/251). If it is a joke, it is not necessarily just a joke. In 'Sur des vers de Virgile', he ventriloquises a reader, giving voice to imagined complaints and confusion in the face of his strange, contrarian, paradoxical writing:

> [B]Voilà un discours ignorant: Voilà un discours paradoxe, en voilà un trop fol: [C]tu te joues souvant, on estimera que tu dies à droit, ce que tu dis à feinte. [B]Oui fais-je, mais je corrige les fautes d'inadvertence, non celles de coustume. Est-ce pas ainsi que je parle par tout? Me represente-je pas vivement? Suffit.' (III.5.875, punctuation according to the Bordeaux Copy, fol. 383v)
>
> [B]This is an ignorant discourse: This is a paradoxical discourse, one that is too mad: [C]You are often playful, people will think you are speaking in earnest when you are making believe. [B]Yes, I say, but I correct the faults of inadvertence, not those of habit. Isn't this the way I speak everywhere? Don't I represent myself to the life? Enough, then. (667).[34]

'Paradoxe' is a surprisingly rare word in the *Essais*. Here, in the first of its two occurrences, it is projected onto a reader accusing Montaigne of being outlandish, outrageous and foolish in his thought and writing,

---

[34] Translation modified. Frame has 'This is ignorant reasoning' and 'paradoxical reasoning'; Screech has 'Here is an ignorant development' and 'Here your argument is paradoxical' (p. 989). Florio gives 'that's an ignorant discourse; that's a paradoxicall relation' (p. 525). I have (partly) followed Florio to retain the sense of 'discours' as refering to both speech and reasoning. See, for instance, Cotgrave's definition: 'A discourse, report, relation, rehearsall of matter; also, a survey, a perusall, examination, pondering of things in the mind.'

accusing him of saying things he cannot possibly believe.³⁵ He accepts the charge ('Oui fais-je') but – again paradoxically – sees in this the 'perfection' of his book: it is in writing his paradoxical, foolish, half-jesting thoughts and, indeed, in contradicting himself (but not the truth), writing what he believes fully in the moment even as he knows his beliefs will at some point change, that he represents himself 'vivement'. It is in writing his 'discours paradoxe', contrarian as well as self-contradictory, claiming to speak truthfully even as he declares his partialness, that he produces a paradoxical – which is to say contrarian, unusual – form of parrhesiastic truth-telling. 'J'ay faict ce que j'ay voulu: tout le monde me reconnoit en mon livre, et mon livre en moy' [I have done what I wanted. Everyone recognises me in my book, and my book in me] (III.5.875/667). This is how he speaks 'par tout'. For his book to represent him, it must be capable of a form of truth-telling full of diversity, inconstancy and contradiction; able to speak fully and sincerely in a way that accommodates his irony ('à feinte'), his contradictory views of a single subject ('tantost un visage, tantost un autre'), and his cognitive dissonance, his knowledge that he will not believe what he currently believes.

Unable to step outside himself, Montaigne could not simply describe his moving and changing mental state. Instead, he tried to capture it as it moved through its different iterations, using his 'forme' to place these alongside one another such that he might be seen fully, 'd'une veue'. The tensions and contradictions that characterise Montaigne's *ethos* are caught 'at a glance' without the need for a totalising view 'en gros': it is in reading his doubtful 'forme' that we recognise these tensions not only in his views and 'opinions' but in his tone, now 'à feinte', now 'à droit'. This further elucidates how the 'truchement de nostre ame' must do more than recount or record his thoughts: we lack both the introspective clarity to see our 'selves' and the requisite detachment that would allow us to step outside the 'here and now' of thinking. 'La parole' becomes a truthful 'truchement' not by producing a comprehensive 'registre' of his

---

[35] The Renaissance sense of 'paradoxe' referred predominantly to mock encomia, arguments made 'à feinte', but also to strange, counterintuitive claims made 'à droit', such as the Stoic 'paradoxes' ('only the wise are free'). One of Montaigne's early readers, Pierre de Saint-Julien de Bailleure, felt the word had been stretched and ought only to refer to true opinions contrary to common belief ('Paradoxe: c'est à dire chose vraye, mais esloignee de la commune opinion'): 'Le mot de Paradoxe n'a pas sa signification si ample que quelques-uns l'ont voulu estendre. L'exercice en la preuve du faulx n'est pas bien proprement Paradoxe' [The word Paradox does not have so broad a meaning as some have stretched it into having. An exercise in proving falsehoods is not properly paradoxical.] See Pierre de Saint-Julien de Bailleure, *Meslanges Historiques et recueils de diverses matieres pour la pluspart Paradoxalles, & neantmoins vrayes* (Lyon: Benoist Rigaud, 1589), fol. E5v ('Advertissement au lecteur') and p. 161.

diverse parts but in the 'commerce' that takes place in and through this 'registre', wherein the writing becomes part of Montaigne's thinking and the movements and shape of writing become those of his 'ame'.

False Consolations

Montaigne's 'registre' serves as a tool with which to know himself and a tool for making himself known. Recent approaches to the *Essais* have focused on the latter of these functions, working in the process to do away with the caricature of the retiree tucked away in his tower.[36] His book may resemble a private journal or domestic ledger, but what makes it noteworthy is, in part at least, its publication and, for all Montaigne's concern with the 'commandement paradoxe', he is no less alert to the public reception of his writing as a 'discours paradoxe'. Despite their stated 'fin domestique et privée', the *Essais* are not the private babbling they sometimes claim to be: throughout, Montaigne is concerned with the communicative function of his book, with the conversation and 'commerce' it affords.[37] And yet there are key moments when it does seem that he is talking to himself.

If talking to yourself is most readily understood as a private act, its social dimension is always lurking in the shadows. Private speech imitates interpersonal dialogue but it also shies away from or anticipates an audience, whether real or imagined, external or internal. 'Si ce n'estoit la contenance d'un fol de parler seul, il n'est jour au quel on ne m'ouist gronder en moy-mesme et contre moy: Bren du fat' [If it did not seem crazy to talk to oneself, there is not a day when I would not be heard growling at myself: 'Confounded fool!'] (I.38.235/173).[38] For Montaigne, this sort of soliloquy is the most natural thing in the world and something he would be seen doing all the time – every hour, as the 1595 text specifies – were he not worried about being taken for a fool or a madman.[39]

---

[36] Notably Desan's *Montaigne: Penser le social* and Boutcher's *The School of Montaigne*.
[37] Montaigne imagines himself writing for no one and still profiting in 'Du dementir', II.18.665/504. On the *Essais* as a confession 'en publicq', see III.5.846/643.
[38] Montaigne uses a turn of phrase rather more vulgar than Frame's 'Confounded fool!': for 'bren'/'bran', Cotgrave gives 'a turd' and 'a sot, an ideot, a ninnie' for 'un fat'. Florio was similarly reluctant to translate this scatological phrase, leaving a space for the reader to complete the clichéd Elizabethan insult 'a turd in your teeth': '(   ) in the fooles teeth'. See William M. Hamlin, *Montaigne's English Journey: Reading the Essays in Shakespeare's Day* (Oxford: Oxford University Press, 2013), p. 56.
[39] The 1595 edition reads: 'il n'est jour *ny heure à peine*, en laquelle on ne me ouist gronder en moy mesme' (emphasis added). See Villey-Saulnier, I.38.235.

A passage from the final chapter of the *Essais* – concerned not with 'bren' [shit] or 'flux' [diarrhoea] but with a rather different sort of evacuation – offers a particularly vivid example of Montaigne's paradoxical truth-telling. His account of how he consoles himself about his kidney stones broadcasts his prattling, his private pep talks, in a way that reveals him 'vivement' precisely when his 'discours' is most self-consciously 'paradoxe'. It is a passage that has been subject to extensive critical scrutiny. It has been read for its attention to embodied cognition and the mind–body problem;[40] as a reflection of medical models of hygiene and pathology, and as a dialogue allegorising faculty psychology;[41] and, through a psychoanalytic lens, as illustrating a 'rhetoric of empowerment based on the mode of the virtual as it is projected by the imagination'.[42] For Blandine Perona, Montaigne's dialogue with himself constitutes the invention of a theatrical role, creating a persona, that of the 'esprit', which invents a version of his ailment with which he is able to live: 'En l'imaginant surmontable, il la surmonte' [In imagining he can overcome it, he overcomes it].[43]

Reading this passage in light of doubtful, paradoxical *parrhesia* reframes the dialogue between Montaigne and his 'esprit' as something other than a psychological interrogation, or a sort of talking therapy, and instead calls attention to its communicative aspect: Montaigne may be reflecting on how he talks to himself, but he is writing to and for his readers. It is a passage in which he examines the efficacy of certain tired and worn-out rhetorical strategies to do with self-control; regimens and behavioural principles that ought to make life a little more bearable. At the same time though, he demonstrates the potential of a strange, unprecedented practice concerned not with persuasion but with open accounting. What's more, for a passage that seems, on the surface at least, to be intensely private, offering a window into Montaigne's soul, it is curiously reliant on Seneca. It shows Montaigne thinking through how he thinks about himself by thinking with quotations from the *Epistles*; with Seneca's use of prosopopoeia; with his reflections on the relationship between part and whole and on what happens when we let loose the mind. What emerges in Montaigne's paradoxical dialogue – a dialogue both with his ventriloquised 'esprit' and with Seneca; a dialogue

---

[40] Charis Charalampous, *Rethinking the Mind–Body Relationship in Early Modern Literature, Philosophy, and Medicine: The Renaissance of the Body* (Abingdon: Routledge, 2016), pp. 35–7.
[41] Jean Starobinski, *Montaigne en mouvement* (Paris: Gallimard, 1982), pp. 333–50.
[42] Kritzman, *The Fabulous Imagination*, pp. 171–80 (p. 172).
[43] Blandine Perona, *Prosopopée et persona à la Renaissance* (Paris: Garnier, 2013), pp. 286–95 (pp. 290–1).

that opens up an exchange with the reader too – is a focus not on the omnipotence, the 'force', of the imagination (this is not a demonstration of 'reason' or the 'will' commanding the self to act in a given way), but rather an account of failure.[44] In recounting this failure though, detailing his habitual recourse to flattery, insincerity and self-contradiction, Montaigne invites us to see him grumbling to himself: he communicates himself fully and truthfully, even as he risks being seen as an ignorant fool.

Montaigne's arguments in favour of 'la gravelle' – 'que c'est pour mon mieux que j'ay la gravelle; que les bastimens de mon age ont naturellement à souffrir quelque goutiere' [that it is for my own good that I have the stone; that buildings of my age must naturally suffer some leakage], and so on (III.13.1090/836) – are, for the most part, in close imitation of Seneca. In terms of 'matière' at least, the source is just one letter, epistle 78. I will return to Seneca shortly. But Montaigne was thinking with another model too, one he acknowledges explicitly in the conclusion to his praise of the stone: Cicero, whose *De Senectute* offered 'argumens, et forts et foibles' [arguments, both strong and weak] on how to handle 'le mal de sa vieillesse' [his disease of old age] (III.13.1095/839).

Consoling yourself – just like talking to yourself – is unusual and paradoxical; the sort of thing one would expect of a 'sot'. In writing up his self-consolation, it is likely that Montaigne had in mind not only Cicero's essay on old age but also one of his works that is now lost: the *Consolatio ad se*. Cicero described this work in a letter to Atticus, noting how, following the death of his daughter, he had done something 'quod profecto ante me nemo, ut ipse me per litteras consolarer' [that I imagine no one has ever done before: I have consoled myself in writing]. 'Totos dies scribo', Cicero continues, 'non quo proficiam quid sed tantisper impedior' [I write all day long, not that I do myself any real good, but just for the time being it distracts me] (*Ad Atticus*, 12.14.3). In consoling himself, Cicero fundamentally changed both the rhetorical and the ethical practices that underpin consolatory writing. This self-aware moment of innovation undermines the relationships of empathy and compassion, of fellow-feeling between friends and within the 'familia', that make consolation what it is. Consoling oneself ought to be impossible, as Han Baltussen has noted, comparing it to another curiosity of self-relation that occupied the ancients at least as far back as Aristotle:

---

[44] On 'acts of will' in Seneca as 'self-directed commands issued in the pursuit of moral self-control' (p. 55), and on the relationship between 'voluntas', Seneca's conception of will or will power, and the broader intellectual history of 'the will' (a 'messy business', p. 59), see Brad Inwood, 'The Will in Seneca the Younger', *Classical Philology*, 95.1 (2000), 44–60.

the fact that you cannot tickle yourself.⁴⁵ It should not be possible to be both consoler and consoled. And, as though to prove the point, Cicero is clear that his paradoxical self-consolation does not work – except that it does, in a way: he writes all day and does himself no good, but in writing all day, distracting and diverting himself, he finds some respite.

Montaigne introduces his own *consolatio ad se* in similar terms: 'Or je trete mon imagination le plus doucement que je puis et la deschargerois, *si je pouvois*, de toute peine et contestation' [Now I treat my imagination as gently as I can, and would relieve it, *if I could*, of all trouble and conflict] (emphasis added). We are a long way from Book 1 chapter 21 on 'la force de l'imagination' and its accounts of how the imagination can cure (or cause) bodily ailments: here it is Montaigne tending carefully and delicately to his sickly mind, and those conditionals underscore from the outset that he knows that this treatment will not be successful.⁴⁶ 'Il la faut secourir et flatter, et piper qui peut. Mon esprit est propre à ce service: il n'a point faute d'apparences par tout; *s'il persuadoit comme il presche, il me secourroit heureusement*' [We must help it and flatter it, and fool it if we can. My mind is suited to this service; it has no lack of plausible reasons for all things. *If it could persuade as well as it preaches, it would help me out very happily*] (emphasis added). Pulling at the threads of Cicero's knotty self-consolation, Montaigne casts into doubt the relationship between himself, his 'imagination' and his 'esprit': is it Montaigne or his spirit, 'propre à ce service', that 'trete [s]on imagination'? And where Cicero drew attention to the novelty and inefficacy of his arguments, Montaigne adds a third quality: his arguments strive to flatter and fool – they are insincere.

Montaigne's account of how he placates himself with false comforts was written amid a flurry of interest surrounding a fake *Consolatio*. In 1583, Carlo Sigonio, famed for his knowledge of Cicero and his uncanny ability to write pure, classical Latin, arranged (via intermediaries) for the printing of what purported to be a newly unearthed copy of

---

⁴⁵ Han Baltussen, 'A Grief Observed: Cicero on Remembering Tullia', *Mortality*, 14.4 (2008), 355–69 (p. 362). See also Han Baltussen, 'Cicero's *Consolatio ad se*: Character, Purpose, and Impact of a Curious Treatise', in *Roman and Greek Consolations: Eight Studies of a Tradition and its Afterlife*, ed. Han Baltussen (Swansea: Classical Press of Wales, 2013), pp. 67–91.

⁴⁶ Montaigne's metaphors imagining philosophy as a 'tres-douce medecine' are conventional and have often been read in light of Sextus' *Outlines*. See Dominique Brancher, '"Ny plus ny moins que la rubarbe qui pousse hors les mauvaises humeurs": La rhubarbe au purgatoire', pp. 303–20, and John O'Brien, 'Si avons-nous une tres-douce medecine que la philosophie', pp. 13–24, both in Demonet and Legros (eds), *L'Écriture du scepticisme chez Montaigne*. What is notable here is the impotence of Montaigne's self-consoling medicine, which lacks the potency, the 'vim medicinae', of Seneca's 'honesta solacia' [honourable consolation] (78.3).

Cicero's lost work. To complement this new discovery, Sigonio wrote a pair of 'orationes' in which he, as an impartial expert, protested rather too much.[47] Sigonio's claims were met with both fanfare and suspicion: in the years following its publication, the work saw a number of printed arguments for and against its authenticity, prime among them the judgement of Lipsius, first printed in the 1584 Plantin edition, in which the *Consolatio* was found not only to be a forgery but a bad one, merely covering old ground, stylistically childish and inept, and entirely lacking the nerves and blood of the man it claimed as its author.[48]

Like Cicero in his letter to Atticus, Montaigne acknowledged the novelty of self-consolation. He presents it as a curiosity for our amusement as much as anything else: 'Vous en plait-il un exemple?' [Would you like an example?] (III.13.1090/836). The attention that the printing of the *Consolatio* garnered across Europe contextualises this offer: Montaigne expected his reader's curiosity to be piqued. To console oneself in writing is, for a humanist working in any period, a rather strange thing to do: it is paradoxical, ethically and rhetorically confused, and not likely to do much good. To do this sort of thing in the mid-1580s, though, is not only to align oneself with Cicero and his false comforts; it is also to invite comparisons with a spurious text, a counterfeit imitation. Encouraging such comparisons seems an odd strategy for the would-be truth-teller.

The 'exemple' Montaigne gives is a rich and complex moment of extended prosopopoeia – not an apostrophe from Montaigne to his 'imagination' but a speech made by the 'esprit' itself.[49] Blandine Perona

---

[47] Cicero [i.e. Pseudo-Cicero], *Consolatio* (Venice: Girolamo Polo, 1583). On Sigonio and his *Consolatio*, see William McCuaig, *Carlo Sigonio: The Changing World of the Late Renaissance* (Princeton, NJ: Princeton University Press, 1989), esp. pp. 291–326, and, for the many editions of this work in the 1580s, see McCuaig's bibliography, pp. 351–2. See also Anthony Grafton, *Forgers and Critics: Creativity and Duplicity in Western Scholarship* (Princeton, NJ: Princeton University Press, 2019 [1990]), pp. 45–8.

[48] *M. Tullii Ciceronis Consolatio... De quo judicium Justi Lipsii subjunctum* (Leiden: Plantin, 1584), pp. 209–10. 'In re & inventione, pleraque protrita & obvia: in phrasi, pueriliter aut inepte imitata. Nihil usquam nervorum aut sanguinis: ac ne color quidem, nisi cum aperta cerussa & fuco' (p. 210). Han Baltussen's analysis of a copybook held in the Bodleian shows just how quickly news and debate surrounding this text spread across Europe: Robert Batt, a student at Oxford, discusses it in a letter to his cousin written less than two months after the *Consolatio*'s publication. See Han Baltussen, 'A Curious Sidelight on the Reception of Ps. Cicero's *Consolatio* (1583)', *Bibliothèque d'Humanisme et Renaissance*, 80.3 (2018), 481–506.

[49] One might expect an enraptured, ecstatic mind to be the object of such an address, as in Rabelais' address to the 'Esprit abstraict, ravy, et ecstatic' [Abstracted Mind, enraptured, true ecstatic] of Marguerite de Navarre in a prefatory poem to *Tiers livre*, p. 341; *Gargantua and Pantagruel*, trans. Screech, p. 399; or for the parts of the mind – 'Reason' and the 'Soul', for instance – to speak to one another, as in François Le Roy's 1499

has noted that, while the 'mise en scène' of the voice of the 'esprit', its 'progressive' introduction, is clearly demarcated, moving from indirect speech ('Il dict que…' [It tells me that…]) to direct speech, the endpoint of the prosopopoeia – the point at which Montaigne starts speaking again in his own voice – is more ambiguous.[50]

> La crainte de ce mal, faict-il, t'effraioit autresfois, quand il t'estoit incogneu: les cris et le desespoir de ceux qui l'aigrissent par leur impatience t'en engendroient l'horreur. C'est un mal qui te bat les membres par lesquels tu as le plus failly; tu és homme de conscience. (III.13.1091)

> 'Fear of this disease,' says my mind, 'used to terrify you, when it was unknown to you; the cries and despair of those who make it worse by their lack of fortitude engendered in you a horror of it. It is an affliction that punishes those of your members by which you have most sinned. You are a man of conscience. (836)

Having found its voice, the 'esprit' begins inventing third-person perspectives and producing its own ventriloquised voices:

> Regarde ce chastiement; il est bien doux au pris d'autres, et d'une faveur paternelle […] Il y a plaisir à ouyr dire de soy: Voylà bien de la force, voylà bien de la patience. On te voit suer d'ahan, pallir, rougir, trembler, vomir jusques au sang. (III.13.1091)

> Consider this chastisement; it is very gentle in comparison with others, and paternally tender […] There is pleasure in hearing people say about you: There indeed is strength, there indeed is fortitude! They see you sweat in agony, turn pale, turn red, tremble, vomit your very blood. (836)

His spirit invites him to step outside himself (as his spirit seems already to have stepped outside him) and imagine a perspective not only looking at him as he suffers nobly but also looking at his 'assistans' [company] and his 'gens' [servants], to look at people looking at him and seeing a reflection of the 'gens du temps passé' [men of past times] (III.13.1091/837).[51] He sees himself not from their perspective exactly but by seeing how they look at him. In this increasingly complex web of

---

Dialogue de consolation entre l'ame et raison. The separation of the mind and body (or of the rational mind and the soul) is a trope; what is surprising is that Montaigne does not go with his 'ecstatic' mind but sticks with the body.

[50] Perona, *Prosopopée et persona à la renaissance*, p. 288.

[51] 'On te voit […] entretenant cependant les assistans d'une contenance commune, bouffonnant à pauses avec tes gens, tenant ta partie en un discours tendu, excusant de parolle ta douleur et rabatant de ta souffrance' [They see you […] keeping up conversation with your company with a normal countenance, jesting in the intervals with your servants, holding up your end in a sustained discussion, making excuses for your pain and minimizing your suffering] (III.13.1091/836–47).

sight lines and projected voices, the 'esprit' complicates things further, anticipating Montaigne's own voice: 'Si tu me dis que c'est un mal dangereux et mortel, quels autres ne le sont?' [If you tell me that it is a dangerous and mortal disease, what others are not?]

The arguments marshalled here are all taken, more or less directly, from Seneca. This is odd: not only is Montaigne's truthful account of his private thoughts entangled with a counterfeit *Consolatio*; his private thoughts aren't his. Montaigne, or rather his 'esprit', is rehearsing maxims and lessons borrowed from one of Seneca's letters in which he advises Lucilius on how to benefit from philosophy when suffering with their shared ailment, catarrh. For Seneca, 'Multum mihi contulerunt ad bonam valetudinem amici' [My friends, too, helped me greatly towards good health] (*Ep.* 78.4), while Montaigne, wryly, notes that 'la compagnie me doibt consoler, estant tombé en l'accident le plus ordinaire des hommes de mon temps' [the company should console me, since I have fallen into the commonest ailment of men of my time of life] (III.13.1090/836). Seneca's tripartite division of disease's trials into fear of death, bodily pain and the interruption of pleasures ('metus mortis, dolor corporis, intermissio voluptatum', *Ep.* 78.6) provides Montaigne with his own commonplacing topics.[52] This proximity comes to a head in a post-1588 addition, where Montaigne quotes Seneca in a close translation: 'morieris non quia aegrotas, sed quia vivis' (*Ep.* 78.6), 'Mais tu ne meurs pas de ce que tu es malade; tu meurs de ce que tu es vivant' [But you will die not of being sick, you die of being alive] (III.13.1091/837).

There are commonalities in *manière* too. Letting loose the mind, as Seneca enthusiastically recommends at the end of *De Tranquillitate animi*, Montaigne's prosopopoeia recalls the flighty, rushing, enraptured letter of Serenus, in which he too talks to himself, repeating the lessons he expected to hear from his tutor and guide. Prosopopoeia's doubling up of voices reveals the 'infirmitas' that these patients, Montaigne and Serenus, suffer: they know what to say, and they can rattle off the regimen they ought to be following, though they struggle to internalise its lessons. Prosopopoeia is common also to consolatory writings

---

[52] See, for instance, disease as *praeparatio mortis*: 'Considere combien artificiellement et doucement elle te desgoute de la vie et desprend du monde' [Consider how artfully and gently the stone weans you from life and detaches you from the world] (III.13.1092/837); bodily pain as heightening health: 'De combien la santé me semble plus belle apres la maladie' [How much more beautiful health seems to me after the illness] (III.13.1093/838); and, on bodily pleasures: 'Regarde sa tardiveté: il n'incommode et occupe que la saison de ta vie qui, ainsi comme ainsin, est mes-huy perdue et sterile' [Consider its lateness; it bothers and occupies only the season of your life which in any case is henceforth wasted and barren] (III.13.1091/836).

and particularly the consolatory dialogue.[53] It is that dialogic quality that allows these texts to model the ethical and rhetorical work of consolation, staging an exchange between consoler and consoled, between teacher and student (Cicero's *Tusculan Disputations*, for instance), between reason and the soul (François Le Roy's 1499 *Dialogue de consolation entre l'ame et raison*), between 'Philosophy' (Boethius) or 'Reason' (Augustine's *Soliloquies*) and the author.[54]

Montaigne's self-consolation lacks the conversational back and forth between characters that typifies Renaissance dialogue: voices in his 'exemple' are constantly projected, ventriloquised and intercalated. In this, it has more in common with prosopopoeia as it is found in Seneca's consolatory letters. In the *Consolatio ad Marciam*, for instance, Seneca speaks at length in three different voices: first as the philosopher Areus; then as Nature; and finally as Marcia's father. And it is not just the consoler's persona that keeps changing. Areus' imagined consolation is directed not at Marcia but at Livia, meaning that it has to be reworked by Seneca – if you can rework something that has not yet been 'worked' – to apply to its new addressee: 'muta personam', he writes, 'te consolatus est' [change the role and it is you who is consoled].[55] Notably, Seneca prefaces his introduction of these exemplary figures and their voices by highlighting his departure from convention, just as Montaigne introduced his own 'exemple': 'Scio a praeceptis incipere omnis, qui monere aliquem volunt, in exemplis desinere. Mutari hunc interim morem expedit [...] Duo tibi ponam ante oculos maxima et sexus et saeculi tui exempla' [I am aware that all those who wish to give anyone instruction begin with precepts and end with examples. But it is desirable at times to alter this practice [...] I shall place before your eyes two examples [Livia and Octavia], the greatest of your sex and century] (*Ad Marciam*, 2.1).[56] In the consolatory works, then, Seneca provides a formal model of a consoler rapidly jumping between different voices and so provides the stylistic framework into which Montaigne could put the reasons and precepts taken from the letters to Lucilius.

---

[53] See Alexandre Tarrête, 'Remarques sur le genre du dialogue de consolation à la Renaissance', *Réforme, Humanisme, Renaissance*, 57 (2003), 133–52.

[54] The conversation between the 'esprit' and Montaigne seems similar, in this regard at least, to the conversation between Augustine and Reason, though it is unlikely that Montaigne knew Augustine's *Soliloquies*. See Takeshi Kubota, *Montaigne, lecteur de la Cité de Dieu d'Augustin* (Paris: Champion, 2019), pp. 13–14, 16.

[55] Translation adapted from Basore, who gives 'change the role – it is you that he tried to comfort'.

[56] On Seneca's use of *exempla*, and the distinction between examples to be imitated and examples to be contemplated, see Jo-Ann Shelton, 'Persuasion and Paradigm in Seneca's *Consolatio ad Marciam* 1–6', *Classica et Mediaevalia*, 46 (1995), 157–88.

The 78th epistle to Lucilius has long been recognised as a source for the arguments gathered by Montaigne's 'esprit' in defence of the stone. But the use of ventriloquised voices in this letter has escaped critical attention. The Stoic tells his friend that those who must suffer pain ought to practise patience. Those who are unable to do this, those who are inexperienced ('imperitos'), have not accustomed themselves to be content in spirit ('non adsueverunt animo esse contenti'): 'Multum illis cum corpore fuit. Ideo vir magnus ac prudens animum diducit a corpore et multum cum meliore ac divina parte versatur, cum hac querula et fragili quantum necesse est' [They have been closely associated with the body. Therefore a high-minded and sensible man divorces soul from body, and dwells with the better or divine part, and only as far as he must with this complaining and frail portion] (*Ep.* 78.10).

What immediately follows this instruction to separate the fragile body from the divine mind is a shift to direct speech: '"Sed molestum est", inquit, "carere adsuetis voluptatibus, abstinere cibo, sitire, esurire"' ['But it is a hardship', he [*or* it] says, 'to do without our customary pleasures, to fast, to feel thirst and hunger'] (*Ep.* 78.11). This persona returns later in the letter, voicing a complaint that Montaigne would echo ('"Dolorem gravem sentio." Quid ergo? [...] "Sed grave est." Quid?' ['I feel severe pain.' What, then? [...] 'But the trouble is serious.' What?], *Ep.* 78.17).[57] Whose voice is this? In the context of the *Epistles*, it can be assumed that Seneca is employing one of his standard rhetorical devices: the introduction of a third-person interlocutor, what Matthew Roller calls Seneca's 'fictive adversary' or 'generalised interlocutor'.[58] The *Epistles* are principally a dialogue with Lucilius, but they are loaded with additional voices, interjecting with queries, rebuttals and requests for clarification.

Montaigne, consciously or otherwise, seems to have misinterpreted this 'inquit' as referring not to the inexperienced *imperitii* but to the body, our weaker, 'fragile and complaining' ('querula et fragili') part. It is a misreading that opens up a dialogue in Seneca's text that otherwise does not exist: a dialogue between mind and body in which the latter, now personified, complains directly to an implied Reason.

---

[57] Compare Montaigne, quoted above: 'Si tu me dis que c'est un mal dangereux et mortel, quels autres ne le sont?' Notably, the text of the *Essais* doubles the ventriloquism, with Montaigne imagining his 'esprit' imagining his response.

[58] Matthew Roller, 'The Dialogue in Seneca's Dialogues (and Other Moral Essays)', in *The Cambridge Companion to Seneca*, ed. Shadi Bartsch and Alessandro Schiesaro (Cambridge: Cambridge University Press, 2015), pp. 54–67. See also Giancarlo Mazzoli, 'Le "voci" dei Dialoghi di Seneca', in *Seneca al suo tempo*, ed. Piergiorgio Parroni (Rome: Salerno Editrice, 2000), pp. 249–60.

In misattributing this moment of ventriloquism, Montaigne invents a model for his own 'exemple' in which he is addressed by his 'esprit' on the subject of his 'corps'. Notably, he inverts the (perceived) relationship that puts Seneca, 'vir magnus ac prudens', in alignment with his 'meliora ac divina pars' and in opposition to the externalised, exterior 'corpus' that addresses him. In the *Essais*, Montaigne, ostensibly concerned with the passing of a very different sort of foreign body, a 'corps' within his own and yet distinct from it, overwrites this Senecan 'inquit' such that it is not the stone but his 'esprit' that is evacuated. Incarnating the 'esprit' in its own 'corps aerée de la voix' [airy body of the voice] (II.6.379/274), Montaigne not only troubles the distinction between interior and exterior, between 'me' and 'not-me': he places himself on the wrong side of the divide.

In giving his 'exemple' of how he talks to himself, Montaigne reveals a plurality of diverse and contradictory voices to reveal the cognitive dissonance or doubleness that he describes elsewhere: his 'esprit' clings on to these 'apparences', these old maxims and commonplaces, even as Montaigne declares them to be white lies and self-soothing flattery. He both believes and doesn't believe them, and we can see, or rather hear, his different, contradictory parts at once. It is an 'exemple' also of the mark left by Seneca – his lessons, sayings, images and techniques – on the habitual patterns of his thinking. The 'esprit' even compares Montaigne, implicitly, with Seneca. The spirit's invitation to imagine a third-person perspective looking at Montaigne as he bears himself nobly (quoted above) has more than a passing resemblance to the account of Seneca steeling himself in preparation for death:

> A voir les efforts que Seneque se donne pour se preparer contre la mort, à le voir suer d'ahan pour se roidir et pour s'asseurer et se desbatre si long temps en cette perche, j'eusse esbranlé sa reputation, s'il ne l'eut en mourant tresvaillamment maintenue. (III.12.1040)[59]

> To see the trouble to which Seneca puts himself to be prepared for death, to see him sweat from the exertion of steeling and reassuring himself, and writhe about interminably on his perch, would have shaken his reputation with me if he had not very valiantly maintained it in dying. (795)

---

[59] Compare III.13.1091/836–7: 'On te voit suer d'ahan, pallir, rougir, trembler, vomir jusques au sang, souffrir des contractions et convulsions estranges, degouter par foys de grosses larmes des yeux, rendre les urines espesses, noires, et effroyables, ou les avoir arrestées par quelque pierre espineuse et herissée' [They see you sweat in agony, turn pale, turn red, tremble, vomit your very blood, suffer strange contractions and convulsions, sometimes shed great tears from your eyes, discharge thick, black, and frightful urine, or have it stopped up by some sharp rough stone]. These are the only instances of the phrase 'suer d'ahan' in the *Essais*.

Ultimately though, from its introduction to its conclusion, it is unclear whether Montaigne's 'traitement' of his imagination works: 's'il persuadoit comme il presche, il me secourroit heureusement' [If it could persuade as well as it preaches, it would help me out very happily] (III.13.1090/836); 'Par tels argumens, et forts et foibles, comme Cicero le mal de sa vieillesse, j'essaye d'endormir et amuser mon imagination, et gresser ses playes. Si elles s'empirent demain, demain nous y pourvoyerons d'autres eschapatoires' [By such arguments, both strong and weak, I try to lull and beguile my imagination and salve its wounds, as Cicero did his disease of old age. If they get worse tomorrow, tomorrow we shall provide other ways of escape] (III.13.1095/839).[60] The curative function of this therapy is placed in doubt: like Cicero in his letter to Atticus, Montaigne finds himself writing all day long and not doing himself any real good. His 'esprit' might know the arguments and the techniques of consolation, but – as the corruption of Seneca's 'inquit' shows – he is on the side of the body: the arguments of the 'esprit', the 'meliora ac divina pars', seem always to stay outside. One would expect his trouble with the stone to be relieved by a certain evacuation. Here in the *Essais* though, the problem is more a matter of retention: Montaigne cannot quite keep his lessons in.

'Feuilles sibyllines'

Why might we, as readers, be interested in listening in on Montaigne as he goes about his strange, foolish habit of talking to himself, of telling himself – whether 'à feinte' or 'à droit' – that his kidney stones are good for him? What is he looking to achieve by offering us this 'exemple'? In 'De l'inconstance de nos actions', he stressed that contradiction and inconstancy are entirely commonplace: 'tout est si plein de tels exemples […] que je trouve estrange de voir quelquefois des gens d'entendement se mettre en peine d'assortir ces pieces' [Everything is so full of such examples […] that I find it strange to see intelligent men sometimes going to great pains to match these pieces] (II.1.332/239). What is the point, then, of giving his reader yet another example?

Montaigne's 'exemple' is self-consciously an object of curiosity and one that is in multiple aspects 'paradoxe': he is consoling himself, or at least trying to; he is praising an ill, a staple of the *paradoxon*, the mock

---

[60] Blandine Perona notes that the spirit's 'habilité rhétorique' [rhetorical skill] might win Montaigne's admiration, 'mais n'a aucune force de conviction' [but it has no force of conviction]. Perona, *Prosopopée et persona à la Renaissance*, p. 288.

encomium tradition.⁶¹ But paradoxical also is his attention to himself, his effort to recognise, examine and reveal his habitual patterns of thought, in all their foolishness, while taking the risk that he will be dismissed as a madman. It is a response to the 'commandement paradoxe' [paradoxical command] issued 'anciennement' by Apollo via his stomach-talking ventriloquist, the raving Pythia whose speech is displaced by divine *enthousiasmos*: 'regardez dans vous, reconnoissez vous, tenez vous à vous' [look into yourself, know yourself, keep to yourself] (III.9.1001/766).

A post-1588 addition to this 'exemple' draws more clearly the connection between the habit of vain self-flattery and the practices of self-knowledge and doubtful veridiction associated with Apollo and the Pythia:

> A faute de mémoire naturelle j'en forge du papier, et comme quelque nouveau symptome survient à mon mal, je l'escris. D'où il advient qu'à cette heure, estant quasi passé par toute sorte d'exemples, si quelque estonnement me menace, feuilletant ces petits brevets descousus commes des feuilles Sybillines, je ne faux plus de trouver où me consoler de quelque prognostique favorable en mon experience passée. (III.13.1092)

> For lack of natural memory I make one of paper, and as some new symptom occurs in my disease, I write it down. Whence it comes that at the present moment, when I have passed through virtually every sort of experience, if some grave stroke threatens me, by glancing through these little notes, disconnected like the Sibyl's leaves, I never fail to find grounds for comfort in some favourable prognostic from my past experience. (837–8)

There is evidence that Montaigne did indeed keep a 'registre' of bodily disorders, one that allowed him always to predict a turn for the better, in his 'journal de voyage', and it can be assumed that this habit continued after his return from Italy in 1581.⁶² Keeping such a 'registre', a sort

---

⁶¹ See, for example, Ortensio Lando's *Paradossi* (Lyon: Gioanni Pullon da Trino, 1543), translated into French by Charles Estienne as *Paradoxes, ce sont propos contre la commune opinion* (Paris: Charles Estienne, 1553), arguing 'Qu'il vault mieux estre maladif, que tousjours sain' [It is better to be sick than always healthy]; and – in addition to his more famous encomium, the *Praise of Folly*, itself framed as a product of renal trouble – Erasmus' preface to his edition of Chrysostom praising gout and the stone, *Divi Joannis Chrysostomi... per Des. Erasmum Roterod.* (Basel: Froben, 1527).

⁶² On the *Journal* as a 'registre medical', see François Rigolot, 'Introduction', *Journal de Voyage* (Paris: Presses Universitaires de France, 1992), pp. xxiii–xxiv. Montaigne's description of this practice aligns him with an empiricist model of medical practice centred on recording 'historia' or 'consilia'. On the relationship between the *Essais* and medical 'historia', see Dominique Brancher, 'Montaigne face à la medecine: écriture sceptique et modèle medical à la Renaissance', *Nouveau Bulletin de la Société Internationale des Amis de Montaigne*, 2 (2012), 41–64, and Dorothea B. Heitsch, *Writing as Medication*

of medical diary, is in part a diagnostic tool, but it is a therapy too: it makes Montaigne feel better.

We might be tempted to read the 'exemple' in this light, to see it as an account first set down as a private record and later copied out into a public 'contrerolle', analogous to the transcription of his reading notes at the end of 'Des livres' (II.10.418–20/305–6). But if we look again at the 'exemple', it is clear that Montaigne isn't recording his symptoms. There is one moment where he does break off into something like this sort of medical record-keeping, but it is a post-1588 addition that is remarkably unlike the rest of the 'exemple', which deals not with 'symptomes' but with maxims and commonplaces: 'Qu'il soit vray! Voicy depuis, de nouveau, que les plus legers mouvements espreignent le pur sang de mes reins' [Here is proof. Now it has happened again that the slightest movements force pure blood out of my kidneys] (III.13.1095/839–40).

The 'exemple' given in the *Essais* – in contrast to the 'exemples' that might have made up a private medical diary, each detailing a new symptom – nonetheless forms part of another set of 'petits brevets descousues' (a phrase that recalls again the 'pieces décousues' (II.10.413/300) of Seneca and Plutarch). Their function is directed not towards consolation but communication and veridiction. With the allusion to the Sibyl's leaves, Montaigne is drawing on a commonplace image of prophetic truth-telling, characterised, as John O'Brien has noted, by vulnerability. While Erasmus took the image as a symbol of certainty ('Sibyllae folium […] id est rem indubitatem' [a leaf from the Sibyl's book, meaning an undoubted fact]), more common is the association, as in Rabelais' account of the Sibylle de Panzoust in the *Tiers Livre*, with doubtful signs that are scattered by the wind and freely interpreted in any way that pleases.[63]

In giving his 'exemple' as the Sibyl offers her leaves, Montaigne exposes himself to scrutiny and interpretation, taking the parrhesiastic risk of speaking openly and sincerely. He makes public his private habits of thought, exposing himself in this most foolish of guises and, at the same time, invites his reader to recognise him in his doubtful, obscure, self-contradictory writing. Under the sign of the Sibyl – whose patronage

---

in *Early Modern France: Literary Consciousness and Medical Culture* (Heidelberg: Universitätsverlag Winter, 2017), pp. 196–200.

[63] John O'Brien, 'Wounded Artifacts: Vulnerability and Montaigne's *Essais*', MLN, 127.4 (2012), 712–31 (pp. 730–1); Erasmus, *Adagia*, I.vii.91, in *Opera omnia Desiderii Erasmi Roterodami*, II-2 (1998), p. 220; *Adages I vi 1 to I x 100*, trans. R. A. B. Mynors, in *Collected Works of Erasmus*, vol. 32 (1982), p. 122; Rabelais, *Tiers livre*, chapters 16–18. On the image of the sibylline leaves as a commonplace denoting *ordo neglectus*, see Eric MacPhail, *Dancing Around the Well: The Circulation of Commonplaces in Renaissance Humanism* (Leiden: Brill, 2014), pp. 75–91.

seems to be declared both 'à feinte' and 'à droit' – Montaigne declares his *membra disjecta* to be a work of truth-telling, albeit one that appears to contradict the basic tenets of good faith.

Montaigne's 'exemple', then, is a 'registre' not of his health nor of his self but of his everyday habits, of his custom of talking to himself. It is an account of how he goes through the rhetorical motions. He is not looking to convince himself by recording these commonplaces culled from a rhetoric of consolation, nor is he looking simply to divert himself.[64] Rather, he is producing an authentic account of how he tells himself things that he knows to be 'apparences'. What makes this significant is that it entails Montaigne writing paradoxically, against the grain of what is considered normal, and it is a paradoxical approach that involves taking a risk – the risk that, in showing us publicly how he talks to himself privately, he will be seen as a fool. 'Bren du fat' [Confounded fool!] (I.38.235/173); 'tu és homme de conscience' [You are a man of conscience] (III.13.1091/836): his assessment of himself might change, but both of these moments are shaped by the conventions of not being seen to talk to oneself in public – not being seen to do something that everyone does and yet no one is willing to admit to.

Montaigne's 'exemple' is not a private interrogation but a half-joking, ridiculous demonstration of who he really is. It begins and ends with Montaigne directly addressing us, his readers, bookending the Senecan interplay of second- and third-person ventriloquism. Having summarised, for our benefit, 'tels argumens, et forts et foibles', the passage immediately following his prosopopoeia is loaded with rhetorical questions and imperatives: 'Or sens je quelque chose qui crosle? Ne vous attendez pas que j'aille m'amusant à recognoistre mon pous' [Do I feel something crumbling? Do not expect me to go and amuse myself testing my pulse], 'Voulez vous sçavoir combien je gaigne à cela? Regardez ceux qui font autrement' [Do you want to know how much I gain by this? Look at those who do otherwise] (III.13.1095/839–40). Montaigne is not talking to himself, he is talking to us, telling us honestly, authentically, truthfully how he does this foolish thing – how he endlessly repeats the rhetorical clichés of Seneca and Cicero.[65] Both in his account of how his 'esprit' customarily addresses him and in his presentation of that

---

[64] As in 'De la diversion', where Montaigne recounts how he teaches others a consolation strategy of 'faking it until you make it'. See Katherine Ibbett, 'Faking It: Affect and Gender in the *Essais*', *Montaigne Studies*, 30 (2018), 69–81.

[65] In this regard, the 'exemple' accords with what Olivier Guerrier has interpreted as an especially social mode of self-care in Montaigne. See Olivier Guerrier, '"Alter remus aquas, alter mihi radat arenas": composition des liens et "souci de soi" chez Montaigne', *Astérion*, 22 (2020), https://doi.org/10.4000/asterion.4756.

account to us, Montaigne is preoccupied constantly with social reputation and perception: not with intimate self-knowledge but with making himself known. It is in this light that we might return to the end of epistle 120, the letter Montaigne drew on so heavily in 'De l'inconstance de nos actions' to articulate a diagnosis (without caring much for the cure) of personal inconstancy. 'Mutamus subinde personam et contrariam ei sumimus, quam exuimus', wrote Seneca. 'Effice ut possis laudari, si minus, ut adgnosci' [We continually change our characters and play a part contrary to that which we have discarded … See to it that men be able to praise you; if not, let them at least identify you] (*Ep.* 120.22). *Ut adgnosci*: present yourself, comport yourself, live your life such that you might be recognised and known. This is Montaigne's aspiration not only in his 'exemple' but in his *Essais*: writing doubtfully, foolishly, paradoxically, he makes himself known to himself and, at the same time, to us.

The 'exemple' is an illustration of a new, paradoxical mode of truth-telling: paradoxical in its praise of illness and in its attempt at *consolatio ad se*; 'paradoxe' also in its hesitation between 'à feinte' and 'à droit' and in its practice of Apollonian self-knowledge. But its central paradox lies in its presentation of Montaigne as double, flattering and inconstant and, at the same time, an authentic, open and sincere truth-teller. This famous passage is innovative, but it is not a deep dive into the murky recesses of the soul, nor does it show Montaigne stepping outside himself to offer an account 'en gros'. Instead, Montaigne takes a risk, making himself vulnerable, and broaches a strange, outlandish form of authenticity that might offer a way forward in a rotten age. Here, his 'livre de bonne foy' is truthful in as much as it writes up the form as well as the content of his rhetorical, rote and insincere patterns on thought. His *parrhesia* looks decidedly unlike a genuine practice of 'speaking from the heart': his words are all borrowed from elsewhere and he doesn't really believe them. And yet it is precisely with Seneca, from whom he took not only the well wishes and motivational messages but the parrhesiastic tradition he is reshaping, that Montaigne developed a 'discours paradoxe' able to respond fully and truthfully to the 'commandement paradoxe'.

Conclusion: Communicating Doubt

Writing nearly fifty years ago, Terence Cave saw in Montaigne's invocation of the Danaïdes an image illustrating the 'problems of writing': 'remplissant et versant sans cesse', the essayist's 'gesture of transference' is no more than an 'empty mime', a disquieting 'counter-example of cornucopian productivity'.[1] The 'papier' to which fragments of 'alien discourse' are attached is 'a place of difference', Cave argued, permitting 'the search for the identity of a *moi*' while ensuring that the search remains incomplete, 'since the self is expressly an entity dissociated from the activity of writing'.[2]

This book has argued that Montaigne thinks with 'ce papier' and, crucially, with Seneca, Plutarch and the 'forme d'escrire' that they facilitate, not as part of an infernal labour of textual and discursive production, but to reveal himself fully and authentically, communicating and recognising his character (*ethos*), his soul, his doubtful, double pattern of thinking. In making this case, I am indebted to Cave's more recent studies of the relationship between literature and cognition. Montaigne's form is, as Cave says of literature more broadly, 'an *instrument* of thought'; his literary and compositional techniques 'perform thought' and do not merely 'exemplify it': 'If you removed those features, the thought would be different.'[3]

Seen in this light, the image of the Danaïdes illustrates not the problems of writing but its affordances. Montaigne draws from Seneca and Plutarch endlessly, but this is not the tired metaphor of a Renaissance return *ad fontes*. His 'commerce' renders this source a 'fontana viva', a living fountain such as he saw on his travels in Italy, and, as he put it in 'De l'art de conférer', 'il faut vivre entre les vivants, et laisser courre

---

[1] Cave, *The Cornucopian Text*, pp. 271–2. See also pp. 278–9.
[2] Ibid., p. 272.
[3] Cave, *Thinking with Literature*, p. 150 (original emphasis).

la riviere sous le pont sans nostre soing, ou, à tout le moins, sans nostre alteration' [we must live among the living, and let the river flow under the bridge, without caring, or, at the very least, without being upset by it] (III.8.929/709).[4] Seneca and Plutarch, those authors Montaigne knew as if they were alive and whose souls he could see moving in their writing, served him as he devised a tool ('util') directed at *conférence* and communication. 'Ma forme essentielle', he writes, 'est propre à la communication et à la production: je suis tout au dehors et en evidence, nay à la societé et à l'amitié [My essential pattern is suited to communication and putting things forth: I am all in the open and in full view, born for company and friendship] (III.3.823/625). The 'forme' of Montaigne's character finds expression in a 'forme d'escrire' that takes shape in his leaky 'commerce' with two dead but vital authors. And it is the leakiness that makes all the difference: his transformative remoulding of those patchwork 'livres solides' produces a form that relies on gaps and seams to respond sympathetically to his liquid, mercurial 'esprit genereux', holding on to it without squeezing too hard. 'Laiss[e] courre la riviere', let it flow: neither the form of the *Essais* nor his 'commerce' with Seneca and Plutarch work to plug the leaks; they work with them.

The form of writing that emerges from Montaigne's 'commerce' with Seneca and Plutarch performs a doubtful way of thinking, which is to say that it both facilitates or conducts doubtful thinking and makes it apparent, rendering Montaigne and his 'subject informe' recognisable on the page. In examining this exchange between one early modern author and his ancient interlocutors, it has not been my aim to trace an intellectual – philosophical or literary – inheritance. Montaigne reworks and subverts several of these authors' defining characteristics and basic assumptions, often by setting one in combination with the other. The *Essais* reveal Montaigne working with Seneca and Plutarch, relying on them not as a model to follow, nor – in spite of the Danaïdes image – as merely a source to be plundered, but as interlocutors to be placed in dialogue: as figures to be seen in fluid and unfixed relation both to each other and to Montaigne himself.

My focus on this relationship with Seneca and Plutarch uncovers one early modern author thinking with his books. But I do not mean

---

[4] *Journal de voyage: partie en italien*, ed. Elisabeth Schneikert and Lucien Vendrame (Paris: Garnier, 2012), p. 200. Describing the garden at Bagnaia (now known as Villa Lante), Montaigne notes that it 'ha l'acqua di fontana viva'. As Vittoria Fallanca has shown, this is an 'evocative phrase, as Montaigne shifts the descriptor "viva", intended for "acqua" [i.e. spring water], to juxtapose it with "fontana" – the order of his words means that it is the fountain as much as the water that is alive'; Fallanca, *The Design of Montaigne's Essais*, pp. 153–8 (p. 153).

to suggest that Seneca and Plutarch are merely illustrative of a broader category of interlocutors in the *Essais*, members of the 'tiers genre', and that one could swap Seneca and Plutarch for another figure – Socrates, say – or another pair of authors – Pliny and Cicero – or set up one or the other with a different partner – Plutarch and Tacitus, maybe, or Seneca and Epicurus – and still find in the *Essais* this doubtful and unresolved mode of writing. Montaigne does, of course, think with all of those figures, and studying their presence in the *Essais* illuminates a whole range of his diverse 'visages', but he repeatedly singles out Seneca and Plutarch for a reason.[5] These authors have been the focus of this study because of the essential role they play in the formation of Montaigne's doubtful writing.

Montaigne's reputation as a French Seneca or a second Plutarch is almost as old as the *Essais* themselves. They stand as 'patrons' for a book that claims not to have any. This study has insisted that they are taken together, as a pair, as one of the foundational doubles in Montaigne's double way of thinking. His affinity with these authors rests on their combination, on their reciprocal, interlocking resemblance: it is in this pair that he recognises a moving, unresolved and authentic mode of saying what one means and meaning what one says. In Seneca and Plutarch together, in the spaces between them and their 'pieces décousues', Montaigne found a framework around which to build his own doubtful way of writing.

Recognising the curious, counterintuitive association of doubtful writing and this pair of dogmatists has allowed me to take a sidelong glance, 'une veue oblique', at one of the most familiar aspects of Montaigne's literary-philosophical project. The 'forme d'escrire douteuse et irresolue' that he identified in Seneca and Plutarch resituates doubt not only in a network of different authorial and philosophical relations (dogmatic rather than Pyrrhonian or Academic), but in its relation to writing. His dealings with Seneca and Plutarch recast doubt such that it becomes naturally associated with communication and especially with literary expression. The Sceptics deploy their *facultas* of opposition in a rhetorical strategy directed towards refutation and *retentio* (whether of 'assent' or of 'assertion') as a step towards suspension and ultimately tranquillity. Their self-purging 'refreins' constitute

---

[5] Nikola Regent, for instance, has read Montaigne's preference for Plutarch against the backdrop of sixteenth-century Tacitean hegemony. See Nikola Regent, 'Montaigne and the Lessons of Ancient History', *Global Intellectual History*, 1.2 (2016), 151–71. Numerous studies already cited have considered the influence of Socrates on the *Essais*. On the parallel pairs of letter writers – Cicero and Pliny, Seneca and Epicurus – see my article, 'Un traict à la comparaison de ces couples'.

a 'dernier tour d'escrime' [fencer's last trick] (II.12.558/418), working not to communicate judgement but to undo it, all the while parrying the hand that looks to seize them by the throat and catch them in the act of saying something positive, forcing them to confess that they know and are certain of one thing at least: that they doubt.[6] The Sceptics are, famously, in want of a 'nouveau langage' but, for all their arguments and disputations, and in spite of Pyrrho's carefree, even careless chatter, their doubtful thinking is one that holds communication in suspicion.[7]

With Seneca and Plutarch, by contrast, doubtful thinking becomes aligned not only with writing and communication but specifically with truthfulness. Communicating doubt is understood to be a necessary component of holding on to one another 'par la parole' (I.9.36/23). Adhering to the 'commandement paradoxe', Montaigne recognises doubt and doubleness to be the condition of human thinking rather than a *facultas* or *dunamis* to be trained and deployed. As a consequence of that recognition, writing and communication – 'commerce' or exchange – are directed not towards *ataraxia* but towards recognising oneself and making oneself recognisable. Seen in the light of Seneca and Plutarch, doubt is understood not as a Sceptical method but as a style, a 'façon' or 'forme' shared and reflected harmoniously by Montaigne's character and his book. He employs this 'façon' as a tool for both thinking and communicating, but it is a tool working to ends quite unlike those to which the Sceptics deployed their *facultas*.

Doubtful writing is therefore not a direct application of Senecan and Plutarchan style to a Sceptical method or objective. It is not a literary expression of a Sceptical philosophy. It is rather a particular mode of doubtful thinking, one that stands alongside Montaigne's engagement with Scepticism, interacting with it without being reduced to or co-opted by it.

Paying attention to Montaigne's strange association of doubt with these authors casts new light on the familiar 'visage' of this Renaissance doubter. But it has not been my aim only to reassess the portrait painted in twentieth-century accounts of a sixteenth-century encounter with Pyrrhonism.[8] Reframing doubt in its Senecan and Plutarchan relation

---

[6] On having the Pyrrhonian by the throat when they say, affirmatively, 'Je doubte', see II.12.527/392, discussed in Chapter 1.

[7] On Pyrrho as a chatterer, see Chapter 1.

[8] We might sketch the shifting approaches to this central preoccupation by pointing to landmark studies of Montaigne and early modern Scepticism, from Villey's evolutionary thesis positing a Sceptical crisis (*Les Sources et l'évolution des Essais*, published in 1908), through Popkin's history of Scepticism as bound up with religious polemic and apologetics (*History of Skepticism*, 1960), to Cave's archipelagic study of Pyrrhonism's shockwaves and their trace in 'perturbations textuelles' (*Pré-histoires*, 1999).

complicates aspects of the *Essais* that have come to the fore over the course of the last two decades of Montaigne studies. I have argued that Montaigne's famous consubstantiality with his book hinges on a conception of authorial association marked by insecurity, temporariness and impermanence, qualities that draw on the *hic et nunc* of writing and judgement to render the book a tool that reveals thinking. Montaigne engages with this tool as a 'registre des essais de ma vie' (III.13.1078/826): a 'registre' that works not to accumulate and stockpile his 'cogitations', nor to paint a portrait 'en gros' as one finds in the lives of illustrious men, but to translate and extend the soul. Seneca and Plutarch shape the *Essais* not as ancient exemplars of moral writing, nor as prototypes for a patchwork, informal genre, but by structuring Montaigne's conception of the relationship between author, cognition and writing. Here too we ought to be alert to the difference at the heart of resemblance: Montaigne's practice of thinking in writing, making his book an extension of himself such that it communicates his soul, resonates with recent cognitive approaches to the relationship between literature and cognition without directly anticipating them. His particular way of conceiving this relationship, rooted in the literary and legal metaphors with which he was familiar, has therefore been the focus of this study.

Montaigne's is a model of authorship that overturns traditional models of *parrhesia*, that 'simple façon' of telling it how it is.[9] Truth-telling in the *Essais* is, as numerous recent studies have demonstrated, conceived as 'simple', 'naïf', 'ouvert', but Montaigne's complex exchange with Seneca and Plutarch, both key figures in the early modern reception of *parrhesia*, establishes a paradoxical reconciliation of simplicity and doubleness such that authenticity and sincerity are marked by contradiction, inconstancy and partialness. It is doubtful writing as developed with Seneca and Plutarch that provides the 'discours paradoxe' responding to the 'commandement paradoxe'.

Authoring, truth-telling, the 'usage' of opinions and of textual 'pieces décousues' are key concepts that are reshaped by the form of Montaigne's doubt. His literary and communicative practices give form to thought in a way that is necessarily doubtful. To return to Terence Cave's comment on literary thinking – a comment not specific to Montaigne but about all literary artefacts – 'If you removed those features, the thought would be different.'[10] Pierre Charron's *De la sagesse* (1601) proves the point.

---

[9] Montaigne uses the collocation 'simple façon' in his parallel celebration of Seneca and Plutarch, II.10.413/300.
[10] Cave, *Thinking with Literature*, p. 150.

Reworking Montaigne's key ideas, sorting them out and putting them in order, Charron produced a systematic account of humankind, virtue and wisdom, proceeding logically through clearly demarcated chapters where the titles accurately reflect the contents.[11] It presents a view 'en gros' of humankind's ignorance but reveals nothing of its author's *ethos*. The difference between the *Essais* as a mode of doubtful writing and Charron's systematised imitation is immediately apparent and helps to illustrate the relationship between Montaigne's form and his thought. But a counterfactual makes the case more strongly still: to imagine a dogmatic, resolved way of thinking written in the style of the *Essais* is to imagine a book that is in fact not dogmatic or resolved at all. It is to imagine a book of the 'tiers genre', not professing Scepticism but nonetheless writing in a way that is 'douteuse en substance' and with a 'dessein plus enquerant qu'instruisant' (II.12.509/377). Montaigne thinks doubtfully by writing doubtfully: hence his claim to have no more made his book than his book had made him (II.18.665/504).

Doubt in the *Essais* is as much about ethics and communication, society and style, as it is about epistemology. The essential benefit of doubtful writing is that it is a mode of thinking that communicates the soul, allowing us to hold on to ourselves, in response to the 'commandement paradoxe' ('tenez vous à vous', III.9.1001/766), and to hold on to each other: 'nous ne sommes hommes, et ne nous tenons les uns aux autres que par la parole' [We are men, and hold together, only by our word] (I.9.36/23).

Seneca and Plutarch are Montaigne's essential companions in his 'commerce', in his exchange with himself, with ancient interlocutors and with his readers. They are the figures he cannot be without: he notes how he cannot tear himself away from Plutarch ('Mais je me puis plus malaiséement deffaire de Plutarque' [But it is harder for me to do without Plutarch], III.5.875/666); how he is led by 'inclination' towards 'imitation du parler de Seneque' (even if he 'estim[e] davantage celuy de Plutarque' [esteems Plutarch's more]) (II.17.638/484). Countless interlocutors, ancient and modern, shaped Montaigne's thinking about doubt, uncertainty, truth, authenticity, sincerity and so on. But it was in

---

[11] Floyd Gray characterised Charron as 'Montaigne', but 'Montaigne with order, with didactic purpose'. See Floyd Gray, 'Reflexions on Charron's Debt to Montaigne', *French Review*, 35 (1962), 377–82 (p. 382). For a more positive view of Charron as an influential figure for seventeenth-century *libertins érudits* (and a writer working in a style more amenable to early seventeenth-century values), see José R. Maia Neto, *Academic Skepticism in Seventeenth-Century French Philosophy: The Charronian Legacy 1601–1662* (Cham: Springer, 2014), esp. pp. 2–3 and 34–40 on the rewriting of the *Essais* 'in a systematic form'.

his 'longue conversation', his endless, leaky exchange with this doubtful pair, that he developed a 'forme d'escrire' that communicates doubtful thinking, a way of writing that makes the movements of the soul recognisable – to author and reader – on the page. 'J'en attache quelque chose à ce papier': thinking in and with writing, Montaigne attached some of his dealings with Seneca and Plutarch to his paper and, in the process, revealed himself fully, authentically and sincerely. His book is 'un livre de bonne foy' written – like those of Seneca and Plutarch – in a 'forme d'escrire douteuse et irresolue'.

Bibliography

Ancient and Early Modern Sources

Aristotle, *L'Organe, c'est à dire l'instrument du discours*, trans. Philippe Canaye ([Geneva]: Jean de Tournes, 1589).
Aristotle, *Metaphysics*, trans. Hugh Tredennick and G. Cyril Armstrong, 2 vols (Cambridge, MA: Harvard University Press, 1933–35).
Aristotle, *Metaphysica, lib. I-XIV. Recensio et Translatio Guillelmi de Moerbeka* (Leiden: Brill, 1995).
Augustine, *Operum D. Aurelii Augustini Hipponensis episcopi*, 11 vols (Antwerp: Plantin, 1576).
Cicero [i.e. Pseudo-Cicero], *Consolatio* (Venice: Girolamo Polo, 1583).
Cicero [i.e. Pseudo-Cicero], *M. Tullii Ciceronis Consolatio ... De quo judicium Justi Lipsii subjunctum* (Leiden: Plantin, 1584).
Cicero, *On Ends*, trans. H. Rackham (Cambridge, MA: Harvard University Press, 1914).
Cicero, *On Old Age. On Friendship. On Divination*, trans. W. A. Falconer (Cambridge, MA: Harvard University Press, 1923).
Cicero, *On the Nature of the Gods. Academics*, trans. H. Rackham (Cambridge, MA: Harvard University Press, 1933).
Cicero, *On the Orator*, trans. H. Rackham and E. W. Sutton, 2 vols (Cambridge, MA: Harvard University Press, 1942).
Cotgrave, Randle, *A Dictionarie of the French and English Tongues* (London: Adam Islip, 1611).
De la Primaudaye, Pierre, *Suite de l'academie française* (Paris: Chaudière, 1580).
De Marconville, Jean, *Traicté de la bonne & mauvaise langue* (Paris: Jean Dalier, 1573).
De Saint-Julien de Bailleure, Pierre, *Meslanges Historiques et recueils de diverses matieres pour la pluspart Paradoxalles, & neantmoins vrayes* (Lyon: Benoist Rigaud, 1589).
Du Val, Antoine, *Les Contrarietez et contredits qui se trouvent en la doctrine de Jean Calvin, Luter, et autres nouveaux Evangelistes de nostre temps* (Paris: Chesneau, 1567).
Erasmus, Desiderius, *Lingua* (Antwerp: Michael Hillenius, 1525).
Erasmus, Desiderius, *Divi Joannis Chrysostomi ... per Des. Erasmum Roterod.* (Basel: Froben, 1527).

Erasmus, Desiderius, *Opera omnia Desiderii Erasmi Roterodami* (Amsterdam: Elsevier, 1969–).
Erasmus, Desiderius, *Collected Works of Erasmus*, ed. R. A. B. Mynors (Toronto: Toronto University Press, 1974–).
Estienne, Charles, *La Dissection des parties du corps humain* (Paris: Simon de Colines, 1546).
Estienne, Robert, *Dictionarium latinogallicum* (Paris: Charles Estienne, 1552).
Fouquelin, Antoine, *La Rhétorique françoise* (Paris: Wechel, 1555).
Furetière, Antoine, *Dictionnaire universel* (La Haye and Rotterdam: Arnoud et Reinier Leers, 1690).
Garasse, François, *Les Recherches des recherches* (Paris: Chappelet, 1622).
Horace, *Satires. Epistles. The Art of Poetry*, trans. H. Rushton Fairclough (Cambridge, MA: Harvard University Press, 1926).
La Boétie, Etienne (trans.), *La Mesnagerie de Xenophon. Les Regles de mariage de Plutarque. Lettre de consolation, de Plutarque à sa femme… Item, un Discours sur la mort dudit Seigneur De la Boëtie, par M. de Montaigne* (Paris: Morel, 1571).
La Croix du Maine, François Grudé de, *Le premier volume de la bibliothèque du sieur de la Croix du Maine* (Paris: Angelier, 1584)
Lando, Ortensio, *Paradossi cioè sentenze fuori del comun parere* (Lyon: Gioanni Pullon da Trino, 1543).
Lando, Ortensio, *Paradoxes, ce sont propos contre la commune opinion*, trans. Charles Estienne (Paris: Charles Estienne, 1553).
Lipsius, Justus, *Justii Lipsii Epistolarum selectarum centuria prima* (Antwerp: Plantin, 1586).
Lipsius, Justus, *Politicorum sive civilis doctrinae libri sex* (Antwerp: Plantin, 1604).
Lucretius, *Titi Lucretii Cari De rerum natura libri sex* (Paris: Rovillius, 1563).
Lucretius, *On the Nature of Things*, trans. W. H. D. Rouse (Cambridge, MA: Harvard University Press, 1924).
Malebranche, Nicolas, *Recherche de la vérité* (1674), in *Œuvres*, ed. Geneviève Rodis-Lewis and Germain Malbreil (Paris: Gallimard, 1979).
Montaigne, Michel de, *Essais de Michel de Montaigne* (Bordeaux: Millanges, 1580).
Montaigne, Michel de, *Les Essais* (Lyon [Geneva]: François le Febvre, 1595).
Montaigne, Michel de, *The Essayes, or Morall, Politike, and Millitarie Discourses*, trans. John Florio (London: Edward Blount, 1603).
Montaigne, Michel de, *Saggi di Michel sig. di Montagna, overa Discorsi naturali, politici, e morali*, trans. Girolamo Canini (Venice: Marco Ginammi, 1633).
Montaigne, Michel de, *L'Esprit des Essais de Michel, Seigneur de Montaigne* (Paris: Charles de Sercy, 1679).
Montaigne, Michel de, *The Complete Works of Montaigne: Essays, Travel Journal, Letters*, trans. Donald M. Frame (Stanford, CA: Stanford University Press, 1957).
Montaigne, Michel de, *The Complete Essays of Montaigne*, trans. Donald M. Frame (Stanford, CA: Stanford University Press, 1958).
Montaigne, Michel de, *Journal de Voyage*, ed. Fausta Garavini (Paris: Gallimard, 1983).

Montaigne, Michel de, *Journal de Voyage de Michel de Montaigne*, ed. François Rigolot (Paris: Presses universitaires de France, 1992).

Montaigne, Michel de, *Essais*, ed. André Tournon (Paris: Imprimerie Nationale, 1998).

Montaigne, Michel de, *Reproduction en quadrichromie de l'Exemplaire de Bordeaux des Essais de Montaigne*, ed. Philippe Desan (Fasano/Chicago: Schena Editore/Montaigne Studies, 2002).

Montaigne, Michel de, *The Complete Essays*, trans. M. A. Screech (London: Penguin, 2003).

Montaigne, Michel de, *Les Essais*, édition Villey-Saulnier (Paris: Presses Universitaires de France, 2004).

Montaigne, Michel de, *Essais*, ed. Emmanuel Naya, Delphine Reguig-Naya and Alexandre Tarrête, 3 vols (Paris: Gallimard, 2009).

Montaigne, Michel de, *Journal de voyage: partie en italien*, ed. Elisabeth Schneikert and Lucien Vendrame (Paris: Garnier, 2012).

Montaigne, Michel de, *Les Essais de Montaigne d'après l'exemplaire de Bordeaux. Villey edition of the Essais with Corresponding Digital Page images from the Bordeaux Copy*, The Montaigne Project, online resource, https://www.lib.uchicago.edu/efts/ARTFL/projects/montaigne/index.html.

Petrarch, *Le familiari*, ed. Vittorio Rossi and Umberto Bosco, 4 vols (Florence: G. C. Sansoni, 1968).

Plutarch, *Vies des hommes illustres*, trans. Jacques Amyot (Paris: Vascosan, 1565).

Plutarch, *Les Œuvres morales et meslées de Plutarque*, trans. Jacques Amyot (Paris: Vascosan, 1572).

Plutarch, *Lives*, trans. Bernadotte Perrin, 11 vols (Cambridge, MA: Harvard University Press, 1914–26).

Plutarch, *Moralia*, trans. Frank Cole Babbitt et al., 15 vols (Cambridge MA, Harvard University Press, 1927–69).

Quintilian, *The Orator's Education*, trans. Donald A. Russell, 5 vols (Cambridge, MA: Harvard University Press, 2002).

Quintus Curtius, *Historia Alexandri Magni* (Basel: Froben, 1545).

Rabelais, François, *Œuvres complètes*, ed. Mireille Huchon (Paris: Gallimard, 1994).

Rabelais, François, *Gargantua and Pantagruel*, trans. M. A. Screech (London: Penguin, 2006).

Ronsard, *Œuvres complètes*, ed. Jean Céard, Daniel Menager and Michel Simonin, 2 vols (Paris: Gallimard, 1993–94).

Seneca, *L. Annaei Senecae Philosophi Stoicorum omnium acutissimi opera quae extant omnia*, ed. Celio Secondo Curione (Basel: [Hervagius], 1557).

Seneca, *Epistres de L. Annæe Seneque, philosophe tres-excellent*, trans. Geoffroy de La Chassaigne, Seigneur de Pressac (Paris: Chaudière, 1582).

Seneca, *Entière traduction des Epistres de Sénèque*, trans. Geoffroy de La Chassaigne, Seigneur de Pressac (Lyon: Ancelin, 1598).

Seneca, *L. Annaei Senecae philosophi opera*, ed. Justus Lipsius (Antwerp: Plantin, 1605).

Seneca, *Œuvres morales et meslées de Seneque*, ed. and trans. Simon Goulart (Geneva: J. Arnaud, 1606).

Seneca, *Epistles*, trans. Richard M. Gummere, 3 vols (Cambridge, MA: Harvard University Press, 1917–25).

Seneca, *Moral Essays*, trans. John W. Basore, 3 vols (Cambridge, MA: Harvard University Press, 1928–35).
Sextus Empiricus, *Sexti Philosophi Pyrrhoniarum hypotyposeon libri III*, ed. and trans. Henri Estienne ([Paris]: Henri Estienne, 1562).
Sextus Empiricus, *Outlines of Pyrrhonism*, trans. R. G. Bury (Cambridge, MA: Harvard University Press, 1933).
Tacitus, *Annals*, trans. Clifford H. Moore and John Jackson, 3 vols (Cambridge, MA: Harvard University Press, 1931).
Virgil, *Aeneid*, trans. H. Rushton Fairclough, 2 vols (Cambridge, MA: Harvard University Press, 1999–2001).

Modern Sources

Almquist, Katherine, 'Du prêt et de l'usufruit des images: le droit de la propriété dans la pensée sceptique de Montaigne', in *L'Écriture du scepticisme chez Montaigne*, ed. Marie-Luce Demonet and Alain Legros (Geneva: Droz, 2004), pp. 169–77.
Anderson, Miranda, *The Renaissance Extended Mind* (Basingstoke: Palgrave, 2015).
Azar Filho, Celso M., 'Sur les rapports entre l'ignorance, la science, la philosophie et le scepticisme chez Montaigne', in *Global Montaigne: Mélanges en l'honneur de Philippe Desan*, ed. Jean Balsamo and Amy Graves (Paris: Garnier, 2021), pp. 303–13.
Balsamo, Jean, *La Parole de Montaigne: littérature et humanisme civil dans les Essais* (Turin: Rosenberg & Sellier, 2019).
Balsamo, Jean, 'Skeletos', in *Dictionnaire de Michel de Montaigne*, ed. Philippe Desan (Paris: Garnier, 2018), pp. 1742–3.
Baltussen, Han, 'Cicero's *Consolatio ad se*: Character, Purpose, and Impact of a Curious Treatise', in *Roman and Greek Consolations: Eight Studies of a Tradition and its Afterlife*, ed. Han Baltussen (Swansea: Classical Press of Wales, 2013), pp. 67–91.
Baltussen, Han, 'A Curious Sidelight on the Reception of Ps. Cicero's *Consolatio* (1583)', *Bibliothèque d'Humanisme et Renaissance*, 80.3 (2018), 481–506.
Baltussen, Han, 'A Grief Observed: Cicero on Remembering Tullia', *Mortality*, 14.4 (2008), 355–69.
Basset, Bérengère, 'Erreur/vérité, mensonge/sincérité, d'Érasme à Montaigne', *Bulletin de la société internationale des amis de Montaigne*, 63 (2016), 73–92.
Baur, Freya, and Teodoro Patera (eds), *Mollesses renaissantes: défaillances et assouplissement du masculin* (Geneva: Droz, 2021).
Bénatouïl, Thomas, 'Les possessions du sage et le dépouillement du philosophe: un paradox socratique et ses reprises stoïciennes', *Rursus: Poiétique, réception et réécriture des textes antiques*, 3 (2008), https://doi.org/10.4000/rursus.213.
Bjørnstad, Hall, 'The Metaphors of Textual Transfer: From Indigestion to Early Modern Tennis', in *Borrowed Feathers: Plagiarism and the Limits of Imitation in Early Modern Europe*, ed. Hall Bjørnstad (Oslo: Unipub, 2008), pp. 215–28.

Boutcher, Warren, *The School of Montaigne in Early Modern Europe*, 2 vols (Oxford: Oxford University Press, 2017).

Boys-Stones, George, 'Plutarch and the Probable Principle of Cold: Epistemology and the *De Primo Frigido*', *The Classical Quarterly*, 47 (1997), 227–38.

Brahami, Frédéric, *Le Scepticisme de Montaigne* (Paris: Presses Universitaires de France, 1997).

Brancher, Dominique, 'Montaigne face à la medecine: écriture sceptique et modèle medical à la Renaissance', *Nouveau Bulletin de la Société Internationale des Amis de Montaigne*, 2 (2012), 41–64.

Brancher, Dominique, '"Ny plus ny moins que la rubarbe qui pousse hors les mauvaises humeurs": La rhubarbe au purgatoire', in *L'Ecriture du scepticisme chez Montaigne*, ed. Marie-Luce Demonet and Alain Legros (Geneva: Droz, 2004), pp. 303–20.

Burrow, Colin, *Imitating Authors: Plato to Futurity* (Oxford: Oxford University Press, 2019).

Butterworth, Emily, 'Censors and Censure: Robert Estienne and Michel de Montaigne', in *Reading and Censorship in Early Modern Europe*, ed. María José Vega, Julian Weiss and Cesc Esteve (Barcelona: Studia Aurea Monográfica, 2010), pp. 161–79.

Butterworth, Emily, '"Un flux de caquet": Excès et éthique de la parole à la Renaissance (le cas de Montaigne, "Sur des vers de Virgile")', in *Mauvaises Langues!*, ed. Florence Cabaret and Nathalie Vienne-Guerrin (Mont-Saint-Aignan: Presses des universités de Rouen et du Havre, 2013), pp. 327–40.

Butterworth, Emily, *The Unbridled Tongue: Babble and Gossip in Renaissance France* (Oxford: Oxford University Press, 2016).

Calhoun, Alison, *Montaigne and the Lives of the Philosophers: Life Writing and Transversality in the Essais* (Newark: University of Delaware Press, 2015).

Castelnérac, Benoît, 'The Method of "Eclecticism" in Plutarch and Seneca', *Hermathena*, 182 (2007), 135–63.

Cave, Terence, *The Cornucopian Text: Problems of Writing in the French Renaissance* (Oxford: Oxford University Press, 1979).

Cave, Terence, *How to Read Montaigne* (London: Granta, 2007).

Cave, Terence, *Live Artefacts: Literature in a Cognitive Environment* (Oxford: Oxford University Press, 2022).

Cave, Terence, 'Montaigne', *Proceedings of the British Academy*, 131 (2005), 183–203.

Cave, Terence, *Pré-histoires: textes troublés au seuil de la modernité* (Geneva: Droz, 1999).

Cave, Terence, 'Thinking with Commonplaces: The Example of Rabelais', in *Retrospectives: Essays in Literature, Poetics, and Cultural History*, ed. Neil Kenny and Wes Williams (London: Legenda, 2009), pp. 38–47.

Cave, Terence, *Thinking with Literature: Towards a Cognitive Criticism* (Oxford: Oxford University Press, 2016).

Cave, Terence, 'The Transit of Venus: Feeling Your Way Forward', in *Montaigne in Transit*, ed. Neil Kenny, Richard Scholar and Wes Williams (Oxford: Legenda, 2016), pp. 9–18.

Cave, Terence, 'Un demi-tour de cheville: Pour une lecture cognitive des *Essais*', *Bulletin de la société internationale des amis de Montaigne*, 74.1 (2022), pp. 109–27.

Cave, Terence, and Kirsti Sellevold, '"Or, ces exemples me semblent plus à propos": une phrase inuagurale dans les *Essais* de Montaigne', in *Éveils: études en l'honneur de J.-Y. Pouilloux*, ed. Valérie Fasseur, Olivier Guerrier, Laurent Jenny and André Tournon (Paris: Garnier, 2010), pp. 64–75.

Céard, Jean, 'Montaigne Anatomiste', *Cahiers de l'Association internationale des études françaises*, 55 (2003), 299–315.

Ceron, Annalisa, 'How to Advise the Prince: Three Renaissance Forms of Plutarchan *Parrhesia*', *History of Political Thought*, 38.2 (2017), 239–66.

Charalampous, Charis, *Rethinking the Mind–Body Relationship in Early Modern Literature, Philosophy, and Medicine: The Renaissance of the Body* (Abingdon: Routledge, 2016).

Clark, Andy, *Natural-born Cyborgs: Minds, Technologies, and the Future of Human Intelligence* (Oxford: Oxford University Press, 2003).

Clark, Andy, and David Chalmers, 'The Extended Mind', *Analysis*, 58 (1998), 7–19.

Claussen, Emma, 'Montaigne's Vagabond Styles: Political Homelessness in the Sixteenth Century', *Forum for Modern Language Studies*, 57 (2021), 283–90.

Colclough, David, *Freedom of Speech in Early Stuart England* (Cambridge: Cambridge University Press, 2005).

Colie, Rosalie L., *Paradoxia Epidemica: The Renaissance Tradition of Paradox* (Princeton, NJ: Princeton University Press, 1966).

Conche, Marcel, *Montaigne et la philosophie* (Paris: Presses Universitaires de France, 1996).

Couton, M., I. Fernandez, C. Jérémie and M. Vénuat (eds), *Emprunt, plagiat, réécriture aux XVe, XVIe, XVIIe siècles* (Clermont-Ferrand: Presses Universitaires Blaise Pascal, 2006).

Couzinet, Marie-Claire, 'Les *Essais* de Montaigne et les miscellanées', in *Ouvrages miscellanées et théories de la connaissance à la Renaissance*, ed. Dominique de Courcelles (Paris: Ecole de chartes, 2003), pp. 153–69.

De Zangroniz, Joseph, *Montaigne, Amyot, Saliat: étude sur les sources des Essais de Montaigne* (Paris: Champion, 1906).

Defaux, Gérard, *Marot, Rabelais, Montaigne: L'Écriture comme présence* (Paris: Champion-Slatkine, 1987).

Delègue, Yves, 'L'Imitation de la vérité', in *Éveils: études en l'honneur de J.-Y. Pouilloux*, ed. Valérie Fasseur, Olivier Guerrier, Laurent Jenny and André Tournon (Paris: Garnier, 2010), pp. 29–43.

Delègue, Yves, *Montaigne et la mauvaise foi* (Paris: Garnier, 1998).

Demonet, Marie-Luce, 'Jeton', in *Dictionnaire de Montaigne*, ed. Philippe Desan (Paris: Garnier, 2018), pp. 988–92.

Demonet, Marie-Luce, 'Le Skeletos de Montaigne ou la leçon de l'anatomie', in *Théâtres de l'anatomie et corps en spectacle*, ed. I. Zinguer and L. Van Delft (Berne: Peter Lang, 2006), pp. 63–88.

Desan, Philippe, *Dix études sur Montaigne* (Paris: Garnier, 2020).

Desan, Philippe, *Les Formes du monde et de l'esprit* (Paris: Presses universitaires de Paris-Sorbonne, 2008).

Desan, Philippe, *Montaigne: Penser le social* (Paris: Odile Jacob, 2018).

Desan, Philippe (ed.), *Dictionnaire de Michel de Montaigne* (Paris: Garnier, 2018).

Desan, Philippe, Déborah Knop and Blandine Perona (eds), *Montaigne: une rhétorique naturalisée?* (Paris: Champion, 2019).
Dionne, Valerie M., *Montaigne: écrivain de la conciliation* (Paris: Garnier, 2014).
Eden, Kathy, *Friends Hold All Things in Common: Tradition, Intellectual Property, and the Adages of Erasmus* (New Haven, CT: Yale University Press, 2001).
Eden, Kathy, 'Literary Property and the Question of Style: A Prehistory', in *Borrowed Feathers: Plagiarism and the Limits of Imitation in Early Modern Europe*, ed. Hall Bjørnstad (Oslo: Unipub, 2008), pp. 21–38.
Eden, Kathy, *The Renaissance Rediscovery of Intimacy* (Chicago: University of Chicago Press, 2012).
Edwards, Catherine, 'Self-Scrutiny and Self-Transformation in Seneca's Letters', in *Seneca: Oxford Readings in Classical Studies*, ed. John G. Fitch (Oxford: Oxford University Press, 2008), pp. 84–101.
Esclapez, Raymond, 'Le Dieu Apollon: des "Dialogues pythiques" de Plutarque aux *Essais* de Montaigne', in *La Moralia et Œuvres morales à la Renaissance*, ed. Olivier Guerrier (Paris: Garnier, 2008), pp. 253–74.
Fallanca, Vittoria, 'The Design of Montaigne's *Essais*', unpublished DPhil dissertation, University of Oxford, 2020.
Foucault, Michel, *Le Courage de la vérité* (Paris: Gallimard, 2009).
Foucault, Michel, *The Courage of Truth*, ed. Frédéric Gros, trans. Graham Burchell (Basingstoke: Palgrave Macmillan, 2011).
Foucault, Michel, *Discours et vérité, précéde de La parrêsia* (Paris: Vrin, 2016).
Foucault, Michel, *Fearless Speech*, ed. Joseph Pearson (Los Angeles: Semiotext(e), 2001).
Foucault, Michel, *Le Gouvernement de soi et des autres* (Paris: Gallimard, 2008).
Foucault, Michel, *The Government of Self and Others*, ed. Frédéric Gros, trans. Graham Burchell (Basingstoke: Palgrave Macmillan, 2010).
Foucault, Michel, *L'Herméneutique du sujet. Cours au Collège de France, 1981–1982* (Paris: Gallimard, 2001).
Foucault, Michel, *The Hermeneutics of the Subject*, ed. Frédéric Gros, trans. Graham Burchell (Basingstoke: Palgrave Macmillan, 2005).
Francis, Scott, 'The Discussion as Joust: *Parrhesia* and Friendly Antagonism in Plutarch and Montaigne', *The Comparatist*, 37 (2013), 122–37.
Friedrich, Hugo, *Montaigne*, trans. Robert Rovini (Paris: Gallimard, 1968).
Frigo, Alberto, '"Un sujet bien mal formé": expérience de soi, forme et réformation dans les *Essais* de Montaigne', *Cahiers de philosophie de l'Université de Caen*, 52 (2015), 69–92.
Frisch, Andrea, *Forgetting Differences: Tragedy, Historiography, and the French Wars of Religion* (Edinburgh: Edinburgh University Press, 2017).
Frisch, Andrea, 'Montaigne and the Ethics of Memory', *L'Esprit créateur*, 46.1 (2006), 23–31.
Frisch, Andrea, 'Montaigne on Memory', in *The Oxford Handbook of Montaigne*, ed. Philippe Desan (Oxford: Oxford University Press, 2016), pp. 648–62.
Fumaroli, Marc, *L'Age de l'éloquence* (Geneva: Droz, 1980).
Garrod, Raphaële, 'La Politesse de l'esprit: Cartesian Pedagogy and the Ethics of Scholarly Exchange', in *Descartes and the Ingenium: The Embodied Soul*

in Cartesianism, ed. Raphaële Garrod and Alexander Marr (Leiden: Brill, 2021), pp. 184–203.
Garrod, Raphaële, 'Subtle Democritus: Natural Philosophy, Ethics, and Poetics in Montaigne's "De Democritus et Heraclitus" (I, 50)', *Montaigne Studies*, 34 (2022), 59–72.
Gilby, Emma, *Sublime Worlds: Early Modern French Literature* (Oxford: Legenda, 2006).
Giocanti, Sylvia, *Penser l'irrésolution: Montaigne, Pascal, La Mothe Le Vayer. Trois itinéraires sceptiques* (Paris: Champion, 2001).
Giocanti, Sylvia, *Scepticisme et inquiétude* (Paris: Hermann, 2019).
Giocanti, Sylvia, 'Un scepticisme sans tranquillité?', *Bulletin de la société internationale des amis de Montaigne*, 55 (2012), 63–90.
Giusti, Elena, 'The Metapoetics of Liber-ty: Horace's Bacchic Ship in Seneca's *De tranquillitate animi*', in *Horace and Seneca: Interactions, Intertexts, Interpretations*, ed. Martin Stöckinger, Kathrin Winter and Andreas T. Zanker (Berlin: De Gruyter, 2017), pp. 239–64.
Grafton, Anthony, *Forgers and Critics: Creativity and Duplicity in Western Scholarship* (Princeton, NJ: Princeton University Press, 2019 [1990]).
Graver, Margaret, 'The Weeping Wise: Stoic and Epicurean Consolations in Seneca's 99th Epistle', in *Tears in the Graeco-Roman World*, ed. Thorsten Fögen (Berlin: De Gruyter, 2009), pp. 235–52.
Gray, Floyd, *Montaigne bilingue: le latin des Essais* (Paris: Champion, 1991).
Gray, Floyd, *Montaigne et les livres* (Paris: Garnier, 2013).
Gray, Floyd, 'Reflexions on Charron's Debt to Montaigne', *French Review*, 35 (1962), 377–82.
Green, Felicity, *Montaigne and the Life of Freedom* (Cambridge: Cambridge University Press, 2012).
Guerrier, Olivier, '"Alter remus aquas, alter mihi radat arenas": composition des liens et "souci de soi" chez Montaigne', *Astérion*, 22 (2020), https://doi.org/10.4000/asterion.4756.
Guerrier, Olivier, 'Le Champ du "possible": de la jurisprudence aux *Essais*', in *L'Écriture du scepticisme chez Montaigne*, ed. Marie-Luce Demonet and Alain Legros (Geneva: Droz, 2004), pp. 159–68.
Guerrier, Olivier, 'Dans la plupart des auteurs, je vois l'homme qui écrit; dans Montaigne, l'homme qui pense', *Montaigne Studies*, 27 (2015), 89–98.
Guerrier, Olivier, *Quand les poètes feignent: 'fantasie' et fiction dans les Essais de Montaigne* (Paris: Champion, 2002).
Guerrier, Olivier, *Rencontre et reconnaissance: les Essais ou le jeu du hazard et de la vérité* (Paris: Garnier, 2016).
Hamlin, William M., *Montaigne's English Journey: Reading the Essays in Shakespeare's Day* (Oxford: Oxford University Press, 2013).
Hartle, Ann, *Michel de Montaigne: Accidental Philosopher* (Cambridge: Cambridge University Press, 2003).
Heitsch, Dorothea B., *Writing as Medication in Early Modern France: Literary Consciousness and Medical Culture* (Heidelberg: Universitätsverlag Winter, 2017).
Helgeson, James, *The Lying Mirror: The First-Person Stance and Sixteenth-Century Writing* (Geneva: Droz, 2012).
Hoffmann, George, *Montaigne's Career* (Oxford: Clarendon Press, 1998).

Hoffmann, George, '"Neither one or the other and both together", *Tiers livre*, 35: How Scholastic Logic Can Help Explain the Marriage Question', *Etudes rabelaisiennes*, 25 (Geneva: Droz, 1991), pp. 79–90.

Hoffmann, George, 'Portrayal from Life, or to Life? The Essays's Living Effigy', *French Forum*, 25.2 (2000), 145–63.

Ibbett, Katherine, 'Faking It: Affect and Gender in the *Essais*', *Montaigne Studies*, 30 (2018), 69–81.

Inwood, Brad, 'The Importance of Form in Seneca's Philosophical Letters', in *Ancient Letters: Classical and Late Antique Epistolography*, ed. A. D. Morrison and Ruth Morello (Oxford: Oxford University Press, 2007), pp. 133–48.

Inwood, Brad, 'The Will in Seneca the Younger', *Classical Philology*, 95.1 (2000), 44–60.

Jeanneret, Michel, 'The Vagaries of Exemplarity: Distortion or Dismissal?', *Journal of the History of Ideas*, 59.4 (1998), 565–79.

Junqueira Smith, Plínio, and Sébastien Charles (eds), *Academic Scepticism in the Development of Early Modern Philosophy* (Cham: Springer, 2017).

Kadue, Katie, *Domestic Georgic: Labors of Preservation* (Chicago: University of Chicago Press, 2021).

Kenny, Neil, '"A propos, ou hors de propos, il n'importe": Relevance Theory and Montaigne', in *Lucidity: Essays in Honour of Alison Finch*, ed. Ian James and Emma Wilson (Cambridge: Legenda, 2016), pp. 20–32.

Kenny, Neil, *Born to Write: Literary Families and Social Hierarchy in Early Modern France* (Oxford: Oxford University Press, 2020).

Kenny, Neil, *Death and Tenses: Posthumous Presence in Early Modern France* (Oxford: Oxford University Press, 2015).

Kenny, Neil, 'La Part du dire dans le contredire, ou l'inconstance des paroles humaines: Léry, Montaigne, Colletet', *Seizième Siècle*, 4 (2008), 255–87.

Ker, James, *The Deaths of Seneca* (Oxford: Oxford University Press, 2009).

Konstantinovic, Isabelle, *Montaigne et Plutarque* (Geneva: Droz, 1989).

Krause, Virginia, 'Confession or *Parrhesia*? Foucault after Montaigne', in *Montaigne after Theory/Theory after Montaigne*, ed. Zahi Zalloua (Seattle: University of Washington Press, 2009), pp. 142–60.

Kritzman, Lawrence D., *The Fabulous Imagination: On Montaigne's Essais* (New York: Columbia University Press, 2009).

Kubota, Takeshi, *Montaigne, lecteur de la Cité de Dieu d'Augustin* (Paris: Champion, 2019).

Langer, Ullrich, 'Montaigne, Scepticism, and Finitude. Montaigne, Horkheimer: Unhelpful Scepticism in a Limited World', in *Global Montaigne: Mélanges en l'honneur de Philippe Desan*, ed. Jean Balsamo and Amy Graves (Paris: Garnier, 2021), pp. 316–26.

Le Cadet, Nicolas, 'La Maxime et le "nouveau langage" des *Essais*', *Nouveau bulletin de la société internationale des amis de Montaigne*, 46 (2007), 85–109.

Legros, Alain, 'Autant la forme que la substance', *Montaigne Studies*, 26 (2014), 79–86.

Legros, Alain, '"*Epékhô*, c'est-à-dire je soutiens, je ne bouge": jeu de paume, histoire et philosophie', in *Global Montaigne: Mélanges en l'honneur de Philippe Desan*, ed. Jean Balsamo and Amy Graves (Paris: Garnier, 2021), pp. 411–23.

Legros, Alain, '*Essais* de 1588 et l'Exemplaire de Bordeaux' (2015), https://montaigne.univ-tours.fr/essais-1588-exemplaire-bordeaux/ [accessed 6 November 2023].
Legros, Alain, *Montaigne manuscript* (Paris: Garnier, 2010).
Legros, Alain, 'Montaigne, son livre, et son roi', *Studi francesi*, 41.2 (1997), 259–74.
Legros, Alain, 'Plutarque annoté par Montaigne', *MONLOE: Montaigne à l'œuvre* (2020), https://montaigne.univ-tours.fr/notes-de-lecture-de-montaigne/plutarque-annote-par-montaigne/ [accessed 6 November 2023].
Leushuis, Reinier, 'Montaigne *Parrhesiastes*: Foucault's Fearless Speech and Truth-Telling in the *Essays*', in *Montaigne after Theory/Theory after Montaigne*, ed. Zahi Zalloua (Seattle: University of Washington Press, 2009), pp. 100–21.
Limbrick, Elaine, 'Was Montaigne Really a Pyrrhonian?', *Bibliothèque d'Humanisme et Renaissance*, 34 (1977), 67–80.
Lyons, John D., *Before Imagination: Embodied Thought from Montaigne to Rousseau* (Stanford, CA: Stanford University Press, 2005).
Machado, Edouardo, 'Foucault, lecteur de Plutarque: de la notion de savoir "éthopoétique" à la construction d'une "esthétique de l'existence"', *Le Télémaque*, 47.1 (2015), 109–20.
Mack, Peter, *Reading and Rhetoric in Montaigne and Shakespeare* (London: Bloomsbury, 2010).
Maclean, Ian, 'Montaigne/Cardano: The Reading of Subtlety/The Subtlety of Reading', *French Studies*, 37.2 (1982), 144–56.
Maclean, Ian, *Montaigne philosophe* (Paris: Presses Universitaires de France, 1996).
Maclean, Ian, 'Montaigne and the Truth of the Schools', in *The Cambridge Companion to Montaigne*, ed. Ullrich Langer (Cambridge: Cambridge University Press, 2005), pp. 142–62.
MacPhail, Eric, *Dancing Around the Well: The Circulation of Commonplaces in Renaissance Humanism* (Leiden: Brill, 2014).
MacPhail, Eric, 'Montaigne and the Theatre of Conscience', *French Studies*, 68.4 (2014), 465–76.
Magnien, Michel, 'Montaigne (re)lecteur des *Tusculanes*', in *La Librairie de Montaigne*, ed. Philip Ford and Neil Kenny (Cambridge: Cambridge French Colloquia, 2012), pp. 157–82.
Magnien-Simonin, Catherine, '*Essais* I, 22: Montaigne lecteur d'un Sénèque français?', *French Forum*, 13.3 (1988), 277–85.
Maia Neto, José R., *Academic Skepticism in Seventeenth-Century French Philosophy: The Charronian Legacy 1601–1662* (Cham: Springer, 2014).
Maia Neto, José R., Gianni Paganini and John Christian Laursen (eds), *Skepticism in the Modern Age: Building on the Work of Richard Popkin* (Leiden: Brill, 2009).
Marchand, Stéphane, 'Sextus Empiricus' Use of *dunamis*', in *Sceptical Paths: Enquiry and Doubt from Antiquity to the Present*, ed. Giuseppe Veltri, Racheli Haliva, Stephan Schmid and Emidio Spinelli (Berlin: De Gruyter, 2019), pp. 23–41.
Mathieu-Castellani, Gisèle, *Montaigne: l'écriture de l'essai* (Paris: Presses Universitaires de France, 1988).

Mathieu-Castellani, Gisèle, *Montaigne ou la vérité du mensonge* (Geneva: Droz, 2000).
Mazzoli, Giancarlo, 'Le "voci" dei Dialoghi di Seneca', in *Seneca al suo tempo*, ed. Piergiorgio Parroni (Rome: Salerno Editrice, 2000), pp. 249–60.
McCuaig, William, *Carlo Sigonio: The Changing World of the Late Renaissance* (Princeton, NJ: Princeton University Press, 1989).
McGowan, Margaret M., *Visions of Rome in Late Renaissance France* (New Haven, CT: Yale University Press, 2000).
McKinley, Mary, 'Montaigne on Women', in *The Oxford Handbook of Montaigne*, ed. Philippe Desan (Oxford: Oxford University Press, 2016), pp. 581–99.
Miernowski, Jan, 'Montaigne on Truth and Skepticism', in *The Oxford Handbook of Montaigne*, ed. Philippe Desan (Oxford: Oxford University Press, 2016), pp. 544–61.
Miernowski, Jan, 'Montaigne, Scepticism, and Finitude. Montaigne, Meillassoux: Helpful Scepticism and the Multiplicity of Worlds', in *Global Montaigne: Mélanges en l'honneur de Philippe Desan*, ed. Jean Balsamo and Amy Graves (Paris: Garnier, 2021), pp. 327–44.
Miernowski, Jan, *L'Ontologie de la contradiction sceptique: pour l'étude de la metaphysique des Essais* (Paris: Garnier, 1998).
Milhe Poutingon, Gérard, 'Le Style du parler simple et naif des Essais', *Bulletin de la société internationale des amis de Montaigne*, 67 (2018), 175–90.
Montaleone, Carlo, 'Montaigne, pratique de l'oubli et erreurs de perspective', *Bulletin de la société internationale des amis de Montaigne*, 68 (2018), 117–30.
Motto, Anna Lydia, and John R. Clark, *Essays on Seneca* (Frankfurt: Lang, 1993).
Naya, Emmanuel, 'Les Mots ou les choses: le "nouveau langage" à l'essai', in *La Langue de Rabelais – La Langue de Montaigne*, ed. Franco Giacone (Geneva: Droz, 2009), pp. 325–49.
Naya, Emmanuel, '"Ne sceptique ne dogmatique, et tous les deux ensemble": Rabelais "on Phrontistere et eschole des pyrrhoniens"', *Études Rabelaisiennes*, 35 (1998), 81–129.
Naya, Emmanuel, 'La Science-fiction pyrrhonienne: des perles aux cochons', *Littératures*, 47 (2002), 67–86.
O'Brien, John, 'All Outward and on Show: Montaigne's External Glosses', in *Self-Commentary in Early Modern European Literature, 1400–1700*, ed. Francesco Venturi (Leiden: Brill, 2019), pp. 165–88.
O'Brien, John, 'Fashion', in *Montaigne after Theory/Theory after Montaigne*, ed. Zahi Zalloua (Seattle: University of Washington Press, 2009).
O'Brien, John, 'Si avons-nous une tres-douce medecine que la philosophie', in *L'Écriture du scepticisme chez Montaigne*, ed. Marie-Luce Demonet and Alain Legros (Geneva: Droz, 2004), pp. 13–24.
O'Brien, John, 'Slavery and Freedom in a Time of Civil War: La Boétie, L'Hospital, and Montaigne', *Early Modern French Studies*, 44.1 (2022), 53–68.
O'Brien, John, 'Wounded Artifacts: Vulnerability and Montaigne's *Essais*', *MLN*, 127.4 (2012), 712–31.
Oddy, Nathalie, 'Presence of Mind: Consubstantiality and Extended Cognition in Montaigne's *Essais*', unpublished DPhil dissertation, University of Oxford, 2022.

Opsomer, Jan, 'Arguments non linéaires et pensée en cercles: forme et argumentation dans les *Questions Platoniciennes* de Plutarque', in *Les Dialogues platoniciens chez Plutarque*, ed. X. Brouillette and A. Giavatto (Leuven: Leuven University Press, 2011), pp. 93–116.

Ossa-Richardson, Anthony, *The Devil's Tabernacle: The Pagan Oracles in Early Modern Thought* (Princeton, NJ: Princeton University Press, 2013).

O'Sullivan, Luke, '"Des responses et rencontres": Frank Speech and Self-Knowledge in Guillaume Bouchet's *Serées*', *Renaissance and Reformation/Renaissance et réforme*, 43.3 (2020), 167–94.

O'Sullivan, Luke, '"Feuilletant ces petits brevets descousus": consolations fausses et l'écriture de la vérité', *Bulletin de la société internationale des amies et amis de Montaigne*, 74 (2022), 187–205.

O'Sullivan, Luke, 'In-Between Authorship in Montaigne's *Essais*', *Early Modern French Studies*, 41.2 (2019), 106–25.

O'Sullivan, Luke, 'On Being Tongue-Tied: *Franchise*, Fluency, and Precarity in Montaigne's "De la vanité"', *Forum for Modern Language Studies*, 59.4 (2023), 616–35.

O'Sullivan, Luke, '"Un traict à la comparaison de ces couples": Seneca's Poets and Epicurean Senecanisms in Montaigne's *Essais*', in *Imitative Series and Clusters from Classical to Early Modern Literature*, ed. Colin Burrow, Stephen Harrison, Martin McLaughlin and Elisabetta Tarantino (Berlin: De Gruyter, 2020), pp. 223–42.

Pade, Marianne, 'Leonardo Bruni and Plutarch', in *Brill's Companion to the Reception of Plutarch*, ed. Sophia Xenophontos and Katerina Oikonomopoulou (Leiden: Brill, 2019), pp. 389–403.

Pade, Marianne, *The Reception of Plutarch's Lives in Fifteenth-Century Italy*, 2 vols (Copenhagen: Museum Tusculanum Press, 2007).

Panichi, Nicola, 'Montaigne and Plutarch: A Scepticism that Conquers the Mind', in *Renaissance Scepticisms*, ed. Gianni Paganini and José Maia Neto (Dordrecht: Springer, 2009), pp. 183–212.

Panichi, Nicola, 'Le Scepticisme qui "gaigne" le jugement: le Plutarque de Montaigne', in *Montaigne: cahiers d'histoire de la philosophie*, ed. Pierre Magnard and Thierry Gontier (Paris: CERF, 2010), pp. 67–80.

Papy, Jan, 'Lipsius' (Neo-)Stoicism: Constancy between Christian Faith and Stoic Virtue', *Grotiana*, 22.1 (2001), 47–71.

Patterson, Jonathan, *Villainy in France, 1463–1610: A Transcultural Study of Law and Literature* (Oxford: Oxford University Press, 2021).

Paul, Joanne, *Counsel and Command in Early Modern English Thought* (Cambridge: Cambridge University Press, 2020).

Perkins, Marina, '"Il guigne seulement du doigt par où nous irons": Underspecification in Montaigne's *Essais*', *Modern Language Review*, 118.3 (2023), 328–48.

Perona, Blandine, *Prosopopée et persona à la Renaissance* (Paris: Garnier, 2013).

Popkin, Richard, *The History of Scepticism from Savonarola to Bayle*, 3rd edn (Oxford: Oxford University Press, 2003).

Pouilloux, J.-Y., 'Autour du *Ei* de Delphes', in *Moralia et œuvres morales à la Renaissance*, ed. Olivier Guerrier (Paris: Garnier, 2008), pp. 293–308.

Pouilloux, J.-Y., *Montaigne: l'éveil de la pensée* (Paris: Garnier, 1995).

Pouilloux, J.-Y., *Montaigne: une vérité singulière* (Paris: Gallimard, 2012).
Prat, Sébastien, *Constance et inconstance chez Montaigne* (Paris: Garnier, 2011).
Prat, Sébastien, 'La réception des *Académiques* dans les *Essais*: une manière voisine et inavouée de faire usage du doute sceptique', in *Academic Scepticism in the Development of Early Modern Philosophy*, ed. Plínio Junqueira Smith and Sébastien Charles (Cham: Springer, 2017), pp. 25–44.
Regent, Nikola, 'Montaigne and the Lessons of Ancient History', *Global Intellectual History*, 1.2 (2016), 151–71.
Regosin, Richard, *Montaigne's Unruly Brood: Textual Engendering and the Challenge of Paternal Authority* (Berkeley: University of California Press, 1996).
Rendall, Stephen, *Distinguo: Reading Montaigne Differently* (Oxford: Clarendon Press, 1992).
Rigolot, François, 'Curiosity, Contingency, and Cultural Diversity: Montaigne's Readings at the Vatican Library', *Renaissance Quarterly*, 64.3 (2011), 847–74.
Robert-Nicoud, Vincent, *The World Turned Upside Down in 16th-Century French Literature and Visual Culture* (Leiden: Brill, 2018).
Rolfe, John C., 'On *Hoc Age*, Plautus Capt. 444', *Classical Philology*, 28 (1933), 47–50.
Roller, Matthew, 'The Dialogue in Seneca's Dialogues (and Other Moral Essays)', in *The Cambridge Companion to Seneca*, ed. Shadi Bartsch and Alessandro Schiesaro (Cambridge: Cambridge University Press, 2015), pp. 54–67.
Russell, Nicolas, *Transformations of Memory and Forgetting in Sixteenth Century France: Marguerite de Navarre, Pierre de Ronsard, Michel de Montaigne* (Newark: University of Delaware Press, 2011).
Sayce, Richard, *The Essays of Montaigne: A Critical Exploration* (London: Weidenfeld and Nicolson, 1972).
Schmitt, Charles B., *Cicero Scepticus: A Study of the Influence of the Academica in the Renaissance* (The Hague: Springer, 1972).
Scholar, Richard, '"J'aime Michel, mais j'aime mieux la verité": Creative Reading and Free-Thinking in Montaigne', *Nottingham French Studies*, 49 (2010), 39–51.
Scholar, Richard, *Montaigne and the Art of Free-Thinking* (Oxford: Peter Lang, 2010).
Screech, M. A., *Montaigne's Annotated Copy of Lucretius* (Geneva: Droz, 1998).
Sellevold, Kirsti, '*J'ayme ces mots...*': *expressions linguistiques de doute dans les Essais de Montaigne* (Paris: Champion, 2003).
Sève, Bernard, *Montaigne: des règles pour l'esprit* (Paris: Presses Universitaires de France, 2007).
Shelton, Jo-Ann, 'Persuasion and Paradigm in Seneca's *Consolatio ad Marciam* 1–6', *Classica et Mediaevalia*, 46 (1995), 157–88.
Smith, Christopher, and Anton Powell (eds), *The Lost Memoirs of Augustus and the Development of Roman Autobiography* (Swansea: Classical Press of Wales, 2009).
Starobinski, Jean, *Montaigne en mouvement* (Paris: Gallimard, 1982).

Steczowicz, Agnieszka, 'The Defence of Contraries: Paradox in the Late Renaissance Disciplines', unpublished DPhil dissertation, University of Oxford, 2004.
Tarrête, Alexandre, 'Remarques sur le genre du dialogue de consolation à la Renaissance', *Réforme, Humanisme, Renaissance*, 57 (2003), 133–52.
Tischer, Ute, '"Nostra faciamus": Quoting in Horace and Seneca', in *Horace and Seneca: Interactions, Intertexts, Interpretations*, ed. Martin Stöckinger, Kathrin Winter and Andreas T. Zanker (Berlin: De Gruyter, 2017), pp. 292–313.
Tournon, André, 'Le Doute investigateur: métamorphoses d'un "refrain" de Plutarque dans les *Essais*', *Nouveau bulletin de la société internationale des amis de Montaigne*, 50 (2009), 5–22.
Tournon, André, *Essais de Montaigne, Livre III* (Paris: Atlande, 2002).
Tournon, André, 'Les Marques de profération dans les *Essais*', in *La Ponctuation à la Renaissance*, ed. Nathalie Dauvois and Jacques Dürrenmatt (Paris: Garnier, 2011), pp. 163–73.
Tournon, André, 'Montaigne et l'"alleure poétique": pour une nouvelle lecture d'une page des *Essais*', *Bibliothèque d'Humanisme et Renaissance*, 33 (1971), 155–62.
Tournon, André, *Montaigne: la glose et l'essai – édition revue et corrigée* (Paris: Champion, 2000).
Tournon, André, 'Les Palimpsestes du "langage coupé"', in *La Langue de Rabelais – La Langue de Montaigne*, ed. Franco Giacone (Geneva: Droz, 2009), pp. 351–69.
Tournon, André, 'La Question du préteur', in *L'Écriture du scepticsme chez Montaigne*, ed. Marie-Luce Demonet and Alain Legros (Geneva: Droz, 2004), pp. 265–72.
Tournon, André, *Route par ailleurs: le 'nouveau langage' des Essais* (Paris: Champion, 2006).
Villey, Pierre, *Les Sources et l'évolution des Essais de Montaigne*, 2 vols (Paris: Hachette, 1908).
Welch, Cara, 'Beyond Stoicism: Plutarch's *Parallel Lives* and Montaigne's Search for a New Noble Ethos', in *Revelations of Character: Ethos, Rhetoric, and Moral Philosophy in Montaigne*, ed. Corinne Noirot-Maguire and Valérie M. Dionne (Newcastle: Cambridge Scholars Publishing, 2007), pp. 99–118.
Williams, Wes, 'Being in the Middle: Translation, Transition, and the Early Modern', *Paragraph*, 29 (2006), 27–39.
Williams, Wes, 'Montaigne on Imagination', in *The Oxford Handbook of Montaigne*, ed. Philippe Desan (Oxford: Oxford University Press, 2016), pp. 679–98.
Wilson, Marcus, 'Seneca's Epistles Reclassified', in *Texts, Ideas, and the Classics*, ed. S. J. Harrison (Oxford: Oxford University Press, 2001), pp. 164–87.
Wilson, Marcus, 'The Subjugation of Grief in Seneca's *Epistles*', in *The Passions in Roman Thought and Literature*, ed. Susan Morton Braund and Christopher Gill (Cambridge: Cambridge University Press, 1997), pp. 48–67.
Winter, Ian, 'L'Emploi du mot *forme* dans les *Essais* de Montaigne', in *Montaigne et les Essais 1580–1980*, ed. François Moureau, Robert Granderoute and Claude Blum (Paris and Geneva: Slatkine Reprints, 1983), pp. 261–8.
Zemon Davis, Natalie, *The Gift in Sixteenth-Century France* (Madison: University of Wisconsin Press, 2000).

Index

Academic Scepticism, 4, 18–25, 219; see also Scepticism
agricultural metaphors, 54–5, 81–2
alertness see attention
Almquist, Katherine, 67
Amyot, Jacques, 8–9, 25–6, 51, 162, 175, 189
anachronism, 77–8, 108–9; see also chronology
antagonism, 55–6, 62, 65, 77, 86–7, 95, 123, 151
Apollo
　double and obscure, 88–91, 119, 170, 186–7
　god of truth and self-knowledge, 169–70, 187, 213, 216
　Temple at Delphi, 52, 99
　see also paradox, *paradoxe*; 'commandement paradoxe'
Aristotle, 1, 20, 55, 57, 90, 148, 156–7, 186, 204–5
　principle of non-contradiction, 95
astheneia, 13, 73; see also *isostheneia*
ataraxia, 62, 74–5, 87, 198, 219–20
attention, 20–1, 80, 132, 135, 144, 145; see also *hoc age*
attunement, 139–40
Augustine, 147, 156–7, 180, 209
authorial association, 13–14, 48–50, 54, 57–8, 61, 72–3, 75–80, 80–3, 161, 199, 221
authority, 17, 54, 56–60, 61

Balsamo, Jean, 117
Baltussen, Han, 204–5

barristers see law
belief see *croyance*
bigarrure, *bigarré* see patchwork
Bjørnstad, Hall, 80
body, 32–9, 88, 90, 106, 119, 210–12
　agility of, 80–1
　anatomy, 115–19, 162
　corps aerée de la voix, 84, 115, 118–19, 188, 211
　in pain, sick, 94, 103, 119, 137–8, 140, 183, 185, 202–16
　see also stone; substance
bonne foi, *bona fides* see good faith
Bordeaux Copy, 1, 6–9, 31–2, 44, 46–7, 55–6, 57–8, 79, 88–91, 108–10, 111, 114, 120, 180, 196–7, 200; see also rewriting
borrowings, 13–14, 45–7, 54–60, 68–73, 76–7, 78–80, 81, 140–3, 155, 168–9, 180–1, 190–3, 199–200, 208–11
　extended transcription or translation of ancient texts, 50–4, 68–73, 103, 208
Boutcher, Warren, 26, 59, 166, 188

Caesar, Julius, 8, 111n57, 155, 159, 164, 168n45
Calhoun, Alison, 164–5
Calvin, Jean, 147
Catullus, 142
Cave, Terence, 10, 76, 139–40, 166, 217, 221
Céard, Jean, 118

certainty see *croyance*
chameleon, 175, 180, 182
Charron, Pierre, 221–2
chronology, 106, 108–15, 119–20, 133–7, 165, 198
Cicero, 28–31, 33, 55, 57, 67–8, 78–80, 94, 101–3, 180, 204–6, 209, 212, 215, 219
Claussen, Emma, 124
cognition
  cogitations, 14, 84, 115, 118, 156, 175, 221
  cognitive dissonance, 16, 94–5, 137–45, 181, 187–8, 211
  embodied cognition, 24n15, 35, 89, 203
  extended cognition, 3, 64, 87–8, 166, 217–18, 221; see also tool
commandement paradoxe see paradox, *paradoxe*
commerce, 1–2, 11, 48, 59, 65, 75, 77, 85–6, 88, 131, 138, 143, 193, 199, 202, 217–18, 222–3
commonplaces, 46, 76, 174–5, 212, 214–16
communalism, 45–9, 65, 68
communication, 11–12, 38, 52–3, 68, 75–7, 85–7, 96–7, 120, 141, 145–6, 151, 153–9, 164–8, 171, 174–5, 177, 178, 181, 188, 194, 202–16, 217–23
consolation, 140–3, 202–16
  consolatory dialogues, 208–9
  consolatory letters, 36, 140–3, 209
  self-consolation, 204–12, 216
constancy, 15, 35, 40, 50–4, 107, 153, 172–3, 177, 178, 180–8, 188–96
consubstantiality, 3, 13, 68, 77, 139, 221
contradiction, 10, 20, 24, 56–7, 60, 66–8, 72–3, 86, 91–7, 106, 112–15, 119, 128–9, 138–9, 141, 144, 152, 181–2, 185–8, 189–96, 199–202, 211, 214–15
contrerolle, 162, 165, 188–96, 197–9, 214; see also *registre*
cornucopia, 48, 65, 217
corps see body

Cotgrave, Randle, 11n26, 17n2, 37n45, 93, 123n4, 189, 202n38
crossings out *see* rewriting
croyance, 18, 64, 75–6, 149, 156, 163, 181, 196–9

daemon, 99, 126–9, 187
Danaïdes, 1, 6–8, 33, 85, 132, 197n28, 217–18
death, 17, 93–4, 103, 135–7, 174, 184, 199, 204–12
  philosophy as *praeparatio mortis*, 34, 36, 44
Demonet, Marie-Luce, 116–18
Desan, Philippe, 90
diary, 89, 105, 110–11, 155, 213–16
digestion, 33, 46, 48, 51, 54, 60, 79–80, 81, 190
digression, 123–32
Diogenes Laertius, 21, 41–2, 162
discontinuity *see* impermanence
disorder, 93, 108–15
dispossession *see* property
dissemblance *see* lying
dogmatism
  dogmatic cadences, 20, 23, 31, 87, 107
  Seneca and Plutarch as dogmatists, 2, 10, 18–25, 219
  tiers genre, 18–25, 87, 92, 107, 196, 219, 222
doubleness
  and cognitive dissonance, 16, 199, 211
  and simplicity, 15, 147–179
  as characteristic of Montaigne's thought and of his book, 10, 12, 14, 85, 91–7, 110–15, 118–19, 122–46, 220
  in Plutarch, 97–8
  of authorial associations, 14, 73, 76, 80, 83
duplicity *see* lying
Du Val, Antoine, 147

Eden, Kathy, 66
Edwards, Catherine, 191
enthousiasmos, 124, 185–7, 208, 213; *see also* Sibyl

Epictetus, 67–8
Epicurus, 45, 219
　and Hermarchus, 93–4
　as 'double', 93–5, 98, 113, 199
　letter writer, 102
equipollence see *isostheneia*
Erasmus, 6n15, 147n1, 174, 213n62, 214
esprit, 14, 64, 74, 127, 138, 177, 186–7, 202–12
　genereux, 88–91, 173, 186–7, 218
　movement of, 32–9, 196, 202
　prosopopoeia of, 16, 202–12
Estienne, Charles, 117, 213n61
example, *exemples*, exemplarity, 16, 62, 148, 165, 189–90, 200, 206, 209–12, 212–16
exchange see *commerce*
exemplaire de Bordeaux see Bordeaux Copy

faces, 1, 14, 19–20, 73, 76–7, 95–6, 98, 187, 194, 196, 219
　noses, 54–60, 77
façon, 3, 36–9, 39–41, 98, 146, 153–61, 168, 179, 180, 182, 190, 220
fantasie see imagination
flattery, 136, 202–12, 216
　Plutarch's essay on, 15, 169–73, 175–6, 178, 191
　self-flattery, *amour de soi-même, philautia*, 170–1, 175, 181
fluids, flow *see* water
folly, 12, 17–18, 44, 125, 160–1, 180–1, 191, 200–1, 202–16
forgetting *see* memory
forme, 14–15, 84–146, 161, 172, 179, 188, 192, 195, 201, 218, 220
　forme d'escrire, 20, 23–4, 84–8, 196, 217–18, 219, 222–3
fortune, 39, 115, 123, 129, 131, 192, 197
　Apelles as figure of, 74
　going with the flow, *rouler au vent*, 74, 81, 127, 129
Foucault, Michel, 58, 159–60, 167, 170, 176–7, 184

frank speech see *parrhesia*
Frisch, Andrea, 63
furor see enthousiasmos

games, 194
　erudite games, 58, 60, 77, 138–9
　fencing, 220
　juggling and acrobatics, 24
　tennis, 80–2
　see also tricks
getting lost, 123–32, 145
gifts, 45, 66–7
Giocanti, Sylvia, 74
Giusti, Elena, 184
good faith, 16, 146, 148–50, 156, 173, 216, 223
Goulart, Simon, 25–6
gravelle see stone
Gray, Floyd, 47–8
Green, Felicity, 37–8

hands
　fingers, pointing, 58, 98–9, 193
　grasp, 7–8, 32, 52, 88, 196–7, 199
　helping, 180–1, 183
　Plutarch's liberal hand, 48
　Sceptical even-handedness, 133–4
Helgeson, James, 174
Heraclitus, 26, 38, 52, 173
hoc age, 28–32
Hoffmann, George, 92
Horace, 72, 180, 186
horses, 28, 59, 69–72, 119, 167, 186
Hydra, 134, 138
hypocrisy, 93–7, 147–8

imagination, *fantasie*, 4, 17, 64, 67, 78, 84, 88–91, 109, 111, 124, 126, 133–5, 179, 180, 205, 212
impermanence, 11, 13–14, 49, 64–5, 68, 73–80, 104–6, 199, 221
inconstancy, 15, 50–4, 80–3, 177, 178, 180–202, 212, 216
indiligent lecteur, 127–30, 132, 146
informe, 1, 14, 84–8, 88–91, 115, 155, 168, 218
ingenium see esprit
inheritance, 2–3, 5–6, 48, 218–19
irony, 47, 57, 72–3

isostheneia, 13, 73–5, 100; see also
     astheneia

jokes, 16, 47, 57, 72–3, 91, 200, 215
judgement, 50, 55, 58–60, 60–5, 68–73, 85–6, 97–8, 109, 133–5, 148, 162–4, 169, 179, 196, 200
     suspension of judgement, *epoché*, *epecho*, 12, 13, 14, 19, 22–3, 50, 62, 73–6, 82, 87, 100, 108, 120, 197–8, 219
     weak and temporary, 48, 73–80, 82
Juvenal, 72

Kenny, Neil, 189, 196
Ker, James, 34
know thyself *see* self-knowledge
Krause, Virginia, 167

La Boétie, Étienne de, 36
Langer, Ullrich, 5
law, 66–7, 137, 180
     barristers, 29, 161
     judge, jury, 156, 169, 175
     legal fictions, 149–50
leaks, leakiness *see* water
Legros, Alain, 9
letters
     Lipsius on letter writing, 106, 145
     Montaigne as letter writer, 101–3, 106–7
     proto-essays, 104–7
     serial, 104–6, 107–8, 110, 113, 120, 137
     see also Seneca
library
     corner of a library, 155
     La Croix du Maine, 2n4, 59
     Montaigne's, 8
     Vatican Library, 26–7
life
     bios mirroring *logos*, 150, 161, 163, 169, 172, 192
     life writing, 115, 155, 161–8, 176, 179, 221
     see also Plutarch; Seneca

Lipsius, Justus, 182, 206
     on letter writing, 106, 113, 145
     on literary property, 46, 61
Livy, 46n8, 99, 143–4
Lucretius, 8, 139–40, 180, 190n16
lying, 14–15, 91, 95, 147, 149, 153–4, 156–8, 171–3, 174, 177, 181

Maclean, Ian, 153
marqueterie, 108, 112, 119, 125, 130
Mathieu-Castellani, Gisèle, 56–7
medicine
     diagnostics, 15, 95, 181, 182–8, 190–1, 196, 213–16
     parrhesiastes as physician, 170–3, 178
     Sceptic as physician, 86–7
     Seneca as physician, 183, 185, 187
     therapy, 15, 202–16
memoir, 155, 162, 166, 194; *see also* diary; life writing
memory, 6–8, 60, 63–5, 78, 94, 155, 168
metals as metaphors for the mind and for cognition
     gold, 137, 144
     mercury, 73, 85, 88, 218
Metrodorus, 94, 138–43, 145
Miernowski, Jan, 5
model *see* patron
multiperspectivalism *see* perspectives, multiple
munusculum see gifts

nonchalance *see* sprezzatura
nose *see* faces

O'Brien, John, 214
office
     clerks and accountants, bookkeeping, 84–6
     office sans nom, 84–5, 95–6, 160, 165–6
open-ended, unresolved, 3, 8, 14, 22, 43, 77, 81–3, 85–6, 88–91, 98–9, 107–8, 111, 112–13

painters, painting, portraits, 74, 84, 143, 164, 187, 192, 221
Panichi, Nicola, 27
paper, 1, 6–8, 47, 64, 76, 83, 85, 102, 132, 150, 213–16, 217, 223
papiers journaux see diary
paradiastole, 123, 196
paradox, *paradoxe*, 16, 103, 127–8, 151, 170, 178, 182, 187–8, 189, 196, 199–201, 202–16, 221
  as outlandish opinion, 182, 189
  as repugnant and contradictory, 96, 182
  'commandement paradoxe', 16, 170, 182, 202, 213, 216, 220–2
  'discours paradoxe', 182, 188, 200–2, 216, 221
  liar paradox, 153–4, 159
  Stoic paradoxes, 66–7, 189
Paré, Ambroise, 116
parrhesia, 15, 87, 136, 145, 149–52, 159–61, 167, 168–79, 181, 185, 187–8, 193, 195–6, 196–216, 220–1
  Plutarch's essay on frank speech and flattery *see* flattery
  Seneca as model of, 102–3
patchwork, 59, 62, 95–6, 123–32, 145, 190–1, 196
patron, 49, 56, 59–60, 72, 77, 88–91, 95–6, 97, 119, 152, 162, 168, 173, 219
Perona, Blandine, 203, 206–7
perspectives, multiple, 6, 11, 12, 16, 20, 22–3, 76–7, 97–100, 111–12, 115–19, 123, 131, 136–7, 187–8, 198, 207–8
Petrarch, 25–6
pieces décousues, 11, 27, 39, 97, 107, 108, 114, 118, 130, 132, 195, 199, 213–14, 219, 221
Pindar, 156
plagiarism, 47, 51, 54, 60, 65, 72
Plato, 1, 20–3, 31, 56, 82, 90, 124–8, 131, 136, 138, 156, 161, 186
Platter, Felix, 117
Pliny the Younger, 30, 102, 219
Plutarch
  as doubtful dogmatist, 11
  editions and manuscripts known to Montaigne, 8–9, 26–7
  in parallel with Seneca, 25–8, 32–9
  life of, 26, 36, 39
  Lives, 9, 15, 25, 33, 155, 162, 168: 'Coriolanus', 29; 'Demosthenes', 199–200; 'Lycurgus', 97–8; 'Lysander', 157; 'Numa Pompilius', 29; 'Paulus Aemilius', 9
  Montaigne's ability to read his soul, 12, 36, 41, 61, 150
  Moralia, 8–9: 'Comment il fault refrener la cholere', 27, 36; 'Comment on pourra discerner le flatteur d'avecq l'amy', 15, 169–73, 175–6, 178; 'De L'Esprit familier de Socrates', 126–31; 'Du premier froid', 99–100; 'Les Dicts notables des Lacedemoniens', 97–8; 'Les Opinions des philosophes', 99; 'Que signifioit ce mot E'i', 50–4
poetry, 1, 124–5
Popkin, Richard, 4
Pouilloux, Jean-Yves, 51–2, 90, 167
Prat, Sébastien, 194–5
property, 13–14, 44–50, 54–60, 60–5, 65–8, 75–6, 80, 137
  common property, common stock, 45–6, 48–9, 54, 58, 68, 72, 82, 141
  loss of, lost, dispossession, 11, 48–50, 63–5, 82, 109
  usufructs, 65–8
  see also getting lost
prosopopoeia, 180–1, 184–5, 187, 200, 203–12, 215
Pyrrhonism, 4, 18–25, 41–2, 74–5, 86–7, 91–3, 153, 219–20
  aphasia, 13, 20–2, 220
  as *dunamis/facultas*, 12, 86–7, 91, 95–6, 219–20
  madness, 11–12
  'nouveau langage', 10, 25, 220
Pyrrho, 18–19, 41–2
Sextus Empiricus, 10, 13, 18, 18–25, 41n53, 86–7, 91, 93n25, 138n24, 205n46

quotation *see* borrowings

Rabelais
  Panurge, 91–2, 96, 120
  Sibylle de Panzoust, 214
  Trouillogan, 91–2, 96–7, 114
record see *registre*
refrains
  phonai skeptikai, 12, 19, 73, 82, 86–7, 120, 153, 219–20
  Plutarch's, 22–4, 50, 173
registre, 15, 58, 61, 63, 84–6, 110–11, 120, 132, 145, 151, 156, 162–8, 179, 188, 201–2, 213–16, 221
repetition, 47, 51–2, 79–80, 148, 185
  inculcation, Stoic tendency *see* Stoics
  parrots, parroting, 59–60, 72, 82
rereading, 106, 111, 113–14, 145–6
  Montaigne as reader of the *Essais*, 49, 63, 85, 111, 114
rewriting, 101, 106, 111, 113–15, 120–1, 135–7, 137–45
  Montaigne crossing out and rewriting in the Bordeaux Copy, 6–9, 13–14, 22–5, 31–2, 44, 46–7, 55–6, 79–80, 88–91, 108–9, 111, 113, 123–32, 133–4, 192–3, 196–7
rhetoric, 52, 57, 86–7, 125, 150–1, 210, 215–16
  artificial, opposed to *parrhesia*, 28–31, 101–3
  canons of, 60–1, 73, 81
  worn out, rote, 203, 215–16
Rigolot, François, 26–7
Rome, 26–7, 77–80, 103, 136, 154
Ronsard, Pierre de, 116

sans forme see *informe*
Scepticism, Sceptics, 2–6, 9–12, 18–25, 74–5, 86–7, 91–7, 100, 119–20, 133–4, 138, 144, 149, 176–8, 197–8, 219–20; *see also* Academic Scepticism; Pyrrhonism
Scholar, Richard, 32, 38–9, 56, 112, 120

self-doubt, 137–45
self-knowledge, 16, 30, 136, 143, 158–9, 169–73, 175, 177, 178–9, 187, 212–16
Seneca
  as doubtful dogmatist, 11
  as prone to repetition *see* Stoics
  Consolatio ad Marciam, 209
  De Beneficiis, 66–7
  De ira, 27, 36
  De Tranquillitate animi, 182–8, 196, 208–9
  editions and manuscripts known to Montaigne, 8, 26–7, 45n2
  Epistulae ad Lucilium, 34–6, 44–7, 100–6, 110, 112–13, 140–3, 180–1, 190–3, 196, 203–4, 208–12, 216
  in parallel with Plutarch, 25–8, 32–9
  life of, 26, 34–7, 39, 116, 163, 174, 211
  saying what he means and meaning what he says, 37, 42, 61, 150
serial epistolography *see* letters
Sève, Bernard, 90, 104
Sextus Empiricus *see* Pyrrhonism
Sibyl, 183, 187
  feuilles sibyllines, 212–16
  Sibylle de Panzoust *see* Rabelais
Sigonio, Carlo, 205–6
simplicity, *simple*, *simplicitas*, 15, 39–43, 111, 137, 145, 147–79, 184–5, 190, 194, 221
Socrates, 20, 23, 99, 126–9, 161, 219
sottise see folly
soul see *esprit*
sprezzatura, nonchalance, 32, 64, 101, 129, 131, 154
Stoics, 40, 72, 182–8
  prone to repetition, 100–1, 103, 183
  Stoic paradoxes *see* paradox, *paradoxe*
stone, 16, 88, 116, 202–16
stultitia see folly
substance, 20, 25, 30–1, 33, 66, 87–8, 90–1, 161, 222

Tacitus, 34, 61, 138, 162–5, 174, 179, 219
temerité, hastiness, rashness, 54, 56, 62, 67–8, 72, 86
theft as metaphor for textual transfer *see* plagiarism
tongue, 14, 147
tool, 10, 15, 48, 77, 80, 87, 113, 145, 157–9, 166–8, 170, 178–9, 182, 194, 197–9, 217–18, 220–1
  outillage mental, 76
Tournon, André, 24, 89, 123, 125, 133–4
tranquillity see *ataraxia*
De Tranquillitate animi see Seneca
translation, 44, 46–7, 69–72, 75–6, 79, 94, 103, 174–6, 208
  language as 'truchement de l'ame', 157–8, 168, 174–6, 179, 195, 201–2, 221
tricks, 54–60, 72–3, 96, 148, 171–2, 220
truth, 18–19, 33, 68, 89, 95, 147–79, 180–216

truth of the schools, 149, 153–4, 156, 173–4
see also *parrhesia*

usage, 65–8, 68–73, 76–7, 81, 85–6, 137–8, 143, 221
usufructs *see* property
util see tool

ventriloquism *see* prosopopoeia; *enthousiasmos*
Vesalius, Andreas, 117
Villey, Pierre, 4
Virgil, 123
visage *see* faces

water, 6–8, 11, 50–4, 77, 85–6, 88–91, 106, 119, 125, 132, 167, 173, 196, 217–18
Williams, Wes, 53
Wilson, Marcus, 104–6

Xenophon, 155

zététique, 89

EU Authorised Representative:
Easy Access System Europe Mustamäe tee 50, 10621 Tallinn, Estonia
gpsr.requests@easproject.com

Printed and bound by CPI Group (UK) Ltd, Croydon, CR0 4YY
17/03/2026
02072698-0005